I0116319

MEDIA
CONVERGENCE
IN JAPAN

EDITED BY
PATRICK W. GALBRAITH
AND JASON G. KARLIN

Media Convergence in Japan

Patrick W. Galbraith and Jason G. Karlin, 2016

First published in 2016 by Kinema Club

Typeset by IntegralDMS

ISBN-10: 0-692-62995-5

ISBN-13: 978-0-692-62995-6

A Kinema Club Book

kinemaclub.org

Table of Contents

Part IV: Convergence of the Virtual and Real

Part V: Affective Convergence

Illustrations

Acknowledgements

Beyond a collection of chapters that assume and deal with the dynamics of convergence, this edited volume is an experiment in convergence. Unlike our previous books this volume is not coming out through a commercial or university press. The reasons for this decision are threefold: access, price and collaborative creativity. These three reasons are interrelated. Trends in the market are such that printed books, especially when targeting an academic audience, have increasingly small print runs and are increasingly inaccessible. This is not simply because printed books are material objects that must be ordered, shipped and stored, but also because the cost of production, in combination with low sales, can lead to prices of US$100 or more. When an edited volume is released for an academic audience, it is often in hardcover and purchased primarily by university libraries, which in turn contributes to a vicious cycle of shrinking sales and higher prices. Readers who cannot afford the purchase and do not have privileged access to university libraries cannot read these books. This inaccessibility is not only unfair, but also unproductive. It leads to exclusively "academic" discussions that are without influence from, and impact on, the world outside of closed "academic" circles. By making *Media Convergence in Japan* available in digital form online and for a price lower than is possible for a print publication, let alone an academic one—for free—we intend to make it accessible to more people. We do this in order to participate in, and contribute to, open and free discussion.

As anyone working in the humanities will attest, writing is not a road to riches. It is not customary to pay researchers to write book chapters, for example. Rather, researchers are asked to contribute to edited volumes, and do so to share ideas, intervene in discussions and receive recognition, which plays a part in securing paid teaching positions. An edited volume is an example of free labor and collaborative creativity. However, not only are researchers not paid to write—and, at some academic journals, must pay to publish—but readers—and, perversely, sometimes even the original writers—have to pay to access what has been written for free. This is not right. If one writes and conveys ideas for little if any monetary gain, then these ideas should be made accessible for as close to free as possible. We have been told that publications in this form do not "count" for much in some academic circles. Well, some academic circles are complicit with the exploitation of free labor and marginalization of large numbers of readers behind publishing protocols (i.e., copyright) and pay walls (i.e., fees for database access or to download articles). If the goal is to produce quality content, then academics who already work towards it should not need a seal of approval from a press or journal. Let the goal of our free labor be for others to read, review and respond to our work freely—to contribute to collaborative and creative thought and action.

This volume was edited and produced by scholars of media convergence in Japan and beyond. Despite not being published by a commercial or university press, it has been as vigorously edited and peer-reviewed as any other—perhaps more so. Each chapter went through two rounds of revisions. First, the editors read and prepared detailed comments that were shared with the contributors. After each contributor made revisions based on these comments, the manuscript was submitted to Kinema Club for editorial review. Kinema Club is an international, informal collective of scholars devoted to the study of Japanese moving images. The collective sent the entire manuscript for external review to two anonymous readers, who provided another set of detailed comments on the manuscript and each of the individual chapters, which informed further revisions. Like the editors of this volume, its contributors and the members of Kinema Club, the external reviewers were uncompensated for their time and labor, which they provided for free as a service to better the field. We thank these two reviewers, whose contribution made this a much better volume.

The process of producing this edited volume was as invigorating as it was exhausting, and many debts were incurred along the way. This volume could not have been completed without the support of Markus Nornes at the University of Michigan and Aaron Gerow at Yale University. We thank them, and all of the members of the Kinema Club Editorial Collective. Marc Steinberg offered advice and encouragement that improved this volume in countless ways. His work is a foundation for us and continues to inspire. Ian Condry cautioned us about the risks of self-publishing. His counsel helped us decide to approach Kinema Club, for which we are extremely grateful. Keiko Nishimura translated Chapter 6. Fiona Jayde designed the cover, and Clifford Ivie kindly provided the frontispiece photo for the Introduction. The cover image came from udocorg, a young Japanese photographer and fashion movie director. His creative work in a precarious media economy is what inspires this exploration of media convergence in Japan. We hope that it contributes in some small way to discussion and understanding of the media worlds that we inhabit and share.

Patrick W. Galbraith and Jason G. Karlin
January 2016

Contributors

Mia CONSALVO is Professor and Canada Research Chair in Game Studies and Design at Concordia University in Montreal. She is the co-editor of *Sports Videogames* and author of *Cheating: Gaining Advantage in Videogames*. She has most recently completed *Atari to Zelda: Japan's Videogames in Global Contexts*, a book about Japan's influence on the videogame industry.

Hideaki FUJIKI is an Associate Professor in the Graduate School of Letters at Nagoya University. He is the author of *Making Personas: Transnational Film Stardom in Modern Japan*, and co-editor of *The Japanese Cinema Book*.

Patrick W. GALBRAITH received his Ph.D. in Information Studies from the University of Tokyo and is currently pursuing a second Ph.D. in Cultural Anthropology at Duke University. He is the author of *Otaku Spaces* and *The Moé Manifesto* and co-editor of *Idols and Celebrity in Japanese Media Culture* and *Debating Otaku in Contemporary Japan*.

Daniel JOHNSON received his Ph.D. in Anthropology and Cinema and Media Studies from the University of Chicago. His research interests include cultures of anonymity and experiences of proximity of space and simultaneity of time in online media.

Jason G. KARLIN is an Associate Professor of media and gender studies in the Interfaculty Initiative for Information Studies at the University of Tokyo. He is the author of *Gender and Nation in Meiji Japan: Modernity, Loss, and the Doing of History* and co-editor of *Idols and Celebrity in Japanese Media Culture*. He is currently completing a book on Japanese television and advertising.

Tara KNIGHT is Associate Dean for the Division of Arts at the Humanities and an Associate Professor of Digital Media at the University of California, San Diego. She is the director of Mikumentary, an ongoing series of short, non-commercial documentary films about Hatsune Miku.

Alex LEAVITT is a Ph.D. Candidate at the Annenberg School for Communication and Journalism at the University of Southern California, where he studies social media and online games from both computational social science and ethnographic perspectives. He has previously been affiliated with Facebook, Sony PlayStation, Disney Interactive, Microsoft Research and MIT.

John LIE is C.K. Cho Professor of Sociology at the University of California, Berkeley. He is the author of numerous works on race, ethnicity and the nation. His most recent book is *K-Pop: Popular Music, Cultural Amnesia, and Economic Innovation in South Korea*.

Dario LOLLI is a Ph.D. student and sessional lecturer in the Department of Film, Media and Cultural Studies at Birkbeck, University of London. His dissertation concerns the globalization of Japanese media franchises, and aims to provide a detailed cultural economy of "Cool Japan" discourse and practices. He is a member of the London Asia Pacific Cultural Studies Forum.

Shunsuke NOZAWA received his Ph.D. in Cultural Anthropology from the University of Chicago and currently is a lecturer in the Interfaculty Initiative for Information Studies at the University of Tokyo. His research interests include social media and speech communities, urbanity and popular culture.

Shinji OYAMA is an Associate Professor of Cultural Studies in the College of International Relations at Ritsumeikan University. His research interests include Japanese creative industries, branding and East Asian cultural economy. Prior to his academic career, Oyama worked for 10 years in the Japanese media industries, equally divided between "old" and "new" media.

Alex YOSHIBA is pursuing a Bachelor's degree in Japanese Studies at the University of California, San Diego. His areas of interest include online gaming, otaku subcultures and contemporary Japanese-American cultural relations.

YOSHIDA Masataka is an Associate Professor at Tohoku University of Art and Design and the author of *Nijigen bishōjo ron* (On Two-Dimensional Cute Girls).

Introduction: At the Crossroads of Media Convergence in Japan

Patrick W. Galbraith and Jason G. Karlin

*Photo by Clifford Ivie. Reproduced with permission.

Japanese media is at a crossroads. In the second half of the twentieth century, the media industries followed a predictable path to increased revenue and audience growth, but today—with a shrinking national population in Japan, migrating audiences and declining sales—the future is less certain. Like the famous "scramble crossing" in Tokyo's Shibuya neighborhood (see image above), the path ahead converges into a jumble of bodies seeking a way forward. Many reach their destination, some compromise by choosing the shortest path, while others turn back, unable to reach the other side before the light changes. More than a few do not even attempt the crossing. Instead they wait—for the next light, for friends, for updates on their mobile phones. Despite the tumultuous flows, there is a rhizomatic quality and organized chaos to the crossroads. The infrastructure is stable and familiar, and movement through the built environment is neither entirely free nor controlled.

Japan prides itself on order, and its media is no exception. The dominant media corporations have long determined the direction and flow of content, but are now losing their preeminent place as agenda-setters and gatekeepers. Whereas newspapers—Japan has the highest circulation in the world[1]—and television—Japanese watch and trust it more than many others in the world[2]—could once count on being able to filter information and set the terms of national discussion, social media has led to an explosive proliferation of channels of communication. This is especially notable after the natural and nuclear disasters that shook Japan on March 11, 2011, which did much to foster skepticism of the mainstream media and its perceived alliance with the state, as well as popularize social media as an alternative source of information (see Chapter 1 and Chapter 2). Today, information is less constrained by the economics and politics of media corporations, and people are more active in commenting on received images and ideas, circulating them and creating alternatives.[3]

Like other post-industrial economies, the passing of each year brings with it much handwringing about the future of media in Japan. The Japanese media, despite its remarkable robustness and resistance to change, is showing signs of distress. Japan's five major newspaper companies have cautiously navigated the digital transition, preferring instead to protect the printed papers that made them rich,[4] but satellite and cable television, online digital media and streaming services—however delayed in their uptake—are beginning to erode the historic power of television. For many in the Japanese media industries, the decreasing number of viewers of television and movies and decreasing revenue from ads in newspapers and magazines provoke a combination of denial and nostalgia for past prosperity. With each countdown, each self-congratulatory retrospective, each announcement of audience ratings and ad revenues, there is a longing to restore Japanese media to what it once was. The gaze is backward to the past, not forward to the future. Can Japan return to the "normal" of an ordered media economy? What is the

---

[1] Mikko Villi and Kaori Hayashi, "'The Mission is to Keep This Industry Intact:' Digital Transition in the Japanese Newspaper Industry," *Journalism Studies* (November 25, 2015):1-18, doi:10.1080/1461670X.2015.1110499.

[2] Yoshimi Shun'ya, "From Street Corner to Living Room: Domestication of TV Culture and National Time/Narrative," in *Mechademia 9: Origins*, ed. Frenchy Lunning (Minneapolis, MN: University of Minnesota Press, 2014), 126-127.

[3] Pamela J. Shoemaker and Tim P. Vos, *Gatekeeping Theory* (London: Routledge, 2009), 130-136.

[4] Villi and Hayashi, "'The Mission is to Keep This Industry Intact.'"

new "normal?" In Japan, as elsewhere, the phenomenon of "convergence"—where old and new media collide—is "throwing media into flux."[5]

Consider a series of moments in recent years when Japanese commentators celebrated the national audience reconstituted. The drama series *Hanazawa Naoki* (10 weekly episodes aired on TBS in 2013) is a rare example of a television program that became a major hit nationally. While few dramas today earn more than a 10% audience share, the final episode of *Hanazawa Naoki* reached 42.2%—the highest rating for a drama in 30 years.[6] Further inspiring commentators, *Hanazawa Naoki* first gained popularity through buzz on social media before becoming a phenomenon discussed in "traditional" media, which seemed to suggest a return of young people to television and a new harmony between old and new media. However, despite the promises of "social television," there is little reason to believe that the unlikely success of *Hanazawa Naoki* will be repeated in the current industry structure of commercial television in Japan. Rather, this drama that bucks the trend of declining ratings and revenue is the exception that proves the rule.

Another moment. While music sales are generally in decline in Japan, the soundtrack to Disney's *Frozen* was an unexpected hit that reached a broad cross-section of Japanese society in 2014. The song "Let It Go" and its Japanese version "Ari no mama de" played everywhere and was practically inescapable that year. Again, the national audience reconstituted. Again, a notable exception. The soundtrack to *Frozen* was the only million-selling album from abroad in Japan that year. More generally, the megahit like "Let It Go" shared across generations has been replaced by a series of smaller, less impactful hits that appeal to fragmented, niche audiences. *Frozen*, which grossed ¥25.48 billion (US$216 million), was a rare example of a highly successful foreign film in Japan.[7] In the last decade, the highest grossing films in Japan mostly have been domestic ones produced in conjunction with television networks.[8] And, as *Hanazawa Naoki* shows,

---

[5] Henry Jenkins, *Convergence Culture: Where Old and New Media Collide* (New York: New York University Press, 2006), 259.

[6] Nakaoku Miki, "Terebi wa dore kurai mirareteita no ka," *Video Research Digest* 5-6 (2014), accessed November 1, 2014, https://www.videor.co.jp/vr-digest/pdf/vrd536_20140506/vrd536_article1.pdf.

[7] Data comes from the Motion Picture Producers Association of Japan, accessed January 8, 2015, http://www.eiren.org/boxoffice_e/2014.html.

[8] The release of Hollywood films is often timed to protect Japanese domestic films from competition. Due to low incidences of online piracy, international film distributors are willing to conform to Japan's delayed release schedule without concern for lost revenue. When Hollywood films do compete with Japanese ones, the results can be remarkable, as when *Love Live! The School Idol Movie* sold more tickets than *Mad Max: Fury Road* in June 2015 and *Yo-Kai Watch the Movie 2: King Enma and the 5 Stories, Nyan!* had higher returns than *Star Wars: The Force Awakens* in December 2015.

the audience for television dramas in Japan is shrinking, meaning that films based on television dramas are less successful.

Japan remains the second largest music market in the world and one of the last bastions of physical CD sales, a seeming anachronism in the age of digital downloads and music streaming services, and here too we see the fault lines of a media system in distress. While the 1990s was marked by bestselling albums by the likes of Utada Hikaru, who broke sales records and enjoyed widespread national support, hits today are supported by small but ardent fan bases. Such fans are encouraged to buy multiple copies of the same CD to obtain limited goods, increased access and special privileges, which is the reason why "idols" (*aidoru*) that are proximate to fans and appeal to them for support are on top of the charts in Japan.[9] Consider that in 2014, the bestselling album (both domestic and international) in Japan was not the soundtrack to *Frozen*, but rather female idol group AKB48's *Tsugi no ashiato*.[10] The trend is even more obvious in terms of sales of CD singles, with all top five spots on the Oricon chart in 2014 monopolized by AKB48; each of these CD singles sold over a million copies. Numbers like these have made AKB48 the bestselling performers in Japanese history with a record 36 million total CD singles sold (as of December 2015). This market dominance is striking—even more so when one notes that AKB48's biggest competition in 2014 came from its own sister groups[11] as well as male idol groups such as Arashi—and it is also telling. AKB48 is a success story in a music market stubbornly holding on to what has worked and continues to work—for now—which obscures experiments in digital distribution and emerging metrics of success beyond the present system. While AKB48 might seem very much like the "national idols" that producers and promoters claim them to be, they are ultimately idols supported by small groups of ardent fans that buy CDs and drive up sales rankings. Describing AKB48 as "national" idols ultimately is prescriptive rather than descriptive.

The *Kōhaku uta gassen* (Red and White Song Contest), an annual year-end special program that pits popular male and female singers against one another, is typically one of the most watched television broadcasts in Japan and a good opportunity to get a sense of the mainstream

---

[9] Patrick W. Galbraith, "AKB Business: Idols and Affective Economics in Contemporary Japan," in *Introducing Japanese Popular Culture*, ed. Alisa Freedman and Toby Slade (London: Routledge, forthcoming).

[10] Data comes from Oricon, accessed January 15, 2016, http://www.oricon.co.jp/rank/ja/y/2014/.

[11] There are more than 130 members (as of December 2015) of AKB48, who are organized into subgroups that compete with one another. Further, AKB48 has sister groups in Japan in Osaka, Fukuoka, Nagoya and Niigata, as well as overseas in Bangkok, Manila, Taipei, Jakarta and Shanghai.

Japanese media market. As the premiere television event of the year, which families watch together during gatherings to welcome the New Year, *Kōhaku* has had staggering viewer ratings in the past. In 1963, for example, 81.4% of Japanese households watched the *Kōhaku* broadcast. By 2015, however, that number had dropped to 39.2%—the lowest in *Kōhaku's* 65-year history.[12] What was once a collective viewing tradition, which Ōta Shō'ichi describes as a "place of solace" (*anjū no chi*) and symbolic coming together for Japanese families (and the Japanese nation), is in decline.[13] Like the Japanese media more generally, *Kōhaku* has been more earnest in its attempts to reconstitute the national audience after the disasters of March 11, 2011, but the annual song contest has become a platform for idols to appeal to their small and fragmented fan bases. Despite Ōta's prediction that *Kōhaku* will endure to produce new forms of community, it instead seems like a return to the past, grasping at and attempting to revive a vanishing tradition, a swan song.

Aired on NHK, the national public broadcaster, *Kōhaku* also provides a glimpse of the pressure points and politics of the Japanese media system. Although South Korean popular culture has thrived in the global market, as tensions between South Korea and Japan have mounted, South Korean performers have disappeared from the *Kōhaku* lineup (see Chapter 5). Social media has been less successful in spreading South Korean music in Japan, where Psy, whose "Gangnam Style" became the most viewed video in the history of YouTube, remains relatively unknown.[14] Tensions also sometimes play out in the performances of Japanese artists. For example, during *Kōhaku* in 2014—which was marked by multiple performances and sing-alongs of "Let It Go," that megahit that brought the nation together—the Japanese pop-rock band Southern All Stars—returning to the broadcast after a 31-year absence—shocked many when its lead singer Kuwata Keisuke seemingly called out conservative Prime Minister Abe Shinzō. Sporting a Hitler mustache, Kuwata sang "Peace and Hi-Lite,"

[12] Kyodo, "NHK Sees Ratings for 'Kohaku' Music Show Sink to Lowest Ever," *The Japan Times*, January 2, 2016, accessed January 15, 2016, http://www.japantimes.co.jp/news/2016/01/02/national/media-national/nhk-sees-ratings-for-kohaku-music-show-sink-to-lowest-ever/.

[13] Ōta Shō'ichi, *Kōhaku utagassen to Nihonjin* (Tokyo: Chikuma Shobō, 2013).

[14] John Lie attributes this to the strength of the "national" in music industries and markets, which apparently impacts even social media flows. See John Lie, *K-Pop: Popular Music, Cultural Amnesia, and Economic Innovation in South Korea* (Oakland: University of California Press, 2015), 111, 137, 156, 222. Others, however, point to transnational "rogue flows" such as the spread of Japanese pornography in China through the internet, which, in conjunction with Chinese social media, has remade Aoi Sola into a media personality in a country where her films are not legally available. See Jamie Coates, "Rogue Diva Flows: Aoi Sola's Reception in the Chinese Media and Mobile Celebrity," *Journal of Japanese and Korean Cinema* 6, no. 1 (2014): 89-103.

which to some sounded like "peace and high right" and a jab at Abe, who, against the backdrop of an increasingly unstable North Korea and powerful China, was endeavoring to reinterpret the Constitution of Japan to allow for military action overseas. Kuwata's voice introduced noise into the orderly *Kōhaku* broadcast, but it was the response that warrants attention: social media commentary and sharing served to briefly turn "Peace and Hi-Lite" into a protest song. Picked up by global media outlets and filtering back into the mainstream media in Japan, this became one of the biggest news stories to come out of *Kōhaku*.[15] Intentional or otherwise, social media turned the moment with Southern All Stars into a political one. Media convergence in Japan has introduced a plurality of voices that disrupt highly staged performances of national unity such as *Kōhaku*. Unlike the dynamic usually associated with the broadcast, the performer is no longer completely under control or in control of the message, which is not transmitted to stable audiences in front of television sets at home with family. The audience is fragmented, mobile and actively involved in curating media flows.

The moment with Southern All Stars was exceptional in a *Kōhaku* broadcast dominated by AKB48, which underscores something important: the resurgence of idols in Japan is the media system's response to crises precipitated by convergence. Idols create a familiar and intimate link to audiences through their appearance across media genres and platforms. Close viewing and interpretation of media through the intertextual links of celebrity is one of the most notable aspects of Japanese media.[16] If, as P. David Marshall suggests, the crossover of media channels contributes to the emergence of "the new intertextual commodity,"[17] then surely Japanese idols are precisely such "image commodities."[18] Even as corporations form "image alliances" with and around idols,[19] audiences form "affective alliances" with and around them.[20] Management

---

[15] See, for example, Philip Brasor, "Snark Levels Were on Full Blast for 'Kohaku,'" *The Japan Times*, January 17, 2015, accessed December 1, 2015, http://www.japantimes.co.jp/news/2015/01/17/national/media-national/snark-levels-full-blast-kohaku/.

[16] Patrick W. Galbraith and Jason G. Karlin, "Introduction: The Mirror of Idols and Celebrity," in *Idols and Celebrity in Japanese Media Culture*, ed. Patrick W. Galbraith and Jason G. Karlin (New York: Palgrave, 2012), 1-32.

[17] P. David Marshall, "The New Intertextual Commodity," in *The New Media Handbook*, ed. Dan Harries (London: British Film Institute, 2002), 69-81.

[18] Gabriella Lukács, *Scripted Affects, Branded Selves: Television, Subjectivity and Capitalism in 1990s Japan* (Durham, NC: Duke University Press, 2010), 24, 47.

[19] Saya S. Shiraishi, "Doraemon Goes Abroad," in *Japan Pop! Inside the World of Japanese Popular Culture*, ed. Timothy J. Craig (New York: M.E. Sharpe, 2000), 289.

[20] Lukács, *Scripted Affects*, 4.

companies (*jimusho*) control the movements of idols and micro-manage their image in order to sell that image to fans, television networks and advertisers.[21] Fan audiences tune in to see idols, and shows featuring them have higher ratings overall, which has led to idols appearing on every conceivable show and all shows converging into one big idol show. Even as genres of television converge, so too does the content of programs and advertisements, which equally carry information about idols and thus intertextual meaning.[22] In short, in response to crises of convergence that pull media apart, a counter convergence occurs with the deployment of idols, who bring together producers, audiences and content.[23]

With the success of AKB48 and other idols in the past decade, there is today an even greater number of young Japanese, especially young Japanese women, aspiring to become media personalities and performers in Japan (see Chapter 9). While this aspiration often means performing on stage and television, this is not always, necessarily or even most importantly the case. Utilizing new technologies and platforms for online self-presentation and promotion, a new generation of net idols and internet celebrities are self-producing and managing their own image and connections with fans and corporations. In the late 1990s and early 2000s, Japanese net idols were typically young women leveraging the technologies of blogs and digital photography to establish a fan base, which they managed through online interaction.[24] Like camgirls, these net idols were an early form of microcelebrity.[25] An outgrowth of this phenomenon, contemporary internet celebrities can draw large fans bases and earn large sums of money (see Chapter 10). The most popular daily videos on YouTube in Japan are from internet celebrities such as HIKAKIN and

---

[21] For a discussion of management companies in Japan, see W. David Marx, "The *Jimusho* System: Understanding the Production Logic of the Japanese Entertainment Industry," in *Idols and Celebrity in Japanese Media Culture*, ed. Patrick W. Galbraith and Jason G. Karlin (New York: Palgrave, 2012), 35-55. Japan has greatly influenced the system of idol production in South Korea, where agencies also have enormous power. See Solee I. Shin and Lanu Kim, "Organizing K-Pop: Emergence and Market Making of Large Korean Entertainment Houses, 1980-2010," *East Asia* 30, no. 4 (December 2013): 255-272.

[22] Jason G. Karlin, "Through a Looking Glass Darkly: Television Advertising, Idols, and the Making of Fan Audiences," in *Idols and Celebrity in Japanese Media Culture*, ed. Patrick W. Galbraith and Jason G. Karlin (New York: Palgrave, 2012), 85-86.

[23] Even this, however, seems in jeopardy. Symbolically, the members of male idol group SMAP, who have been pillars of Japanese television and drawn together a national audience since the 1990s, threatened to leave their management agency and upset its powerful position in the system in January 2016.

[24] Gabriella Lukács, "The Labor of Cute: Net Idols, Cute Culture, and the Digital Economy in Contemporary Japan," *positions: east asia cultures critique* 23, no. 3 (2015): 487-513.

[25] Theresa M. Senft, *Camgirls: Celebrity and Community* (New York: Peter Lang Publishing, 2008).

Hajime Shachō (notably still Japanese celebrities, but self-producing and online). Rather than celebrating potential liberation from the Japanese media system, HIKAKIN reproduced it in June 2013, when he founded the first Japanese management agency for YouTube celebrities. Called uuum, the agency has a net worth of ¥281 million (US$2.34 million) (as of December 2015). Revenue comes from ads and tie-ups with advertisers for products and services featured in videos. Much of this is familiar from the way that "traditional" media functions, which speaks to a convergence of old and new. Today, Japanese corporations are drawn to internet celebrities such as HIKAKIN because they promise to connect them with the audience that has migrated away from mainstream media and advertising.

What is Convergence?

Convergence means a coming together of two or more things, but, in discussions of media, there is some disagreement as to what is coming together, how and why.[26] Though often associated with the spread of digital media technology, networked devices and the internet, media convergence describes something that is not reducible to technological change. Derek Johnson identifies connections between convergence and licensing and franchising in the United States in the 1950s, which is long before what might be called the digital revolution.[27] Similarly, in Japan, connections have been made between convergence and character franchising in the media and material culture of the 1960s.[28] Rather than something to do with technology per se, convergence points to a complex network of relations that impact how media is produced and consumed. Approached this way, discussions of convergence have been ongoing in media studies for decades.[29] Undoubtedly, however, it was Henry Jenkins who popularized the term in academic circles with *Convergence Culture: Where Old and New Media Collide* (2006). As the book title suggests, Jenkins emphasizes that the phenomenon of convergence is marked by old and new media coming together in multitudinous sites of "tension and

---

[26] August E. Grant and Jeffrey F. Wilkinson, *Understanding Media Convergence: The State of the Field* (Oxford: Oxford University Press, 2009).

[27] Derek Johnson, *Media Franchising: Creative License and Collaboration in the Culture Industries* (New York: New York University Press, 2013), 31.

[28] Marc Steinberg, "Anytime, Anywhere: *Tetsuwan Atomu* Stickers and the Emergence of Character Merchandising," *Theory, Culture and Society* 26, no. 2-3 (2009): 113-138.

[29] The academic journal *Convergence* was founded in 1995. For an example of scholarship on convergence in the 1990s, see Thomas Elsaesser, "Convergence, Divergence, Difference," in *Cinema Futures: Cain, Abel or Cable? The Screen Arts in the Digital Age*, ed. Thomas Elsaesser and Kay Hoffmann (Amsterdam: Amsterdam University Press, 1998), 9-26.

transition."[30] For Jenkins, "[c]onvergence alters the relationship between existing technologies, industries, markets, genres and audiences."[31] In other words, categories and relations in the media that have been fixed, stable and separate are coming together.

In contrast to discussions that emphasize or focus exclusively on technological change, Jenkins argues for the need to consider "the cultural levels" of convergence.[32] This does not mean ignoring technological change, but rather broadening the scope of analysis to include the logic by which media industries and audiences operate. Jenkins notes three simultaneously occurring aspects of convergence: one, technological convergence, or devices that can perform multiple functions; two, corporate convergence, or massive multinational corporate conglomerates that own and produce media across platforms; and three, receptive convergence, or audiences coming together across boundaries, bringing together channels simultaneously, multitasking across platforms and creatively interacting with media and others.[33] Convergence, then, points to "the flow of content across multiple media platforms, the cooperation between multiple media industries, and the migratory behavior of media audiences who will go almost anywhere in search of the kinds of entertainment experiences they want."[34] Just as corporations consolidate to produce content that flows across multiple media platforms, so too do "lives, relationships, memories, fantasies, [and] desires also flow across media channels."[35] Convergence occurs in devices, companies and consumers.

When considering the cultural levels of convergence, active audiences are crucial, and they call attention to shifting dynamics of power. Jenkins explains:

Convergence...is both a top-down corporate-driven process and a bottom-up consumer-driven process. Media companies are learning how to accelerate the flow of media content across delivery channels to expand revenue opportunities, broaden markets, and reinforce viewer commitments. Consumers are learning how to use these different media technologies to bring the flow of media more fully under their

---

[30] Henry Jenkins, "The Cultural Logic of Media Convergence," *International Journal of Cultural Studies* 7, no. 1 (2004): 33.

[31] *Ibid.*, 34.

[32] Jenkins, *Convergence Culture*, 14-15.

[33] *Ibid.*, 16; and Jenkins, "The Cultural Logic of Media Convergence," 34.

[34] Jenkins, *Convergence Culture*, 2.

[35] *Ibid.*, 17.

control and to interact with other consumers...Sometimes, corporate and grassroots convergence reinforce each other, creating closer, more rewarding relations between media producers and consumers. Sometimes, these two forces are at war.[36]

On the one hand, media companies are interested in "extension" and the expansion of potential markets by moving content across platforms and delivery channels; "synergy" and the economic opportunities of owning and controlling multiple manifestations; and the "franchise" of branded content. On the other hand, consumers are interested in archiving, discussing, annotating, appropriating, remixing and circulating media content. At this intersection, "the power of the media producer and the power of the media consumer interact in unpredictable ways."[37] However, Jenkins argues that "the cultural shifts, the legal battles, and the economic consolidations that are fueling media convergence...will determine the balance of power in the next media era."[38] In its demand for greater access to information and content and control over them, the active audience might become an activist one (see Chapter 1 and Chapter 2). Then again, what Jenkins calls the "participation gap" may end up marginalizing populations worldwide.[39] One might also point out that those with the desire and means to participate might be subjugated to the agenda of powerful media companies, which own, provide and have a controlling interest in information and content.[40]

In the coming together of producers and consumers in convergence culture, at least three issues should be flagged as potentially politically significant: one, inequalities both between corporate producers of content and consumers (who are also producers, but without equal rights) and between consumers with differing access to technology, media and commodities (and thus are less visible and valued by corporations and communities); two, corporations encouraging active audiences, but still wanting to control content or selectively assert their right of ownership; and three, corporations profiting off consumers, whose productive activity spreads media and generates value but remains unremunerated.[41]

---

[36] *Ibid.*, 18.

[37] *Ibid.*, 2.

[38] *Ibid.*, 17.

[39] *Ibid.*, 23. The participation gap is an issue of not only differential access to media technologies, but also differential literacy.

[40] Where the content is user generated, the issue is of the ownership of the platform.

[41] For a discussion of productive activity online being "off the books," see Jaron Lanier, *Who Owns the Future?* (New York: Simon and Schuster, 2014).

On this last point, Jenkins insightfully highlights "the work—and play—spectators perform in the new media system."[42] As an example, Jenkins draws attention to videogame companies that find success by incorporating the productive activity of fan communities,[43] which others point to as a model case of the cultivation and exploitation of "immaterial" labor.[44] Certainly the "prosumer" that Jenkins identifies is nothing if not an ideal immaterial laborer: active, mobile and flexible, as well as social, networked and communicative.[45]

Jenkins' discussion of convergence is influential, but not without limits. Jenkins himself notes that he is focusing almost exclusively on the US, which raises questions about media systems elsewhere.[46] As Marshall states in his work on celebrity and power in contemporary culture, the "national and the transnational," as much as new media, "need much further work."[47] Upon examination, Jenkins' position on the national and the transnational in convergence is somewhat ambiguous. On the one hand, he is a believer in "pop culture cosmopolitanism," whereby "[n]either images nor viewers fit into circuits or audiences that are easily bound within local, national, or regional spaces."[48] On the other hand, national context, and even cultural context, seems to matter:

> The rate of convergence will be uneven within a given culture, with those who are most affluent and most technologically literate becoming the early adopters and other segments of the population struggling to catch up. Insofar as these trends extend beyond a specifically American context, the rate of convergence will also be uneven across

---

[42] Jenkins, *Convergence Culture*, 3.

[43] Jenkins, "The Cultural Logic of Media Convergence," 40.

[44] Nick Dyer-Witheford and Greig de Peuter, *Games of Empire: Global Capitalism and Videogames* (Minneapolis, MN: University of Minnesota Press, 2009), 212-213. Some examples of productive activity among gamers include modding (modifications of commercially released games), MMOs (online games where players are running massive experiments in community- and team-building), machinima (creating "cinema" from in-game "footage") and more. Much of this has its roots in a hacker culture based on self-organization and networked cooperation, but corporations capture some of the value of this productive activity. One wonders whether or not hacker culture—as it bleeds into fan culture in the form of "otaku," for example—is necessarily opposed to private property and capitalist relations. See Lawrence Eng, "Strategies of Engagement: Discovering, Defining, and Describing Otaku Culture in the United States," in *Fandom Unbound: Otaku Culture in a Connected World*, ed. Mizuko Ito, Daisuke Okabe and Izumi Tsuji (New Haven: Yale University Press, 2012), 85-106.

[45] Maurizio Lazzarato, "Immaterial Labor," in *Radical Thought in Italy: A Potential Politics*, ed. Paolo Virno and Michael Hardt (Minneapolis:, MN University of Minnesota Press, 1996), 133-147.

[46] Jenkins, *Convergence Culture*, 12, 17-18; and Jenkins, "The Cultural Logic of Media Convergence," 42.

[47] P. David Marshall, *Celebrity and Power: Fame in Contemporary Culture* (Minneapolis, MN: University of Minnesota Press, 2014), xxviii-xxix.

[48] Jenkins, *Convergence Culture*, 158.

national borders, resulting in the consolidations of power and wealth within the "have" nations and some shift in the relative status and prominence of developing nations.[49]

Now, it is clear that what Jenkins is getting at here is relative technological development as it relates to relative affluence, but his use of phrases such as "a given culture" next to "a specifically American context" and "national borders" suggests that different cultures of convergence might exist in different contexts as media is produced and circulated within and across national borders (see Chapter 4 and Chapter 5). Japan, for example, is not significantly less affluent than the US, and is certainly not a technologically underdeveloped nation, but its media culture, including media convergence, seems to take somewhat different forms than those that appear in Jenkins' account.

Convergence as Divergence

Optimistic claims that transnational flows would bring the world together in a sort of global cultural convergence have been met with critiques of the friction engendered by these flows.[50] Despite the inexorable process of globalization, national contexts—localized, linguistically, legally bounded systems—still matter in the production, circulation and reception of media. It follows that convergence occurs in different ways in different national contexts, which is to say that in discussions of convergence in context we need to pay attention to divergence. For his part, Jenkins is aware that convergence and divergence are "two sides of the same phenomenon."[51] However, because of his position in the US and consideration of media convergence in primarily that national context, there is still room to consider how the coming together of different technologies, industries, markets, genres and audiences plays out in different places and times. In this section, we introduce the Japanese media system in its national context in the second half of the twentieth century.

In the decades after the Second World War, the Japanese media and advertising industries consolidated to produce a distinct media environment that has been relatively immune to outside threats and internal upstarts.

---

[49] *Ibid.*, 35.

[50] See Anna Lowenhaupt Tsing, *Friction: An Ethnography of Global Connection* (Princeton: Princeton University Press, 2005); and Seth Perlow, "On Production for Digital Culture: iPhone Girl, Electronics Assembly, and the Material Forms of Aspiration," *Convergence: The International Journal of Research into New Media Technologies* 17, no. 3 (August 1, 2011): 245-269.

[51] Jenkins, *Convergence Culture*, 10.

Once consolidated, it became intensely focused on the domestic market, which was large enough to be attractive in and of itself (see Chapter 3). Over time, as Japanese industries prioritized the domestic, a robust media system took shape that made little room for foreign offerings, which began to disappear from the mainstream. Since satellite and cable television were slow to catch on, NHK and Japan's five commercial broadcasters had an almost completely unchallenged position as providers of television programming (see Chapter 4). Even as late as the 1990s, with a recessionary economy and widespread instability, Japanese broadcasters still imported only 3% of their content.[52] Gabriella Lukács notes that Japanese broadcasters at the time courted Japanese audiences with dramas that centered on popular Japanese performers, who audiences approached intertextually as dense carriers of information about lifestyles.[53] By deploying idols and reinforcing "affective alliances" with them and their trendy lifestyles of the moment, broadcasters were able to reconstitute a fragmenting national market. At the same time, they also emptied the content of rerun value (when the moment is over, the content is untrendy) and export value, because audiences outside of Japan did not know Japanese performers the same way or desire their lifestyles. The result was that Japan did not import or export much television content in the 1990s—with notable exceptions such as dramas in East Asia[54] and anime more broadly—and diverged from North America and other parts of the world.

The music industry took a similar path as Japanese producers came to assert a tighter grip on Japanese consumers by deploying Japanese performers. Since sales of domestic music surpassed sales of foreign music in Japan in 1967,[55] the overall trend has been toward a larger and larger share of the market for Japanese performers. Sales were driven by media appearances and promotion, which intensified in Japan from the 1970s.[56] During the instability of the 1990s, the music industry turned further inward. The music produced in a largely closed system after 1991 was called "J-pop," which was a branding strategy to situate Japanese

---

[52] Lukács, *Scripted Affects*, 33.

[53] *Ibid.*, 29-31, 43, 51-52.

[54] Koichi Iwabuchi notes that some in Taiwan and other parts of East Asia were attracted to Japanese television dramas and the lifestyles that they projected, which accounts for export success there. See Koichi Iwabuchi, *Recentering Globalization: Popular Culture and Japanese Transnationalism* (Durham, NC: Duke University Press, 2002). For an example of regional convergence around shared content, see Thomas Lamarre, "Regional TV: Affective Media Geographies," *Asiascape: Digital Asia* 2 (2015): 93-126.

[55] Shuhei Hosokawa, "Popular Entertainment and the Music Industry," in *A Companion to the Anthropology of Japan*, ed. Jennifer Robertson (Oxford: Blackwell Publishing, 2005), 306.

[56] Galbraith and Karlin, "Introduction."

music on the world stage.[57] In practice, J-pop was a performance of the global, where Japanese artists incorporated English words and world beats into their performances. In this, J-pop expressed not only the dream of performing on the world stage as a globalized Japanese, but also marked a return to Japan (the "J" in J-pop) and served to domesticate the foreign in Japan.[58] As Japanese performed the global at home, there was increasingly less room for non-Japanese performers in Japan. For example, in 1991, Tama, a Japanese garage band, sold more records in Japan than MC Hammer—by a factor of two to one—and almost as many records as Madonna.[59] As Guy de Launey pointed out at the time, Japan was one of the largest music markets in the world, but there was an increasingly small piece of the pie for performers from outside of Japan.[60] This was not simply a matter of taste, as de Launey rightly noted by examining aspects of the Japanese media system that structurally marginalize foreign music.[61] Media appearances and promotion, advertisements and live shows make Japanese performers an intimate part of everyday life in Japan. Not speaking the Japanese language and not appearing regularly in the Japanese media puts performers from outside of Japan at a disadvantage compared to idols such as AKB48, who have near constant exposure. To understand J-pop, we must bear in mind that difference comes not from any essential Japanese character, but rather from a divergent series of industrial structures and practices that gave rise to distinct features produced and reproduced within the Japanese media system.

In the late 1990s, a significant example of divergence occurred in the Japanese mobile-phone market, which was dominated by feature-rich handsets produced exclusively for Japan. These devices operated mobile data services on closed networks such as NTT DoCoMo's i-mode and KDDI's EZweb.[62] The relatively advanced technology of these mobile phones—which could not only access a walled version of the internet, but also included digital cameras and wallets long before

[57] Michael K. Bourdaghs, *Sayonara Amerika, Sayonara Nippon: A Geopolitical Prehistory of J-Pop* (New York: Columbia University Press, 2012), 224.

[58] Mōri Yoshitaka, "J-Pop: From the Ideology of Creativity to DiY Music Culture," *Inter-Asia Cultural Studies* 10, no. 4 (2009): 475-479.

[59] Guy de Launey, "Not-so-Big in Japan: Western Pop Music in the Japanese Market," *Popular Music* 14, no. 2 (May 1995): 210.

[60] *Ibid.*, 204.

[61] *Ibid.*, 211-220.

[62] Larrisa Hjorth, *Mobile Media in the Asia-Pacific: Gender and the Art of Being Mobile* (London: Routledge, 2008), 79-118.

their introduction with smartphones in other parts of the world—did not function outside of Japan.[63] As was the case with media, Japanese providers had the infrastructure to serve a domestic market so robust that they did not need to expand overseas; at the same time, the highly specialized and integrated system made it hard for providers from outside of Japan to break into the market.[64] As Kenji E. Kushida argues, "politics and regulatory structures shaped a specific set of competitive dynamics, which in turn shaped the choices of technology, standards, and corporate strategies that ended up isolating Japan's domestic telecommunications market from global markets."[65] The technology and infrastructure in Japan also supported new cultural forms such as "cell-phone novels." Networked mobile phones afforded young women, who posted and read episodic stories online while on trains, with new opportunities for self-expression, while also integrating their labor into the emerging digital economy.[66] One cell-phone novel, *Deep Love* (2003), was rereleased as a printed book that sold 2.6 million copies, but it is unlikely that many people outside of Japan have ever heard of it, much less read it on a mobile phone. This is an example of divergent technology and infrastructure leading to divergent media production, distribution and consumption. The phenomenon of divergent development is pronounced enough in Japan to earn comparisons with the Galapagos Islands.

What is Media Mix?

In the Japanese context, an important term in the discussion of convergence is "media mix" (*media mikkusu*). Put simply, media mix refers to a system of media and commodities in relation to one another. The term was popularized in the 1980s, but refers to practices of character franchising that emerged in Japan in the 1960s.[67] In 1963, Tezuka Osamu created *Tetsuwan Atomu* (known in the US as *Astro Boy*), an animated television

---

[63] Mizuko Ito, "Introduction: Personal, Portable, Pedestrian," in *Personal, Portable, Pedestrian: Mobile Phones in Japanese Life*, ed. Mizuko Ito, Daisuke Okabe and Misa Matsuda (Cambridge, MA: MIT Press, 2005), 1-18.

[64] Kenji E. Kushida, "Entrepreneurship in Japan's ICT Sector: Opportunities and Protection from Japan's Telecommunications Regulatory Shift," *Social Science Japan Journal* 15, no. 1 (Winter 2012): 3-30.

[65] Kenji E. Kushida, "Leading without Followers: How Politics and Market Dynamics Trapped Innovations in Japan's Domestic 'Galapagos' Telecommunications Sector," *Journal of Industry, Competition, and Trade* 11, no. 2 (September 2011): 280.

[66] Gabriella Lukács, "Dreamwork: Cell Phone Novelists, Labor, and Politics in Contemporary Japan," *Cultural Anthropology* 28, no. 1 (2013): 44-64.

[67] Marc Steinberg, *Anime's Media Mix: Franchising Toys and Characters in Japan* (Minneapolis, MN: University of Minnesota Press, 2012), viii.

series based on his popular comic book by the same name. Struggling with funding, Tezuka sought out sponsors for promotional tie-ups with *Tetsuwan Atomu*. The result was that the characters of *Tetsuwan Atomu* existed not only in comic books and cartoons, but also on commodities that they promoted and that promoted them. For example, *Tetsuwan Atomu* character stickers were offered as a premium with the purchase of Meiji's marble chocolates, which simultaneously advertised the series and attracted consumers; both ratings of the television series and sales of the chocolates increased. Put another way, the deployment of *Tetsuwan Atomu* characters created synergy and inspired consumption across media and material forms.[68] A huge success, *Tetsuwan Atomu* subsequently became a model for media mix in Japan. "Whereas traditionally the method of selling a product was to advertise and sell a product based on its content," explains Kusakawa Akira, "after *Tetsuwan Atomu* companies would advertise and sell products by overlapping the commodity image with a character image."[69] This overlapping is characteristic of media mixes.

Media mix has its roots in the very analog world of printed comic books, hand-drawn animation and stickers, but in many ways resembles media convergence, which challenges implicit assumptions about digital media technology being key to the phenomenon. In this way, media mix encourages us to consider media convergence in a different place and time and in different ways. Certainly industrial strategies of extension, synergy and franchising are aspects of media convergence that we see in media mix. Certainly corporations, audiences and media forms are coming together in both. The discussion of media mix, however, places more emphasis on characters and affective relationships with them (a dynamic familiar from work on idols in Japan).[70] In his work on character franchising in Japan, Marc Steinberg explicitly connects media mix to Jenkins' discussion of media convergence in the US,[71] but also highlights some differences. In the media mix, the emphasis is not on a coherent narrative or world unfolding across media forms—the "transmedia

---

[68] *Ibid.*, 19. Noting that "economic motivation alone cannot account for the centrality of character merchandising to anime," Steinberg argues that affective engagement with characters was central to anime's success. Affective engagement with characters will be familiar to many from the example of Mickey Mouse and the Walt Disney success story in the US, which resonates strongly with the example of *Tetsuwan Atomu* in Japan.

[69] Kusakawa Akira, *Atomu no ko-ra wa kōya o mezasu: Terebi anime 20-nen shi* (Tokyo: Rippu Shobō, 1981), 31, cited in Steinberg, *Anime's Media Mix*, ix.

[70] For example Lukács, *Scripted Affects*.

[71] Marc Steinberg, "Condensing the Media Mix: Multiple Possible Worlds in *The Tatami Galaxy*," *Canadian Journal of Film Studies* 21, no. 2 (Fall 2012): 72.

storytelling" that Jenkins identifies in *The Matrix*[72]—but rather the franchising of characters, which can exist simultaneously in diverging narratives and worlds.[73] Rather than emerging forms of storytelling, the discussion of media mix draws our attention to the deployment of characters and the economy of affect that exists around them.[74]

Compared to media convergence, the discussion of media mix could do more to address issues of ownership. There is a tendency to celebrate how different actors come together to produce media and material for the mix. Since media mix was originally an industry term that described "a method of advertising that used multiple media forms to deliver an advertising message to potential consumers,"[75] its leanings are clear. As work on convergence has shown, however, the productive activity of consumers and their relationship to media industries should not go unproblematized.

Steinberg's work already suggests some of the issues, which we can unpack here. To return to the example of *Tetsuwan Atomu* in Japan in the 1960s, in the media mix, the characters were "environmentalized" and made "ubiquitous."[76] As the characters proliferated, they became an intimate presence in everyday life.[77] Children grew up in a media environment and in relation to the characters of *Tetsuwan Atomu*, which became part of their shared social imaginary and world. Historical accounts tell of Japanese children not only playing with and as *Tetsuwan Atomu* characters, but also using the character stickers they received with the purchase of Meiji chocolates to transform everyday objects into character merchandise, and therefore expand their attachments and points of access to the media world. These children were, as part of their practices of play, imaginatively inhabiting a media world, expanding it through spreading character images, turning everyday objects into character merchandise and advertising *Tetsuwan Atomu* to others, who

---

[72] Jenkins, *Convergence Culture*, chapter three.

[73] For example, Tezuka Osamu's *Tetsuwan Atomu* comic books did not necessarily have the same story as the television anime, which is to say that the narrative worlds diverged from one another, despite coexisting in space and time as part of the same media mix. For more, see Steinberg, "Condensing the Media Mix," 76-79.

[74] In her work on media mixes, which is cited by Jenkins (*Convergence Culture*, 109-110) and in dialogue with him, Mizuko Ito states that "different national contexts have certain areas of specialization." See Mizuko Ito, "Mobilizing the Imagination in Everyday Play: The Case of Japanese Media Mixes," in *Mashup Cultures*, ed. Stefan Sonvilla-Weiss (London: Springer, 2010), 94. The area of specialization in the national context of Japan might be affective economics in the deployment of idols and characters. In this sense, moving forward in the discussion of media convergence in Japan, we perhaps have more to learn from Jenkins' approach to *American Idol* than transmedia storytelling in *The Matrix*.

[75] Steinberg, *Anime's Media Mix*, 139.

[76] Steinberg, "Anytime, Anywhere," 113-117.

[77] Steinberg, *Anime's Media Mix*, 79, 165-166.

might join them in play. In her research on more contemporary Japanese media mixes such as *Yu-Gi-Oh!*, anthropologist Mizuko Ito observed children engaged in what she calls "hyper sociality," or "social exchange augmented by the social mobilization of elements of the collective imagination."[78] Although Ito for the most part does not consider issues of ownership, because it seems that children at play are freely making use of and collectively sharing anime characters, these elements of their collective imagination that are socially mobilized were provided by corporations, which profit from people buying into and sharing media worlds. On this point, Steinberg argues that "working to follow and produce connections, organizing...relations to the media-commodities, and thereby extending the life of the character" is productive activity and immaterial labor, which entails "the real subsumption of life...under a... regime of image circulation and capital accumulation."[79] For Steinberg, this represents a form of "endocolonization," or cultivation of hearts and minds to make them productive for capital.[80]

Beyond issues of access and literacy, a critical approach to media mix exposes tension between collective and corporate ownership. Characters are part of a collective imagination and social world, but also owned by corporations, which use characters as a "regulatory mechanism" to produce divergent series and force "their convergence at the level of economics and desire."[81] The resulting entanglements are anything but simple. Ōtsuka Eiji—one of Steinberg's primary interlocutors and a former employee of the Kadokawa Corporation, which helped define media mix in Japan in the 1980s—makes this point well in his discussion of world and variation. From his position in the industry, Ōtsuka suggests that in media production, someone provides a "world," which he also describes in terms of a "grand narrative" or underlying order; inside this world, "variation" occurs, which he also describes in terms of "small narratives."[82] Ōtsuka proposes that media corporations most often provide worlds, but small narratives in these worlds are not just, for example, episodes in an anime series, but also fan creations (ie., fanzines) that tell different stories using existing characters or original characters that could exist in a given world. In this way, Ōtsuka makes the labor of production in media worlds similar for "professionals"

---

[78] Ito, "Mobilizing the Imagination in Everyday Play," 87.

[79] Steinberg, *Anime's Media Mix*, 167-169.

[80] *Ibid.*, 167.

[81] *Ibid.*, 190.

[82] Ōtsuka Eiji, "World and Variation: The Reproduction and Consumption of Narrative," in *Mechademia 5: Fanthropologies*, ed. Frenchy Lunning (Minneapolis, MN: University of Minnesota Press, 2010), 99-116.

and "amateurs."[83] A tension emerges in corporations, which incorporate fan creativity into strategies of ownership and profit making, but also empower consumers as creators potentially independent of corporations.[84]

Echoes of Ōtsuka's approach to media mix can be heard in ongoing discussions of media industries in Japan. Kitabayashi Ken, working for the Nomura Research Institute, calls for Japanese corporations to "use otaku and their activities," which is to say to develop an "integrated" model of active, productive, communicative fans working for and with corporations.[85] An interesting example is fanzines, which Kitabayashi explains as follows:

> A unique feature of fanzine publishing is that it is somewhat recognized by the commercial publishing industry. Most fanzine content consists of parodies of commercial publications and often seems to infringe on copyrights and neighboring rights of the original creators...However, its function as a place for testing has been widely recognized in the commercial publishing industry as being indispensable for promoting the comics business and, therefore, the existence of fanzines has been tactically accepted within the industry...Such a structure of the Japanese comics industry, which recognizes the existence and makes active use of fanzines as a home for testing, is rarely seen elsewhere.[86]

While Kitabayashi is correct that the tolerance for fanzines displayed by commercial publishers in Japan is striking in comparison to places such as the US, the "integrated" model that it suggests is not unique to Japan. Fan activities, as Jenkins, Ito and many others note, are increasingly mainstream in convergence culture around the world.[87]

The case of fanzines in Japan makes clear that the productive activity of fans is good for business, which is why fanzines have not only been allowed, but even encouraged to expand to an unprecedented extent in that country. Consider that there are thousands of fanzine events in Japan, with the largest, the Comic Market, drawing over 550,000 fans to Tokyo to

---

[83] Ian Condry makes a similar argument in his discussion of characters and worlds as platforms for creative action for both professionals and fans. See Ian Condry, *The Soul of Anime: Collaborative Creativity and Japan's Media Success Story* (Durham, NC: Duke University Press, 2013), 58-64.

[84] Ōtsuka, "World and Variation," 107, 113.

[85] Kitabayashi Ken, "The *Otaku* Group from a Business Perspective: Revaluation of Enthusiastic Consumers," *NRI Papers* 84 (December 1, 2004): 6-7. Compare this with Jenkins, "The Cultural Logic of Media Convergence," 42.

[86] Kitabayashi, "The *Otaku* Group from a Business Perspective," 6.

[87] Ito, "Mobilizing the Imagination in Everyday Play," 82.

buy and sell printed copies of fanzines featuring their favorite characters from comics, anime and other media.[88] To put this into perspective, San Diego Comic-Con, a massive event boasting an impressive line up of Hollywood stars, draws around 130,000 people.[89] In a *Wired* report on fanzines in Japan, Daniel H. Pink proposes three reasons why the flouting of copyright law is tolerated: one, fanzine events allow corporations and creators to observe fans and learn what they like; two, fanzine creators broaden and deepen the talent pool and become the next generation of creative professionals; and three, fanzines are a form of customer care that not only do not diminish sales of comics, anime and other media, but in fact invigorate them by allowing fans of characters to express and share their love, which tends to reinforce existing attachments and bring fans back to commercial releases.[90] In addition, corporations treat fanzine events as marketing opportunities in at least two ways: one, corporations advertise new and upcoming character media and merchandise directly to their core audience; and two, core audiences take existing characters and markets them to other fans in the form of fanzines. Building on Pink's insights, we can say that active, productive and communicative fans invigorate media worlds, affirm and deepen existing attachments to characters and spread images of those characters to where they can be encountered by new fans. All of this productive activity among fans is free marketing and free labor for corporations.

Like fanzines, Hatsune Miku—a virtual idol produced by dispersed fan networks spanning the globe—is another noteworthy example of the productive activity of fans and affective alliances between corporations and fans brought together by characters (see Chapter 8). No one person is Miku's producer, since anyone with the Vocaloid software can produce music with her. Some of this music has been popular enough to be released on CDs, rank on the Oricon charts and make its way into karaoke boxes in Japan. While some use separate software to make videos of Miku dancing, others draw fan art, costume and perform as her, write fan fiction and/or produce figurines and character merchandise. Anthropologist Ian Condry argues that Miku is a "platform" for "collaborative creativity."[91] For Condry, "creativity grows out of social energy arising from a collective

[88] This figure is from the summer 2015 event.

[89] This estimate is from the 2015 event.

[90] Daniel H. Pink, "Japan, Ink: Inside the Manga Industrial Complex," *Wired*, October 22, 2007, accessed December 1, 2015, http://www.wired.com/techbiz/media/magazine/15-11/ff_manga.

[91] Ian Condry, "Post-3/11 Japan and the Radical Recontextualization of Value: Music, Social Media, and End-Around Strategies for Cultural Action," *International Journal of Japanese Sociology* 20, no. 1 (November 1, 2011): 12-15.

interest in Miku."[92] Condry refers to this social energy and collective interest, which are key to his analysis of contemporary media culture, as "the soul" and "the social in media."[93] Despite the infectious positivity of such discussions of Miku, we nonetheless wonder who provides and profits from the platform, and how. Facebook is a social media platform, but that does not change the fact that a corporation owns it and capitalizes on users spending free time on the platform and freely sharing data, which is collected and sold to interested parties.[94]

Given all of this, it should come as no surprise that the Kadokawa Corporation, which did much to conceptualize media mixes integrating fan activity in Japan in the 1980s, has recently merged with Dwango, known for Niconico (formerly Nico Nico Douga), a video-sharing site and source of immense social and creative activity in contemporary Japan.[95] For example, it was through fan-produced videos uploaded on Niconico that Hatsune Miku became an idol with global star power. At a time of media convergence, Kadokawa's merger with Dwango looks suspiciously like an attempt to harvest the value of productive activity online. None of this is to diminish or dismiss the creativity of fans, the value of whose social lives and activities is certainly not completely captured by corporations, just as Kadokawa-Dwango profiting from people making free use of characters and platforms is not necessarily a simple example of exploitation. However, when discussing media mixes, scholars need to think about differential ownership; profit sharing, privacy and surveillance; and the freedom and limitation of creative action. We must keep in mind that social life and activity is the "factory" for post-industrial economies. This social factory thesis is precisely why autonomous Marxists at times advocate a refusal of

---

[92] Condry, *The Soul of Anime*, 63.

[93] *Ibid.*, 2, 29.

[94] Although Condry clearly wants to avoid a political economy approach, his own move to refer to the social, productive, creative activity of human beings in terms of "soul" cannot help but lead to critiques of the "soul at work." See Franco Berardi, *The Soul at Work: From Alienation to Autonomy*, trans. Francesca Cadel and Guiseppina Mecchia (Los Angeles: Semiotext(e), 2009). More specifically, the question is how the soul and the social in media are put to work. As a corrective to certain strands of contemporary political theory, Franco Berardi argues that collectives are not boundless positive energy and potential, but rather groups of human beings with limited libidinal energy, which is channeled and capitalized on in manageable circuits. This channeling and feeding off of libidinal energy can serve to exhaust and pacify collectives, as well as divert channeling libidinal energy into other action.

[95] Ōtsuka Eiji has expressed apprehension regarding this merger. See Ōtsuka Eiji, *Media mikkusu-ka suru Nihon* (Tokyo: East Press, 2014). In particular, Ōtsuka seems concerned that the labor of fans producing content for Niconico will be integrated into corporate structures. Whereas Ōtsuka was a champion of media mix in the 1980s when it meant developing new forms of storytelling and franchising, he seems to have a different response to today's media convergence, which seeks to consolidate ownership and integrate fan/free labor.

capitalist relations, which are seen as parasitic relations feeding off of life itself. For the fan, however, free labor in the social factory and social media worlds is a life sustaining "labor of love" (see Chapter 9). In the convergence of corporate and fan interests in affective alliances around idols and characters, we observe how one can actually desire capitalist relations, but also struggle to interact with and through media more freely. The direction suggested by this discussion is no less than a political economy of social media worlds.

Conclusion

Media Convergence in Japan is a collection of chapters by a group of scholars from around the world brought together by a shared interest in media and Japan. The contributors recognize that as Japanese media circulates globally, scholars need a better understanding of the dynamics that produce it, which are changing. One of the goals of the edited volume is to take the general concept of convergence and work through it in a specific time and place. However, as the editors of the volume, we are strongly against reproducing discourses of "Japanese-ness," which assert that Japan and Japanese media and culture are unique and incommensurate with the rest of the world. That is not what *Media Convergence in Japan* is about. It is not what the body of work on media convergence in Japan, at its best, has been about, even when it seems that "media convergence" is contrasted with "media mix."[96] Media convergence and media mix are not different phenomena, but rather different analytic emphases. If convergence points to a coming together of two or more things, media mix points to a system of media and commodities in relation to one another.

Media Convergence in Japan is divided into five sections, which at times correspond with and at times depart from familiar divisions in the discussion of media convergence. As Terry Flew explains, media convergence encompasses at least five major kinds of convergence: technological, industrial, social/cultural, textual and political.[97] Although this volume is divided into five sections, the sections consciously do not reproduce the five major kinds of convergence. That said, the five sections are not meant to be an alternative list of the major kinds of convergence. Rather, the chapters simply converge on different themes, which are

---

[96] For his part, Steinberg is clear that differences (real or imagined) between media convergence and media mix should not be conflated with or reduced to reified national differences in discussions of "Japan" (Steinberg, "Condensing the Media Mix," 73, 87).

[97] Terry Flew, "Media Convergence," Encyclopaedia Britannica Online, January 8, 2014, accessed January 16, 2016, http://www.britannica.com/topic/media-convergence.

organized into different sections: Media Convergence After 3/11, Industrial Convergence, Cultural Convergence, Convergence of the Virtual and Real and Affective Convergence. Each section and chapter brings together the five major kinds of convergence in media convergence in different ways. In some, the focus is technological and industrial, while in others it is social/cultural and political.[98] As is the case with media convergence as a phenomenon, lines are crossed and blurred as things come together.

Returning to scramble crossing in Shibuya, the traffic lights begin to flash and the flow of bodies subside. What was a chaotic jumble slowly starts to clear in anticipation of oncoming traffic. New arrivals pool on street corners and wait for the next light in a cycle without end. Some look at the screens of their mobile phones, while the attention of others is captured by massive display screens integrated into the sides of buildings. Images of idols flash across those screens and stare down from massive posters plastered onto the sides of buildings. AKB48 is on one screen, HIKAKIN on another; AKB48 is on one poster, Arashi on another. Music from loudspeakers on narrow side streets associated with hip youth culture drifts into scramble crossing. The music is all recent J-pop songs played for a fee, which producers pay to promote their performers. If one waits here long enough, the music starts to become familiar. A kiosk is crowded with people buying newspapers, magazines and comic books for the train ride home. In a space so saturated with media—overflowing with information, proliferating with images and identities—nothing seems certain. As old and new media come together, much changes and much stays the same. So it goes with media convergence in Japan. Awash in image and sound, we wait for the light to change.

Works Cited

Berardi, Franco. *The Soul at Work: From Alienation to Autonomy.* Translated by Francesca Cadel and Guiseppina Mecchia. Los Angeles: Semiotext(e), 2009.

Bourdaghs, Michael K. *Sayonara Amerika, Sayonara Nippon: A Geopolitical Prehistory of J-Pop.* New York: Columbia University Press, 2012.

Brasor, Philip. "Snark Levels Were on Full Blast for 'Kohaku.'" *The Japan Times.* January 17, 2015. Accessed December 1, 2015. http://www.japantimes.co.jp/news/2015/01/17/national/media-national/snark-levels-full-blast-kohaku/.

---

[98] While not entirely absent in the edited volume, textual convergence gets somewhat less discussion overall, because the textual is overrepresented in scholarship on media in Japan.

Coates, Jamie. "Rogue Diva Flows: Aoi Sola's Reception in the Chinese Media and Mobile Celebrity." *Journal of Japanese and Korean Cinema* 6, no. 1 (2014): 89-103.

Condry, Ian. "Post-3/11 Japan and the Radical Recontextualization of Value: Music, Social Media, and End-Around Strategies for Cultural Action." *International Journal of Japanese Sociology* 20, no. 1 (November 1, 2011): 4-17.

———. *The Soul of Anime: Collaborative Creativity and Japan's Media Success Story.* Durham, NC: Duke University Press, 2013.

De Launey, Guy. "Not-so-Big in Japan: Western Pop Music in the Japanese Market." *Popular Music* 14, no. 2 (May 1995): 203-225.

Dyer-Witheford, Nick, and Greig de Peuter. *Games of Empire: Global Capitalism and Videogames.* Minneapolis, MN: University of Minnesota Press, 2009.

Elsaesser, Thomas. "Convergence, Divergence, Difference." In *Cinema Futures: Cain, Abel or Cable? The Screen Arts in the Digital Age,* edited by Thomas Elsaesser and Kay Hoffmann, 9-26. Amsterdam: Amsterdam University Press, 1998.

Eng, Lawrence. "Strategies of Engagement: Discovering, Defining, and Describing Otaku Culture in the United States." In *Fandom Unbound: Otaku Culture in a Connected World,* edited by Mizuko Ito, Daisuke Okabe and Izumi Tsuji, 85-106. New Haven: Yale University Press, 2012.

Flew, Terry. "Media Convergence." Encyclopaedia Britannica Online, January 8, 2014, accessed January 16, 2016, http://www.britannica.com/topic/media-convergence.

Galbraith, Patrick W. "AKB Business: Idols and Affective Economics in Contemporary Japan." In *Introducing Japanese Popular Culture,* edited by Alisa Freedman and Toby Slade. London: Routledge, forthcoming.

Galbraith, Patrick W., and Jason G. Karlin. "Introduction: The Mirror of Idols and Celebrity." In *Idols and Celebrity in Japanese Media Culture,* edited by Patrick W. Galbraith and Jason G. Karlin, 1-32. New York: Palgrave, 2012.

Grant, August E., and Jeffrey F. Wilkinson. *Understanding Media Convergence: The State of the Field*. Oxford: Oxford University Press, 2009.

Hjorth, Larrisa. *Mobile Media in the Asia-Pacific: Gender and the Art of Being Mobile*. London: Routledge, 2008.

Hosokawa, Shuhei. "Popular Entertainment and the Music Industry." In *A Companion to the Anthropology of Japan*, edited by Jennifer Robertson, 297-313. Oxford: Blackwell Publishing, 2005.

Ito, Mizuko. "Introduction: Personal, Portable, Pedestrian." In *Personal, Portable, Pedestrian: Mobile Phones in Japanese Life*, edited by Mizuko Ito, Daisuke Okabe and Misa Matsuda, 1-18. Cambridge, MA: MIT Press, 2005.

———. "Mobilizing the Imagination in Everyday Play: The Case of Japanese Media Mixes." In *Mashup Cultures*, edited by Stefan Sonvilla-Weiss, 79-97. London: Springer, 2010.

Iwabuchi, Koichi. *Recentering Globalization: Popular Culture and Japanese Transnationalism*. Durham, NC: Duke University Press, 2002.

Jenkins, Henry. "The Cultural Logic of Media Convergence." *International Journal of Cultural Studies* 7, no. 1 (2004): 33-43.

———. *Convergence Culture: Where Old and New Media Collide*. New York: New York University Press, 2006.

Johnson, Derek. *Media Franchising: Creative License and Collaboration in the Culture Industries*. New York: New York University Press, 2013.

Karlin, Jason G. "Through a Looking Glass Darkly: Television Advertising, Idols, and the Making of Fan Audiences." In *Idols and Celebrity in Japanese Media Culture*, edited by Patrick W. Galbraith and Jason G. Karlin, 72-93. New York: Palgrave, 2012.

Kitabayashi, Ken. "The *Otaku* Group from a Business Perspective: Revaluation of Enthusiastic Consumers." *NRI Papers* 84 (December 1, 2004): 1-8.

Kusakawa Akira. *Atomu no ko-ra wa kōya o mezasu: Terebi anime 20-nen shi.* Tokyo: Rippu Shobō, 1981.

Kushida, Kenji E. "Entrepreneurship in Japan's ICT Sector: Opportunities and Protection from Japan's Telecommunications Regulatory Shift." *Social Science Japan Journal* 15, no. 1 (Winter 2012): 3-30.

———. "Leading without Followers: How Politics and Market Dynamics Trapped Innovations in Japan's Domestic 'Galapagos' Telecommunications Sector." *Journal of Industry, Competition, and Trade* 11, no. 2 (September 2011): 279-307.

Kyodo. "NHK Sees Ratings for 'Kohaku' Music Show Sink to Lowest Ever." *The Japan Times*, January 2, 2016, accessed January 15, 2016, http://www.japantimes.co.jp/news/2016/01/02/national/media-national/nhk-sees-ratings-for-kohaku-music-show-sink-to-lowest-ever/.

Lamarre, Thomas. "Regional TV: Affective Media Geographies." *Asiascape: Digital Asia* 2 (2015): 93-126.

Lanier, Jaron. *Who Owns the Future?* New York: Simon and Schuster, 2014.

Lazzarato, Maurizio. "Immaterial Labor." In *Radical Thought in Italy: A Potential Politics,* edited by Paolo Virno and Michael Hardt, 133-147. Minneapolis, MN: University of Minnesota Press, 1996.

Lie, John. *K-Pop: Popular Music, Cultural Amnesia, and Economic Innovation in South Korea.* Oakland: University of California Press, 2015.

Lukács, Gabriella. *Scripted Affects, Branded Selves: Television, Subjectivity and Capitalism in 1990s Japan.* Durham, NC: Duke University Press, 2010.

———. "Dreamwork: Cell Phone Novelists, Labor, and Politics in Contemporary Japan." *Cultural Anthropology* 28, no. 1 (2013): 44-64.

———. "The Labor of Cute: Net Idols, Cute Culture, and the Digital Economy in Contemporary Japan." *positions: east asia cultures critique* 23, no. 3 (2015): 487-513.

Marshall, P. David. "The New Intertextual Commodity." In *The New Media Handbook*, edited by Dan Harries, 69-81. London: British Film Institute, 2002.

———. *Celebrity and Power: Fame in Contemporary Culture*. Minneapolis, MN: University of Minnesota Press, 2014.

Marx, W. David. "The *Jimusho* System: Understanding the Production Logic of the Japanese Entertainment Industry." In *Idols and Celebrity in Japanese Media Culture*, edited by Patrick W. Galbraith and Jason G. Karlin, 35-55. New York: Palgrave, 2012.

Mōri, Yoshitaka. "J-Pop: From the Ideology of Creativity to DiY Music Culture." *Inter-Asia Cultural Studies* 10, no. 4 (2009): 474-488.

Nakaoku Miki. "Terebi wa dore kurai mirareteita no ka." *Video Research Digest* 5-6 (2014), accessed November 1, 2014, https://www.videor.co.jp/vr-digest/pdf/vrd536_20140506/vrd536_article1.pdf.

Ōta Shō'ichi. *Kōhaku utagassen to Nihonjin*. Tokyo: Chikuma Shobō, 2013.

Ōtsuka Eiji. *Media mikkusu-ka suru Nihon*. Tokyo: East Press, 2014.

———. "World and Variation: The Reproduction and Consumption of Narrative." In *Mechademia 5: Fanthropologies*, edited by Frenchy Lunning, 99-116. Minneapolis, MN: University of Minnesota Press, 2010.

Perlow, Seth. "On Production for Digital Culture: iPhone Girl, Electronics Assembly, and the Material Forms of Aspiration." *Convergence: The International Journal of Research into New Media Technologies* 17, no. 3 (August 1, 2011): 245-269.

Pink, Daniel H. "Japan, Ink: Inside the Manga Industrial Complex." *Wired*, October 22, 2007, accessed December 1, 2015, http://www.wired.com/techbiz/media/magazine/15-11/ff_manga.

Senft, Theresa M. *Camgirls: Celebrity and Community*. New York: Peter Lang Publishing, 2008.

Shin, Solee I., and Lanu Kim. "Organizing K-Pop: Emergence and Market Making of Large Korean Entertainment Houses, 1980-2010." *East Asia* 30, no. 4 (December 2013): 255-272.

Shiraishi, Saya S. "Doraemon Goes Abroad." In *Japan Pop! Inside the World of Japanese Popular Culture*, edited by Timothy J. Craig, 287-308. New York: M.E. Sharpe, 2000.

Shoemaker, Pamela J., and Tim P. Vos. *Gatekeeping Theory*. London: Routledge, 2009.

Steinberg, Marc. 2009. "Anytime, Anywhere: *Tetsuwan Atomu* Stickers and the Emergence of Character Merchandising." *Theory, Culture and Society* 26, no. 2-3 (2009): 113-138.

———. "Condensing the Media Mix: Multiple Possible Worlds in *The Tatami Galaxy*." *Canadian Journal of Film Studies* 21, no. 2 (Fall 2012): 71-92.

———. *Anime's Media Mix: Franchising Toys and Characters in Japan*. Minneapolis, MN: University of Minnesota Press, 2012.

Tsing, Anna Lowenhaupt. *Friction: An Ethnography of Global* Connection. Princeton: Princeton University Press, 2005.

Villi, Mikko, and Kaori Hayashi. "'The Mission is to Keep This Industry Intact': Digital Transition in the Japanese Newspaper Industry." *Journalism Studies* (November 25, 2015): 1-18. doi: 10.1080/1461670X.2015.1110499.

Yoshimi, Shun'ya. "From Street Corner to Living Room: Domestication of TV Culture and National Time/Narrative." In *Mechademia 9: Origins*, edited by Frenchy Lunning, 126-142. Minneapolis, MN: University of Minnesota Press, 2014.

Part I:
Media Convergence After 3/11

Precarious Consumption After 3.11: Television Advertising in Risk Society

Jason G. Karlin

For about three days after March 11th 2011, Japan's television networks broadcast continuous uninterrupted news coverage of the aftermath of the earthquake and tsunami in northeast Japan and the emerging crisis at the Fukushima nuclear reactor. The constant news coverage was a profound disruption in the experience of everyday life for most Japanese, including those who were mostly unaffected spectators to the greater tragedy. Television in Japan is, among other things, a technology of time control that modulates the diurnal cycle.[1] Since the spread of television into Japanese homes during the 1960s, the various genres of programs established what Yoshimi Shun'ya describes as a "national timetable" (*kokuminteki jikanwari*) that structures postwar conceptions of time and the flow of daily events. Beginning with morning news and information shows, the daily television schedule gives way to daytime dramas and "wideshows"—which are followed by early evening news and golden time variety, quiz shows and dramas—before concluding with the nightly news and late-night variety programs. About 89% of all Japanese watch television on any given day.[2]

The regularity and repetition of television contains the potential for disruption that constitutes the spectacle of television to provide coverage of live media events. In the days following 3.11, a singular frame replaced the flow of time experienced through the daily television-programming schedule. Morning and evening became undifferentiated, and unfamiliar newscasters donning helmets in news studios reported the events in a hypnotic cycle punctuated by new announcements, videos, and reports of the hundreds of aftershocks. Even the broadcasting of commercials was suspended, only to be replaced by the airing of unrelated public service announcements inserted as substitutes for paid ads. As the experience of time became disconnected from the rhythms

---

[1] Yoshimi Shun'ya, "Terebi ga ie ni yatte-kita: Terebi no kūkan, terebi no jikan," *Shisō* 956 (Dec. 2003): 26-48.

[2] NHK Hōsō Bunka Kenkyūjo, *2010-nen kokumin seikatsu jikan chōsa hōkokusho* (Feb. 2010), accessed November 21, 2012, http://www.nhk.or.jp/bunken/summary/yoron/lifetime/pdf/110223.pdf.

of everyday life, an uncanny feeling of both repulsion and attraction suffused each new report and aftershock.

The disruption to regular television broadcasting in Japan resulting from the events of 3.11 is an unprecedented event that may help us to better understand the role of media and celebrity in our everyday lives. According to Mary Ann Doane, television's principle of structuration is time.[3] It is the basis by which television defines its content of information as a continuous flow and the measure by which it designates the rate of advertising. As the endless stream of images flash across the screen, television signifies the present. However, as Doane notes, amid the continuous flow of information, there are "moments with an impact which disrupts the ordinary routine—moments when information bristles."[4] These events, like the quake on 3.11, are catastrophes that are unexpected discontinuities in the regular flow of television time. If most news stories are defined by their resolution within a limited period of time, a catastrophe is outside of time. "It interrupts television's regular daily programming, disrupting normal expectations about what can be seen and heard at a particular time."[5] While the catastrophe is an event that affirms television's status as a medium of live information, it is also an event that is irreconcilable with the corporate interests of commercial broadcast television. In short, catastrophes create negative associations that commercial brands seek to avoid. During a catastrophe, the broadcasting of television commercials is suspended since images of death and suffering cannot be reconciled to the image that brands seek to project.

This chapter will explore how Japanese commercial television negotiates the unexpected and contingent, whether a catastrophe such as 3.11 or the loss of commercial sponsors. Consolidated around five key terrestrial broadcast stations, Japanese commercial television has faced negligible competition in the past from satellite or cable television. Like many sectors of the Japanese economy, commercial television engages in anti-competitive practices that seek to prevent new entrants and to mitigate risk (see Chapter 4). However, Japanese television today faces its greatest existential threat from media convergence. Despite their tight grip on the television market, commercial television broadcasters are facing unprecedented challenges from new media as mobile phones, video games, and PCs compete for time and attention. Indeed, daily

---

[3] Mary Ann Doane, "Information, Crisis, Catastrophe," in *Logics of Television: Essays in Cultural Criticism*, ed. Patricia Mellencamp (Bloomington: Indiana University Press, 1990), 222.

[4] *Ibid.*, 228.

[5] *Ibid.*, 232.

media usage of cell phones has climbed from 18 minutes in 2009 to more than 74 minutes per day in 2014.[6] As a result, the overall audience share for Japanese television has declined in the last decade, with few programs attracting more than 10% of the national audience. Owing to media convergence, audiences have developed increasingly migratory behavior that seeks out new platforms and dispersed media content; and consumers—empowered by social media—have become more active in their relationship to content producers and sponsors.[7] In the following, this chapter will analyze how Japan's commercial television broadcasters manage risk associated with media convergence. In what ways have new technologies of social media altered the perception of risk? What are the consequences of risk management for the Japanese media industry?

Media and Risk

The experience of life in modern capitalist societies is, as Anthony Giddens has noted, "apocalyptic" owing to the heightened perception of new and unexpected risks. With themes of disaster common in Japanese popular culture, risk is embedded in the narratives of national identity in contemporary Japan.[8] The characterization of modernity as a "risk society" is not to suggest that modernity is any more precarious than earlier times. Instead, Giddens argues, the distinctiveness of modern life is rather in the way assessments of risk and contingency are built into modern institutions. Everyday life, with its routinization of work and play, form a framework for cultivating a sense of being that is essential to ontological security. In other words, the habits and routine of our ordinary lives insulate us from the anxieties arising from modernity. As Anthony Giddens notes, "the abstract systems of modernity create large areas of relative security for the continuance of day-to-day life."[9] The repetition of television in Japan, including idols and celebrities, operating together with the day-to-day routines reproduced by it, form a structure of social stability and identity formation.

Since Japanese television is predicated on an intimate connection with its audience through idols and celebrities, the constant news coverage

---

[6] Media Kankyō Kenkyūjo, *Media Teiten Chōsa (Tōkyō) 2014*, June 10, 2014, accessed March 16, 2015, http://www.media-kankyo.jp/wordpress/wp-content/uploads/teiten2014.pdf.
[7] Henry Jenkins, *Convergence Culture: Where Old and New Media Collide* (New York: New York University Press, 2006).
[8] See Susan J. Napier, "Panic Sites: The Japanese Imagination of Disaster from *Godzilla* to *Akira*," *The Journal of Japanese Studies* 19, no. 2 (1993): 327-351.
[9] Anthony Giddens, *Modernity and Self-identity: Self and Social Life in the Late Modern Age* (Stanford: Stanford University Press, 1991), 133.

following 3.11 also disrupted established patterns of social interaction and community. As Patricia Mellencamp argues, the flow of time on television is a system of economics—both material and libidinal.[10] With the experience of everyday life mediated by familiar personalities whose regular appearance on television and other media create a sense of connectedness and identity, the loss of this supportive social network of imagined relations was a profound violation of the routines of everyday life in contemporary Japan. The social deprivation resulting from the sudden loss of a familiar, though mediated, relationship is no longer a trivial concern in our increasingly media-saturated culture.[11] One should not dismiss the importance of social networks, including mediated relationships to celebrities, on our everyday lives. Celebrities form the structure of our sense of identity and allow us to conceptualize our relationship to the wider world. Moreover, they facilitate social practices within society by organizing patterns of social exchange, accumulation, and consumption.

In the days of catastrophe coverage following 3.11 when regular broadcasting and commercials were suspended, Japan's idol-industrial complex was left without the means of directly addressing its audience. Fearing the loss of exposure, Japanese idols and celebrities took to social media as means of confirming the integrity of the "celebrity public sphere."[12] Many posted messages of condolences on their official blogs, while others took the lead in soliciting charitable donations from fans (figure 1). Through their public expressions of grief, celebrities appear in the public sphere to stand in for real citizens. Lynn Spigel describes this as "celebrity citizenship," by which she argues that celebrities affirm their status in the national community through the performance of public service.[13]

---

[10] Patricia Mellencamp, "TV Time and Catastrophe, or *Beyond the Pleasure Principle* of Television," in *Logics of Television: Essays in Cultural Criticism*, ed. Patricia Mellencamp (Bloomington: Indiana University Press, 1990): 240-262.

[11] Julie Lather and Emily Moyer-Guse, "How Do We React When Our Favorite Characters Are Taken Away? An Examination of a Temporary Parasocial Breakup," *Mass Communication and Society* 14, no. 2 (February 28, 2011): 196–215.

[12] Lynn Spigel, "Entertainment Wars: Television Culture after 9/11," *American Quarterly* 56, no. 2 (2004): 235-270.

[13] *Ibid.*, 250-255.

Figure 1. The "Celebrity Public Sphere."

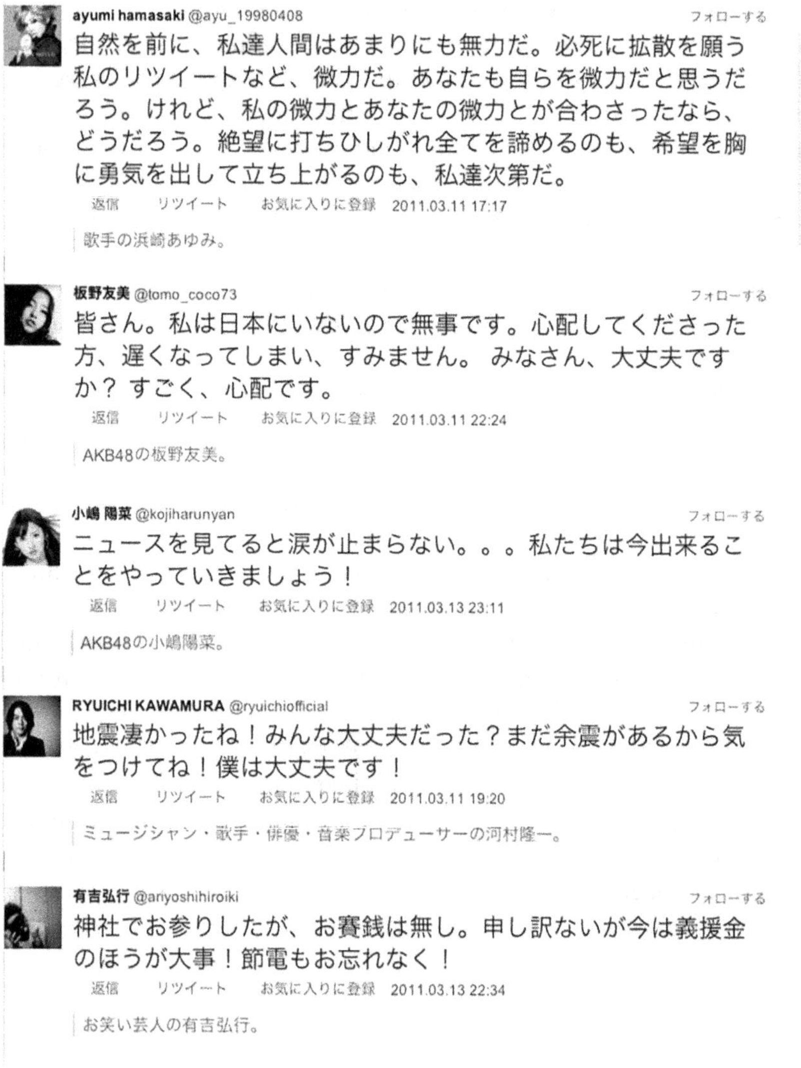

ayumi hamasaki @ayu_19980408 　　　　　　　　　　　フォローする

自然を前に、私達人間はあまりにも無力だ。必死に拡散を願う
私のリツイートなど、微力だ。あなたも自らを微力だと思うだ
ろう。けれど、私の微力とあなたの微力とが合わさったなら、
どうだろう。絶望に打ちひしがれ全てを諦めるのも、希望を胸
に勇気を出して立ち上がるのも、私達次第だ。

返信　　リツイート　　お気に入りに登録　2011.03.11 17:17

歌手の浜崎あゆみ。

板野友美 @tomo_coco73 　　　　　　　　　　　　　フォローする

皆さん。私は日本にいないので無事です。心配してくださった
方、遅くなってしまい、すみません。 みなさん、大丈夫です
か？ すごく、心配です。

返信　　リツイート　　お気に入りに登録　2011.03.11 22:24

AKB48の板野友美。

小嶋 陽菜 @kojiharunyan 　　　　　　　　　　　　フォローする

ニュースを見てると涙が止まらない。。。私たちは今出来るこ
とをやっていきましょう！

返信　　リツイート　　お気に入りに登録　2011.03.13 23:11

AKB48の小嶋陽菜。

RYUICHI KAWAMURA @ryuichiofficial 　　　　　　　フォローする

地震凄かったね！みんな大丈夫だった？まだ余震があるから気
をつけてね！僕は大丈夫です！

返信　　リツイート　　お気に入りに登録　2011.03.11 19:20

ミュージシャン・歌手・俳優・音楽プロデューサーの河村隆一。

有吉弘行 @anyoshihiroiki 　　　　　　　　　　　　フォローする

神社でお参りしたが、お賽銭は無し。申し訳ないが今は義援金
のほうが大事！節電もお忘れなく！

返信　　リツイート　　お気に入りに登録　2011.03.13 22:34

お笑い芸人の有吉弘行。

Note: Japanese celebrities Hamazaki Ayumi, Itano Tomomi, Kojima Haruna, Kawamura Ryuichi, and Ariyoshi Hiroiki took to social media (ie., Twitter) to reach their fans and supporters in the wake of 3.11.

The Japanese mainstream media's relentless promotion of idols and celebrities in the period after the triple disaster in Fukushima is a reflection of the importance of consumption to Japan's precarious post-industrial economy. Rather than a sign of economic prosperity, the intensification of the idol industry in recent years, after a period of decline in the 1990s, is a product of Japan's unsustainable consumption-based media system thrown into crisis by globalization and convergence. In modern societies, institutionalized systems of risk, such as consumer markets, are highly unpredictable and unstable, since much of what we consume is defined more in terms of its exchange rather than use value. Like all institutionalized risk cultures, consumer culture too in Japan engages in the reflexive monitoring of risk. Just as the Hollywood star system provided a guarantee or promise against loss on investment for the film industry, idols are an immunity against instability since they regulate and ensure regular consumption in post-industrial society. For the media industry, idols and celebrities colonize the future by dispersing risk into a more manageable system for regulating consumer desire.

In Japanese consumer society, two media institutions share a close reciprocal relationship in the management of risk. The first is ad agencies. Unlike in the US and the UK, Japan's advertising agencies manage both creative production and media buying. Because media-buying power is consolidated around two large "full-service" advertising agencies, Dentsu and Hakuhodo, clients primarily pay commissions for advertisement placement in the media rather than creative. Without independent creative agencies competing for clients, the production of television ads is driven more by marketing managers than by agency creative units. Dentsu's annual revenue in 2014 amounted to ¥4.642 trillion or roughly US$39 billion; Hakuhodo's annual revenue in 2014 totaled ¥1.131 trillion or roughly US$9 billion.[14] As a total of its revenue, television advertising accounts for most of Dentsu's and Hakuhodo's revenue. Though internet advertising has increased in recent years, it is still much smaller than television. One of the primary functions of ad agencies in Japan is to manage risk through public relations, including the leverage they exercise against media companies in return for advertising revenue. Beyond just the creative production of advertising and the buying of media, ad agencies engage in damage control and image management. They use their considerable power and influence to manage risk, especially by limiting damage to the image of one of their brands.

The second media institution, which manages risk for corporate brands, is talent agencies or management companies (*jimusho*). Japan's talent agencies—which create, train and manage the careers of media

[14] Dentsu, "2014-nendo renketsu kessan gaikyō to jiki gyōseki mitōshi," May 14, 2015, http://www.dentsu.co.jp/ir/data/pdf/2015EAPREJ0.pdf, accessed June 10, 2015; and Hakuhodo DY Holdings, "2015-nen 3-gatsu-ki tsūki renketsu kessan gaiyō," May 13, 2015, accessed June 10, 2015, https://www.hakuhodody-holdings.co.jp/ir/pdf/博報堂DY2015年3月期通期決算説明会資料.pdf.

performers—are by comparison mostly small, privately owned companies. They produce popular celebrities who will generate media attention and avoid scandals or public relations problems for the media companies and their advertisers. Most agencies exert strict control over their performers, not only in the direction of their careers, but also in their personal lives. In order to maintain their youthful or "boyish" image, few of the male idols managed by the agency Johnny's & Associates are permitted to marry. The female idols in AKB48 and its "sister" groups are banned from romantic relationships as a means of preserving their chaste and pure image. These infringements into the private lives of celebrities might be enforced by the *jimusho*, but are dictated by the corporations for whom they are sponsoring. "*Jimusho* face major repercussions when their stars get in trouble for personal scandal—first and foremost because companies have invested in using their 'clean' image to promote their products."[15] In short, the role of talent agencies is to manage the risk associated with the personalities or human capital that sponsor goods and services through their commercial endorsements.

In general, the media institutions of ad and talent agencies have served, with varying degrees of success, to mitigate risk in the advertising and entertainment industries. Ad agencies limit risk or negative exposure by withholding or threatening to withhold advertising from those media outlets that report on information harmful to the image of their corporate clients; and talent agencies restrict access to popular celebrities as a means of containing scandals. However, due to social media's rising popularity in Japan, the role of old media to serve as gatekeepers to prevent negative publicity or as agenda setters to limit the salience of stories that are unfavorable to advertisers has been greatly weakened in recent years. Social Networking Services (SNS) have been rapidly growing in popularity with more than 57% usage among all Japanese in 2013.[16] LINE, Google+, Facebook, and Twitter respectively are the most popular SNS in Japan, and their usage is expected to continue to grow. News stories or scandals that might have been contained in the past, now risk becoming viral on Japanese social media. Without the means of controlling public discourse in Japan, society's institutions and corporations have become hypersensitive to criticism, and media companies—especially commercial television—have become highly averse to risk.

---

[15] W. David Marx, "The Jimusho System: Understanding the Production Logic of the Japanese Entertainment Industry," in *Idols and Celebrity in Japanese Media Culture*, ed. Patrick W. Galbraith and Jason G. Karlin (London: Palgrave, 2012), 51.

[16] Japanese Ministry of Internal Affairs and Communications, Institute for Information and Communications Policy (IICP), "Jōhō tsūshin media no riyō jikan to jōhō kōdō ni kan-suru chōsa," April 2013, accessed April 8, 2015, http://www.soumu.go.jp/iicp/chousakenkyu/data/research/survey/telecom/2014/h25mediariyou_1sokuhou.pdf.

Television and Catastrophe

Within seconds of the quake at 2:46 p.m. on March 11, 2011, Japan's commercial television broadcasters interrupted their regular programming to provide constant news coverage of the evolving triple disaster. For around 60 consecutive hours, Japanese television covered news of the disaster, recovery efforts, and the more than 1,500 aftershocks without commercial interruption.[17] In other words, for nearly three days, Tokyo's commercial broadcast networks did not broadcast any commercials. With each passing hour, the networks had to balance their responsibilities as licensed commercial broadcasters with the financial exigencies of operating a television network. Unlike public broadcaster NHK, the privately-owned networks rely entirely on commercials to finance their operating costs. When would it be appropriate to resume regular programming? How long could they financially sustain not broadcasting any commercials? Generally, catastrophe coverage, with its open-ended disruption of everyday life, "ceases only when it has an answer or becomes exhausted from repetition."[18] However, in the case of the triple disaster on 3.11, narrative closure of the catastrophe was precluded by not only the scale of the tragedy and relief efforts, but the continuous evolving crisis at the Fukushima Dai'ichi Nuclear Power Plant.

TV Tokyo, the smallest of the five commercial broadcasters, was the first to concede—it resumed regular programming at 11:56 p.m. on March 12 after about 33 hours. Most of the other commercial networks were able to hold out for about another 28 hours. TV Asahi went the longest without broadcasting a commercial for a total of 74 hours.[19] The only other times that commercial broadcasters refrained from airing commercials was when Emperor Hirohito passed away in 1989 (for 46 hours) and during the Great Hanshin earthquake in 1995 (for 36 hours). As television struggled to resume its regular schedule, the president of TV Asahi estimated that not broadcasting commercials likely cost the network upwards of ¥1.5 billion (US$15 million).[20]

---

[17] Of the roughly 1,500 aftershocks in those three days, 19 registered above *shindo-5* on the Japan Meteorological Agency seismic intensity scale.

[18] Patricia Mellencamp, "TV Time and Catastrophe, or *Beyond the Pleasure Principle* of Television," in *Logics of Television: Essays in Cultural Criticism*, ed. Patricia Mellencamp (Bloomington: Indiana University Press, 1990): 252.

[19] CM Sōgō Kenkyūjo, "Kieta CM, sai-sutāto shita CM: Shōhisha no hanou to hyōka wa?" *CM Index* 301 (April 2011), 7.

[20] "TV-kakukyoku 'CM jishū' de dageki 'genshū wa 10-oku en-dai kōhan," *Sankei shinbun*, April 17, 2011, accessed April 17, 2011, http://headlines.yahoo.co.jp/hl?a=20110417-00000105-san-bus_all.

Despite resuming their regular programming from March 14, corporate sponsors were skittish about having their products and services advertised against the backdrop of mounting death tolls from the tsunami and reports of radiation emanating from Fukushima. In addition, since many companies were experiencing sustained disruptions in distribution, they were reluctant to sponsor ads for products that they were unable to supply. In the media and advertising industries in Japan, where crisis management and protecting corporate image is paramount, the risk of public relations is about managing so-called *fushōji* (lit. inauspicious events). Japan's large advertising agencies, such as Dentsu and Hakuhodo, have sections within their corporate structure specifically for managing such media crisis.[21] As the industry term used to describe the "unexpected" and "contingent," *fushōji* are the uncontrollable events within capitalism that disrupt normalcy. Most *fushōji* are scandals arising from criminal or unethical behavior by a corporation or one of its representatives, including the celebrity "image characters" that appear in commercial endorsements. The catastrophe of 3.11, however, was an unprecedented *fushōji* in postwar Japanese advertising.

(Not) Serving the Public Interest

In the week after March 14, when regular programming had generally resumed, most commercials were public service announcements (PSA). For the month of March 2011, PSA were broadcast more than 20,000 times, which is the same number of times that all automobile commercials are aired in one year in Japan (figure 2).[22] Corporate sponsors, who had contracted and paid for their advertising space many months in advance of the disaster, requested the networks not broadcast their ads. In response to these requests, the commercials can neither be filled with dead air nor replaced with ads from other sponsors. Therefore, when advertisers elect to pull their ads, the commercial time slots are filled with PSA produced by AC Japan. AC Japan is a private, non-profit organization that distributes and promotes PSA from various non-profit organizations. In recent years, PSA have become a kind of insurance policy for when sponsors withdraw ads. In addition to advertising agencies and talent agencies, PSA increasingly have become a third way that the Japanese media industry

---

[21] Honma Ryū, *Dentsū to genpatsu hōdō: Kyodai kōkoku-nushi to ōte kōkoku dairiten ni yoru media shihai no shikumi* (Tokyo: Akishobō, 2012), 19.
[22] Typically, PSA are only broadcast about 130-150 times each month. "AC Japan no kōkyō kōkoku CM shinsai-go ni 'yaku-2-man-kai' hōsō," Oricon Style, May 27, 2011, accessed May 29, 2011, http://www.oricon.co.jp/news/88154/full/.

manages risk. Whenever an ad is pulled, sponsors are expected to pay a cancellation fee, and the ad space is donated to the broadcasting of PSA that serve the public interest. In this way, AC Japan's PSA serve the media industry's needs by providing assurances against the unpredictable and precarious nature of the capitalist system. Just as the insurance industry exists to manage the risks inherent in modern capitalist societies, the mass media too finds new ways to limit and to contain risk.

Figure 2: Television Commercials Broadcast in March 2011.

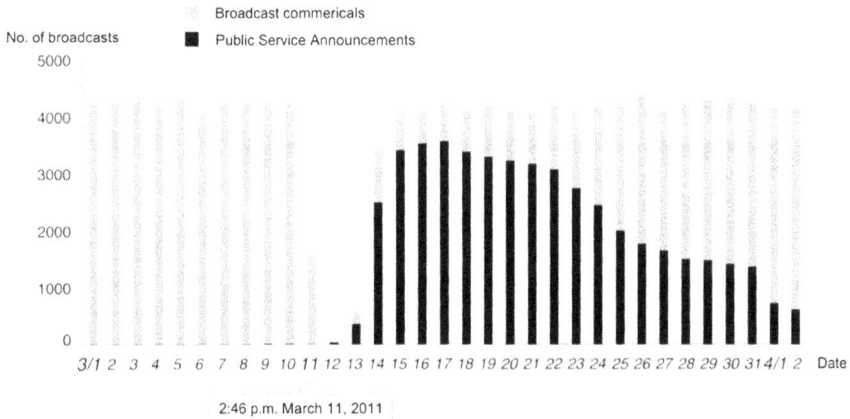

Note: CM Sōgō Kenkyūjo, "Kieta CM, sai-sutāto shita CM: Shōhisha no hanō to hyōka wa?" *CM Index* 301 (April 2011): 8.

AC Japan's public service messages appear in both print and broadcast media. Across its more than 40-year history, AC Japan has produced PSA on issues ranging from conservation, volunteerism, blood donations, and the handicapped to international exchange and assistance. Many relate to public morals and behavior so as to cultivate forms of publicness that serve the general welfare of society. The content of AC Japan's PSA follows particular guidelines. For example, it cannot merely raise social problems, but must also provide some means of remedy. As tools of social policy, PSA are an important means of changing public attitudes and behavior. The costs of production of the pubic service announcements are paid for by AC Japan from the annual membership fees of its roughly 1,200 member organizations, which are mostly media, advertising and other general companies.[23] Its PSAs are created by 47 separate advertising

---

[23] AC Japan's membership fee income for fiscal year 2011 totaled ¥160 million (US$ 1.6 million). At the time of the 2011 Tohoku earthquake, of the 67 members of AC Japan's board of directors, seven were affiliated with Japan's electric utility companies.

agencies in Japan to support around 10 non-profit organizations involved in public welfare activities. Unlike the Ad Council in the US, AC Japan must avoid all government interference. Whereas PSA in the US might be produced by government agencies, AC Japan—as an independent private entity—selects the themes and pays the costs of the production of PSAs.

Amid the period of high-speed growth, AC Japan was founded in 1971 to rectify the erosion of public morals. Its first public service announcement was a TV commercial in 1972 about throwing cigarette butts onto train tracks. AC Japan was modeled after the American Ad Council, which was established in 1941 for the purpose of mobilizing the advertising industry for the war effort by encouraging enlistment in the military, the purchase of war bonds, and conservation of war materials. Saji Keizō (1919-1999), who was the president of the Suntory Corporation, proposed the establishment of the predecessor to AC Japan after visiting the US in 1969.[24] With the world's attention focused on Japan ahead of the Osaka Expo in 1970, he believed that the persuasive power of advertising could be harnessed to improve public manners and morals.[25] For Saji and the others in advertising and industry who worked to establish AC Japan, PSA were about using advertising for the greater good of society. For Japan's five key broadcasting networks, which generate revenue from the selling of time to corporate sponsors, the benefits of PSA were less clear. Though granted broadcast licenses by the state, they are under no obligation to air PSA as a condition of serving as a public trustee. Instead of donating time for the airings of PSA, Japan's commercial broadcast networks have been broadcasting them mainly as fillers in the event a corporate sponsor pulls a particular ad.

Since the establishment of PSAs by AC Japan was modeled after the Ad Council but differed in their purpose and application, it is necessary to briefly mention the history and regulatory background of PSAs in the US. The Federal Radio Act of 1927 declared the airwaves public property and established the standard of licensure that broadcasters serve "the public interest, convenience and necessity." As a result, television broadcasters in the US are obliged to demonstrate their statutory public service. Along with broadcasting the news, PSAs constitute their main contribution to the public interest. According to the Federal Communications Commission (FCC), a PSA is defined as an advertisement "for which no

---

[24] AC Japan was established originally as the Kansai Kōkyō Kōkoku Kikō in 1971 before it became incorporated as the Kōkyō Kōkoku Kikō in 1974. It wasn't until 2009 that it changed its name to AC Japan.

[25] Kōkyō Kōkoku Kikō, ed. *Kōkyō Kōkoku Kikō 20-nenshi* (Osaka: Kōkyō Kōkoku Kikō, 1992), 14-19.

charge is made and which promotes programs, activities or services of Federal, State or local governments or the programs, activities or services of nonprofit organizations or any other announcements regarded as serving community interests."[26] This "donation" of time at no cost for the airing of PSAs by television broadcasters partly fulfills their public service obligation (while also insulating them from competition for access to the public airwaves). However, since the FCC has no quantitative requirements for PSAs, most are aired late at night when few people are watching. Recently, the prioritizing of profits over public service has led to a decline in the number of PSAs in the US, and many public service advertising campaigns are now paid in order to ensure optimal time placement.[27] In the US, PSAs generally are broadcast during unsold advertising time as a way of affirming broadcasters commitment to serve the public interest.

In Japan, however, PSAs are broadcast merely as a stopgap for commercials that are taken off the air at the request of advertisers. For Japanese commercial broadcasters, their obligation to serve the public interest is less clearly defined under the law. According to the Broadcast Act of 1950, which was established under the direction of the Allied Occupation authorities, the purpose of regulating broadcasting is "to conform to public welfare and to achieve its sound development."[28] Reflecting the Occupation's concern with democraticization and demilitarization, the law emphasized the principles of wide dissemination, freedom of expression, and the development of sound democracy. Though commercial broadcasters are required to apply for renewal of their broadcast license every five years, the approval process does not require them to demonstrate service to the public interest. Instead, since the Broadcast Act entrusts the Japan Broadcasting Corporation (NHK) with the role of serving the public welfare through its status as a public broadcaster, commercial broadcasters have no obligation to serve the public interest by airing PSAs.

---

[26] Federal Communications Commission, FCC 80-557 (September 25, 1980), accessed August 27, 2013, http://transition.fcc.gov/Bureaus/Mass_Media/Databases/documents_collection/80-557.pdf.

[27] Craig L. LeMay, "Public Service Announcements, Broadcasters, and the Public Interest: Regulatory Background and the Digital Future" (working paper, Institute for Policy Research, Northwestern University, Evanston, 2001).

[28] Ministry of Internal Affairs and Communications, "The Broadcast Act" (Act No. 132 of 1950), accessed August 29, 2013, http://www.soumu.go.jp/main_sosiki/joho_tsusin/eng/Resources/laws/pdf/090204_5.pdf.

Figure 3. Public Service Announcements.

Note: The PSA (left), "Greetings Are Magic," which teaches the importance of daily greetings, was broadcast 1,682 times in March 2011; and the PSA (right) for the Japan Cancer Society aired 2,865 times.

Because PSA in Japan are intended as replacements for regular commercials pulled at the request of sponsors, such as a celebrity scandal, the PSAs broadcast after 3.11 were utterly discontinuous with the realities of life amid catastrophe. With the same commercials broadcasting incessantly from March 14, many people criticized the PSA for being "inappropriate" and "too repetitive." One, emphasizing the importance of consideration (*omoiyari*), showed a high school boy helping an old woman up the stairs. An animated PSA emphasized the importance of daily greetings with animal cartoon characters named "sayona-raion" ("goodbye" lion) and "konban-wani" ("goodnight" alligator) to a light-hearted jingle punctuated by the lyric *"popopopōn."* Yet another urged women to have cervical and breast cancer tests (figure 3). Some on social media began to to remix the PSA, especially the one on the importance of greetings, to produce new meanings. The participatory culture of Japan's netizens produced an outpouring of MAD movies, music remixes, and parodies of the PSA.[29] Under mounting criticism, AC Japan was forced to apologize and to produce new PSA that better reflected the somber national mood in the wake of the earthquake and tsunami and the uncertainty of the Fukushima nuclear crisis.

From March 23, AC Japan began broadcasting new public service announcements with messages that were specifically tailored to the conditions after the Tohoku earthquake. Created quickly and reflecting the somber mood of the nation, the commercials were visually restrained to include only text and narration. SMAP was one of the first celebrities to

---

[29] "Greetings Are Magic," Know Your Meme, last modified April 15, 2014, http://knowyourmeme.com/memes/greetings-are-magic-あいさつの魔法。.

appear in a PSA created by Hakuhodo entitled "I believe in the strength of Japan" (*Nihon no chikara o shinjiteiru*). The commercial was broadcast 2,439 times in the month after it was first broadcast on March 23.[30] Each line of the PSA is solemnly stated by a different member of SMAP:

> You are not alone.
> We, and all of us, are here together.
> Making mutual concessions and helping one another...
> Strongly believing in the future...
> This is the time to come together.
> I believe in the strength of Japan.

The PSA concludes with Tōtasu Matsumoto, the lead singer of the group Ulfuls, who are perhaps best know for their 2001 cover of Sakamoto Kyū's 1964 song "Ashita ga aru sa" (There's Always Tomorrow). Matsumoto says, "Japan is a strong country. It may be a long path [back to recovery], if we all persevere (*ganbareba*) together, we can definitely overcome it."

One of the distinct rhetorical tropes that emerged in public discourse, including these PSA, following 3.11 is the notion of *ganbaru* (to persevere). The Japanese term *ganbaru*, which means "work hard" or "do your best" is often used as an exhortation to persevere in the face of difficulty or hardship. The historical anthropologist Amanuma Kaoru has described this notion of *ganbaru* as the "ethos of the Japanese nation," which he likens to Max Weber's concept of the Protestant work ethic.[31] According to the scholar Tada Michitarō, the term originated in the higher schools of the late Meiji period and became popular around the early Shōwa period, mostly in relation to sports.[32] In the postwar period, the expression has come to serve more generally as an ideological cudgel to work hard in order to achieve success. This appeal to the virtues of hard work, diligence, and sacrifice echo prewar government campaigns to promote austerity and savings. In the immediate postwar, to rebuild Japan and to achieve economic prosperity, official and nongovernment groups urged self-restraint to promote national savings. These postwar campaigns "emphasized production over consumption to persuade the people that hard work and frugality would stave off poverty and dependence on state

---

[30] "Kongetsu no CM kōkando, shinsaku toppu 10," *CM Index* 302 (May 2011): 10.

[31] Amanuma Kaoru, *Nihonjin wa naze ganbaru no ka: Sono rekishi, minzokusei, ningen kankei* (Tokyo: Daisanshobō, 2004).

[32] Tada Michitarō, *Shigusa no Nihon bunka* (Tokyo: Kadokawa Shoten, [1978] 1990), 26.

assistance."[33] In the everyday language of postwar Japan, as it achieved economic prosperity, the expression *ganbaru* has become common as a term of moral encouragement, especially during times of hardship.[34]

Figure 4. "What Can I Do Now [to help]."

Note: Members of the idol group AKB48 urge viewers to think about the real needs of the people in the disaster area in this PSA.

With the specter of power shortages forcing blackouts and disruptions in supply that were leading to hoarding (especially of toilet paper) in the weeks after 3.11, the media rallied to exhort sacrifice and self-restraint. In another series of public service announcements from AC Japan, which were created by Dentsu, various celebrities and idols urged the nation to conserve, sacrifice, and refrain from consumption. The spots were titled, "What I can do now [to help]" (figure 4). In these PSA, a different celebrity holds up a placard while reading a slogan:

[33] Sheldon Garon, *Molding Japanese Minds: The State in Everyday Life* (Princeton: Princeton University Press, 1997), 171.

[34] During the Great Hanshin Earthquake of 1995, some mental health care professionals avoided using the expression with victims of psychological trauma since it was felt to be an insensitive platitude that would make victims feel as if they were alone. See Endō Kennosuke, "Ronsetsu nōto: Ganbaranakute-ii—Hanshin daishinsai," *Mainichi shinbun*, Tokyo morning edition, February 26, 1995, 5.

Unplug electrical appliances that are not in use.
Be more diligent in turning off lights.
Don't rashly buy up items.
Don't buy unnecessary items.
Think about the real needs of the people in the disaster area.
Don't be deceived by false rumors.
Stop useless emails and telephone calls.

If celebrities and idols can organize a culture of consumption and exchange, then the rationalization after 3.11 was that they could also be effective as tools of public policy to urge conservation. The contradiction or double bind of these icons of consumption now urging viewers to refrain from ritualized forms of consumption and leisure was not lost on many. Where they had previously served the aims of advertisers to maximize consumption, now they were being flipped to admonish viewers not to consume. One user on Twitter, reflecting the participatory potential of remix culture, replaced the message from the PSA featuring members of the idol group AKB48 with an injunction to stop buying multiple copies of the same audio CD (figure 5). This subversion of the text displayed on the placard held by these idols criticized how AKB48 encourages its fans to purchase multiple copies of their single CDs in exchange for voting tickets in their annual general election. This event, like other events created by the group's production company, exploit fan affect in order to maximize consumption.

Figure 5. "Stop Buying Multiple Copies of the Same CD."

Note: This Photoshoppped image was first tweeted by user tebukuro_kun on April 4, 2011, and was retweeted more than 11,000 times (http://twitpic.com/4gtxcb). In addition, it was posted widely on blogs and other social media.

In the wake of the catastrophe, many events were canceled or postponed across Japan. Popular domestic travel locations were vacated by cancellations, and consumers became reluctant to spend. In contrast to George W. Bush, who after 9.11 implored Americans to shop and enjoy their lives in order to effect a rapid return to normalcy, AC Japan mobilized celebrities to urge the nation to modify its normal patterns of consumption and everyday life. Instead of a quick return to normalcy, the Japanese people were expected to make collective sacrifices for the welfare of the nation. As a result, a mood of "self-restraint" (*jishuku*) settled over the nation that included voluntary conservation efforts and a decline in consumer spending, even in areas far removed from the disaster.[35] The ease with which the Japanese nation shifted to a mode of self-restraint and sacrifice seemed to invoke a certain nostalgia for the past. Hearkening back to not only the spirit of collective suffering during the war, the catastrophe invoked nostalgic memories of the

---

[35] A survey of Japanese companies in Shizukoka, for example, conducted in late March found that around 70% were experiencing significant declines in sales owing to the national mood of self-restraint. See "'Jishuku de uriage-gen' 7-wari," *Yomiuri shinbun*, Shizuoka morning edition, April 8, 2011, 24.

hardship and sacrifice that fueled Japan's postwar recovery. Amid already heightened levels of concern about their image and reputation, many Japanese corporations announced donations to charities. Worried about appearing unsympathetic or inconsiderate to those in need, corporations responded by denying a return to normalcy. In particular, many brands were anxious about resuming their normal advertising campaigns that are generally centered on idols and celebrities. As cherry blossom season (*hanami*) began in late March, Tokyo Governor Ishihara Shintarō remarked at a press conference "This isn't the time for drinking and chatting."[36]

We Now Return to Your Regularly Scheduled Program

For Japan, a return to normalcy should have meant a resumption of the logic of consumption. As the lubricant for the capitalist machine in Japan, idols and celebrities are foremost devices for advertising goods and services. Nonetheless, negotiating a return to normalcy was complicated by the immense scale of the recovery efforts and the ongoing crisis at the Fukushima Dai'ichi Nuclear Power Plant. Some in the business sector began to refer to this "consumer self-restraint" (*shōhi jishuku*) as "the fourth disaster" after the triple disaster.[37] An editorial appearing in the *Yomiuri shinbun* on April 7, asserted that the excessive mood of self-restraint was robbing the nation of its vitality.[38] On April 8, the governor of Miyagi Prefecture, which was one of the areas hardest hit by the earthquake and tsunami, met with the Prime Minister and his cabinet to urge greater action: "For the disaster area to recover, the whole of Japan must recover. I'd appreciate your taking the lead in ending this excessive mood of self-restraint and reviving consumption."[39] As fear of economic stagnation grew, Economics Minister Yosano Kaoru responded by saying, "it's about time that the Japanese nation returned to everyday life."[40]

On a normal day, Japan's commercial broadcasters air commercials from about 500 companies. On March 15, when regular programming resumed, only 119 companies consented to having the commercials of their brands broadcast on television.[41] Besides PSA, many of the commercials

---

[36] Jiji Press, Ltd., "Hanami wa jishuku o=hisaisha ni hairyo hitsuyō-Ishihara-tochiji," March 29, 2011, accessed May 4, 2011, http://www.jiji.com/jc/c?g=soc&k=2011032900919.

[37] Naitō Kō, "'Shōhi no jishuku' no seitai," *Nikkei Business Online*, March 30, 2011, accessed July 9, 2013, http://business.nikkeibp.co.jp/article/money/20110329/219215/.

[38] "Shasestu: Iki-sugita jishuku wa katsuryoku o ubau," *Yomiuri shinbun*, morning edition, April 7,

[39] "'Kado no jishuku' ni kakuryō ya chiji kugen," *Yomiuri shinbun*, morning edition, April 9, 2011, 4.

[40] *Ibid.*

[41] CM Sōgō Kenkyūjo, "Kieta CM, sai-sutāto shita CM: Shōhisha no hanou to hyōka wa?" *CM Index* 301 (April 2011), 8.

broadcast over the next month were somber corporate announcements expressing condolences, soliciting donations, announcing recovery efforts or urging conservation. In the month after the earthquake, more than 150 of these "special commercials" (*rinji CM*) were produced and aired in lieu of the usual television commercials in Japan featuring celebrities and idols (figure 6).

Figure 6: Types of Television Commercials Broadcast after March 11, 2011.

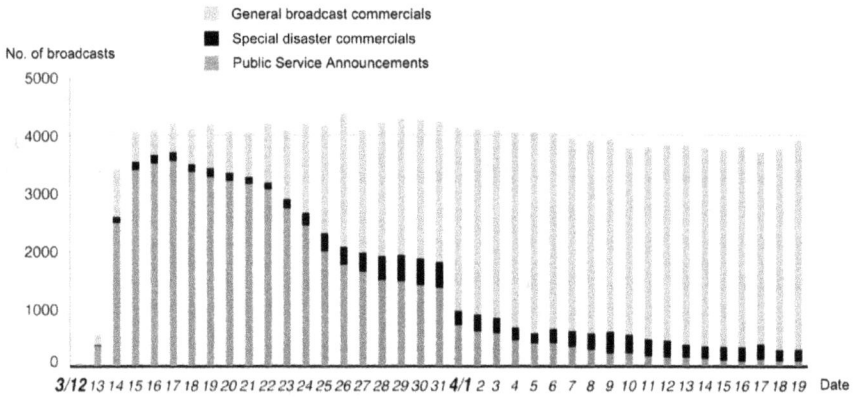

Note: CM Sōgō Kenkyūjo, "Sono-go no CM onea gaiyō to shinsai taiou CM," *CM Index* 302 (May 2011), 19.

One of the few special commercials to feature celebrities was a series of spots by Suntory that showed artists, actors, talents and musicians solemnly singing Sakamoto Kyū's early 1960s hits "Ue o muite arukō" (I Will Keep My Head Up as I Walk) and "Miagete-goran yoru no hoshi o" (Look Up at the Stars in the Night).[42] Cutting between shots of Japanese celebrities each singing a verse of the songs in a recording studio, the subdued tone of the commercials invoked nostalgic memories of Japan's past (figure 7). In the postwar period, Sakamoto's music has undergone an historical shift in its meaning to become today the nostalgic anthem of post-bubble Japan. From the early 1960s, Sakamoto signified the optimism and hope of the post-recovery period, as Japan returned to the international stage. When he tragically died in a plane crash in 1985, Japan was at the height of its economic prosperity. For a generation that had not experienced his music originally in the 1960s, the revival of his music amid the crash of JAL 123 triggered much soul-searching about not

---

[42] The commercials were first broadcast on April 4 and aired 407 times in April (March 20-April 19). "Sono-go no CM on'ea gaiyō to shinsai taiō CM," *CM Index* 302 (May 2011): 24.

only the causes of the crash, but the precarious future of Japan. Michael Bourdaghs describes Sakamoto as "the unshakable ghost haunting a once high-flying empire."[43] In the aftermath of 3.11, Sakamoto's music provided a melancholic refrain that referenced the memory of Japan's postwar recovery and the desire to return to the prosperity of the past. The narrative of the nation that emerged from these discourses affirmed a sense of history by celebrating the values of perseverance and sacrifice. Commercials, such as these, aimed to help audiences transition back into the flow of everyday television viewing centered around idols and celebrities.

Figure 7. Japanese actress Takeuchi Yūko sings a verse from "I Will Keep My Head Up as I Walk" (Ue o muite arukō) in this special commercial from Suntory.

Note: This series of special commercials, which was first broadcast on April 6, featured 71 different celebrities.

Television in Crisis

Nearly three years after 3.11, another "catastrophe" was visited on Japanese television that resulted in the unprecedented suspension of television advertising and its replacement by PSA. On January 15, 2014, Nippon Television (NTV) began airing a new TV drama on Wednesday nights called *Ashita Mama ga Inai* (Tomorrow Your Mother Won't Be Here). The

---

[43] Michael K. Bourdaghs, *Sayonara Amerika, Sayonara Nippon: A Geopolitical History of J-Pop* (Chicago, IL: University of Chicago Press, 2012), 111.

drama focused on the lives of orphaned children living in a privately run group home (figure 8). The program depicted the lives of orphaned and abandoned kids in a style that aims more to be entertaining than didactic. It featured two of Japan's most popular kid actors, Mana Ashida and Suzuki Rio, in a story that sought to soften its complex subject with elements of fantasy. While eschewing realism in its depiction of the lives of orphans, it drew on the topicality of the issue of children born out of wedlock. In particular, the character played by Ashida is nicknamed "Post" because she was abandoned in a "baby postbox" (*akachan posuto*).

Figure 8. The NTV Drama *Ashita Mama ga Inai* (Tomorrow Your Mother Won't Be Here).

Note: The website for the television drama as it appeared on the NTV website (http://www.ntv.co.jp/ashitamama/).

The nickname used in the drama was a reference to the baby hatch program "Konotori no yurikago" (stork's cradle) established by Jikei Hospital in Kumamoto Prefecture on May 10, 2007 to deal with cases of infant abandonment and infanticide. In Kumamoto Prefecture, there had been three incidents in as many years in which the abandoned bodies of newborn infants were discovered. In one incident, an unemployed eighteen-year-old girl killed her female infant immediately after giving birth and buried her in the yard. Another involved a twenty-one-year-old trade school student who suffocated her newborn infant after giving birth in a toilet. Like similar programs in Germany, the Japanese baby hatch program was created in order to provide a safe and anonymous means for infant adoption.

On it first day of operation, a three-year old child was left in the baby hatch. This incident attracted immense media attention and scrutiny, particularly because of the age of the child. In its first year, a total of 17 children were deposited. All originated from outside of Kumamoto, 60% were married, and 40% were from single parents. In 90% of the cases the deposited children had at least one sibling.[44] In the next year, 25 additional children were deposited. In its six years of operation up to 2014, there have been more than 92 children deposited. More recently, on October 3, 2014, the dead body of a newborn infant was deposited in the hatch. Although the purpose of the baby postbox is to protect children and to prevent women from committing criminal acts of infanticide and abandonment, such systems that allow parents to give up their infants anonymously have been criticized for promoting the shirking of parental responsibility and issues related to human rights such as the right of an individual to know his or her origins. Many experts believe that any system that allows parents to anonymously surrender their parental rights should only be the method of last resort in preventing infanticide.

After its first episode, the television drama faced harsh criticism from two parties who called on NTV to stop broadcasting the program. First, the National Council for Children's Group Homes (Zenkoku Jidō Yōgo Shisetsu Kyōgikai) asserted that the show was "creating misunderstanding and prejudice towards the children and workers in protective institutions." Claiming that the drama depicted the treatment of children in group homes as akin to "pets in a pet shop," they framed the issue as a violation of the human rights of orphaned children and damaging to the morale of its workers.[45] The organization distributed press releases citing cases of discrimination against children in its facilities after the broadcasting of

---

[44] Kashimi Yoshida, "Japanese Baby Hatches and Unmarried Mothers/Children Born Out of Wedlock: A Comparison with German Babyklappen and American Safe Haven Laws," *Ars Vivendi Journal* 5 (August 2013): 26-27.

[45] Zenkoku Jidō Yōgo Shisetsu Kyōgikai, "Jidō yōgo shisetsu de seikatsu suru kodomo-tachi he no gokai to henken, jinken shingai o makanaide kudasai: Renzoku dorama 'Ashita, Mama ga Inai' ni tsuite," January 20, 2014, accessed November 3, 2014, http://www.zenyokyo.gr.jp/whatsnew/140121kougi.pdf.

the program. Second, Jikei Hospital objected to the use of nicknames such as "Post," arguing that such epithets would be traumatic for those children who already were the victims of domestic abuse. Though Jikei Hospital had never used the term "baby postbox" to refer to its baby hatch program, the term was used widely in the Japanese media. They argued that unlike the police, schools or hospitals, audiences would be unable to differentiate fiction from reality because they lack other sources of knowledge about the conditions of group homes.[46] Despite these allegations, NTV resolved to broadcast all nine weekly episodes of the drama.

Before the third-weekly episode of the show broadcast on January 29, 2014, all eight sponsors had withdrawn their ads. The sponsors included such familiar companies as Subaru, Mitsubishi Estate, Kao, Kobayashi Pharmaceutical, and Nissin Foods. Several of the sponsors stated that the program was not a suitable environment for broadcasting their commercials. This was the first time in the history of Japanese television that all commercial sponsors had withdrawn their ads for a program in response to a controversy regarding the content of a program. A marketing consultant with more than 20 years of experience in the advertising industry, noted "I cannot recall a case where the sponsor's name was removed from a program on account of the show's contents. The only other cases have been when the sponsor itself has withdrawn after some inauspicious event (*fushōji*) or when all of Japan has suffered some misfortune (such as a disaster or the death of the emperor). The situation this time is an exception among exceptions."[47] On the January 28 broadcast, the drama aired entirely with all its commercials replaced by PSA from AC Japan. For Japanese television viewers of NTV, this represented an experience similar to the days after 3.11.

For sponsors fearing a backlash from consumers for their support of a program that was charged with violating human rights, the audience's response on social media was unexpected. In an analysis of 5,000 tweets on Twitter from January 29 to February 26, 2014, few expressed support for the criticisms made by Jikei Hospital and the National Council for Children's Group Homes.[48] Instead, many more expressed supported for NTV, defining the controversy as a struggle over freedom of expression:

[46] Jikei Hospital, "Nihon Terebi dorama 'Ashita, Mama ga Inai' hōsō ni atarimashite," accessed November 2, 2014, http://jikei-hp.or.jp/tv_mama/.
[47] "'Ashita Mama' naze suponsā wa teikyō o ketsudan? Kōkoku-nushi, dairiten, Ni-tere no gosan no karakuri," *Business Journal*, January 29, 2014, accessed February 2, 2014, http://biz-journal.jp/2014/01/post_3985.html.
[48] The Twitter analysis was conducted with RowFeeder (http://rowfeeder.com/), using the Japanese hashtag "AshitaMama." Results of the study found that postings were most active on Wednesdays at the time of the broadcast; and 24% of tweets were re-tweets, mostly of news reports about the controversy.

NTV, don't give up! Protect freedom of expression.
#ntv #AshitaMama

#AshitaMama Even without sponsors, keep fighting!!

#AshitaMama Those who say "show some consideration" [to the children in orphanages] only want us to look away from their misery. The reality is far worse.

Despite the attention on social media, the controversy surrounding the drama did not translate into a significant ratings increase for NTV. Audience share peaked at 15% during its third weekly broadcast on January 29, 2014 when all commercial sponsors had withdrawn their ads, but averaged only 12.8% over its entire nine episodes.[49]

After NTV refused to stop broadcasting the program, Jikei Hospital and the National Council for Children's Group Homes petitioned the Broadcast Ethics and Program Improvement Organization (BPO) to investigate the drama for ethics violations. The BPO is a non-profit, non-governmental organization that serves to improve the quality of broadcasting and promote higher ethical standards while ensuring freedom of speech and expression. It was formed in 1997 by NHK and the Japan Commercial Broadcasters Association. On May 21, 2014, the BPO announced that it would not hear the petition, citing no evidence that the content of the drama had violated its rules on broadcast ethics.[50] While the drama relied on numerous clichés about orphanages and lacked the seriousness that its subject demanded, the BPO found no evidence that the rights of any party had been violated and defended the use of nicknames as an issue of freedom of expression.[51] Despite affirming NTV's right to broadcast the drama, the BPO's announcement had no impact on the position of the program's corporate sponsors. In the end, the "controversy" surrounding the drama, including the involvement of the BPO, only increased the perception of risk and produced a greater reluctance to produce challenging, original content.

---

[49] Video Research Ltd., "Shichō data: Shūkan kō setai shichōritsu bangumi 10," accessed May 2, 2015, http://www.videor.co.jp/data/ratedata/backnum/2014/index.htm.

[50] The BPO is composed of three committees: Committee for the Investigations of Broadcasting Ethics, Broadcast and Human Rights Committee, and the Broadcasting Committee for Youth Programming. The later two committees, which were petitioned, both declined to hear the case.

[51] Broadcasting Ethics & Program Improvement Organization, "'Jidō yōgo shisetsu kanren dorama e no mōshitate' shinri taishōgai to handan," May 20, 2014, accessed May 21, 2014, http://www.bpo.gr.jp/?p=7612.

In the past, Japanese television was more inclined to incur risk, though often producing content that was crude, offensive, and degrading to women. From the late 1990s, the National PTA of Japan's (Nippon PTA Zenkoku Kyōgikai) criticisms of the content of television programs directly led to the establishment of the BPO. Despite the lowbrow culture of much Japanese television in the past, its dramas and other information programs were more likely to address social and political issues without concern that sponsors would withdraw their ads. Today, due to media convergence, advertisers have become highly sensitive to complaints or claims about the content they sponsor. Following the controversy over the drama, one journalist and social media consultant declared that, "TV is dead." Writing in a widely noted online column, he lamented that "television has become a platform entirely incapable of taking risks. There is now no difference between commercial broadcasters and NHK."[52] The fear that he and others have expressed about the future of Japanese television is that this risk aversion among sponsors merely will result in more variety shows centered on popular idols. To understand the popularity of idols in contemporary Japan, one must understand how television and advertising are promoting idols as a means of minimizing risk.

Conclusion: In Idols We Trust

In this chapter, I have described the Japanese media's management of risk following the catastrophe of March 11, 2011. As a disruption to the uneventfulness of everyday life, the events of 3.11 precipitated a mood of self-restraint, savings, and work that was detrimental to consumer spending. This self-restraint resulted in a 2.4% decline in consumer spending in 2011, and the slump continued in 2012 with household spending shrinking by an additional 1.8%.[53] Abenomics, the set of policy measures implemented by Prime Minister Abe Shinzō in 2012, has sought to stimulate the Japanese economy by fostering greater consumer spending. Advertisers, responding to the decline in consumer spending, increased their expenditures on advertisements in 2012 for the first time in five years with spending on television advertising, in particular, increasing by 3%.[54]

---

[52] Kanda Toshiaki, "Ashita, kōkoku-nushi ga inai. Nihon Terebi no Ashita, Mama ga Inai," *Yahoo! Japan News*, January 28, 2014, accessed February 3, 2014, http://bylines.news.yahoo.co.jp/kandatoshiaki/20140128-00032067/.

[53] Ministry of Internal Affairs and Communication, Statistics Bureau, "Kakei shōhi shisū, futari ijō no setai," June 14, 2013, accessed June 29, 2013, http://www.stat.go.jp/data/gousei/soku10/index.htm.

[54] Dentsu, "2012-nen no Nihon no kōkokuhi," February 21, 2013, accessed February 22, 2013, http://www.dentsu.co.jp/news/release/2013/pdf/2013016-0221.pdf.

Even before the events of 3.11, several factors have contributed to a heightened aversion to risk in the Japan television and advertising industries. First, the rise and widespread adoption of social media has increased the potential for negative publicity. Second, shrinking audiences and declining profits have made Japanese media companies less likely to take risks that might alienate audiences and/or threaten the support of their corporate sponsors. With media convergence, Japanese corporations have become even more concerned about managing their public image. There is a heightened sense of vigilance about preventing "inauspicious events" that might generate negative publicity. As a result, corporations and institutions, especially the media, have become highly averse to risk. The safe middle ground of consensus, often dictated by the past, has made Japanese society reluctant to innovate or to take risks. On television, this · means that the popularity of idols on television has increased since they are carefully managed by their talent agencies to avoid controversies that might jeopardize corporate sponsors. While they might not contribute to innovative or challenging programming on Japanese television, they do ensure a regular and predictable audience of loyal fans.

Following from the work of Anthony Giddens, I argue that the study of risk in consumer society is a means of understanding the control of time, or what he terms the "colonisation of the future."[55] Since risk concerns the future, only through the monitoring of risk can modern society tame the future. As a nation whose history has been marked by numerous disasters, both natural and manmade, Japan is born into risk. The discourses of futurism in Japan, especially in the post-bubble period, are preoccupied not only with anxiety about the future, but relentless attempts to both monitor and to manage risk. Whether the looming demographic crisis arising from its declining fertility rate or the problems of its inward-looking (*uchimuki*) and passive youth, Japan is ever vigilant of potential threats to society. In short, normality is carefully managed in postwar Japan to ensure a state of staged uneventfulness.

Although the unexpected or contingent might provide new opportunities, Japanese media institutions instead are engineered to avoid risk. Rather than embracing the contingent nature of risk inherent in capitalist social processes, the Japanese media are ever vigilant in monitoring risk arising from the dislocations of capital. In this regard, the idol industry in Japan functions as a "disembedded mechanism" for the circulation of goods and services. For Giddens, disembedded

---

[55] Giddens, *Modernity and Self-Identity*, 111.

mechanisms are symbolic mediums of exchange that are interchangeable across a plurality of contexts. The idol industry is a medium for the exchange of goods penetrating nearly all aspects of social and economic life in contemporary Japan. Amid the complexity and interconnectedness of modern institutions, it is necessary to understand that the role of idols is not confined merely to that of media performers. Though the idol industry serves the purpose of mass entertainment, they also are a means of maximizing and ensuring consumption in risk society.

Works Cited

Amanuma Kaoru. *Nihonjin wa naze ganbaru no ka: Sono rekishi, minzokusei, ningen kankei.* Tokyo: Daisanshobō, 2004.

Bourdaghs, Michael K. *Sayonara Amerika, Sayonara Nippon: A Geopolitical History of J-Pop.* Chicago, IL: University of Chicago Press, 2012.

Broadcasting Ethics & Program Improvement Organization (BPO). "'Jidō yōgo shisetsu kanren dorama e no mōshitate' shinri taishōgai to handan." May 20, 2014. Accessed May 21, 2014. http://www.bpo.gr.jp/?p=7612.

CM Sōgō Kenkyūjo. "Kieta CM, sai-sutāto shita CM: Shōhisha no hanō to hyōka wa?" *CM Index* 301 (April 2011): 7-12.

———. "Kongetsu no CM kōkando, shinsaku toppu 10," *CM Index* 302 (May 2011): 7-17.

———. "Sono-go no CM on'ea gaiyō to shinsai taiō CM." *CM Index* 302 (May 2011): 19-25.

Dentsu. "2012-nen no Nihon no kōkokuhi." February 21, 2013. Accessed February 22, 2013. http://www.dentsu.co.jp/news/release/2013/pdf/2013016-0221.pdf.

Doane, Mary Ann. "Information, Crisis, Catastrophe." In *Logics of Television: Essays in Cultural Criticism*, edited by Patricia Mellencamp, 222-239. Bloomington: Indiana University Press, 1990.

Endō Kennosuke. "Ronsetsu nōto: Ganbaranakute-ii—Hanshin daishinsai." *Mainichi shinbun*, Tokyo morning edition, February 26, 1995, 5.

Federal Communications Commission. FCC 80-557 (September 25, 1980). Accessed August 27, 2013. http://transition.fcc.gov/Bureaus/Mass_Media/Databases/documents_collection/80-557.pdf.

Garon, Sheldon. *Molding Japanese Minds: The State in Everyday Life.* Princeton: Princeton University Press, 1997.

Giddens, Anthony. *Modernity and Self-identity: Self and Social Life in the Late Modern Age.* Stanford: Stanford University Press, 1991.

Honma Ryū. *Dentsū to genpatsu hōdō: Kyodai kōkoku-nushi to ōte kōkoku dairiten ni yoru media shihai no shikumi.* Tokyo: Akishobō, 2012.

Japanese Ministry of Internal Affairs and Communications, Institute for Information and Communications Policy (IICP). "Jōhō tsūshin media no riyō jikan to jōhō kōdō ni kan-suru chōsa." April 2013. Accessed April 8, 2015. http://www.soumu.go.jp/iicp/chousakenkyu/data/research/survey/telecom/2014/h25mediariyou_1sokuhou.pdf.

Jenkins, Henry. *Convergence Culture: Where Old and New Media Collide.* New York: New York University Press, 2006.

Jikei Hospital. "Nihon Terebi dorama 'Ashita, Mama ga Inai' hōsō ni atarimashite." Accessed November 2, 2014. http://jikei-hp.or.jp/tv_mama/.

Kanda Toshiaki. "Ashita, kōkoku-nushi ga inai. Nihon Terebi no Ashita, Mama ga Inai." *Yahoo! Japan News.* January 28, 2014. Accessed February 3, 2014. http://bylines.news.yahoo.co.jp/kandatoshiaki/20140128-00032067/.

Kōkyō Kōkoku Kikō, ed. *Kōkyō Kōkoku Kikō 20-nenshi.* Osaka: Kōkyō Kōkoku Kikō, 1992.

Lather, Julie, and Emily Moyer-Guse. "How Do We React When Our Favorite Characters Are Taken Away? An Examination of a Temporary Parasocial Breakup." *Mass Communication and Society* 14, no. 2 (February 28, 2011): 196–215.

LeMay, Craig L. "Public Service Announcements, Broadcasters, and the Public Interest: Regulatory Background and the Digital Future." Working paper, Institute for Policy Research, Northwestern University, Evanston, 2001.

Marx, W. David. "The *Jimusho* System: Understanding the Production Logic of the Japanese Entertainment Industry." In *Idols and Celebrity in Japanese Media Culture*, edited by Patrick W. Galbraith and Jason G. Karlin, 35-55. London: Palgrave, 2012.

Media Kankyō Kenkyūjo. *Media Teiten Chōsa (Tōkyō) 2014.* June 10, 2014. Accessed March 16, 2015. http://www.media-kankyo.jp/wordpress/wp-content/uploads/teiten2014.pdf.

Mellencamp, Patricia. "TV Time and Catastrophe, or *Beyond the Pleasure Principle* of Television." In *Logics of Television: Essays in Cultural Criticism*, edited by Patricia Mellencamp. Bloomington: Indiana University Press, 1990, 240-262.

Ministry of Internal Affairs and Communications, Statistics Bureau. "Kakei shōhi shisū, futari ijō no setai." June 14, 2013. Accessed June 29, 2013. http://www.stat.go.jp/data/gousei/soku10/index.htm.

Ministry of Internal Affairs and Communications. "The Broadcast Act" (Act No. 132 of 1950). Accessed August 29, 2013. http://www.soumu.go.jp/main_sosiki/joho_tsusin/eng/Resources/laws/pdf/090204_5.pdf.

Naitō Kō. "'Shōhi no jishuku' no seitai." *Nikkei Business Online.* March 30, 2011. Accessed July 9, 2013. http://business.nikkeibp.co.jp/article/money/20110329/219215/.

Napier, Susan J. "Panic Sites: The Japanese Imagination of Disaster from *Godzilla* to *Akira*." *The Journal of Japanese Studies* 19, no. 2 (1993): 327-351.

NHK Hōsō Bunka Kenkyūjo. *2010-nen kokumin seikatsu jikan chōsa hōkokusho* (Feb. 2010). http://www.nhk.or.jp/bunken/summary/yoron/lifetime/pdf/110223.pdf.

Spigel, Lynn. "Entertainment Wars: Television Culture after 9/11." *American Quarterly* 56, no. 2 (2004): 235-270.

Tada Michitarō. *Shigusa no Nihon bunka*. Tokyo: Kadokawa Shoten, [1978] 1990.

Video Research Ltd., "Shichō data: Shūkan kō setai shichōritsu bangumi 10." Accessed May 2, 2015. http://www.videor.co.jp/data/ratedata/ backnum/2014/index.htm.

Yoshida, Kashimi. "Japanese Baby Hatches and Unmarried Mothers/ Children Born Out of Wedlock: A Comparison with German Babyklappen and American Safe Haven Laws." *Ars Vivendi Journal* 5 (August 2013): 25-41.

Yoshimi Shun'ya. "Terebi ga ie ni yatte-kita: Terebi no kūkan, terebi no jikan." *Shisō* 956 (Dec. 2003): 26-48.

Zenkoku Jidō Yōgo Shisetsu Kyōgikai. "Jidō yōgo shisetsu de seikatsu suru kodomo-tachi he no gokai to henken, jinken shingai o makanaide kudasai: Renzoku dorama 'Ashita, Mama ga Inai' ni tsuite." January 20, 2014. Accessed November 3, 2014. http://www.zenyokyo.gr.jp/ whatsnew/140121kougi.pdf.

Networking Citizens through Film Screenings: Cinema and Media in Post-3.11 Social Movements

Hideaki Fujiki

Film screening events conducted by citizens have become a notable practice among social movements in the wake of the nuclear catastrophe in Fukushima on March 11, 2011. Even though they are less spectacular than the anti-nuclear demonstrations that took place in front of the Prime Minister's Official Residence and other sites in (and outside) Japan, screening events have been no less significant in constructing and expanding the networks of media and citizens, the sharing of knowledge and concerns, and the coordinating of action. These networks have developed to protest the networks of dominant capital and governmental power that have promoted nuclear energy. In this chapter, I will discuss the significance of citizens' film screening events not only in terms of anti-nuclear protests and social movements but also as they relate to media convergence in contemporary Japanese society. If one sees a film-screening event as only a one-time activity, it would seem to have little influence on society; however, framing it as a crucial part of wider networks enables us to locate its significant social potential.

A citizens' screening event is usually organized as an independent screening (*jishu jōei*), and typically combines the communal watching of an independent film with a presentation by a guest speaker and a general discussion.[1] Since the 3.11 earthquake, such screening events have been held at a variety of public venues such as city halls, community centers, schools, and cafes in areas all over Japan, from Hokkaido to Okinawa. These screenings take place randomly, sometimes overlapping. I will discuss these screenings not as isolated, spatially fixed events, but as a porous process that produces temporarily emerging hubs where citizens, media, knowledge, shared concerns and actions become connected to each other in complex ways so as to generate, expand, and/or empower their networks. Here, my primary focus is not on the relation between

---

[1] Because of this combination, I translate *"jishu jōei kai"* not simply as a "film screening," but as a "film screening event" or "screening event."

a filmmaker and his or her film, but on the dialogic interactions among the organizer, the film, the guest speaker (who may be the filmmaker), and other participants. This necessarily leads us to deal with the film not as an autonomous medium, but in view of its transmedial connections with other media, especially social media (including email, mailing lists, Twitter, and the wider internet). Through this examination, I will show that citizens' screening events and their networks present both opportunities and problems for anti-nuclear activism as well as for social movements and socio-cultural politics in contemporary Japan.

Since the 1980s, numerous scholars have discussed the network as a key concept in the analysis of social movements,[2] but Manuel Castells's conception is of particular use to consider its relations with political power and media. Notably, he has described contemporary society as "the network society," one conditioned by digital networks of communication, the flows of finance and labor, the space of flows, and timeless time. Taking his view, we can see that the power of domination, which is usually sustained by capital and government, is both structurally networked and exercised in the very process of networking. But counter-power can intervene by reprogramming or switching networks of communication.[3] I will further push forward this view from two different angles. For one thing, while Castells and other media scholars of social movements pay exclusive attention to new media or what Castells calls mass self-communication, I will make film-screening events the central subject of my discussion and then highlight both how they are distinct from and cooperative with new media. Moreover, I will deal with networks not simply of communication, but of media, knowledge, concerns, and actions that are linked under the historical and performative concept of "citizens," a concept characterized by self-proclamation, political nuance, equality, and openness while also involving certain contradictions and conflicts.

In this argument, I also intend to reconsider convergence culture in the realm of media. Like Henry Jenkins, I assume that a "story" in his terms, or a "network" in mine, can endlessly grow beyond one medium

---

[2] These include Alberto Melucci, *Nomads of the Present: Social Movements and Individual Needs in Contemporary Society* (Philadelphia: Temple University Press, 1989); Mario Diani and Doug McAdam, eds., *Social Movements and Networks: Relational Approaches to Collective Action* (Oxford, UK: Oxford University Press, 2003); Nick Couldry and James Curran, *Contesting Media Power: Alternative Media in a Networked World* (Lanham, MD: Rowman and Littlefield, 2003); and Jeffrey Broadbent, *Environmental Politics in Japan: Networks of Power and Protest* (Cambridge, UK: Cambridge University Press, 1998).
[3] Manuel Castells, *The Rise of the Network Society*, second ed. (Oxford, UK: Blackwell, 2000); *Communication Power* (Oxford, UK: Oxford University Press, 2009).

across different media platforms while audiences actively participate in its construction and reconstruction.[4] However, whereas Jenkins is primarily interested in the tripartite alliance between industry, media, and audiences, I am more interested in political tensions between citizens and corporate-governmental power. Indeed, most films that citizens use for their screening events are independent of major film production and distribution companies. Crucially, this condition allows filmmakers and citizens to maintain a critical distance from corporate-governmental power. In addition, as I will examine a screening event as something unique and irreducible to one medium rather than a mere gateway to multiple media in transmedia storytelling, I see the transmedial relation between one platform and another not as flat, but as uneven. Taking citizens' screening events as a prime example of convergence culture, I will explore how they have been operating, and could operate, as a complex nexus of the networks of media, knowledge, concern, action, and citizens vis-à-vis the dominant political-economic power.

Facilitating a Network of Media

A citizens' film screening event can be seen as a hub in which a variety of media are linked, resulting in a network of media. In contrast to movie theater exhibition, it is usually organized as a one-off independent screening event (*jishu jōei kai*) in a public space like a city hall, school, or cafe. This practice emerged by the late 1950s when the National Conference for Promotion of Independent Film Screenings (Jishu Eiga Sokushinkai Zenkoku Kyōgikai) was founded, but it grew significantly in the 2000s and 2010s. Two main factors arguably brought about this growth: the development of information technology and the eruption of new crises, especially the nuclear catastrophe in Fukushima. In this context, citizens' film-screening events have enjoyed reciprocal relations with new media. DVDs, the internet, and social media have boosted the upsurge of screening events while each screening in turn has played a pivotal role in facilitating a network of media including new media. Citizens' film screening events have grown together with this form of media convergence and divergence.

For Jenkins, convergence and divergence are "two sides of the same phenomenon."[5] Convergence results when different media industries collaborate, content flows, and consumers migrate across multiple media

---

[4] Henry Jenkins, *Convergence Culture: Where Old and New Media Collide* (New York: New York University Press, 2006).
[5] *Ibid.*, 10.

platforms. This linkage of one medium with another simultaneously can be seen as an extension from one medium to another, hence divergence. I would like to adopt this approach, but we should also note that a network of media develops centering on a screening event through the process of information, knowledge, concern and action flowing in two partly overlapping but different directions. In one direction, which can be called the centripetal direction, a screening event mobilizes a network of media by driving multiple media to focus attention on it, as the media users are planning, organizing, and promoting it, and members of their networks express their interests in it. This transmedial chain has a certain range of possible starting points, for example, when an organizer tries to find information online about an appropriate film for an event, or, even before that, when she becomes inspired by a social media message introducing another screening event. During the planning of an event, the organizers exchange opinions and contact the filmmaker or his/her agency, the managers of possible venues, a guest they want to invite, and other related people through email, the internet, and other social network services (including mailing lists, Facebook, Twitter, and blogs). Meanwhile, they advertise the event through social network services, fliers, newsletters, and local newspapers. The receivers of the information further use media to transmit it. In this way, the mobilization for an upcoming screening event makes multiple media converge.

In the other direction, which can be called the centrifugal direction, a screening event constructs a network of media through the process of multiple media diffusing information about the event and its theme and also turning attention to related issues. This enables both the participants and non-participants to further think about the issues—in this case, the issues related to radioactive contamination and nuclear power plants— and take action. To begin with, advertising and promoting the event— which can also be seen in the centripetal direction—have this function. But the screening of the film as well as the Ustream webcasting of the guest's presentation and the resulting audience discussion more fully fulfill a centrifugal role in sharing the ongoing communication with audiences both within and outside the venue. Some audiences may use Twitter to share the live discussion in order to raise wider concern about the problem of radioactivity. Other important media in the centrifugal dynamic are DVDs of the screened film, the rest of the director's oeuvre and films on related topics by other directors, as well as books on related issues by the filmmaker or other authors. These media are frequently sold at the screening venue. While they have a certain commercial purpose, they are also expected to share knowledge about the issues at hand with people elsewhere. For instance, on June 30, 2012, I attended the screening of Kamanaka Hiromi's *Living with Internal Exposure* (2012) at the Tahara Culture Hall in Aichi Prefecture. DVDs of this film and her other films including *Hibakusha at the End of the World* (2003) and *Rokkasho Rhapsody* (2006) and her books were being sold. Similarly, fliers for other events concerning similar social problems, brochures, and copies of newspaper articles on related issues were placed at the reception desk, with the aim of extending the audience's engagement with these issues beyond that particular event. Moreover, after the event, some audience members post their reviews or impressions on their blogs, Facebook pages, and on Twitter, while the event or its organizer is occasionally covered in local newspapers. Most productively, at some screenings of Kamanaka's film the organizers were encouraged to begin issuing newsletters (*mini-comi*) or launch a website.[6] In this way, a screening event may generate a sustainable media network. In short, a screening event drives diverse types of media to form a network, functioning as a juncture where information and concerns relating to the event itself converge and from which ones linked to related issues diverge.

It is significant to note that this process suggests that film-screening events cannot stand alone without being linked with other types of media. Indeed, we can see that this type of citizens' independent screening owes much to the development of media technology. In Japan, the independent film screening can be tracked back to the Prokino (the Proletarian Film League of Japan) in the late 1920s and early 1930s, during which leftist intellectuals (such as Sasa Genjū and Iwasaki Akira) and laborers organized events to screen their own documentary films in community centers and factories. This type of non-theatrical film screening was more fully legitimated in the late 1950s, when critics and fans successfully organized a public screening of *Battleship Potemkin* (1925) defying the Ministry of Finance and the major distribution companies. This resulted in the foundation of the National Conference for the Promotion of Independent Film Screenings.[7] In the late 1960s, the documentary filmmaker Ogawa Shinsuke's production team began to screen their films in non-theatrical public spaces in cooperation with Beheiren (Citizen's

---

[6] For examples of *mini-comi*, see Miyazu Mitsubachi Project, "Mitsubachi note" and ELDNACS, "6peace free paper." For the websites, see http://rokkasho-rhapsody.jimdo.com and http://www.eldnacs.jp/freepaper/.

[7] Yamada Kazuo, "Kankyaku wa eiga o kanri dekiru: Jishu eiga jōei undō no imi suru mono," *Eiga hyōron* 17, no. 9 (1960): 36-39.

League for Peace in Vietnam) and university students' councils (*gakusei jichikai*) in many parts of the country.[8] From a less political standpoint, the 1970s also saw the rise of independent cinephile screening groups, who later established art cinema theaters or citizens' cinemas as in the case of Nagoya Cinémathèque.[9] These independent screening practices overlapped with the use of other media such as hand-made fliers and a kind of low-budget newsletter called mini-comi—which citizens made and used as an alternative to mass media.[10] But the potential expansion and complexity in the convergence and divergence of media seem to have been more limited in the case of the links between the film screenings and other non-digital media than in the later independent screening practices associated with digital media. Indeed, Koizumi Shūkichi, the founder of the independent film production and distribution company, Group Gendai, has pointed out that independent film-screenings became a common practice only after 2001, when they actively invited citizens to organize screening groups and to show his documentary film, *Sense of Wonder: The Present from Rachel Carson*, in public spaces. This practice was extended to *Hibakusha* and *Rokkasho Rhapsody*, by Kamanaka Hitomi (also affiliated with Group Gendai), which further contributed to the nation-wide expansion of citizens' independent film screening events.[11] Although no statistical data is available, this statement by Koizumi seems to oversimplify the history because DVDs and VHS, personal computers, and portable digital projectors had were already widely available by the late 1990s.[12] Nevertheless, the further development of digital technologies made it much less expensive and logistically much easier both for citizens to organize screening events and for public places to host them. This occurred while the expansion of the internet and social media enabled screening events to become a nexus of transmedial networks as we saw above.

---

[8] Abé Mark Nornes, *Forest of Pressure: Ogawa Shinseki and Postwar Japanese Documentary* (Minneapolis, MN: University of Minnesota Press, 2007), 39-53.

[9] Jiang Jieun, "Nihon ni okeru shimin eigakan no taitō to tenkai," *Eizōgaku* 71 (2003): 13-14.

[10] Maruyama Hisashi, *Rōkaru nettowāku no jidai: Mini-comi to chiiki to shimin undō* (Tokyo: Nichigai Associates, 1997).

[11] Koizumi Shūkichi, "Dokyumentari seisaku to jōei no jissai," in *Series Nihon no kokyumentari 1: Dokyumentari no miryoku*, ed. Satō Tadao (Tokyo: Iwanami Shoten, 2009), 151.

[12] For instance, inspired by Paper Tiger Television in New York, a somewhat experimental project, "Independent Video plus Screening" (jishu bideo + jōei) was organized by The Association for the People's Media (Minshū no media renrakukai) in the early 1990s. See Matsubara Akira, "Paper Tiger TV to Nihon no media undō," in *Media to kassei: What's Media Activism*, ed. Hosoya Shūhei (Tokyo: Impact Shuppankai, 2012), 38-46. Regrettably, further research on the relations between independent screenings and technology has yet to be conducted.

Nowadays, almost all independent filmmakers or their production groups set up their own websites to call for citizens to organize independent screenings of their films, but perhaps Kamanaka and her allied company Group Gendai/NPO TVE Japan (Kankyō Terebi Torasuto) do so the most actively and strategically in both economic and political terms. For instance, each website for her individual films has clear instructions explaining the procedure for organizing a screening event so that anyone can easily follow it.[13] Instructions, with humorous illustrations drawn by the Nagano citizens' group Rokkasho Kaigi in Ueda on the basis of their experience are also available.[14] Both provide instructions about how to establish a committee for the event, its planning (the schedule, the division of roles, the reservation of a venue, and so on), balancing expenses and revenue (obtaining the rights for screening the film, purchasing the DVD, renting a facility for the venue, the projector and other equipment, advertising expenses, income by admissions, etc.), advertising and promotion, setting up a contract with the agent, paying commissions off the sale of DVDs and books, the management of the event (e.g., setting up, reception, ushering, moderating and chairing, selling goods, and operating equipment), and further steps after the event. The filmmaker only charges for the cost of the DVD (¥3,700 in December 2013) and its rights (by multiplying the number of tickets sold by ¥500) so that those who are interested in organizing an event can feel peace of mind about taking a financial risk, while the filmmaker and agent make a (moderate yet constant) profit.[15] Politically, this serves as encouragement for citizens to mobilize their own social movements. After all, this is an excellent example of facilitating the network of media that film-screening events drive in cooperation with new and traditional media. Kamanaka and Group Gendai are increasingly pursuing this kind of venture, launching the distribution of behind-the-scenes documentaries about the making of her films, a mailing list called Bunbun News, and video letters titled Kama Repo or Kamanaka Report, among other media practices.

By 2011, the ubiquity of new media had come to be taken for granted, despite the fact that access remained uneven and unequal across

---

[13] See "Kamanaka Hitomi," accessed March 19, 2014, http://kamanaka.com/selfscreening.

[14] "Rokkasho kaigi in Ueda ban: Jishu jōeikai no tsukurikata," accessed March 19, 2014, http://kamanaka.com/wp/wp-content/themes/kamanaka-com/common/doc/jouei_tsukurikata_6rapuagain_version.pdf.

[15] "Naibu hibaku o ikinuku," accessed December 11, 2013, http://www.naibuhibaku-ikinuku.com/. It is arguable that with their own financial strategy described here, Kamanaka's team has gained more profits through the screening events by citizens than many other independent filmmakers.

geographic areas and social groups.[16] Despite, or because of this fact, citizens' independent film screening events kept expanding. Indeed, in 2012, more than 60 organizers held public screenings of Kamanaka's films in Japanese towns every month—for instance, more than 97 such screenings took place in October 2012 alone.[17] It is true that new media have come to take a central role in social movements and citizens' activism in recent years. However, how can we account for this growth of citizens' film screenings? In effect, new media and screening events have mutually vitalized relations, thereby fostering a wider media network. And yet, the screening event also has integral features that make it impossible to argue that it is merely an equivalent to new media. In order to explore this unique potential, I will examine the functions of the screening event as a nexus of the networks of knowledge and of citizens.

Building a Network of Knowledge, Concerns, and Actions

Citizens' screening events function as the hubs of wider media networks, by creating what I call intimate public spheres. In this sphere, the participants—who are not limited to those attending the event—have dialogues about particular social issues and share their concerns about the impact on people's lives. Knowledge and concern relating to these issues and the suffering they cause converge into the event through the expanding network of media (including the film) as well as a corresponding network of participants (including the guest and the audiences), and then the knowledge and concerns that are shared and amplified through the dialogue diverge from there to thinking and action through the growing networks of media and participants after the event.

The issues facing post-3.11 social movements are not simple. They have been recognized not simply as an environmental problem, but as an array of social injustices.[18] The nuclear disaster led to a surge of criticism of socio-political power structures for victimizing, exploiting, and deceiving citizens. In this case, "power structures" means the network derogatorily

---

[16] Leah A. Lievrouw, *Alternative and Activist New Media: Digital Media and Society* (Cambridge, UK: Polity, 2011), 12.

[17] "Mitsubachi no haoto to chikyū no kaiten," accessed November 22, 2012, http://888earth.net/trailer.html.

[18] Indeed, Simon Avenell is critical of the historical continuation of the anti-nuclear Japanese activism for considering the issue solely from a human-centered perspective. See his "From Fearsome Pollution to Fukushima: Environmental Activism and the Nuclear Blind Spot in Contemporary Japan," *Environmental History* 17, no. 2 (2012): 244-276. Yet, it should be also noted that the connection of nuclear power with environmental injustice is a global phenomenon. See, for instance, Danielle Endres, "From Wasteland to Waste Site: The Role of Discourse in Nuclear Power's Environmental Injustices," *Local Environment* 14, no. 19 (2009): 917-937.

named *genshiryoku mura* or the "nuclear power village" comprised of bureaucrats, politicians, the Tokyo Electric Power Company (TEPCO) and its affiliates, and scientists (labeled *goyōgakusha* or "opportunist scholars"). There are also perceptions that the mass media lent support to the village and are still doing so. Indeed, rather than acknowledging this role, the mass media are mounting a *kizuna* (bonds) media campaign and propagating a myth of safety (*anzen shinwa*) even after the catastrophe. The "bonds" campaign (the fundamental meaning of which here is not financial bonds but human bonds) propagates the idea that, no matter where people live in Japan, the population must proportionately share the burdens of Fukushima (e.g., consuming contaminated foods and making space for radioactive rubble in landfills) without interrogating the responsibility of TEPCO and the government. It is arguable that this idea even echoes the idea of "*ichioku sōzange*" (a national confession of guilt that prevailed when Japan was defeated in World War II). At the same time, citizens have become aware that the national government and the electric companies have bought off some residents in the areas surrounding the nuclear power plants and that this has resulted in a discrepancy between urban and rural areas in terms of what Ulrich Beck would call the distribution of the risk of radioactive pollution.[19] Whether they are accurate or nor, such interpretations and representations of the disaster as the symbolic consequence of social injustice function as major triggers for citizens' participation in protesting the nuclear power plants.

And yet, protest and social mobilization do not merely manifest in the form of demonstrations, which have drawn the most attention. In fact, there are a variety of activities. Here I would like to highlight the five most vital, correlated phases of the social movement: (1) obtaining information (e.g., petitioning the government for its internal documents, attending open hearings and explanatory meetings by the government or companies, and collecting information via mass and social media); (2) forming and expanding a network or group; (3) sharing and building knowledge (through symposia, lectures, study meetings, mass and social media); (4) expressing wishes and opinions (through voting, demonstrations, submitting petitions, negotiating with the government, corporations and the mass media via phone, fax or in person, pursuing lawsuits, recalls, requests for city regulations, and demanding compensation); (5) supporting people who are suffering, accepting children and adults from the stricken areas, and measuring the radioactive doses of air, land

---

[19] Ulrich Beck, *Risk Society: Towards a New Modernity*, trans. Mark Ritter (London: Sage, 1992), especially Chapter I.

and foods for the residents); and (6) strategically planning and steering all these forms of activism. Film screening events have the potential to make a contribution to the sharing and building of knowledge as well as to the creation and expansion of networks, and, less conspicuously, to the expression of goals. From a wider perspective, screening events, albeit indirectly, may serve to promote a network in which all the phases are connected to each other.

At a screening event, the film and the guest speaker are usually the primary, if not sole, catalysts for the participants to share knowledge and concerns. The guest is often the filmmaker, but he or she might also be a journalist, scientist or any other person, as at the event I attended in my neighborhood in Nagoya in September 2013, when a former professor in molecular biology was invited to talk about radioactive contamination at Fukushima and Chernobyl while the film screened was the documentary *Fukushima: We Won't Forget* (*Wasurenai Fukushima*, 2013). The organizer as well as the film and guest speaker that are selected for such an event are not neutral, but explicitly critical of the seeming alliance between the government, corporations and the mass media. Typically, the fact that they share this stance and the goal of countering the dominant power is clear prior to the event. As many critics have pointed out, this prior knowledge relies on what social media have communicated while it is exactly what the mass media neglects to communicate.

To be sure, mass media and social media cannot be reduced to a binary opposition (as I will discuss below). However, it is clear that mass media have predominantly taken the side of the government and the corporations that have sought to resolve the problem of the nuclear catastrophe by emphasizing the necessity of "bonds" and national cooperation, the safety of food and affected regions, the effectiveness of the decontamination (*josen*), and the hopeful rehabilitation and return of the former residents to the contaminated areas (*kison*). In comparison, social media have created a space for skeptical views on this framing by the dominant power. By using Twitter and the wider internet, freelance journalists, scientists, lawyers and critics have castigated the "nuclear village" and posted different accounts of the "real" level of radiation from those released by the authorities, while television broadcasts and, to a lesser extent, major newspapers (with some exceptions, like *Tokyo shinbun*) have given no space to these alternative views. Our Planet TV, IWJ (Independent Web Journal), Citizens' Nuclear Information Center (Genshiryoku Shiryōshitsu), and other alternative media organizations have taken a leading role in advancing this trend, broadcasting press conferences, gatherings, protests and demonstrations, tweeting and retweeting comments on such events, and archiving images of and comments on them.[20] Numerous citizens' groups and their individual members have exchanged and/or transmitted information and ideas through their websites, blogs, Facebook pages, mailing lists, and tweets, and by linking their websites and blogs to each other.[21] Opposing opinions obviously abound on the internet and other social media; some blogs stress the safety of areas in Fukushima and oppose the discourse of radioactive hazard.[22] However, it is fair to say that critical responses to nuclear power have primarily circulated on social media, more than in the mass media. Activists often call this type of network "*tsunagari*" (links), using the concept of linking as a counter-concept against the bonds (*kizuna*) that the government, corporations, and mass media have promoted.

Because the organizers of screening events relating to the post-3.11 situation are mostly linked to this network of counter-power knowledge, they naturally select mostly films that were produced independently from the nuclear power companies and hence can resist political pressure by the nuclear village. An increasing number of films—mostly documentaries but also some fiction—on the aftermath of 3.11 have been made, but those most frequently shown at citizens' screenings include Shinomiya Hiroshi's *Fukushima: We Won't Forget* (*Wasurenai, Fukushima*, 2013), Shimada Kei's *Fukushima, Rokkasho, and Proposal to the Future* (*Fukushima, Rokkasho, and Mirai e no teigen*, 2014), Hayakawa Yumi's *Women from Fukushima* (*Kidasan and genpatsu, and Nihon*, 2013), and Ian Thomas Ash's *A2-B-C* (2013) as well as Kamanaka's *Surviving Internal Exposure* (*Naibu hibaku o ikinuku*, 2012).[23] These films are certainly not uniform in representing the issues. For instance, some of them take different views on the effectiveness of the government's decontamination measures, as seen when one compares *Surviving Internal Exposure* and Doi Toshikuni's *Iitate Village: Radiation and Return* (*Iitate mura: Hōhsanō to kison*, 2013). This may be less because of

---

[20] Nicola Liscutin well illustrates them, especially Our Plant TV and IWJ. See her "Indignez-Vous!: 'Fukushima,' New Media and Anti-Nuclear Activism in Japan," *The Asia-Pacific Journal: Japan Focus* 9, issue 47, no. 1 (November 21, 2011), accessed December 11, 2013, http://www.japanfocus.org/-Nicola-Liscutin/3649.

[21] One of the most notable examples of the groups is Citizens' Commission on Nuclear Energy and Association for Citizens and Scientists Concerned about Internal Radiation Exposures (ACSIR). I would like to add Mirai ni Tsunageru Tokai Net as a most active group or network in Tokai area, which is one of the most significant resources for my research.

[22] For instance, see "Ganbare. Fukushima," accessed December 12, 2013 http://www47.atwiki.jp/info_fukushima/.

[23] It should also be noted that pre-3.11 films and/or films produced overseas, such as *Radiation* (2003), *Rokkasha Rhapsody* (2006), *Ashes to Honey* (Kamanaka Hitomi, *Mitsubachi no haoto to chikyū no kaiten*, 2010), *Controverses nucléaires* (Wladimir Tchertkoff, 2004), and *Das Schönauer Gefühl* (Frank Dietsche, 2008), are shown at independent screening events.

the filmmakers' different visions than because the situations and people's interpretations of them have changed over time. Yet, while some films on Fukushima highlight the unity of the family and community,[24] most films shown at citizens' screening events are more concerned with revealing political and social problems. Moreover, they stand in sharp contrast with the Ministry of the Environment's film *Living in Fukushima* (2013). This sort of propaganda film portrays the safety of foods, the effectiveness of decontamination, and the promising recovery of the contaminated town and the possible return of its former residents as a beautiful story of overcoming difficulties without interrogating the government and TEPCO's responsibility for the catastrophe. As its last scene shows, it turns toward resolving the difficult situations by dealing with them as a matter of personal feelings (*kimochi*) rather than socio-political problems while foregrounding the scenic landscape and personal engagement in combination with the voice-of-God narration and moderately emphatic non-diegetic music. In contrast, the films at citizens' screening events illuminate residents' anxiety about constant radioactive contamination, their psychological conflicts regarding their work and lives, their distrust of the electric company, and/or their complaints about the government's measures.[25]

When viewing such a film at a screening event, the audiences do not merely receive the information presented in it. Rather, they participate in an event that functions both as a nexus of networked knowledge and as an intimate public sphere. By the intimate public sphere, I mean that it combines some (but not all) features of what scholars have delineated as the public sphere and the intimate sphere. Most notably, in his 1962 book *The Structural Transformation of the Public Sphere*, Jürgen Habermas characterizes the public sphere as a site of rational communication or dialogue among "citizens" in the "life-world" that vie for rationalization in the bureaucratic and capitalist "system."[26] Since its first publication, however, this model, which is based on the male bourgeois educated "citizens" in eighteenth-century Europe, has been criticized especially for its phallocentric homogenous nature and its rationalist assumptions.[27]

---

[24] A good example is Toyoda Naomi and Noda Masaya's *The Will: If Only There Were No Nuclear Power Plant* (2013).

[25] For a more detailed analysis of the films, see my "Problematizing Life: Documentary Films on the 3.11 Nuclear Catastrophe," in *Negotiating Nuclear Disaster: 'Fukushima' and the Arts, eds.* Kristina Iwata Weikgenannt and Barbara Holthus (London: Routledge, forthcoming).

[26] Jürgen Habermas, *The Structural Transformation of the Public Sphere: An Inquiry into a Category of a Bourgeois Society*, trans. Thomas Burger and Frederick Lawrence (Cambridge, UK: Polity, 1989).

[27] A good overview is provided in Saitō Jun'ichi, *Kōkyōsei* (Tokyo: Iwanami Shoten, 2000), 15.

Nevertheless, this whole debate on the public sphere gives us a useful framework for understanding the screening event as a site of dialogic communication among participants.

Set up as a combination of a film, a talk and a discussion, the dialogic communication here contains a plurality of standpoints constituted by the film, the organizer, the guest, and the audience members. Thus, a screening event differs from normalized movie viewing in a theater, where the audience has a primary relationship with the screened film and leaves after the screening ends. At a screening event, the film plays more ambiguous roles. While the film is a weighty source of knowledge and affect for the participants, it may be just a pretext or appetizer for the organizer and other participants to discuss the main issues. For instance, at the screening event of *Fukushima: We Won't Forget* I attended in my neighborhood, the participants hardly touched on the film in their discussion, even though the film poses important issues, including some relating to the filmmaker's ethics vis-à-vis the residents and his treatment of Pilipino women in the stricken areas who are ignored in other films. At this point, citizens' screening events depart from film criticism and film festivals (except specifically targeted film festivals like the Peace Film Festival and the Organic Foods Film Festival) where the films are their main focus. What is more vital for the citizens' screening event is that it constitutes a learning process whereby the participants come to feel, know, and understand the issues not merely through watching the film, but through their dialogic communication in participation with the film, the guest's talk, and the general discussion. This is crucial for screening events concerning nuclear energy and radioactive pollution in that the topic requires a wide range of interdisciplinary knowledge drawing from physics, medicine, and biology to law, politics, sociology, geography, culture, and the actual circumstances on the ground. In addition, the audiences have the potential to bring related topics to the discussion, for example when one elderly woman introduced the problem of the planned facilities for nuclear fusion in Toki City in Gifu Prefecture at a screening of *Fukushima, Rokkasho, and Proposal to the Future*, which I attended in Nagoya in April 2013. Thus, the audiences do not only receive the knowledge from the film and guest speaker but also participate in cultivating new knowledge through their dialogic interactions with each other as well as with the film and guest.

It should be noted here that the dialogue is not a full debate in which the promoters and protesters vent their own opinions at one another. Rather, the event can be seen as an intimate sphere, where the participants can express concerns about each other as well as for the people who suffer from the problems being discussed. The political scientist Saitō Jun'ichi makes a theoretical distinction between the public sphere and the intimate sphere: "while the former emerges on the basis of a common issue on which people focus as something that lies *between* them, the latter is formed and maintained on the basis of people's concerns about and consideration of the concrete other's life and livelihood."[28] At the screening event, the participants might articulate their criticism of political and economic power structures, but not of other citizens, except in venting their frustration with "rightwing internet users" (*netto uyoku*)—many members of which participate in the promotion of nuclear power—or the majority of people in society who have little concern about these issues. After all, the event is a site where people who already share a political stance (and, to a lesser extent, those who do not, but have been invited by someone else or just happened to attend) get together.[29]

Here, the political thinker Seyla Benhabib's conception of the intimate sphere helps us to explore a key characteristic of the screening event further. She suggests that the intimate sphere is a relatively closed entity, resulting in a certain ambivalent nature: while it lacks differences and disputes among its participants, it can empower them to act politically outside it, that is, in the public sphere.[30] To extend this view, the screening event, on the one hand, may create a homogenous community where people with the same beliefs are united, though dialogue and the concept of "citizens," which I will discuss later, could mitigate this risk. On the other hand, it allows the participants to openly express and discuss their concerns, which they might feel hesitant to do outside the sphere because of a fear of being regarded as "political" or "troublesome." This is partly because the growth of consumerism since the 1970s has created a social atmosphere in which someone expressing political concerns—such as about nuclear power plants—is deemed dangerous, and partly because the governmental-corporate and mass media promotion of post-3.11 Japan as still safe and structured by "bonds" has generated peer pressure, which makes expressing opposing opinions—such as that radiation still lingers and is contaminating foods, and harming children's health—

---

[28] *Ibid.*, 92.

[29] Questioners for the screening events of Kamanaka's films also indicate this trend. I would like to thank her for her having shared the documents with me.

[30] Seyla Benhabib, *The Reluctant Modernism of Hannah Arendt* (London: Sage, 1996), especially 211-215. See also, Saitō, *Kōkyōsei*, 95-99.

detrimental to the friendly atmosphere.³¹ Furthermore, the revision of
the Fundamental Law of Education under the first Abe Shinzō cabinet
in 2005 made it a taboo for educators to express disagreement with
government policy at school. Against this background, the screening
event can give the participants a sense of security and can empower them
towards frank expression and discussion. Citizens can feel grounded by
an awareness of their and others' concrete lives, livelihoods and dignity,
at a remove from the tendency of the government and corporations
to downplay citizens' concerns and to strive towards investing in more
abstract goals like "the national" (*kokumin*) and "consumers" (*shōhisha*)—
investments that tend to favor the state and the corporations.

As such, citizens' screening events can be seen as a blend of the
public sphere and the intimate sphere, in which the participants rebuild
knowledge about certain issues through dialogic communication while
sharing their concerns about and empathy with each other and the
victims. This heightened knowledge and sense of concern has the potential
to diverge from the screening site to the outside world through media
networks. At this point, the event functions not only as a site for sharing
and building knowledge, but also as one where participants can express
their hopes. Organizing this kind of event in itself has this function in
that it transmits messages against nuclear energy. And yet, the citizens'
screening differs from the on-street demonstration insofar as it serves to
create dialogic communication, and enhance the network of knowledge
and shared concern. In the screening event, this mutual understanding, not
just mimetic stimulation, would drive action. For instance, the organizer
of the screening of *Fukushima: We Won't Forget* in my neighborhood is both
a mother and a childcare worker. She was inspired by her friend, also a
mother of a small child, who had organized a screening of *Surviving Internal
Exposure*. In the discussion portion of the event, she said that her friend had
made her realize that even a single citizen like her can do something. In
effect, unlike normalized film watching in a theater or other viewing space,
participating in screening events is not confined to the film screening.
Rather, audiences are expected and encouraged to extend their knowledge
and concerns beyond the intimate public sphere to taking action outside it.

Making Citizens' Network

While the screening event acts as a nexus of networks of media, knowledge
and shared concern, it simultaneously functions as a core from which

---

³¹ This kind of community problem is well represented in the documentary film *A2-B-C* (2013) and the
fiction film, *Odayakana nichijō* (2012).

citizens can generate and expand their networks. More precisely, when citizens organize a screening event on radiation or the post-3.11 situation, the citizens and the event have a reciprocal relationship. For one thing, organizing the event can lead the citizens to strengthen their networks through working together, to include new participants in the event and even to reach out to non-participants through the network of media, knowledge, and shared concern we saw above. The very process of planning and steering the event demands cooperation, thereby creating unity among the staff, who often include volunteers previously unknown to each other.

Concurrently, the concept of "citizens" makes it possible for anyone to participate in the event and thus join the network. So far I have used "citizens" as a rather general term, but we should consider it as a discursively and performatively constructed historical concept. Indeed, in recent years scholars have analyzed the genealogy of "citizens" or "*shimin*" in postwar Japan.[32] There is not sufficient space here to explain in detail, but these scholars seem to agree that the concept of "citizens" changed on three levels from the late 1940s through the 1990s: its implicated political stance vis-à-vis the government changed from resistive to cooperative; its concerns shifted from such abstract ideas as "peace" and "democracy" to concrete issues concerning lives and livelihoods; and its implied mode of political involvement moved from voluntary and diverse to voluntary but normative. These transformations occurred as Japanese society saw the emergence of such citizens' groups as The Voiceless Voice (Koenaki Koe, 1960-) and Citizen's League for Peace in Vietnam (Beheiren, 1965-1974), both of which focused on the struggle over the US-Japan Security Treaty, the rise of the proposal style of civic activism in the 1970s, which replaced the demonstrations of the 1960s, and the institutionalization of civic activities by NPOs in the 1990s. Certainly, even in the 1980s and 1990s, citizens' resistive stance did not completely disappear, as can be seen in the foundation of the Association for Citizens' 30 Opinions (Shimin no Iken 30 no Kai) in 1988 and the growth of the anti-nukes movement after the 1986 nuclear power plant accident in Chernobyl.[33] In the 2000s,

---

[32] Important works include Kurihara Akira, "Shimin seiji no ajenda: Seimei seiji no hō e," *Shisō* 908 (2000): 5-14; Akihiro Ogawa, *The Failure of Civil Society?: The Third Sector and the State in Contemporary Japan* (Albany, NY: State University of New York Press, 2009); and Simon Avenell, *Making Japanese Citizens: Civil Society and the Mythology of the Shimin in Postwar Japan* (Berkeley: University of California Press, 2010).

[33] See Gonoi Ikuo, *"Demo" to wa nanika: Henbō suru chokusetsu minshushugi* (Tokyo: NHK Shuppan, 2012), 127-129; and Higuchi Naohito, "Mirai no 'yogensha' to shite no shakai undō: 'Risuku shakai' no keiji," in *Shakai undō no shakaigaku*, ed. Ōhata Hirotsugu *et al.* (Tokyo: Yūhikaku, 2004), 20-22.

however, demonstrations became much more visibly resurgent with such currents of activism as the Peace Walk, the Global Justice Movement, and the Precariat Movement protesting the Iraq War and neoliberal measures by the government. The post-3.11 anti-nuclear movement should be placed in this context. As I have noted, for the protesters, nuclear power is not simply an environmental issue, but also a matter of social justice. Yet, unlike the violent demonstrations in the 1960s, contemporary demonstrations allow families or mothers with children to join without worry thanks to the restraints on violence initiated by the Peace Walk movement, as well as to the joyfulness introduced by the form of "sound demonstrations," in which participants play music and dance.[34] In line with this trend, post-3.11 Japan has seen the nation-wide establishment of citizens' groups by mothers, most notably the National Network of Parents to Protect Children from Radiation (Kodomotachi o Hōshanō kara Mamoru Zenkoku Nettowāku), and has become an important driver of film-screening events.

We can observe how, shaped by these historical circumstances, some characteristic features of the concept of "citizens" act to bolster social movements, including screening events. On the one hand, the concept accommodates contradictory and conflicting factors and meanings. Unlike "the masses," "citizen" implies an independent individual, but in many cases the term still indicates something abstract and general. Differing from "elite," it is not an exclusive concept in terms of ability and class. It can also be distinguished from ethnicity and gender/ sexuality insofar as it is not classified by visibly or invisibly nuanced physical differences. Nor can it have anything to do with the implication of a geographical and spatial boundary like "the national" (*kokumin*) or "imperial subjects" (*kōmin*), though administrators and intellectuals once used "*shimin*" to differentiate people in urban areas from ones in rural areas and/or to be somewhat synonymous with the national.[35] In addition, whatever a person's political leanings, anyone can call himself or herself a "citizen." Nevertheless, once this pluralistic, open-minded term is used by conservative political actors, its meaning can change. For instance, despite their self-proclamation as "citizens," the Association of Citizens against Special Privilege for Korean Residents in Japan (Zainichi Tokken o

---

[34] For the sound demonstration, see Mōri Yoshitaka, *Sutorīto no shisō: Tenkanki to shite no 1990-nendai* (Tokyo: Nihon Hōsōkyōkai, 2009); Gonoi, *"Demo" to wa nanika*; and Itō Masaki, *Demo no media ron: Shakai undō no yukue* (Tokyo: Chikuma Shobō, 2013).

[35] See Oguma Eiji, *"Minshu" to "aikoku": Sengo Nihon no nashonarizumu to kōkyōsei* (Tokyo: Shinyōsha, 2002), Chapter 16; and Avenell, *Making Japanese Citizens*, Chapters 1 and 3.

Yurusanai Shimin no Kai, or Zaitokukai) promotes racism, nationalism, and political extremism.

While it entails contradictions and conflicts, the concept of "citizens" has at least four significant implications, which are not simply reducible to such a neutral, colorless description as pluralistic or complex. First, anyone can proclaim himself or herself a citizen. Certainly, the modern concept of citizenship necessarily sets up a boundary between "citizens" and others (e.g., "foreigners," social outcasts, criminals, and illegal immigrants),[36] but it is arguable that the boundary is not essentially fixed. Yet, my point here is not whether everyone has the rights to actually become a citizen approved by the government, but rather that the term allows a person to define his- or herself more freely than, say, other terms designating social groups, like "the masses," which tends to be used by the "elite."[37] The aspect of self-proclamation allows one to define his or her own social position while creating a symbiotic relationship with other "citizens" defined as people occupying the same social position. Second, the combination of the concept of "citizens" with the anti-nuclear movement creates a certain political nuance. While "citizens" in a capitalist country are simultaneously "consumers" and anyone can call himself or herself a "citizen," the former may be differentiated from the latter in terms of whether they have (or articulate) political concerns. In addition, even though "citizens" (*shimin*) is usually categorized as an administrative and hence depoliticized term by municipal governments, as we have seen, "citizens" sometimes use municipal facilities like a city hall for the purpose of holding (albeit loosely defined) political gatherings like screening events. Third, the concept is based on the ideal of equality. Surely, there are often discrepancies in their skills, abilities, and roles; for instance, the famous journalists, scholars, or film directors who call themselves "citizens" may receive special treatment and monetary rewards for their talks. They, however, are not slotted into an institutional hierarchy as in a company or a governmental organization. In addition, the overarching concept always involves the risk of making invisible inequality among "citizens," but it serves to offer a common ground for anyone to participate in society and politics. This

---

[36] There is insufficient space here to discuss citizenship and global citizenship, which have been actively debated in the social sciences in recent years. A good overview is provided in Fukuwara Takashi and Yamada Ryūsaku, ed., Shiteizunshippu *ron no shatei* (Tokyo: Nihon Keizai Hyōronsha, 2010).

[37] While I argue that "the masses" have tended to be defined by others rather than by people self-identifying, this concept also certainly has complex historical and social implications. See, for instance, my "'Taishū' to shite no eiga kankyaku," in *'Sengo' Nihon eigaron: 1950-nendai o yomu*, ed. Mitsuyo Wada-Marciano (Tokyo: Seikyūsha, 2012), 121-142.

leads to the final implication I would like to highlight—its openness. If the concept of "citizens" is free from any geographical or racial category, anyone can become a citizen, regardless of his or her physical traits, blood relations, and the country or place where he or she comes from— though an administrative concept of "citizens" or citizenship may block this potential by defining the national as citizens versus foreigners. The person also can choose not to become a "citizen," or can leave the citizens' group he or she has joined. This suggests that anyone can enjoy an equal relationship with one another through the shared identity of "citizen." These four implications are not necessarily in concert. Even though those who call themselves "citizens" believe themselves to be open-minded, others who don't often identify themselves as "citizens" may feel segregated from the former due to a difference in educational background or the lack of an overlapping political consciousness. Thus, the concept of "citizens" involves contradictions and frictions. Still, we can say that this unstable nature itself is a feature of "citizens," embracing a wide range of possibilities and diversities.

It is against this background that citizens organized the film screening events I have discussed in this chapter. Consequently, they seem to highlight several realities in the relations between citizens' networking and the screening event. One relates to the ambivalent quality of the intimate public sphere I discussed above. While the open-minded nature of the concept of "citizens" allows for the participation of people from diverse social positions and hence distinguishes the screening event from a closed homogenous community, its political nuance may cause the aforementioned unbalanced range of audience members. That is, as the questionnaires filled out at the screenings of Kamanaka's films suggest, many participants of citizens' screening events hold the same political standpoint (i.e., anti-nukes), while people with opposing political beliefs barely attend them.[38] Those who occupy the political middle ground, or so-called non-political people, do participate in these events and in the questionnaires often describe their experience by emphasizing the contrast in their thinking before and after the event. One wrote: "[The event] made me realize that I did not know anything. I came to feel that the news on TV and the internet were not telling the truth, and indeed they did not inform anything [important about the accident of the nuclear power plant and radioactivity]."[39] Nevertheless, it cannot be denied

---

[38] The questionnaires Kamanaka and a citizen group have kindly shared with me do not provide systematic data for many reasons. Nevertheless, they clearly indicate this tendency.

[39] From the questionnaires about the event entitled "The Screening Event of *Surviving Internal Exposure* and Kamanaka Hitomi's Live Talk," which was held in Shinshū University, Nagano City, on June 26, 2011.

that the political nuance of "citizens" vis-à-vis governmental power as well as such specific advocacy as anti-nuclear activism may make non-political people feel reluctant to join the events. Still, there is also the possibility that, if the citizens' network expands and permeates into people's everyday lives, it may make it common to think about politics through participating in such events, so that the depoliticized could be re-politicized.

Another implication of the concept of "citizens" in its relation with screenings is its influence on the connection between people through the process of crystalizing their concerns about each other on the basis of their concrete lives, livelihoods, and dignity. On one level, the films that citizens select for their screening events mostly show concrete images of how residents and ex-residents (and animals) in Fukushima lead lives disrupted by 3.11. Their sense of dignity, then, is often underscored in contraposition with the conduct and attitude of the corporations and government, which have put the highest priority on economic development and urban-centered national prosperity. The corporations and government are more eager to promote the construction of nuclear power plants by offering funding and employment to residents than to respect the residents' own ways of living. In effect, the images of these ways of living shown screenings are likely sites of common concern for "citizens"—the concept under which an alliance between the people on screen and the audience, in order to resist corporate and governmental power, becomes possible. It should be further added that such concerns about actual people and their concrete livelihoods differentiate citizens' screening events from the Communist Party and its affiliated organizations insofar as the latter are mostly concerned with maintaining their ideological and organizational integrity. Indeed, citizens' groups are often cautious about interference by such organizations, even though the latter also partake in the anti-nuclear movement.[40]

Finally, the combination of the screening event with the implications inherent to the concept of "citizens" enables people to create a network beyond what can be called territorial *tōjisha-shugi* or "affected party-ism." The Japanese term *tōjisha-shugi* is also used as the legal term that can be translated as the "adversarial system," but in the Japanese context it often connotes that only the party directly concerned or, in our case, the residents living in the neighborhood of the exploded nuclear power plant have the right to speak about a problem.[41] On one level, this admonishes an

---

[40] Tokai Net members have shared this feeling with me. This, of course, suggests a complication in citizens' openness.

[41] There was a boom of "*tōjisha*" in Japanese intellectual discourses in the 2000s. See, for instance, Nakanishi Masashi and Ueno Chizuko, *Tōjisha shuken* (Tokyo: Iwanami Shoten, 2003).

outsider not to comment irresponsibly on the circumstances in Fukushima. However, doing so risks isolating the residents from people outside their area because it prohibits outsiders from offering spontaneous suggestions and assistance to the residents. Moreover, this idea can be exploited by the neoliberal notion that *tōjisha* should take the responsibility for their own fate because they had accepted the construction of the nuclear power plant in their region. However, if we can separate this term from the notion of the territory or the area where the residents live or used to live, we can unlock much more positive potential. That is, by sharing the knowledge and affect relating to these circumstances through watching a film about them and discussing the issues, we all can become *tōjisha* or affected parties, even though we are not physically living in the stricken areas. In fact, even someone living in the area may not be a *tōjisha* because, for instance, he is only concerned about his own life and employment by the electric company while having no concern about the neighbors or ex-neighbors who are terrified by the continuing spread of radioactive contamination. After all, the coupling of "citizens" with the screening event could serve to build and expand a network of *tōjisha* by sharing their concerns about the problem and having dialogues about it unconstrained by territorialism.[42] Vitally, *tōjisha* do not need to live there or to be directly involved with the case, but are open to people from all areas and social positions. In other words, they are connected only, but most crucially, by shared concerns and dialogue about each other, including those who are directly affected by the problem.

Citizens' screening events are meaningful both in that they are organized by "citizens," and in that they allow the "citizens" to make and remake their networks to empower each other and to resist government and corporate power. The screening event also has the potential to drive the expansion of citizen networks to their family, on- and off-line friends, and beyond, through the networks of media, and shared concern and knowledge. As a remarkably successful case, screenings of Kamanaka's films have led to sustainable networks as seen in the establishment of the citizens' groups like Rokkasho Kaigi in Ueda in Nagano Prefecture and Green Green in Uonuma, Shizuoka Prefecture, as well as trans-local networks such as Rokkasho Rhapsody Again. As one organizer in Yamagata succinctly stated, the film-screening event is both a site of rich learning to inspire thinking and a site that brings about many encounters.[43]

---

[42] I got this idea from the film director Mikami Chie's talk on the issue of the US military bases in Okinawa, which was held at the citizens' screening event of her *The Targeted Village* (*Hyōteki no mura*, 2013) in Shintomiza, a historic cinema theater in Ise City, Mie Prefecture, on February 1, 2014.
[43] Matsui Ai, "Jishu jōeikai o tsūjite," *Yamagata shinbun* (August 7, 2011).

Confronting Difficulties

Film screening events have been held in multiple areas in a somewhat random and sometimes overlapping fashion. As such, they constitute nexuses of multi-layered networks of media, knowledge and shared concern, which end up linking citizens. So far I have illuminated mainly the positive aspects and potential of this form of citizens' social activism. However, it is also true that the practice faces many problems and difficulties, as do other kinds of citizens' activism that make up the post-3.11 social movement. In this last section I will briefly focus on four points.

In the first place, citizens' activism is faced with the question of how to create a network out of depoliticized "consumers," who arguably are largely guided by networks of capital. It is obvious that sports events like the Olympics, popular music concerts, idols and stars on television and the internet, and other entertainments and commercial products attract such tremendous numbers of people that they cannot bear comparison with social movements, even in cases such as anti-nuclear demonstrations saw a boom in popularity in 2012. Capital-oriented events and products stimulate people's desire to consume, not only in a variety of phantasmagoric ways but also in constantly circulative ways, for example as the Olympics are held every four years while no citizens' activism—including screening events—is stably or regularly organized. Ideas of linking this commercial drawing power with citizens' political power have been proposed, and recent activists do attempt to incorporate some aspect of enjoyment, such as music and dance, into their protests. Nevertheless, current political indications suggest that the government has by and large overwhelmed this attempt by targeting and using the depoliticized public as "tacit approvers" of their policies. Some popular musicians, most notably Miyake Yōhei, have successfully turned their fans on to politics (albeit on a small scale,) but this is still rare.[44] Most stars seem to be under pressure from the creative industries that control their performance dates, publicity, and salaries. In this context, citizens always have to confront the question of how and to what extent their screenings can expand their network in competition with corporate-governmental power backed up by capital.

Another difficulty relates to the essential fragility of citizens' networks. These networks should be always open without any institutional

---

[44] Miyake stood as a candidate from the officially authorized political party Greens Japan for the election of the members of the House of Councilors in July 2013 and gained as many as 176,970 votes. For more detail, see Andō Kenji, "Miyake Yōhei-shi, naze 17-manbyō kakutoku de rakusen?" *The Huffington Post*, July 23 2013, accessed October 5, 2015, http://www.huffingtonpost.jp/2013/07/22/miyakeyouhei_n_3634080.html.

and emotional restraint—you can join or leave whenever you like. Unlike hierarchical institutions such as private companies or official organizations, they also should be equal in their relationships. This means that the network depends on exchanges of information and ideas as well as a sense of mutual trust between one citizen and another. It follows that their decisions are not made in a top-down manner but democratically, thereby ensuring inefficiency and instability. Should they become hierarchical organizations for the sake of efficiency and stability, they would lose the very characteristics that define both citizens and their networks. In addition, not all citizens can focus on activism as their primary occupation. Nor do all of them have the specialized knowledge and skills concerning social, political, and scientific issues like nuclear power and radiation. Although the growth of social media has made it easier to find talented participants in different fields and to assist one another, in reality it is often difficult to do so. Moreover, in some cases, corporations or the government co-opts citizens,[45] and established political organizations or agents provocateurs may also disrupt their activism. The intervention of "extremists" (*kagekiha*) have more often than not led the police and the mass media to attach negative labels to citizens' groups, resulting in splitting existing networks and/or the loss of potential connections to other people.[46] In addition to these disruptions from outside, there are conflicts and contestations within the social movement. For instance, some participants oppose nuclear power plants but support the government's measures of decontaminating the land in Fukushima and the nationwide processing of (possibly radioactive) rubble and waste from the Tohoku area, while others do not. These realities all suggest that social movements concerning themselves with nuclear energy cannot simply be reduced to a binary opposition between power versus counter-power, or the government-corporations-mass media versus the citizens, played out in social media and film screening events. While gigantic capital-oriented power puts pressure on citizens' networks, these networks also contain their own fragility, conflicts, and instability, and sometimes they manage to expand while at other times they split apart.

---

[45] Such cases tend to be repressed because organizers fear retaliation and are thus hesitant to expose them to the public. Nevertheless, we can see resources, documents, and testimonies such as Uemura Shinsaku and Yamamoto Kenji, *Shimin undō no jidai desu: Shimin ga shuyaku no 21-seiki* (Tokyo: Dai 3 Shobō, 2011), 136-137; "Kintoku Genpatsu ga dekinakatta machi de," NHK Nagoya, June 29, 2012; Lectures, "Do you know Ashihama?: Genpatsu o tometa machi 'Ashihama' ni manabu," February 22, 2014.

[46] Uemura and Yamamoto, *Shimin undō no jidai desu*, 207-208. Similar cases already happened in the late 1960s. See Andō Takemasa, *Nyūrefuto undō to shiminshakai: "60-nendai" no shisō no yukue* (Tokyo: Sekai Shisōsha, 2013), 133-135.

The relative effectiveness of social movements (including screening events) should also be considered. Although citizens' screenings and anti-nuclear demonstrations have flourished since March 11, 2011, the current LDP government is nevertheless promoting the exporting of nuclear reactors and the restarting of the nuclear power plants that are still inactive as I am writing this in 2014.[47] The post-3.11 anti-nuclear movement has frequently been hailed as successful because it managed to shut down all 54 nuclear power plants in Japan,[48] but the current government policy trivializes citizens' voices with the seeming strategic intention to nullify this activism. This in turn poses the question of how citizens can create sustainable networks to resist power and achieve their goals (while avoiding making maintenance of the network its own end, as a dogmatic party would do). Lastly, there is also the important question of how and to what extent citizens have created, and could create, a global network. To be sure, numerous anti-nuclear demonstrations and gatherings have been held in various places, including Germany, Taiwan, India, Switzerland, UK, Korea, Australia, Canada, France and the US in response to the 3.11 nuclear catastrophe in Fukushima. Some Japanese independent organizations such as the Citizens' Nuclear Information Center (CNIC) transmit information concerning radiation and nuclear energy, and Japanese independent films on these issues have been shown at film festivals, universities, and other public spaces outside Japan while related foreign films have been screened in small theaters and citizens' screening events inside Japan. International organizations like Safecast and Greenpeace are also active. Still, citizens' screenings as well as other activism should explore a more globally sustainable network. This is important especially because the promoters of nuclear energy have their own global nuclear lobby.[49]

Citizens' independent film screening events have played a unique and significant role in post-3.11 social movements as well as more generally in media convergence. They have functioned as nexuses within multi-layered networks of media, knowledge, shared concern, action, and citizenship. This function has been realized in cooperation with new media such as social networking technology, DVDs, and the internet. At the same time, the screening event is distinctive in that it motivates people

---

[47] "Kōyaku mushi no saikadō suishin: Enerugi keikaku seifu an," *Tōkyō shinbun*, February 26, 2014), accessed February 27, 2014, http://www.tokyo-np.co.jp/s/article/2014022690071137.html.

[0]Oguma Eiji, *Genpatsu o tomeru hitobito: 3.11 kara Kantei-mae made* (Tokyo: Bungei shunjūsha, 2013), 287-295.

[49] Collin Kobayashi, *Kokusai genshiryoku robī no hanzai: Cherunobuiri kara Fukushima e* (Tokyo: Ibunsha, 2013).

to watch a film together in a physically bound concrete space and operates as an intimate public sphere where the participants conduct dialogues and share concerns about each other, the issues, and the residents directly affected by the catastrophe, in defiance of geographical restraints and differences in social position. It also serves to foster a kind of non-territorial *tōjisha-shugi*. In effect, with the characteristics of the concept of "citizens"—self-proclamation, political nuance, equality, and openness—the screening events are not only vital in the anti-nuclear movement, but also suggestive for social movements in general, epitomizing a rich potential for interpersonal relations, learning, and networking among citizens, albeit with certain difficulties. It is at this point that citizens' film screening events can be productively seen as an especially politically significant form of convergence culture in contemporary Japan.

Works Cited

Andō Takemasa. *Nyūrefuto undō to shimin shakai: "60-nendai" no shisō no yukue*. Tokyo: Sekai Shisōsha, 2013.

Avenell, Simon. *Making Japanese Citizens: Civil Society and the Mythology of the Shimin in Postwar Japan*. Berkeley: University of California Press, 2010.

———. "From Fearsome Pollution to Fukushima: Environmental Activism and the Nuclear Blind Spot in Contemporary Japan." *Environmental History* 17, no. 2 (2012): 244-276.

Beck, Ulrich. *Risk Society: Towards a New Modernity*. Translated by Mark Ritter. London: Sage, 1992.

Benhabib, Seyla. *The Reluctant Modernism of Hannah Arendt*. London: Sage, 1996.

Broadbent, Jeffrey. *Environmental Politics in Japan: Networks of Power and Protest*. Cambridge, UK: Cambridge University Press, 1998.

Castells, Manuel. *The Rise of the Network Society*, second ed. Oxford, UK: Blackwell, 2000.

Communication Power. Oxford, UK: Oxford University Press, 2009.

Couldry, Nick, and James Curran. *Contesting Media Power: Alternative Media in a Networked World*. Lanham, MD: Rowman and Littlefield, 2003.

Diani, Mario, and Doug McAdam, eds., *Social Movements and Networks: Relational Approaches to Collective Action*. Oxford, UK: Oxford University Press, 2003.

Endres, Danielle. "From Wasteland to Waste Site: The Role of Discourse in Nuclear Power's Environmental Injustices." *Local Environment* 14, no. 19 (2009): 917-937.

Fujiki Hideaki. "'Taishū' to shite no eiga kankyaku." In *'Sengo' Nihon eigaron: 1950-nendai o yomu*, edited by Mitsuyo Wada-Marciano, 121-142. Tokyo: Seikyūsha, 2012.

———. "Problematizing Life: Documentary Films on the 3.11 Nuclear Catastrophe." In *Negotiating Nuclear Disaster: 'Fukushima' and the Arts*, edited by Kristina Iwata Weikgenannt and Barbara Holthus. London: Routledge, forthcoming.

Fukuwara Takashi, and Yamada Ryūsaku, eds. *Shiteizunshippu ron no shatei*. Tokyo: Nihon Keizai Hyōronsha, 2010.

Gonoi Ikuo. *"Demo" to wa nanika: Henbō suru chokusetsu minshushugi*. Tokyo: NHK Shuppan, 2012.

Habermas, Jürgen. *The Structural Transformation of the Public Sphere: An Inquiry into a Category of a Bourgeois Society*. Translated by Thomas Burger and Frederick Lawrence. Cambridge, UK: Polity, 1989.

Higuchi Naohito. "Mirai no 'yogensha' to shite no shakai undō: 'Risuku shakai' no keiji." In *Shakai undō no shakaigaku*, edited by Ōhata Hirotsugu, Sei Gentetsu, and Higuchi Naoto, 15-30. Tokyo: Yūhikaku, 2004.

Itō Masāki. *Demo no media ron: Shakai undō no yukue*. Tokyo: Chikuma Shobō, 2013.

Jenkins, Henry. *Convergence Culture: Where Old and New Media Collide*. New York: New York University Press, 2006.

Jiang Jieun. "Nihon ni okeru shimin eigakan no taitō to tenkai." *Eizōgaku* 71 (2003): 5-26.

Kobayashi Collin. *Kokusai genshiryoku robī no hanzai: Cherunobuiri kara Fukushima e.* Tokyo: Ibunsha, 2013.

Koizumi Shūkichi. "Dokyumentarī seisaku to jōei no jissai." In *Series Nihon no dokyumentarī 1: Dokyumentarī no miryoku*, edited by Satō Tadao, 144-159. Tokyo: Iwanami Shoten, 2009.

Kurihara Akira. "Shimin seiji no ajenda: Seimei seiji no hō e." *Shisō* 908 (2000): 5-14.

Lievrouw, Leah A. *Alternative and Activist New Media: Digital Media and Society.* Cambridge, UK: Polity, 2011.

Liscutin, Nicola. "Indignez-Vous!: 'Fukushima,' New Media and Anti-Nuclear Activism in Japan." *The Asia-Pacific Journal: Japan Focus* 9, Issue 47, No. 1 (November 21, 2011), http://www.japanfocus.org/-Nicola-Liscutin/3649.

Maruyama Hisashi. *Rōkaru nettowāku no jidai: Mini-comi to chiiki to shimin undō.* Tokyo: Nichigai Associates, 1997.

Matsubara Akira. "Paper Tiger TV to Nihon no media undō." In *Media to kassei: What's media activism*, edited by Hosoya Shūhei, 38-46. Tokyo: Impact Shuppankai, 2012.

Matsui Ai, "Jishu jōeikai o tsūjite," *Yamagata shinbun* (August 7, 2011).

Melucci, Alberto. *Nomads of the Present: Social Movements and Individual Needs in Contemporary Society.* Philadelphia: Temple University Press, 1989.

Mōri Yoshitaka. *Sutorīto no shisō: Tenkanki to shite no 1990-nendai.* Tokyo: Nihon Hōsōkyōkai, 2009.

Nakanishi Masashi, and Ueno Chizuko. *Tōjisha shuken.* Tokyo: Iwanami Shoten, 2003.

Nornes, Abé Mark. *Forest of Pressure: Ogawa Shinseki and Postwar Japanese Documentary*. Minneapolis, MN: University of Minnesota Press, 2007.

Ogawa, Akihiro. *The Failure of Civil Society?: The Third Sector and the State in Contemporary Japan*. Albany, NY: State University of New York Press, 2009.

Oguma Eiji. *"Minshu" to "aikoku": Sengo Nihon no nashonarizumu to kōkyōsei*. Tokyo: Shinyōsha, 2002.

———. *Genpatsu o tomeru hitobito: 3.11 kara Kantei-mae made*. Tokyo: Bungei Shunjūsha, 2013.

Saitō Jun'ichi. *Kōkyōsei*. Tokyo: Iwanami Shoten, 2000.

Uemura Shinsaku, and Yamamoto Kenji. *Shimin undō no jidai desu: Shimin ga shuyaku no 21-seiki*. Tokyo: Dai 3 Shobō, 2011.

Yamada Kazuo. "Kankyaku wa eiga o kanri dekiru: Jishu eiga jōei undō no imi suru mono." *Eiga hyōron* 17, no. 9 (1960): 36-39.

Part II:
Industrial Convergence

Convergence and Globalization in the Japanese Videogame Industry

Mia Consalvo

For contemporary media scholars, convergence means more than technologies or content coming together in one box.[1] It instead alludes to the convergence of content across media platforms, and the joining together of media producers and consumers in the production and negotiation of that content—through user-generated content, greater feedback mechanisms for consumers, or fan-driven media campaigns. Yet apart from a sidebar mentioning the importance that both Western and Japanese fans have played in the global popularity of Japanese anime, most examples that Henry Jenkins cites in *Convergence Culture*, and the majority of work done by other media scholars, focuses on Western media products and companies.[2]

This essay addresses that omission and advocates further investigation regarding the Japanese game industry by studying three companies successful in developing and publishing games, along with a range of other activities. Those companies are Bandai Namco, Square Enix, and Konami. I chose these three for several reasons. First, all released annual reports for 2007, which formed the starting point of analysis. Second, the companies have had long histories and have all weathered multiple console releases, as well as evolving cultural, technological, social, and political developments. None of the three are principally console manufacturers, like Sony and Nintendo. Those companies would make comparisons more difficult, as hardware and software production are different undertakings. And finally, I chose companies that acted as both developers and publishers and who had diversified holdings. Not all Japanese videogame companies are this diverse in their ownership and business strategies; it is exactly their diversity that makes these three companies particularly interesting and important.[3]

---

[1] Henry Jenkins, *Convergence Culture: Where Old and New Media Collide* (New York: New York University Press, 2006); Henry Jenkins, "The Cultural Logic of Media Convergence," *International Journal of Cultural Studies* 7, no. 1 (2004): 33-43.

[2] Jenkins, *Convergence Culture*, 156-161.

[3] Other contenders considered, and to be expanded on in a future edition of this paper, include Capcom, Sega, Koei, and Atlus.

This essay investigates how these companies are negotiating the "convergence culture" that Jenkins writes about. Next, it examines how they are responding to a problem unique to Japan—the graying of the nation. Lastly, it questions how globalization plays a role in Japanese game business strategies.

First, however, let me give a brief description of each company. The oldest is Bandai Namco. Bandai began in the 1950s producing various toys, mostly metallic cars. It created the Sailor Moon and Power Rangers brands, released Tamagotchi in 1996, and in 2005 acquired Namco.[4] Namco started out producing mechanical rocking horses, later acquiring the Japanese division of Atari and entering the coin-operated game market. In 1980 Namco released the global blockbuster Pac-Man, and in 1993 the company merged with Aladdin's Castle Inc., to become the world's largest arcade company.[5] Bandai Namco now comprises business units that include game development, arcades, toys and toy-related products, spa facilities, tourist hotels, online services, anime production, and restaurants.

Konami incorporated in 1973, when it began to manufacture amusement machines.[6] It created the hit arcade game *Frogger* in 1981, and has since produced some of the best-known games in game history, including the *Castlevania* (1986-2008), *Contra* (1987-2007), *Silent Hill* (1999-2008), and *Metal Gear* (1987-2008) series, along with *Dance Dance Revolution* (1998) and the soccer series *Winning Eleven* (1995-2008). Currently, Konami has three business segments. Its Digital Entertainment segment comprises home videogame software, card games, and amusement arcade machines. The Health and Fitness segment operates sports clubs and develops health-related products and services. Lastly, the Gaming and System segment develops, manufactures, and supplies gaming machines and casino management systems.

The final company, Square Enix, is the product of another merger, in 2003, of two Japanese developer/publisher stalwarts best known for their *Final Fantasy* (1987-2016) and *Dragon Quest* (1986-2016) series. Enix was founded in 1975, while Square began operations in 1986. Square Enix continues to release games in the *Final Fantasy* and *Dragon Quest* series, along with developing games for emerging markets in China and Korea. In

---

[4] For more on the history of these companies, see Bandai's official history at http://www.bandai.co.jp/e/corporate/history.html and a Wikipedia entry profiling the company at http://en.wikipedia.org/wiki/Bandai (accessed October 10, 2008).

[5] Information taken from http://en.wikipedia.org/wiki/Namco (accessed October 10, 2008).

[6] Konami Corporation, Annual Report 2007, Tokyo, Japan.

2005, Square Enix acquired Taito Corporation, which started operating in 1953 as a manufacturer of small vending machines. Taito went on to expand its arcade business, developing the global hit *Space Invaders* in 1978. Square Enix segments its business into numerous areas, including offline games, online games, mobile phone content, publications, and amusements.

Convergence Culture Meets Japan's Media Mix

Jenkins writes how content moves across platforms, as well as how media consumers interact with content, identifying sites of negotiation where convergence occurs.[7] One site transforms media franchises from a central text with derivative works related to it to, instead, places where "each media manifestation makes a distinct but interrelated contribution to the unfolding of a narrative universe."[8] If thought about as a continuum, universes range from encapsulating a strong "center-periphery" model to systems that are much less centralized.

The "center-periphery" model was first widely exploited in the West with the success of George Lucas's *Star Wars* series in the 1970s and 1980s. Although most often credited with creating a market for media-related consumables and collectibles, *Star Wars* also helped establish the idea of a media universe, creating opportunities for further consumption, but also for providing new pieces of the *Star Wars* story (as well as adaptations) through novels, comics, and videogames. During that time, most of what was released was created by professional storytellers (or designers) rather than by fans of the series, a situation that would change quickly.[9]

Western media corporations have mostly continued to follow a "center-periphery" paradigm, claiming a particular canon for some universe, either through films (*Star Wars*), books (Tolkien and Middle Earth), or a television series (*Star Trek*). In contrast, the background that companies such as Bandai Namco and Konami have in toys and amusements sets up a different form of engagement with the world of cross-media and cross-product promotion; unlike in the American model, here central characters or a theme or world are created, then gradually filled in by various media products, none of which may take center stage.[10] Bandai's

---

[7] Jenkins, "The Cultural Logic."

[8] *Ibid.*, 40.

[9] More recent franchises such as the Harry Potter books have entered a playing field where readers-turned-fans have also become active producers in the Potterverse. The fan site HarryPotterfanfiction.com, for example, boasts over 50,000 stories and podcasts created by fans, and receives over 40 million hits per month.

[10] Perhaps the best-known example would be Sanrio's Hello Kitty, which started life in 1974 simply as a brand, with content waiting to flesh out the form.

Gundam character line, for example, began in 1979 as part of an anime series, followed by a toy series in 1980, a series of movies starting the next year, and continuing with new toy lines, anime (TV) productions, films, and videogames. Importantly, these are all key components of the Gundam universe, with no one piece being the center. Such assemblages constitute what Ito terms a "media mix" which includes games "as one component of a broader media ecology that includes anime, manga, trading card games, toys, and character merchandise."[11]

Bandai Namco stresses such linkages, calling them synergies, which "integrate character merchandising with technical development capabilities and a location network."[12] That synergy includes the networked arcade game *Mobile Suit Gundam: Senjō no Kizuna* (2007)— which sixteen people can play concurrently—and the 2006 construction of the theme park "Namco Wonder Park Hero's Base." In similar ways, Square Enix draws from elements of its business to expand the *Final Fantasy* universe, which has never featured a core text or storyline, but instead creates features and elements that make each iteration of *Final Fantasy* feel familiar (including the appearance of specific animal races such as the chicken-like chocobos, a character named Cid, crystals, and a common currency). Currently Square Enix takes the *Final Fantasy* universe and uses films to tell some stories ("Advent Children"), games to tell more (including games such as *Crisis Core* [2007], which steps outside the numbered franchise and tells a story of a character from *Final Fantasy VII* [1997]), and other products or services to keep the universe expanding. Other elements include the MMOG, *Final Fantasy XI* (2002), mobile phone games such as *Dirge of Cerberus: Lost Episode* (2006), collectibles, music CDs, and mp3's from the games.

The Graying of Japan

Top sellers in places like the United States and Europe draw from developers and publishers spread around the globe. One European Top 20 list, for example, includes games from Nintendo, Konami, Activision, EA, Ubisoft, and Sega.[13] In contrast, Japan remains insular in its appetite for game titles. Charts listing the top one hundred games sold in Japan in 2005 show the first non-Japanese game listed being the #70 title *Ratchet*

---

[11] Mizuko Ito, "The Gender Dynamics of the Japanese Media Mix" (paper presented at the Girls and Games Workshop, UCLA, 2006).

[12] Bandai Namco Games, Annual Report 2007, Tokyo, Japan.

[13] "Top 20 Publishers 2007," *Game Developer* (2008), accessed October 10, 2008, http://www. gamedevresearch.com/top-20- publishers-2007.htm.

& Clank 4 produced by Insomniac Games in California. In 2007, the first non-Japanese entry was Rockstar Games' *Grand Theft Auto: San Andreas* at #35, selling slightly more than 400,000 copies. To compare, the top seller in 2007 was *Wii Sports* (Nintendo), which sold almost two million units, and #2 was *Monster Hunter Freedom 2* (Capcom) for the PSP with almost 1.5 million units, suggesting that Western games have a rough time gaining entry or popularity in the Japanese market.[14] Because of those historical tendencies, Japanese game companies have found a ready market at home, with little fear of outside competition.

However, even if game and related product sales in Japan are favorable (as they have been for Konami), and even if Japanese game companies have had a near monopoly on game sales in Japan itself, convergence and a turn to global audiences are becoming necessities not options. Much has been made of the declining birth rate in Japan—the "graying of Japan"—with two annual reports specifically concerned with the aging of the Japanese market as a "risk factor." In this context, the possibilities of convergence help to shore up a games market that has started to contract due to the shifting demographics of Japanese society. This challenge in part drives the creation of game-related products such as Square's 2001 film *Final Fantasy: The Spirits Within* (Hironobu Sakaguchi and Motonori Kakakibara), to spur potential interest beyond the traditional core of young boys and men. A converged media culture has added more revenue flows, as Japanese game companies have placed greater emphasis on going global with their media mix—something that they have been doing for years with varied degrees of success—as another key way of managing the declining local market.

Going Global with a Converged Culture

The media mix or convergence culture which Japanese companies have been developing has of necessity made its way to Western markets, often beginning through unofficial channels. Jenkins explains that "western youth is asserting its identity through its consumption of Japanese anime and manga....A new pop cosmopolitanism is being promoted by corporate interests both in Asia and in the West."[15] Scholars have begun to map this trend, pointing to how anime fans see the material as more

[14] *Wii Sports* may be an unfair comparison, as it came free with the Wii console; thus I have included the #2 ranked game as a better comparison. "2005 Top 100 Best selling Japanese console games," *The Magic Box* (2006), available online at http://www.the-magicbox.com/Chart-BestSell2005.shtml; Daemon Hatfield, "The Japan 100, 2007 Edition," IGN (2008), accessed October 10, 2008, http://ps3.ign.com/articles/845/845026p1.html.
[15] Jenkins, "The Cultural Logic," 41.

complex and thought-provoking than most Western media, as well as how "all things Japan" come to be seen as "cool" in the West.[16] That trend has historical roots which span at least 150 years, with similar fads or interest in "all things Japanese" influencing the Impressionists in Europe, and other intellectuals and middle class citizens as time passed, as Susan Napier has noted.[17] Games (and their related products) appear to be another piece of that Japanese cultural "cool," on which the media industry capitalizes.

Steady calls for globalization of a media mix in annual corporate reports may seem puzzling, since games from Japan have been an integral part of the history of the game industry since Nintendo revitalized the US market in the mid-1980s.[18] From that time, Japanese game developers, publishers, and console manufacturers have gone from dominating output to, at minimum, assuming a central role in the industry's continuing development. Yet financial documents reveal another view of Japanese companies. While Bandai Namco, Square Enix, and Konami all have global operations, percentages of income and sales gained from abroad are rather meager. Across the three, the Japanese market accounts for three-quarters or more of sales and revenue. The remaining income is gathered from North America, Europe, and Asia. ("Asia" here refers to a select few countries—China, Hong Kong, Taiwan, and Korea—and is a minor player.) It is easy to see why Japanese companies are so nervous about their shrinking domestic market: it represents the vast majority of their sales. Consequently, Japanese companies are desperately seeking to diversify, and do so in ways that go beyond a few internationally known blockbuster titles or series. Even if revenues are comparatively small, the global operations of Japanese game companies have been key to the development of the industry generally, as Japanese games and firms have contributed much in the way of cultural (if not economic) influence on the global games industry.

Yet now, those companies desire to broaden their markets, expand operations, or more carefully develop opportunities for international sales. Konami talks of "bolstering overseas business development," while Bandai

---

[16] Susan Napier, *From Impressionism to Anime: Japan as Fantasy and Fan Cult in the Mind of the West* (New York: Palgrave, 2007).

[17] *Ibid.* See also Mia Consalvo, "Visiting the Floating World: Tracing a Cultural History of Games Through Japan and America" (paper presented at the Digital Games Research Association Conference, Tokyo, Japan, September 2007).

[18] Mia Consalvo, "Console Video Games and Global Corporations: Creating a Hybrid Culture," *New Media & Society* 8, no. 1 (2007); Oavid Sheff, *Game Over: How Nintendo Conquered the World* (New York: Vintage, 1994).

Namco states that one of their "key business strategies...is strengthening overseas businesses."[19] Square Enix reports that overseas sales from games such as *Kingdom Hearts II* (2005) and *Final Fantasy XII* (2006) "contributed substantially to earnings and profits."[20] Bandai Namco also realized gains from abroad, which "supported domestic operations," which had seen a decline in sales and profits in the past year.[21] In the 1980s and 1990s Japanese companies produced a disproportionate share of software and hardware sold globally, meaning that even poorly localized games could sell well. Early game fans derided the translation and localization efforts of those games, which often featured badly broken English. Yet the development of a more competitive global market with more companies and genres of games that might be regionally appropriate has changed the parameters for competition. Japanese companies must now be more diligent in how they pursue overseas markets, carefully developing or adapting selected media products that (re)deploy successful product universes.

Thus Konami will have employees in North America, Europe, and Asia "create, produce and offer products and services targeting local markets...[and] each local operating base will [also] build a system that will enable the global rollout of certain products and services."[22] Echoing interests in convergence, Konami sees opportunities both for global successes like *Metal Gear*, as well as the creation of content tied to particular regions and interests, that is, not simply Japanese content repackaged for sale elsewhere.

Bandai Namco is moving their strategy beyond localization of Japanese products and the development of overseas content: "Instead of development that is based on the framework of 'products for Japan' and 'products for overseas' we will emphasize cooperation between Japan and overseas bases and implement worldwide development from the planning stage."[23] What this might mean is the development of content that in its raw form might draw from common themes, characters, or universes, but is then localized or "culturalized" to respond best to the interests of a variety of markets. Perhaps this indicates the formation of another layer or level to convergence. In addition to a fictional media universe drawing from a theme or character to create a diversity of content across multiple media platforms, convergence might entail that process working across

---

[19] Konami, 15; Bandai Namco, 9.
[20] Square Enix Company Limited, Annual Report 2007, Tokyo, Japan.
[21] Bandai Namco, 9.
[22] Konami, 16.
[23] Bandai Namco, 14.

regions and markets as well, carefully adapted not only for a technical platform, but for particular communities or nation states. Convergence just gained another order of complexity.

Conclusions

This essay has applied the concept of convergence to a slice of the Japanese game industry, to see how they are adapting to new demands. Japanese companies like Bandai Namco or Konami have a broadly diversified set of business segments, managing businesses that would seem to have nothing to do with games or even amusements. Yet at the same time, they have certain segments, such as toys and arcades, which help them create greater synergies or convergences across media forms as well as fictional universes. Japanese game companies operate primarily in domestic markets, where they dominate, and are now trying to diversify their revenue streams through more skilful use of their media mixes, and through the (re)capture of global markets, which have become much more demanding in terms of quality of content and familiarity of products. It can be done. Many Western individuals claim to love anime for its complex themes and lack of simplistic endings, suggesting that there is still interest in Japanese products abroad, in games, in anime, and in many other related artifacts. Yet how wide that market may be is an open question. Japanese game companies will need to consider such questions and challenges as they move forward with plans for greater expansion. They have moved beyond the creation of basic product lines to more sophisticated and inter-related products, as well as from the export of crudely localized products to more carefully "culturalized" ones. They are also questioning whether one-way exports are the answer, or if simply setting up offices abroad and having them make "local" games and artifacts is the right approach. For now, they continue to struggle with the logics of convergence, in a constantly changing global media universe.

Works Cited

Bandai Namco Games, Annual Report 2007, Tokyo, Japan.

Consalvo, Mia. "Console Video Games and Global Corporations: Creating a Hybrid Culture." *New Media & Society* 8, no. 1 (2007): 117-137.

———. "Visiting the Floating World: Tracing a Cultural History of Games Through Japan and America." Paper presented at the Digital Games Research Association Conference, Tokyo, Japan, September 2007.

Ito, Mizuko. "The Gender Dynamics of the Japanese Media Mix." Paper presented at the Girls and Games Workshop, UCLA, 2006.

Jenkins, Henry. "The Cultural Logic of Media Convergence." *International Journal of Cultural Studies* 7, no. 1 (2004): 33-43.

———. *Convergence Culture: Where Old and New Media Collide.* New York: New York University Press, 2006.

Konami Corporation, Annual Report 2007, Tokyo, Japan.

Napier, Susan. *From Impressionism to Anime: Japan as Fantasy and Fan Cult in the Mind of the West.* New York: Palgrave, 2007.

Sheff, Oavid. *Game Over: How Nintendo Conquered the World.* New York: Vintage, 1994.

Square Enix Company Limited, Annual Report 2007, Tokyo, Japan.

When the Media Do Not Quite Converge: The Case of Fuji TV vs. Livedoor

Shinji Oyama and Dario Lolli

A simple walk in downtown Tokyo is enough to assure any commentator that it is indeed appropriate to speak about convergence in relation to the Japanese media environment: crowds of students enjoy manga, video games or television on the move with their mobile devices, interactive digital billboards in subway stations detect the demographics of viewers as they pass by, while behind the windows of internet cafes groups of young people engage in hectic "tag battles" on the popular social media platform Niconico.[1] As such, Japanese media convergence would seem to fit the image usually associated with this new global phenomenon—namely the integration of "old" and "new" media enabled by digital technologies, the experience of accessing multiple media contents on mobile and interconnected devices, and the emergence of new cultural practices that are transforming and mixing the once autonomous spheres of media production and consumption.[2] In its most evident uses, the term convergence suggests a common ground in which different technological, economic or political stakes unite in a single point or logic—usually innovation and market expansion and a deterministic belief that such a convergence process is inevitable and irreversible. In spite of this popular narrative, however, contemporary academic research has suggested how frictions and fragmentations are the paradoxical preconditions of what often appears as an ineluctable convergence.[3] If we shift our view from media consumption to consider the practices of the Japanese creative industries, in particular, it is possible to see how a deterministic idea of media convergence starts to blur into a more fragmented, uncertain and open-ended process.[4]

---

[1] Hamano Satoshi, "The Generaticity of Nico Nico Douga: The New Type of Creativity Enabled by Metadata," *Genron: Portal for Critical Discourse in Japan*, May 14, 2012, http://global.genron.co.jp/2012/05/14/the-generativity-of-nico-nico-douga/.

[2] Henry Jenkins, *Convergence Culture: Where Old and New Media Collide* (New York: New York University Press, 2008); and Charles Leadbeater, *Living on Thin Air: The New Economy* (London: Penguin, 2000).

[3] James Hay and Nick Couldry, "Rethinking Convergence/Culture: An Introduction," *Cultural Studies* 25, no. 4-5 (2011): 473-486; and Peter Ludes, *Convergence and Fragmentation: Media Technology and the Information Society* (Bristol: Intellect, 2008).

[4] "Tokushū: Nerawareta Horiemon," *Aera* (January 30, 2006): 21-32.

This chapter will focus on a key, but still under researched aspect of Japanese media convergence, the industrial integration of "old" media groups and "new" media companies.[5] More specifically, we will analyze a process that has long dominated the debate on media convergence in Japan, the so-called "convergence between broadcasting and communication" (*hōso to tsūshin no yūgo*), in order to broaden our understanding of media convergence in relation to the social, economic and political dimensions of the Japanese mediascape.[6] The argument we would like to pursue here is that the international debate on Japanese media convergence has been mainly shaped by, and narrowed down to, a limited consideration of a *particular* segment of the Japanese creative industries and the new consumption practices emerging in the digital environment. In other words, the recent global popularity of Japanese media products like anime and manga has sparked much interest in their production and consumption, often linking them to broader debates about transmediality and convergence.[7] This perspective has promoted the image of Japan at the forefront of media convergence processes, thanks to the strong transmedia nature of its popular culture. Seen from the broader perspective of the whole of Japanese creative industries, however, media convergence in Japan appears rather as an uneven process, involving industrial actors and political stakes that are often difficult to detect from the study of the consumption of popular culture.

In what follows, we will focus on the uneasy interaction of "traditional" media groups with the "new media" industries emerging from the development of digital technologies, primarily the internet. This often-neglected view on Japanese convergence does not solely imply a focus on the diversity of the industrial actors involved in these processes, but also to the fact that their operations have direct effect on a media market

---

[5] Since considering a medium as new or old is only a perspectival matter constantly troubled by remediation. See J. David Bolter and Richard A. Grusin, *Remediation: Understanding New Media* (Cambridge, MA: MIT Press, 1999), the persistent recourse to the "old"/"new" binary betrays particular assumptions about origin, modernity and progress that require an "archaeological" methodology to be unraveled. See Jussi Parikka, *What Is Media Archaeology?* (Cambridge: Polity Press, 2012). In this chapter, we decided to deploy this simplistic dichotomy in a purely descriptive and strategic way, as we believe that it nonetheless captures the different prestige/power relations and work ethos characterizing Japan's "old" mass communication industries (*masukomi gyōkai*) and the "new" internet companies (*netto kigyō*), the emerging industrial sectors primarily dependent on digital technologies.

[6] Suzuki Yūji, "'Tsūshin hōso yūgō' no genzai, kako, mirai: 'TV bangumi netto haishin' gannen ni okeru kōsatsu," *NHK Hōso Bunka Kenkyūjo Nenpō* 53 (2009): 7-46; and Suzuki Yūji, "'Tsūshin to hōso no yūgō' wa dō giron sateta no ka," *Hōso kenkyū to chōsa* (October 2006): 14-31.

[7] Jenkins, *Convergence Culture*.

that consistently exceeds and ultimately encompasses that of popular products like anime and manga. After providing a brief overview of the diversity of the Japanese creative industries involved in convergence, we will analyze how they have ambivalently coped with the forces of globalization and liberalization, concentrating in particular on the case of the so-called Livedoor incident—the ultimately failed attempt by a new media company to take over the powerful old media player Fuji TV in 2005. This case study is particularly enlightening, as it will challenge the universal notion of media convergence on several counts. On the one hand, it highlights how old Japanese media groups have been reacting to the challenges of convergence and globalization in a very nation-centric way, sometimes at odds with the neoliberal logic that leads convergence processes elsewhere.[8] On the other hand, it also shows how old media groups in the Japanese media industries are operating in a different sphere (and politics) than those companies usually associated with the subcultures so often featured in academic research and governmental "Cool Japan" policies.[9]

The chapter will conclude with some considerations based on the cultural and political implications of this case in the context of convergent media policies in Japan. Although it is impossible to generalize how Japanese media groups across different sectors will respond to convergence and neoliberal globalization, the case of Livedoor points to some historical specificities in the way new technologies have been arranged, economically and politically, in the evolving Japanese media environment. This chapter, therefore, will try to suggest that an understanding of multiple and sometimes "not-quite-converging" convergences can better capture the complexity and diversity of media convergence in different cultural contexts around the world.

Media Convergence and Japan

In 2006, when Henry Jenkins gave renewed currency to the idea of media convergence, he envisioned it as a series of cultural changes

---

[8] Tim Dwyer, *Media Convergence* (Maidenhead: Open University Press, 2010), 18; and Dal Yong Jin, ed. *Global Media Convergence and Cultural Transformation: Emerging Social Patterns and Characteristics* (Hershey, PA: IGI Global, 2011), xv.

[9] Michal Daliot-Bul, "Japan Brand Strategy: The Taming of 'Cool Japan' and the Challenges of Cultural Planning in Postmodern Age," *Social Science Japan Journal* 12, no. 2 (Winter 2009): 247-266. It should be noted that the word "subculture" is used here in its Japanese sense of "niche consumption." See Eiji Ōtsuka, "World and Variation: The Reproduction and Consumption of Narrative," *Mechademia* 5, no. 1 (2010): 99-116, not in the socio-political meaning of oppositional culture usually found in British cultural studies. See Stuart Hall and Tony Jefferson, *Resistance through Rituals: Youth Subcultures in Post-War Britain* (London: Routledge, 2006).

dependent on increasing digitization, transmediality and collaboration.[10] Although many of these processes can be easily detected in any advanced capitalist country like Japan, the industry arrangements that allow for such changes might not always be the same in every cultural context, rendering the notion of a singular convergence insufficient to capture the variety of what rather appears as a set of recurrent but disarticulated processes.[11] The collision of "old" and "new" media anticipated by Jenkin's *Convergence Culture*, therefore, has to be located in the contingent social, industrial and political organization of a specific country. In Japanese media studies, this perspective has so far found only partial scrutiny, and the changing media environment of contemporary Japan has been mostly considered through the lenses of consumer experiences and entertainment media. The constant blurring in Japanese otaku subcultures of assumed categories such as producers and consumers or original and derivative works,[12] for instance, has led many scholars to focus specifically on their fan practices, overemphasizing the role of Japanese fans as active co-producers or "prosumers" (producer-consumer) of media contents.

In his book, Jenkins acknowledges quite often that the remarkable cultural changes brought about by convergence are not only the result of consumer-driven processes, but also of the alarming concentration of resources into the hands of a powerful and limited number of transnational media corporations.[13] Yet, it is his focus on the participatory productions by consumers—the *culture* of convergence—which has most powerfully captured the imagination of media scholars working on Japan. Japanese media convergence, that is, has been mainly linked to the national or transnational consumption of globally popular products like anime, manga and their related transmedia commodities.[14]

---

[10] Jenkins, *Convergence Culture*, 2-3.

[11] Hay and Couldry, "Rethinking Convergence/Culture," 490.

[12] Azuma Hiroki, *Otaku: Japan's Database Animals*, trans. Jonathan E. Abel and Shion Kono (Minneapolis, MN: University of Minnesota Press, 2009); and Otsuka, Eiji. "World and Variation: The Reproduction and Consumption of Narrative," *Mechademia* 5, no.1 (2010): 99-116

[13] Jenkins, *Convergence Culture*, 3.

[14] See Jaqueline Berndt and Bettina Kuemmerling-Meibauer, ed., *Manga's Cultural Crossroads* (New York: Routledge, 2013); Condry, *The Soul of Anime;* Daliot-Bul, "Japan Brand Strategy," 247-266; Mizuko Ito, "Technologies of the Childhood Imagination: Yugioh, Media Mixes, and Everyday Cultural Production" in *Structures of Participation in Digital Culture*, ed. Joe Karaganis (New York: Social Science Research Council, 2007), 88-111; Hye-Kyung Lee, "Participatory Media Fandom: A Case Study of Anime Fansubbing," *Media, Culture & Society* 33, no. 8 (2011): 1131-1147; Hye-Kyung Lee, "Between Fan Culture and Copyright Infringement: Manga Scanlation," *Media, Culture and Society* 31, no. 6 (2009): 1011-1022; and Marc Steinberg, *Anime's Media Mix: Franchising Toys and Characters in Japan* (Minneapolis, MN: University of Minnesota Press, 2012).

The Japanese government—particularly the powerful Ministry of Economy, Trade and Industry (METI)—has further contributed to this confusion by conflating media convergence with the marketing of anime and manga. In June 2010, METI established the Creative Industries Promotion Office, which was appointed with the specific task of supporting the international promotion of the Japanese creative industries through a specific plan of cultural policies named "Cool Japan."[15] What is interesting about this support program is the way it bridges industry and government in order to promote the content industries central to Cool Japan policies. Cool Japan, a term originally coined by American journalist Douglas McGray more than ten years ago, has become a buzzword in contemporary Japanese society, establishing its own discursive space in an endless stream of popular and academic articles, television series, government reports and industry white papers.[16] In spite of this popularity, Cool Japan policies remain quite ambiguous in relation to convergence and the creative industries, and limited and biased above all by the adoption of a global orientation. Although based on transmediality and meant to promote the Japanese creative industries at large, Cool Japan places at the center of its strategies products like manga and animation, which are already popular in the global market. In 2012, manga and anime brought in around ¥34 billion in international licensing sale, but this ultimately amounts to only a fraction of the total revenues produced by what are usually known as the "core" creative industries, with the Japanese broadcasting industry alone generating revenues for as much as ¥3,891 billion.[17] In 2011, METI identified eight industrial sectors to be supported by Cool Japan policies: fashion, foods, contents, local produces, houses, tourism, art and design. Amongst those, only the so called "content industries"—the industries based on the development of intellectual properties, but specifically those of anime, manga and video games—can be considered part of what media scholars usually refer to as the "core cultural industries": broadcasting, the film industries, the internet industry, the music industries, print and electronic publishing,

---

[15] Daliot-Bul, "Japan Brand Strategy," 247-266; Mihara Ryūtarō, *Kūru Japan wa naze kirawareru-no-ka: "Nekkō" to "reishō" o koete* (Tokyo: Chūo Kōron, 2014); Nissim Otmazgin, "A Tail That Wags the Dog? Cultural Industry and Cultural Policy in Japan and South Korea," *Journal of Comparative Policy Analysis: Research and Practice* 13, no. 3 (2011): 307-325; and Katja Valaskivi, "A Brand New Future? Cool Japan and the Social Imaginary of the Branded Nation," *Japan Forum* 25, no. 4 (2013): 485-504.

[16] Douglas McGray, "Japan's Gross National Cool," *Foreign Policy* 130 (May/June 2002): 44-54.

[17] Ministry of Internal Affairs and Communications, *Jōhō tsūshin hakusho 2014* (Tokyo: Ministry of Internal Affairs and Communications, 2014).

video and computer games, advertising and marketing.[18] Broadcasting and the internet are regulated by the Ministry of Internal Affairs and Communications (MIC), so METI and Cool Japan have no say in this huge and influential industry, much to METI's chagrin.[19]

Accordingly, Cool Japan's focus on the content industries of anime and manga has created an impression, particularly outside Japan, that these niche genres are far more valuable than they actually are. This, coupled with Jenkin's convincing discussion of consumers' active participation in convergence processes, has been very influential in the way media convergence has been thought and researched in the context of Japanese media studies. In his recent book on the global popularity of Japanese animation, for instance, Ian Condry represents convergence as a bottom-up process, the social energy that drives communications between creators, fans and media texts constituting what he terms the "soul of anime."[20] Although Condry does not directly mention media convergence, this phenomenon is nonetheless pivotal for his main argument of the connectivity of anime, as it constitutes the necessary technological background of "media systems and delivery platforms."[21] As such, media convergence is seen as enabling new ways of experiencing a medium like Japanese anime today and a main factor behind its increasing success worldwide. Condry, in particular, moves forward Jenkin's discussion of a participatory culture of convergence when he states that "technological platforms only work because people contribute their energy" or that "anime can extend our understanding of globalization from below."[22] In this sense, the book's underlying idea that a perspective on the collaborative efforts of producers and consumers offers a good vantage point to understand media convergence is certainly embraceable. Yet, it

---

[18] David Hesmondhalgh, *The Cultural Industries* (London: Sage, 2007), 12-13. Notwithstanding some of METI's claims, however, the video game industry usually transcends METI's control (Shin Kiyoshi, "'Gēmu' no nai Nihon no kontentsu sangyō seisaku wa nanika kanchigai shitenai ka?" *AGORA: Genron Platform*, April 18, 2013, accessed November 18, 2014, http://agora-web.jp/archives/1530740.html. In 2012 manga and anime generated ¥34 billion in overseas licensing sales, whereas video games made as much as ¥300 billion (Humanmedia, Inc., "Sekai shijō ni muketa Nihon kontentsu no shinshutu 2013," accessed November 25, 2014, http://humanmedia.co.jp/database/PDF/release3.pdf.

[19] Multiple government agencies have stakes in Japanese media convergence. METI regulates hardware, the Ministry of Internal Affairs and Communications regulates broadcasting, and the Agency for Cultural Affairs regulates intellectual property. In addition, there are as many as nine laws in the area of broadcasting and communications. The introduction of the overarching Communication and Broadcasting Act (Jōhō Tsūshin Hō) was proposed in 2008 and approved by the cabinet in 2010.

[20] Condry, *The Soul of Anime*.

[21] *Ibid.*, 73.

[22] *Ibid.*, 212, 215.

also presents the blind spot of not detecting the economic frictions and political interests that are as much part of convergence as the new modes of collaboration that it increasingly facilitates.

From a different perspective, Mark Steinberg has recently discussed convergence in relation to the development of anime and the practice of media franchising in Japan.[23] Media franchising—or the development of transmedia commodities—is commonly known by Japanese media producers by the term "media mix." Steinberg timely connects the analysis of this Japanese practice with the global debate initiated by Jenkins around transmedia storytelling, the technique developed under convergence of creating huge fictional "storyworlds" distributed in "instalments" through different media platforms.[24] Steinberg's objective, however, is broader than simply tracing the Japanese development of transmedia storytelling, and his interest lies rather in mapping a comprehensive genealogy of Japanese anime that precedes historically the development of digital technologies and theoretically the creative practice of synergistic media production. Through the development of the media mix system in Japan, Steinberg is able to consider different aspects of convergence, not only the social and economic functioning of transmedia commodities but also the vertical integration of different media industries under the initiative of leading corporations like Kadokawa publishing. The idea underlined by the book that the media mix equates to Japanese media convergence, therefore, is original and strategically consistent, although at the same time partial if put in relation to the entire economy of the Japanese media industries. After all, the development of media franchises based on anime characters is a phenomenon only relative to the Japanese entertainment sector, so it is unable to encompass entirely all the economic and political stakes involved in broader convergence processes like the merging of broadcasting and communication.

A rare exception to this general interest in Japanese media convergence through the perspective of entertainment media is Dal Yong Jin's comparative study on the strategies of convergence developed by East Asian electronic giants Sony and Samsung.[25] His article is a welcome addition to this debate as it considers convergence through the lenses of industrial competition and refrains from looking at it only in terms of

---

[23] Steinberg, *Anime's Media Mix*.

[24] Jenkins, *Media Convergence*, 93-130.

[25] Dal Yong Jin, "Corporate Strategies in Media Convergence: A Comparative Study of Sony Vs. Samsung as Transnational Cultural Industries," in *Global Media Convergence and Cultural Transformation: Emerging Social Patterns and Characteristics*, ed. Dal Yong Jin (Hershey, PA: IGI Global, 2011), 340-353.

the consumption of popular culture. Yet, for Jin, convergence is mainly the strategy of many consumer electronic industries of integrating the production and distribution of cultural texts like film, music or video games in order to better sell the electronic equipment necessary for their reproduction. A similar strategy of integrating the production of both "software" and "hardware" is certainly not new and has been also considered by Steinberg in his analysis of the media mix. Pursued by Sony since the late 1980s, it is usually known to scholars of political economy as the concept of "synergy"—the ideal of increasing the corporate profitability by vertically integrating partner industries.[26] As our case study will show, however, the reduction of convergence to the practice of industrial synergy is only marginally helpful to explain the complex and contradictory processes involved in digital media convergence today.

As we shall argue, recent works in Japanese media studies have been receptive to the international debate on media convergence and have tried to connect it to the specific coordinates of the contemporary Japanese mediascape. So far, however, the majority of these researches have been mainly focused on the observation of convergence from the perspective of cultural consumption and popular culture. The aim of this chapter is to introduce a different perspective by focusing on the often mutually suspicious relationship between Japan's "old" media groups (*masukomi gyōkai*) and "new" media internet companies (*netto kigyō*). These actors constitute the "core" of the Japanese creative industries and engender profound effects in the ways media convergence develops within the country, and how tens of millions of people experience the media both inside and outside Japan.

The Core of the Japanese Creative Industries

To understand the complex and uneven path in which media convergence in Japan has been taking place, it is necessary to give closer attention to the biggest actors involved in the processes, to those companies that are generally considered the core of the creative industries. In the contemporary Japanese context, this means "old" media groups and "new" internet companies. Old media generally include the four "core" mass communication industries (*masukomi gyōkai*) of broadcasting, publishing, newspapers and advertising. These traditional and largely national media industries have not always reacted with enthusiasm to the new opportunities represented by convergence and globalization, in

---

[26] See David Hesmondhalgh, *The Cultural Industries* (London: Sage, 2007), 166; and Yoneji Masuda, *Managing in the Information Society: Releasing Synergy Japanese Style* (Oxford: Basil Blackwell, 1990).

contrast to anime, manga and video games that have developed global ambitions with or without the support from "Cool Japan" policies.

"Old" Media

The reasons for the "old" media's peculiar behavior can be partially found in the structural organization of these industries, their privileged relations with the government and the national regulations that have helped discourage innovation and risk-taking in the media sector. As is well known, the largest actors in the Japanese media are NHK (the world's largest public broadcasting corporation) and the five big commercial media groups that own television and newspaper through cross-ownership. These de-facto oligopolies include *Yomiuri shinbun* and Nippon Television, *Asahi shinbun* and TV Asahi, *Sankei shinbun* and Fuji Television, *Mainichi shinbun* and TBS, and the *Nihon keizai shinbun* and TV Tokyo. The old media also includes large publishing groups such as Kōdansha, Kadokawa and Shogakukan, and large advertising agencies like Dentsu and Hakuhodo. The list of these major players has not changed much for about 50 years, testifying to a lack of competition and disruptive technological innovation. Furthermore, these old media groups are notoriously conservative in many respects: they rarely hire outside a limited number of elite universities, and they submit job hunting university students to the same formal and generic recruitment process that is not different from that in the manufacturing or banking sectors. Many old media companies are famous for exceptionally generous salaries, far better than in global manufacturing companies like Toyota or new media companies where financial reward is skewed drastically in favor of founders and top management. In a recent study on the highest average salaries in Japanese companies, the five Tokyo-based television companies featured in the top ten positions, with Fuji television hitting the number one spot for many years.[27] In addition, broadcasters generally hire a significant number of graduates based on their family relationship with large advertisers, politicians, regulators, or other celebrities. Many important ruling LDP politicians have their sons and daughters working at one of the large broadcasters, advertising agencies or newspapers. Among current cabinet members (at the time of writing), Prime Minister Abe Shinzō's wife worked at Dentsu and his nephew is now at Fuji Television, METI chief Obuchi Yūko (and daughter of late Prime minister Obuchi Keizō) worked at TBS, and Minister for Reconstruction Takeshita Wataru worked at NHK.

---

[27] "Shui wa Fuji 1506-man-en saishinban 'kōkyūyo kigyō' jōi 100-sha," *Nikkan Gendai*, July 26, 2014, accessed November 15, 2014, http://www.nikkan-gendai.com/articles/view/news/152127.

In brief, and in contrast to some global discourses surrounding the creative class,[28] these big media companies are not particularly interested in hiring graduates with a creative bent as administrators. From the perspective of these groups, this is hardly seen as a problem, as most of the creative work is outsourced for a cheap price to a large number of small production companies and independent creators—as, for instance, in the case of television and animation.[29] In television production, the exploitation of this outsourced labor has been so severe that otherwise reluctant regulators have intervened to protect production studios.[30] Instead of the flexible and creative environment usually celebrated by the literature on the creative industries, the working conditions in the biggest Japanese media industries seem rather to conform to the "strict rules, regulation and management" typical of Japanese corporate culture.[31] The Japanese government, more specifically the Ministry of Internal Affairs that regulates broadcasting policies, has been reluctant to change regulations in order to promote competitiveness in this highly protected sector that has produced little growth and employment, and shown little appetite to go digital or global. If anything, Japanese regulators have helped these media oligopolies to maintain their privileged positions, effectively precluding ownership change in this sector or the introduction of overseas investment.[32]

From the perspective of these powerful oligopolies, therefore, the double challenge represented by globalization and media convergence did not appear immediately as an opportunity to seize but potentially as a threat to their own remarkable privileges. In the inevitable shift in the balance of power brought about by new internet media, these media groups reacted with a mix of contempt, suspicion and fear to the emergence of new media actors and what they represented, showing above all a strong reluctance to merge or collaborate with them.[33]

---

[28] Richard L. Florida, *The Rise of the Creative Class: And How It's Transforming Work, Leisure, Community and Everyday Life* (New York, NY: Basic Books, 2002), xii, 404.

[29] See Shibayama Masayuki, "4-bun no 1 ni suginai seisaku gaisha no nenshū," *President*, June 29, 2009, accessed November 28, 2014, http://president.jp/articles/-/3594; and Yoshitaka Mōri, "The Pitfall Facing the Cool Japan Project: The Transnational Development of the Anime Industry under the Condition of Post-Fordism," *International Journal of Japanese Sociology* 20, no. 1 (November 2011): 30-42.

[30] See Ministry of Internal Affairs and Communications, *Jōhō tsūshin hakusho* 2014 (Tokyo, Ministry of Internal Affairs and Communications, 2014).

[31] Morris Low, Shigeru Nakayama, and Hitoshi Yoshioka, *Science, Technology and Society in Contemporary Japan* (Cambridge, UK: Cambridge University Press, 1999), 140.

[32] Ministry of Internal Affairs and Communication, "Hōsōkyoku ni taisuru gaishi kisei ni tsuite," April 14, 2005, accessed November 15, 2014, http://www.soumu.go.jp/main_sosiki/joho_tsusin/policyreports/joho_tsusin/joho_bukai/pdf/030414_3_2.pdf.

[33] This reluctance can be also explained by the fact that in Japan the shrinking of the "old" media market is, if irreversible, still noticeably slower than in other developed economies.

"New" Media

In Japan, the new media industries are generally considered under the label of *netto gyōkai* (internet industries), a sector that has rapidly grown during the last 20 years. These new industries are challenging the dominance of old media oligopolies for the time and attention of the about 100 million Japanese currently using the internet.[34] One of the biggest and in many ways representative convergent new media actors is Yahoo! Japan. A joint venture between US-based Yahoo (which hold 35.5%) and the Japanese internet company SoftBank (which owns 36.4%), Yahoo! Japan retains substantial operational autonomy. Yahoo! Japan offers different services from Yahoo Inc. and, unlike its US counterpart, is a market leader ahead of its competitors in many areas, including search engine, auction, news and other key services.[35] Along with a few other new media actors, Yahoo! Japan is amongst the biggest media groups in Japan with annual sales of ¥386 billion.[36] In spite of its growing influence the management teams of many of these new media companies are generally much younger than those working in traditional media groups, since there is significantly more flexibility and mobility in their particular job markets. To provide some data, the average age of the 6,291 employees of Yahoo! Japan is 33, earning on average ¥6.7 million. In contrast, the average age of the 6,112 employees at the broadcaster Fuji Media Holdings, the parent company of Fuji Television, is 44 years old with an average salary of ¥15 million. These figures are also reflected at the very top: Yahoo! Japan's CEO is 47 years old, while Fuji's CEO is 68 years old and its chairman is 76 years old.[37] Large new media companies are becoming increasingly popular amongst graduate and mid-career professionals, as they can offer—on top of reasonably competitive salaries—more dynamic working environments and opportunities for upward mobility that are not determined solely by age.[38]

What media convergence has brought to Japan, therefore, is not simply the technological and industrial merging of computers,

---

[34] Ministry of Internal Affairs and Communication, *Jōhō tsūshin hakusho 2014*.

[35] ComScore, "2013 Japan Digital Future in Focus," October 14, 2013, accessed November 25, 2014, http://www.comscore.com/Insights/Presentations-and-Whitepapers/2013/2013-Japan-Digital-Future-in-Focus.

[36] Based on the published results from the last fiscal year, the other largest new media companies include online retailer and media portal Rakuten (annual sale of ¥443.4 billion), online adverting and media company Cyberagent (¥162.4 billion), social gaming company GREE (¥152.2 billion) and DeNA (¥202.4 billion), which operates in mobile gaming and e-commerce.

[37] Based on corporate data published on Yahoo! Finance in 2014, http://stocks.finance.Yahoo.co.jp/stocks/profile/?code=4676.T and http://stocks.finance.Yahoo.co.jp/stocks/profile/?code=4689.T.

[38] "Gekihen, Tōdaisei no shūkatsu!: Shin-gosanke wa kono sansha!" *Tōyō keizai*, March 31, 2014, accessed November 15, 2014, http://toyokeizai.net/articles/-/34081.

telecommunications and broadcast media or the increasing overlapping of the spheres of media production and consumption, but rather a complex cultural process that is undermining the gerontocratic structure of old media, the cozy relationship between them and the government, and the image of Japanese corporate culture at large. No case study is more helpful to illustrate these tense and complex dynamics of media convergence than the rise of Livedoor and the lingering legacy that its fall has had over the media industries in Japan.

Old and New Media Collide: Fuji TV vs. Livedoor

Livedoor is an internet startup founded by University of Tokyo dropout and serial entrepreneur Horie Takafumi, or Horiemon, the nickname—actually a play on the name of the popular manga character Doraemon—for which he is known to the public with either affection or contempt. Horie started his business in 1996 while still a university student, and rose to public prominence and even cult status thanks to a number of widely reported buyouts as well as his quick wit and defiant attitude in numerous appearances on national television. His young style—characterized by jeans, sneakers and spiky hair—appeared in stark contrast to middle-aged corporate executives in dark suits, highlighting his disdain for conservative Japanese corporate culture. In spite of this, however, he is neither popularly regarded as being stylish or attractive, and he is mostly associated with the young, geeky and unpopular male subculture of internet users that form the base of his supporters. He is famous for being a ruthless rationalist, a free market fundamentalist and someone who is ready to repudiate any tradition that he deems meaningless, including much of old corporate-Japan's routines and practices.

Horie listed his company on Mothers, a stock market for startups equivalent to Nasdaq in North America, and used the newly raised capital to buy a defunct internet-service provider that was renamed Livedoor in 2004. Chiefly through financial engineering and a series of mergers and acquisitions, the capitalization of Livedoor rose to about ¥935 billion at its peak in early 2004. Livedoor's business was based on a Yahoo-style portal site, called Livedoor, from which visitors could get access to different e-commerce services including travels, auctions, VoIP phone calls and a used car market. Since traffic to the portal was key to its business success, Horie tried eagerly to pursue various opportunities for publicity, such as a failed attempt to buy the troubled professional baseball team Osaka Kintetsu Buffaloes. In February 2005, however, the then 32-year-old Horie mounted a takeover bid for Nippon Broadcasting System (NBS), a relatively insignificant radio station that, because of a complicated system of cross-shareholdings, would have given him indirect control of Japan's largest commercial television Fuji Television with annual sales of ¥470 billion. What surprised everybody about this deal was that Livedoor, with revenues of merely ¥30 billion, was able to raise the nearly ¥70 billion required for the acquisition. It was widely reported that American investment bank Lehman Brothers had given Livedoor the money in exchange for the issue of Moving Strike Convertible Bonds, which— to put it simply—gave Lehman a sure way to make a huge profit at the expense of other shareholders.[39] The involvement of Lehman Brothers and its reported grotesque profits further highlighted the affinity between Livedoor and American-style finance capitalism.

Led by the then 65 years old CEO Hieda Hisashi—a perfect representative of old media by virtue of his advanced age, resistance to change (he is still a chairperson at the age of 76 at the time of writing in 2015), and hostility to American management style—Fuji Television fought a melodramatic battle in court and over the airwaves against Horie, who was depicted as a challenger and destroyer of a complacent system of old media, traditionally considered immune from hostile takeovers and the "dog eat dog" world of American investment banks. Nonetheless, Livedoor had acted by playing with the rules of global financial capitalism, buying shares during after-hours trading enabling it to avoid disclosure. The two-month conflict—a national media event in many respects, in which every move and details were reported minute by the minute—was finally resolved in April 2005 through a forced settlement in which Livedoor sold its stake in Fuji TV for a handsome profit, while Fuji TV had to make an investment in Livedoor in return.

In this national media frenzy, the old media system often referred to Livedoor and the new media in general with the term "*kyogyō*" (shady business), a derogative word identifying an industry that is not creating tangible goods or serving an important public interest (like "old media" journalism), and thus lacking any social value.[40] Livedoor and new media were also represented as contaminated too much by neoliberal capitalism, with news media accusing them of putting shareholders' interest and profit before that of their audience or employees.[41] Horie made almost

---

[39] "Lehman ga Raibu-kabu baikyaku tenkan shasai no hanbun o kabushiki kōkan," *47 News*, March 18, 2003, accessed November 15, 2014, http://www.47news.jp/CN/200503/CN2005031801005077.html.

[40] On January 27, 2006, TV Asahi's popular talk show *Asamade nama terebi* ran a special program focusing on the "Livedoor shock" in which the main topic of discussion was whether Livedoor was some kind of "shady business" (*kyogyō*).

[41] See "Netto kigyō ga TV o nomikomu," *Aera* (January 23, 2006): 33-34; and "Tokushū 'Horiemon' ni hyōka o kudasu," *Shokun!*, May 2005, 138-171.

daily national television appearances, but his provocative personality did not help either. He owned a private jet that he reportedly used to travel to exotic South Pacific resorts with young models, making frequent remarks boasting how money can buy everything and encouraging young people to make a quick buck with the publication of books titled *Making Money Is Winning* and *The Worship of Money*.[42]

More importantly, what emerged from the media coverage of the row was the strong resistance to convergence expressed in different ways by the old media groups. Up to that point, media convergence had mostly remained a technological possibility for broadcasters, meaning that the old oligopolistic media groups had maintained the luxury to decide when, how much, and in what terms they would be willing to put their contents on the internet. This luxury was suddenly and severely threatened. Livedoor certainly promised to offer many services enabled by the convergence between television/radio and the internet that would have enriched the audience's experience.[43] The fierce resistance to this convergence mustered by old media groups like Fuji TV and NBS, however, was mostly based on melodramatic and naïve arguments, often lacking any concrete internet strategy and expressing distrust for what they considered Livedoor's management style of "money can buy anything."[44] The entire body of NBS' employees collectively even issued an open letter in which they claimed Livedoor was lacking any "love for the listeners" or "understanding of broadcasting and media's mission as a public institution," and was therefore not deserving to become their owner.[45] Watanabe Sadao, the chairperson of the Yomiuri Group, summarized the sentiments of old media groups when he attacked Horie saying that "prestigious media [such as NBS, Fuji and no doubt his own Yomiuri] should not be the target of any kind of takeover [by supposedly

---

[42] Horie Takafumi, *Kasegu ga kachi: Zero kara hyakuoku-en ore no yarikata* (Tokyo: Kobunsha, 2004); and Horie Takafumi, *Okane wa itsumo tadashii* (Tokyo: Futabasha, 2011).

[43] See the report of the press conference by Kobayashi Nobuya and Okada Yūka, "Horie-shachō 'Livedoor + Nippon Hōsō' de Yahoo tsuigeki," *IT Media News*, February 8, 2005, accessed October 10, 2015, http://www.itmedia.co.jp/news/articles/0502/08/news095.html. Those in the media who are frustrated by the old media's rigid control voiced a varying degree of sympathy, if not support, for Livedoor. For example, respected freelance video journalist Tetsuo Jimbo voiced his support in a blog posting (http://www.jimbo.tv/commentary/000007.php) on March 11, 2005.

[44] This is the exact expression that then Keidanren chairperson and former Toyota president Okuda used in order to criticize Livedoor ("Kane sae areba wa mazui Okuda Keidanren-kaichō ga hihan," *47 News*, February 21, 2005, accessed November 15, 2014, http://www.47news.jp/CN/200502/CN2005022101002527.html.

[45] This March 3, 2005 letter can still be read at the NBS website, http://www.1242.com/info/seimei/ (accessed on November 28, 2014).

not prestigious new media]."[46] Many commentators writing for popular magazines running special sections on Horie made fun of NBS and Fuji, speculating that this improvised adherence to some journalistic mission was mostly to cover for their concerns that their famously high salaries and perks would be abruptly cut, echoing the general sentiment shared by many spectators.[47]

If the merger had gone through, it could have arguably accelerated media convergence in Japan and became one of the pioneering cases in online television services globally, especially considering this was at least three to five years before the appearance of internet television providers such BBC iPlayer, Hulu or Netflix. None of this, however, happened. Instead, Horie had managed to infuriate the interconnected system of the old media and political establishment, including Japanese prosecutors. In January 2006, his home and office in the prestigious office-residence complex Roppongi Hills were raided in front of the cameras of all the national TV channels, as this had already been leaked to the major media.[48] The Livedoor incident ignited a wide scale market sell-off. Japan's Nasdaq index-equivalent Mother collapsed at the news of Livedoor's raid and lost more than 90% of its value going from its peak at 2,800 to hovering around 300 for most of the last ten years. Livedoor was delisted from the stock market on April 14, 2006 before the prosecution had even started. In March of the following year, Horie was convicted of fraud (inflating the firm's profit) and sentenced to two-and-a-half years in jail, surprising many observers for the rigidity of the punishment. This, however, did not stop Horie's provocations. On the day he was imprisoned, he was answering the journalists alongside his long-time ally and founder of the notorious anonymous textboard 2channel, Nishimura Hiroyuki. They both wore the same black T-shirt with the big white caption "go to jail" followed by a list of other big corporations involved in similar frauds cases but who got away without any prosecution at all. Horie sought to depict himself as the innocent victim of a "*kokusaku sōsa*" (a national investigation driven by the political interest to punish the morally wrong).[49]

---

[46] "Watanabe zen-ōnā Horie-shachō giri 'Kōkyu-na media baitai o manē gēmu de shihai suru no wa machigai," *Nikkan Sports*, March 14, 2005, accessed June 5, 2013, http://www.nikkansports.com/ns/baseball/f-bb-tp0-050314-0037.html.

[47] "Saraba Horiemon!," *Aera*, February 6, 2006, 23-33, 72-79; "Tokushū: Nerawareta Horiemon," *Aera*, January 30, 2006, 21-32; and "Heisei Horiemon jiken," *Bungei Shunjū*, May 2005, 94-127.

[48] In fact, Nikkei and NHK had started reporting the investigation even before it had started. See "NHK to Nikkei Livedoor sōsaku chakushu temae ni kyōsei sōsa hōdō," *Asahi shinbun*, January 16, 2006, accessed July 9, 2014, http://www.asahi.com/national/update/0116/TKY200601160282.html.

[49] The interview Horie gave before being imprisoned can be seen in full on YouTube at https://youtu.be/C-ckiH80H2k (accessed July 9, 2014).

The Livedoor case, however, was not the only instance in which an emerging internet company mounted a hostile takeover bid for a major broadcaster. In October 2005, Rakuten, Japan's largest online retailer with well-known ambitions to become a portal media platform, bought close to a 20% share of TBS for as much as ¥120 billion. Rakuten's CEO Mikitani Hiroshi proposed a merger to the broadcaster in a bid to increase the range of contents for Rakuten's portal and to create a "world class media company" through convergence between internet and television.[50] A former banker at the prestigious Industrial Bank of Japan and a graduate of Harvard Business School, Mikitani is a less controversial figure than Horie, though he is also a strong believer in market capitalism and an advocate of deregulation. Mikitani also fought widely reported public and courtroom battles against TBS. TBS strenuously resisted Rakuten's proposal containing, which contained concrete plans regarding new "convergent" services for consumers. The case was once again based on a biased understanding of the market economy, as TBS repeatedly condemned Rakuten for buying the shares "without TBS' consent" and by demanding that Rakuten unload its TBS shares before any talk about a possible merger could even start.[51] After a prolonged court battle and public outcry, TBS was allowed by existing shareholders to introduce "a poison pill"—a strategy used by corporations to discourage hostile takeovers at the cost of existing shareholders.

In the aftermath of these incidents involving Livedoor and Rakuten, MIC—the regulatory agency responsible for broadcasting policies and licensing—took action in order to protect the old broadcasting companies and their mutual interests. In particular, it released a new broadcasting law in April 2008 that allows a broadcaster to operate under a holding company and to put local TV stations under its umbrella. The law prohibits a shareholder from owning more than 33% of voting rights in the holding company, thereby effectively overthrowing Rakuten's aim of controlling TBS and preventing the likes of Livedoor from ever mounting a similar bid. Mikitani and Rakuten sold their shares back to TBS at a considerable loss, signaling once again the old media broadcasters' dominance over Japanese media convergence.

---

[50] Horikoshi Isao, "Sekai ni tsūyo suru media gurūpu o tsukuru: TBS-kabu shutoku no Rakuten," *Nikkei Business Publications*, October 13, 2005, accessed November 20, 2014, http://itpro.nikkeibp.co.jp/article/NEWS/20051013/222785/.

[51] "TBS ni yabureta, Rakuten Mikitani-shachō no 'dōri'," *Nihon keizai shinbun*, April 1, 2009, accessed November 28, 2014, http://www.nikkei.com/article/DGXZZO11050770U0A710C1000000.

Coupled with these measures, the Livedoor incident engendered a chilling effect on the new media sector, with some observers quoting it as a defining moment in the abrupt end of the Japanese startup boom that blossomed in the early 2000s.[52] Although big new media companies like GREE, DeNA or Cyberagent are still attractive to top university graduates, Livedoor's and Horie's spectacular fall has tarnished the image of this sector in profound ways, decreasing the appetite for risk of many young entrepreneurs and repositioning the future of convergence in the hands of the old media system. Therefore, an overarching view of convergence—one that depicts multiple stakes uniting in technological progress and industrial concentration—seems far from "convergent" when seen from the perspective of Japan and the case of the Livedoor incident. This case reveals how the deterministic narrative of a linear, progressive and inevitable integration of "old" and "new" media needs to be assessed, in Japan as well as elsewhere, through the complex articulation of global processes with local socio-cultural and politico-economic specificities, such as the industrial organizations and regulatory policies of each country as well as the social status and prestige relative to specific industrial sectors.[53]

Conclusion

The Livedoor incident is an interesting lens through which to observe the development of media convergence in Japan. It redirects our attention to practices and operations in the "core" of the Japanese creative industries still enjoying considerable influence and prestige, but thus far somehow overshadowed by the disproportionate attention given to the consumption of those globally successful media contents generally packaged under the heading of Cool Japan. Despite all the hype surrounding Cool Japan, the country still remains—with perhaps the notable exception of gaming—a relatively minor exporter of popular culture. Moreover, those working for old media groups enjoy a prestige, influence and visibility that are still unmatched by employees of new media companies—let alone those working in the anime and manga industries, whose marginal standing is sustained only by their central place in the discourses of Cool Japan. It is the "core" sector of the Japanese creative industries that funds, distributes and have life-and-death power over the vast majority of media contents

---

[52] Mizukoshi Yutaka, "Benchā ni taisuru wakamono no yume ga shibonda: Livedoor jiken no 'tsumeato' o aratamete furikaeru," *Nikkei Business Online*, July 21, 2011, accessed July 14, 2014, http://business.nikkeibp.co.jp/article/topics/20110715/221497/.

[53] See Dwyer, *Media Convergence*, 3.

in the domestic market—including, of course, much of anime and manga production. As the struggle between Fuji TV and Livedoor hopefully has shown, we believe that media convergence could be productively assessed outside the common focus on convergence as "culture" in order to shed new light on such factors as the competition within the domestic market, specific industrial organization and the political regulations within each country.

In an exemplary way, the Livedoor case captures the complex power struggle inherent in any convergence process as they are "called upon by the hegemonic demands of the neoliberalization project."[54] As we have seen, this "project"—as far as large Tokyo-based television stations are concerned—has been so far strongly countered in Japan by the aid of MIC and the oligopolistic position of old media groups, which so far have managed to fend off the double challenges arising from globalization and new media. Whatever the case may be, it would be misguided to see these old media groups as the saviors of the country from the threat of neoliberal policies, as much as Horie and his faith in the market should not be seen as the champions of entrepreneurship against an obsolete system and stagnant national economy. On the one hand, Horie's market fundamentalism was in line with many neoliberal assumptions underlying much of the discourse on creativity, digitization and convergence found in many quarters of the post-Fordist world.[55] On the other, however, it was not only in the name of progressive politics that the Japanese government acted in the interests of the old media against financial capitalism and international competition. Behind Horie's prosecution, it was evident that there exists a shared interest in protecting a power system that has long kept the biggest media actors in line with the government at the cost of a more democratic and diverse mediasphere. It would also be wrong to generalize that the Japanese government always act in the interest of the status quo at the cost of new challengers. In the telecommunications sector, there are many cases in which the government, through various regulatory shifts, firmly provided opportunities for entrepreneurs while protecting them from large incumbent firms.[56] If anything, then, the Livedoor incident highlights the divergent and unresolved tensions between political, commercial and democratic interests in Japanese convergent media policies.

---

[54] *Ibid.*, 18.

[55] See Dwyer, *Media Convergence*; Eran Fisher, *Media and New Capitalism in the Digital Age: The Spirit of Networks* (Basingstoke: Palgrave Macmillan, 2010); and Jim McGuigan, *Cool Capitalism* (London: Pluto, 2009).

[56] See Kenji Kushida, "Entrepreneurship in Japan's ICT Sector: Opportunities and Protection from Japan's Telecommunications Regulatory Shift," *Social Science Japan Journal* 15, no. 1 (Winter 2012): 3-30.

After almost ten years since the rise and fall of Livedoor, Japanese media convergence seems to be entering into a new phase. In fact, it has taken until 2009 for Fuji TV and TBS to launch their own on-demand sites, which still do not offer live streaming but only access to select contents, with more content added only gradually since then. In 2012, the five Tokyo-based television networks and Dentsu created Motto TV—an on-demand but not streaming service platform—which characteristically only supports a half-dozen specially designed, made-in-Japan television sets and Android OS enabled devices, but not computers! Indeed, the user experience of Motto TV was so poor that it closed its services in March 2015. In its place, the five broadcasting networks and large ad agencies launched TVer in October 2015, a similar streaming platform, a month after the official launch of Netflix Japan in September. Furthermore, the recent merger of Dwango—the operator of the popular video-sharing platform Nico Nico Douga headed by 46-year-old Kawakami Nobuo (who, unlike Horie, seems to be well-liked by older media kingpins)—with Kadokawa publishing drew a lot of media attention. This is a rare case in which a new media company had acquired a relatively large old media corporation. One of the main aims of this merger is the mobilization of Dwango's knowhow to develop global online business platforms to capitalize on Kadokawa's large library consisting of contents related to manga, anime and light novels.[57] It is, of course, impossible to foresee how much of an impact these new steps will have on the development of media convergence in Japan. Whatever the outcome, the Livedoor incident is an important and useful reminder that the frictions and divergences are the key to better understanding media convergence in its specific local and historical articulations.

Works Cited

47 News. "Kane sae areba wa mazui Okuda Keidanren-kaichō ga hihan." February 21, 2005. Accessed November 15, 2014. http://www.47news.jp/ CN/200502/CN2005022101002527.html.

———. "Lehman ga Raibu-kabu baikyaku tenkan shasai no hanbun o kabushiki kōkan." March 18, 2003. Accessed November 15, 2014. http:// www.47news.jp/CN/200503/CN2005031801005077.html.

Aera. "Netto kigyō ga TV o nomikomu." January 23, 2006.

---

[57] "Kadokawa Dwango wa wakai saino o sekai e tsunage," *Nihon keizai shinbun*, May 17, 2014, accessed November 15, 2014, http://www.nikkei.com/article/DGXDZO71357780X10C14A5EA1000/.

————. "Saraba Horiemon!" February 6, 2006.

————. "Tokushū: Nerawareta Horiemon." January 30, 2006.

Asahi shinbun. "NHK to Nikkei Livedoor sōsaku chakushu temae ni kyōsei sōsa hōdō." January 16, 2006. Accessed July 9, 2014. http://www.asahi.com/national/update/0116/TKY200601160282.html.

Azuma Hiroki. *Otaku: Japan's Database Animals.* Translated by Jonathan E. Abel and Shion Kono. Minneapolis, MN: University of Minnesota Press, 2009.

Berndt, Jaqueline, and Bettina Kuemmerling-Meibauer, ed. *Manga's Cultural Crossroads.* New York: Routledge, 2013.

Bolter, J. David, and Richard A. Grusin. *Remediation: Understanding New Media.* Cambridge, MA: MIT Press, 1999.

Bungei Shunjū. "Heisei Horiemon jiken." May 2005.

Condry, Ian. *The Soul of Anime: Collaborative Creativity and Japan's Media Success Story.* Durham, NC: Duke University Press, 2013.

Daliot-Bul, Michal. "Japan Brand Strategy: The Taming of 'Cool Japan' and the Challenges of Cultural Planning in Postmodern Age." *Social Science Japan Journal* 12, no. 2 (Winter 2009): 247-266.

Dwyer, Tim. *Media Convergence.* Maidenhead: Open University Press, 2010.

Fisher, Eran. *Media and New Capitalism in the Digital Age: The Spirit of Networks.* Basingstoke: Palgrave Macmillan, 2010.

Florida, Richard L. *The Rise of the Creative Class: And How It's Transforming Work, Leisure, Community and Everyday Life.* New York, NY: Basic Books, 2002.

Hall, Stuart, and Tony Jefferson. *Resistance through Rituals: Youth Subcultures in Post-War Britain.* London: Routledge, 2006.

Hamano Satoshi. "The Generaticity of Nico Nico Douga: The New Type of Creativity Enabled by Metadata." *Genron: Portal for Critical Discourse in Japan*, May 14, 2012. http://global.genron.co.jp/2012/05/14/the-generativity-of-nico-nico-douga/.

Hay, James, and Nick Couldry. "Rethinking Convergence/Culture: An Introduction." *Cultural Studies* 25, no. 4-5 (2011): 473-486.

Hesmondhalgh, David. *The Cultural Industries*. London: Sage, 2007.

Horie Takafumi. *Kasegu ga kachi: Zero kara hyakuoku-en ore no yarikata*. Tokyo: Kobunsha, 2004.

———. *Okane wa itsumo tadashii*. Tokyo: Futabasha, 2011.

Horikoshi Isao. "Sekai ni tsūyo suru media gurūpu o tsukuru: TBS-kabu shutoku no Rakuten." *Nikkei Business Publications*. October 13, 2005. Accessed November 20, 2014. http://itpro.nikkeibp.co.jp/article/NEWS/20051013/222785/.

Ito, Mizuko. "Technologies of the Childhood Imagination: Yugioh, Media Mixes, and Everyday Cultural Production." In *Structures of Participation in Digital Culture*, edited by Joe Karaganis, 88-111. New York: Social Science Research Council, 2007.

Jenkins, Henry. *Convergence Culture: Where Old and New Media Collide*. New York: New York University Press, 2008.

Jin, Dal Yong, ed. *Global Media Convergence and Cultural Transformation: Emerging Social Patterns and Characteristics*. Hershey, PA: IGI Global, 2011.

———. "Corporate Strategies in Media Convergence: A Comparative Study of Sony vs. Samsung as Transnational Cultural Industries." In *Global Media Convergence and Cultural Transformation: Emerging Social Patterns and Characteristics*, edited by Dal Yong Jin, 340-353. Hershey, PA: IGI Global, 2011.

Kobayashi Nobuya, and Okada Yūka. "Horieshachō 'Livedoor + Nippon Hōsō' de Yahoo tsuigeki." *IT Media News*. February 8, 2005. Accessed

October 10, 2015. http://www.itmedia.co.jp/news/articles/0502/08/news095.html.

Kushida, Kenji. "Entrepreneurship in Japan's ICT Sector: Opportunities and Protection from Japan's Telecommunications Regulatory Shift." *Social Science Japan Journal* 15, no. 1 (Winter 2012): 3-30.

Leadbeater, Charles. *Living on Thin Air: The New Economy*. London: Penguin, 2000.

Lee, Hye-Kyung. "Between Fan Culture and Copyright Infringement: Manga Scanlation." *Media, Culture and Society* 31, no. 6 (2009): 1011-1022.

———. "Participatory Media Fandom: A Case Study of Anime Fansubbing." *Media, Culture & Society* 33, no. 8 (2011): 1131-1147.

Low, Morris, Shigeru Nakayama, and Hitoshi Yoshioka. *Science, Technology and Society in Contemporary Japan*. Cambridge, UK: Cambridge University Press, 1999.

Ludes, Peter. *Convergence and Fragmentation: Media Technology and the Information Society*. Bristol: Intellect, 2008.

Masuda, Yoneji. *Managing in the Information Society: Releasing Synergy Japanese Style*. Oxford: Basil Blackwell, 1990.

McGray, Douglas. "Japan's Gross National Cool." *Foreign Policy* 130 (May/June 2002): 44-54.

McGuigan, Jim. *Cool Capitalism*. London: Pluto, 2009.

Mihara Ryūtarō. *Kūru Japan wa naze kirawareru-no-ka: "Nekkō" to "reishō" o koete*. Tokyo: Chūo Kōron, 2014.

Ministry of Internal Affairs and Communication (MIC). "Hōsōkyoku ni taisuru gaishi kisei ni tsuite." April 14, 2005. Accessed November 15, 2014. http://www.soumu.go.jp/main_sosiki/joho_tsusin/policyreports/joho_tsusin/joho_bukai/pdf/030414_3_2.pdf.

————. *Jōhō tsūshin hakusho 2014*. Tokyo, Ministry of Internal Affairs and Communications, 2014.

Mizukoshi Yutaka. "Benchā ni taisuru wakamono no yume ga shibonda: Livedoor jiken no 'tsumeato' o aratamete furikaeru." *Nikkei Business Online*. July 21, 2011. Accessed July 14, 2014. http://business.nikkeibp. co.jp/article/topics/20110715/221497/.

Mōri, Yoshitaka. "The Pitfall Facing the Cool Japan Project: The Transnational Development of the Anime Industry under the Condition of Post-Fordism." *International Journal of Japanese Sociology* 20, no. 1 (November 2011): 30-42.

Nihon keizai shinbun. "Kadokawa Dwango wa wakai saino o sekai e tsunage." May 17, 2014. Accessed November 15, 2014. http://www. nikkei.com/article/DGXDZO71357780X10C14A5EA1000/.

————. "TBS ni yabureta, Rakuten Mikitani-shachō no 'dōri'." April 1, 2009. Accessed November 28, 2014. http://www.nikkei.com/article/ DGXZZO11050770U0A710C1000000.

Nikkan Gendai. "Shui wa Fuji 1506-man-en saishinban 'kōkyūyo kigyō' jōi 100-sha." July 26, 2014. Accessed November 15, 2014. http://www. nikkan-gendai.com/articles/view/news/152127.

Nikkan Sports. "Watanabe zen-ōnā Horie-shachō giri 'Kōkyu-na media baitai o manē gēmu de shihai suru no wa machigai." March 14, 2005. Accessed June 5, 2013, http://www.nikkansports.com/ns/baseball/f-bb-tp0-050314-0037.html.

Otmazgin, Nissim. "A Tail That Wags the Dog? Cultural Industry and Cultural Policy in Japan and South Korea." *Journal of Comparative Policy Analysis: Research and Practice* 13, no. 3 (2011): 307-325.

Ōtsuka, Eiji. "World and Variation: The Reproduction and Consumption of Narrative." *Mechademia* 5, no. 1 (2010): 99-116.

Parikka, Jussi. *What Is Media Archaeology?* Cambridge, UK: Polity Press, 2012.

Shibayama Masayuki. "4-bun no 1 ni suginai seisaku gaisha no nenshū." *President*. June 29, 2009. Accessed November 28, 2014. http://president. jp/articles/-/3594.

Shin Kiyoshi. "'Gēmu' no nai Nihon no kontentsu sangyō seisaku wa nanika kanchigai shitenai-ka? *AGORA: Genron Platform*, April 18, 2013. Accessed November 18, 2014. http://agora-web.jp/archives/1530740. html.

Shokun! "Tokushū 'Horiemon' ni hyōka o kudasu." May 2005.

Steinberg, Marc. *Anime's Media Mix: Franchising Toys and Characters in Japan*. Minneapolis, MN: University of Minnesota Press, 2012.

Suzuki Yūji. "'Tsūshin hōso yūgō' no genzai, kako, mirai: 'TV bangumi netto haishin' gannen ni okeru kōsatsu." *NHK Hōso Bunka Kenkyūjo Nenpō* 53 (2009): 7-46.

———. "'Tsūshin to hōso no yūgō' wa dō giron sareta no ka." *Hōso kenkyū to chōsa* (October 2006): 14-31.

Tōyō keizai. "Gekihen, Tōdaisei no shūkatsu!: Shin-gosanke wa kono sansha!" March 31, 2014. Accessed November 15, 2014. http://toyokeizai. net/articles/-/34081.

Valaskivi, Katja. "A Brand New Future? Cool Japan and the Social Imaginary of the Branded Nation." *Japan Forum* 25, no. 4 (2013): 485-504.

Part III:
Cultural Convergence

Obasan and Kanryū : Modalities of Convergence of Middle-Aged Japanese Women Around South Korean Popular Culture and Gender Divergence in Japan

John Lie

While newspaper headlines in Japan and South Korea in 2012 frequently featured the territorial dispute over Takeshima/Tokdo (Dokdo)— insignificant islets in the ocean which in turn has two contending nomenclature (Sea of Japan [Nihonkai] and East Sea [Tonghae])—the more remarkable phenomenon was the South Korean popular cultural expansion in Japan. Beginning with food in the 1980s, South Korean cultural products and performers have steadily carved larger niches in the Japanese archipelago. The proximate source of the Korean Wave (initially called *Kanryū*) in 2003 and 2004 was the explosive popularity of the South Korean television drama *"Fuyu no sonata"* (*Kyŏul yŏng'a* in Korean, *Winter Sonata* in English, and often called by the contraction *Fuyusona* in Japan) and the ensuing enthusiasm for South Korean television drama (commonly called *Kandora*, a contraction of *Kankoku dorama* or South Korean drama).[1] The recent rise of K-pop in Japan is equally remarkable.[2]

The emergence of the Korean Wave fandom in Japan, given the troubled relationship between the two countries, is noteworthy in and of itself and signifies something of a popular cultural convergence between Japan and South Korea. Yet just as remarkable is the demographic characteristic of the nascent subculture, which was initially almost exclusively female and middle-aged. The development of fandom generates social convergence, creating official organizations and informal networks of fans—including creating something of a mecca for the Korean Wave fandom (geographical

---

[1] As one barometer, see the cornucopia of cultural commentaries in the form of books on *Fuyusona* in Japan. Already by 2006, a review of the literature yielded several books and over a score of articles: Hasegawa Kei, "Kanryū būmu to jendā," in Mizuta Muneko, Hasegawa Kei, and Kitada Yukie, eds. *Kanryū sabukarucha to josei* (Tokyo: Shibundō, 2006), 47-57.

[2] The sheer amount of print materials on K-pop is staggering. For overviews, see *Seoul de 100% tanoshimu K-Pop kanzen gaido* (Tokyo: Kinema Junpōsha, 2012); and *Seoul hon-Kanryū K-Pop 2013* (Tokyo: Ei Shuppansha, 2012). For magazines, see among others *ODINA, K-Pop Wave,* and *A-Music*.

convergence), and seeking linguistic and cultural knowledge (linguistic and cultural convergence). Many of them were largely innocent of the information technology and the social media before their transformation as *Kandora* fans (technological convergence). They moreover expanded their interest beyond the genre of television drama to embrace not only other popular culture genres (genre convergence) but also actively introduced South Korean popular culture, especially to their younger counterparts, including in some cases their daughters (generational convergence). The Korean Wave fandom in Japan is a striking example of multifaceted convergences born of a distinct subculture and group identity. Finally, the Korean Wave fandom in Japan points to one manifest mode of divergence: gender.

The Korean Wave Fandom in Japan

In the beginning was *Fuyusona*. Originally aired in South Korea in 2002, by its reprised broadcast in 2004, it had become a blockbuster, establishing both *Fuyusona* and *Kanryū* as buzzwords in Japan.[3] By the late 2000's *Kandora* fandom had become something of an institution in Japan, populated mostly by middle-aged and older women usually called somewhat pejoratively as *obasan*, which is a kinship term for "aunt" but is generally used to refer to middle-aged women. In contemporary usage, it has accrued negative connotations. Whereas young women are prized for being *kawaii* (cute), *obasan* is by definition not cute. A woman of certain age with sexual appeal is often called *jukujo* (mature women) but not *obasan*. Neither is *obasan* associated with professional women—with social standing and cultural prestige—and therefore carries the implication of being an ordinary housewife. Some less-than-complimentary character traits in the discourse include being nosy, gossipy, and bossy.[4]

Kandora obasan did not discover or import South Korean television drama. Two intertwining undertows facilitated the Korean Wave's smooth sailing in Japan in the 2000s: the post-Cold War relaxation of intra-East Asian geopolitical tensions and the improved images of

---

[3] For early studies of South Korean television drama's expansion into Japan and elsewhere, see Mōri Yoshitaka, ed., *Nisshiki Kanryū* (Tokyo: Serika Shobō, 2004); Hirata Yukie, *Han'guk ŭl sobi hanŭn Ilbon* (Seoul: Ch'aek Sesang, 2005); Ishita Saeko, Kimura Kan, and Yamanaka Chie, eds., *Posuto Kanryū no media shakaigaku* (Kyoto: Minerva Shobō, 2007); Yi Hyanjin [Yi Hyang-jin/Lee Hyangjin], *Kanryū no shakaigaku*, trans. Shimizu Yukiko (Tokyo: Iwanami Shoten, 2008); Pak Chang-sun, *Hallyu, Han'guk kwa Ilbon ŭi dŭrama chŏnjaeng* (Seoul: K'ŏmyunik'eisyŏnbuksŭ, 2008); Chua Beng Huat and Koichi Iwabuchi, eds., *East Asian Pop Culture* (Hong Kong: Hong Kong University Press, 2008); and Mark James Russell, *Pop Goes Korea* (Berkeley: Stone Bridge Press, 2008).

[4] For an overview of *obasan* and its pejorative stereotype, see Tanaka Hikaru, *"Obasan" wa naze kirawareru-ka* (Tokyo: Shūeisha, 2011).

South Koreans.[5] If the South Korean commonsense reviled Japan as the erstwhile colonial oppressor, the Japanese stereotype cast South Korea as a poor country under military dictatorship. From the 1980s, however, Japanese journalists and tourists conveyed increasingly positive depictions of South Korea, cresting in 2002 with the joint hosting of the World Cup that generated an impressive amount of bonhomie.[6] Put differently, South Korea often ranked among the country least liked by Japanese people in opinion surveys from the 1970s, but by 2002 the likes had superseded the dislikes. Beyond shifting Japanese perceptions lies a transformed South Korea. The South Korea of *Fuyusona* is a country of great natural beauty, an affluent society of elegance and sophistication, and a land of romance and gallant, handsome heroes. A devoted fan recalls that when she went to South Korea on a packaged tour 20 years ago (around 1990), she encountered pushy vendors and rude pedestrians.[7] Older women recall the country not only as poor but also as a destination of sex tours that their husbands and other male acquaintances indulged in.[8] However, a decade later, when she viewed the 2000 South Korean film *Irumāre Il Mare*; in Korean *Siwŏlae*, meaning "Love That Transcends Time"), she was struck by a completely different vision of the country, which was crystallized by her immersion in *Fuyusona* soon thereafter. Rather than urban poverty and rustic behavior, she found romance and elegance. Soon thereafter she visited Seoul and found South Koreans to be kind and generous. Thereafter, she was under *Kandora's* thrall: she had been swept away by the Korean Wave.

From suspicion or ignorance on matters South Korean, chance viewing, sheer curiosity, or insistent recommendation from friends tether *Fuyusona* fans (who often call themselves *"pen"* after the Japanese pronunciation of the Korean pronunciation of the English word "fan") to the experience of *hamaru* (entrapped, entranced, and enthralled). The rhetoric of *hamaru*

[5] The significance of popular culture in enhancing popular perceptions of Japan and South Korea in both countries should not be underestimated. See, for example, Kwon Yongseok, *"Kanryū" to "Nichiryū"* (Tokyo: NHK Bukkusu, 2010), 35-45. For an overview of Japanese images of South Korea, see Tei Taikin, *Kankoku no imēji*, exp. ed. (Tokyo: Chūō Kōron Shinsha, 2010). For an early study of South Korean consumption of Japanese popular culture, see Paku Sun'e [Pak Sun-ae] and Tsuchiya Reiko, eds., *Nihon taishū bunka to Nikkan kankei* (Tokyo: Sangensha, 2001). For a pioneering study of transnational cultural flow in East Asia, see Iwabuchi Kōichi, *Toransunashonaru—Japan* (Tokyo: Iwanami Shoten, 2001).

[6] John Lie, *Zainichi (Koreans in Japan): Diasporic Nationalism and Postcolonial Identity* (Berkeley: University of California Press, 2008), 146-152.

[7] Mikazuki Kanna, *Kankoku onna hitoritabi* (Tokyo: Chūkei Shuppan, 2012), 4-7.

[8] See John Lie, "The Transformation of Sexual Work in Twentieth-Century Korea," *Gender & Society* 9, no. 3 (1995): 310-327.

discloses sentiments somewhere between religious conversion and falling in love. *Fuyusona* was not just a compelling melodrama—a common connotation of *hamaru* is to be hooked—but it became a way of life, focused especially on the protagonist Bae Yong Joon (Pae Yong-jun) as a semi-deity of romance.[9] Widely known in Japan as Yon-sama (Honorable Yon[g]), he was 30 years old at the time of the filming of *Fuyusona* and still commands a legion of devoted fans or, in a cult-like language, *kazoku* (family).

Beauty and charisma are central ingredients of any star system and the modern entertainment industry, exemplified by Hollywood, banks on good looks and charismatic presence. Bae is hardly the only *ikemen* (the contraction of *iketeru men*, literally "mask or mug that goes" but meaning gorgeous men) as the Korean Wave cannot be extricated from its attractive stars. Although tastes vary, a longstanding ideal among Japanese women is androgynous and even effeminate. Bae has an effeminate visage and gentle demeanor far removed from the conventional assumption about South Korean masculine behavior (and also distinct from the stereotypical middle-aged Japanese man).[10] One woman recalls that the first time she saw Bae's face on the cover of a glossy magazine, she was convinced that Bae was a female star, perhaps a former Takarazuka performer. Takarazuka is a renowned all-female revue that performs musical theater with cross-dressing leads frequently capturing the heart and soul of female fans.[11] *Berusaiyu no bara* (*The Rose of Versailles*, often called *Berubara*) exemplifies Takarazuka aesthetics: a torrid romantic love affair in an exotic locale, featuring an effeminate and charismatic (fe)male hero(ine). *Berubara* set one standard of an ideal male beauty (and behavior) and generated many imitators in girls' manga.[12] To take another example, BL (Boys' Love, or manga dealing with gay male characters in love, formerly called *yaoi*) presents another

---

[9] To gauge his enduring appeal, see the special feature on Bae in the fan magazine *Aishiterut!! Shin Kankoku Dorama* 1 (December 2012).

[10] Hayashi Kaori, for example, reveals that her favorite scene from *Fuyusona* exemplified Bae's kindness, especially that women are taken care of in the drama. See Hayashi Kaori, *"Fuyusona" ni hamatta watashitachi* (Tokyo: Bungei Shunjū, 2005), 14. On South Korean popular culture and "soft masculinity," see Sun Jung, *Korean Masculinities and Transcultural Consumption* (Hong Kong: Hong Kong University Press, 2011), 35-39.

[11] See Jennifer Robertson, *Takarazuka* (Berkeley: University of California Press, 1998).

[12] Ikeda Riyoko, *Berusaiyu no bara*, 5 vols. (Tokyo: Shūeisha, 1972-1973 [2009]). The Takarazuka version debuted in 1975. In spite of its significance in making sense of Japanese popular culture, there is surprisingly little commentary. This may be yet another manifestation of the gender divide: "subculture" sections of large Japanese bookstores tend to be replete with books on male subcultures. See, however, for *Berubara*, Asahi Shinbunsha, ed., *Ikeda Riyoko no sekai* (Tokyo: Asahi Shinbunsha, 2012).

way in which a beautiful, effeminate male protagonist becomes the fantasy object of desire and love.[13]

Appeal is not merely a matter of appearance, however. Fans often note the timbre of the star's voice. This is naturally the case for singers but the principle holds surprisingly strongly for actors as well. A housewife in her 40s recalls overhearing Bae talking on television and finding his voice "electric." *Fuyusona* was originally broadcast in a dubbed version but a clamor from the audience restored the original Korean soundtrack. A crucial element of this counterintuitive move (very few Japanese people understand Korean) is that many listeners found Bae's voice, as well as those of other actors, resonant and seductive. In this regard, many Japanese viewers, especially women, are habituated to watching foreign films and reading subtitles, a non-trivial factor in the popularity of Korean-speaking *Kandora*. Needless to say, K-pop's appeal combines physical attractiveness and vocal allure.

Beauty not only is but as it does: it is not just an aesthetic of appearance but also of behavior and character. He must be noble in spirit, kind at heart: a prince charming who is as beautiful outwardly as he is inwardly, in face as in heart. Thus, Bae is handsome but also beautiful: not a muscled, macho man (Arnold Schwarzenegger fans tend to be men in Japan) but kind, gentle, and gallant. Bae certainly captures the Japanese female aesthetic of effeminate male beauty.[14] The ideal is not a powerful patriarch but a gallant gentleman.

Beyond the seemingly straightforward appeal of South Korean stars lies a curious cultural logic that sustains them as safe and approachable objects of love and fantasy. In the post-World War II period, an influential ideal of beauty in Japan was dominated by the projected Western standards of masculine and feminine perfection, usually embodied in Hollywood stars. Even today, it is common to see models for expensive products that stress beauty, elegance, and sophistication to be Western. As a simple binary, the Japanese were said to be short and stocky, narrow-eyed and flat-faced, whereas the Westerners were the polar opposite. At the same time, many Japanese regarded foreigners as different and

---

[13] The genre is vibrant enough to generate a re-telling of Japanese and world history, including Hori Gorō, *BL Shin Nihonshi* (Tokyo: Gentōsha, 2006); and Kiryū Misao, *Sekai bōizu rabu taizen* (Tokyo: Bungei Shunjū, 2012).

[14] Some commentators are wont to expatiate on the Confucian character of South Korean stars. Although it is difficult to deny that the rhetoric of Confucian tradition is widely invoked in South Korea, it is misleading to see that as a crucial component of their attraction for Japanese women. It is fair to say that they have had enough of Confucian and post-Confucian patriarchy that promotes male boorishness.

distant, definitely unattainable. For *Kandora* and K-pop stars, they are at once similar to but different from Western or Japanese stars.[15] It is something of a commonsense among *Kandora* fans that South Koreans are like Western stars in being tall and attractive but they seem more approachable because they look basically Japanese. Not being Japanese makes them, however, less threatening than if they were Japanese because as foreigners they seem safely distant. Thus, South Korean stars are beautiful and exotic, but not too different; comforting and familiar, but not too similar.[16] In short, they occupy the right distance.

Cultural distance allows imagination to take flight. If we were to trace middle-aged Japanese women's girlhood fantasies about romantic love, then we would find among others the influence of manga, such as *Berubara*, movies, Takarazuka, and even pop-music lyrics, all of which valorize first love (*hatsukoi*) and pure love (*jun'ai*), but usually in an exotic place, far away from urban Japan. It is certainly not wrong to say that *Kandora* stories are often fairy tales and that *Fuyusona* can be read as a hybrid of fairy tales and fantasies, a curious amalgam of *Cinderella* and *Jane Eyre* among others.[17] Yet we should remember that the most common theme of classical European fairy tales, such as those of the Grimm Brothers and Hans Christian Andersen, is parental cruelty and not romantic love.[18] *Kandora* and middle-aged Japanese women's taste is much closer to Disney Princess stories in the United States but with a twist: not so much happily-ever-after but the valorization of love's purity and its everlasting memory. The suspension of belief is facilitated by taking place far away from everyday life of Japanese (or, for that matter, even South Korean) viewers. While the favored locus used to be France in the 1970s, as in *Berubara*, South Korea became a plausible place by the 2000s. It is also not an accident that the Bae character in *Fuyusona* ends up being blind before being united with his first and true love, very much like Mr. Rochester in *Jane Eyre*. That is, there are at least two conditions

---

[15] See, for example, Tanaka Chizuko, *Kanryū desu ga sore ga nani ka?* (Tokyo: Gamu Shuppan, 2009), 69-71. It is possible that the popularity of *Kandora* stars signifies the waning hegemony of Westernized beauty ideals in Japan, which may in turn be related to the declining significance of American cultural hegemony in Japan. Indeed, there is a larger argument about the Korean Wave as a counter-hegemonic cultural flow.

[16] Some commentators suggest that the rise of South Korean stars indicates the decline of Western hegemony, especially in terms of beauty ideals. One should question the extent to which the projected Western ideal was hegemonic in the past. It seems, rather, they were idealized *faute de mieux*.

[17] See Mizuta Muneko, "Gendai no otogibanashi 'Fuyu no sonata' no monogatari no kōzō," in Mizuta Muneko, Hasegawa Kei, and Kitada Yukie, eds., *Kanryū sabukaruchua to josei* (Tokyo: Shibundō, 2006), 93-110.

[18] Maria Tatar, *The Hard Facts of Grimms' Fairy Tales* (Princeton: Princeton University Press, 1997).

of possibility for pure and true love: the suspension of disbelief requires its exotic location (enabling fantasy to be unimpeded by the reality principle) and that the course of true love not run smoothly (not only for the necessity of dramatic tension but also the imperfect catharsis of the resolution). The story is cathartic, a form of double healing (*iyasareru*): a happy ending (the fantasy fulfilled) but not the sort for ordinary people (the fantasy deflected).[19] It is crucial to *Fuyusona*'s success that the story is about first love and a love that moreover endured all manners of obstacles that end in, like *Jane Eyre*, with the hero blind but finally united with his love. What survives intact is the ideal and memory of pure love.

The reality principle is in fact inescapable in the life of so-called *obasan* (childrearing, housework, and so on and on) or even for young girls (parents, schoolwork). The rhetoric of *hamaru* and the fantasy of falling in love constitute a conversion experience that provide a new meaning in life or a newfound *raison d'être*. The humdrum reality of most middle-aged and middle-class fans is living a life of quotidian routine and housework. Life is alas typically less than romantic and exotic but most Japanese women grow up with tales of romance and romantic heroes. That is, like Madame Bovary, few can escape the lure of thinking that there is another, better life: more meaningful, more "me." Except for the happy few, most express low-level contentment—a decent husband, decent children—but something remains clearly amiss. Enter South Korean stars and the shock of the old: the rekindled passion, if not of the actual personal experience then the long-simmering ideal of true love. Against the unremarkable reality of everyday life and relationships is the rekindling of romantic love, and especially the glow of pure first love.

Modalities of Convergence

Whatever the structure of appeal of *Kandora* for women described as *obasan*, once they have become entrapped (*hamaru*) in it they experience a series of convergences.

The first is *social convergence*: the convergence of fans or the crystallization of fandom. Many women experience the indifference of, and even criticisms from, family members and neighbors who find their newfound enthusiasm—manifesting itself in everything from becoming more lively and fun-loving to being more youthful and better dressed—

---

[19] The thematic of "healing" *(iyashi)* is very much part of the contemporary Japanese discourse that pays obeisance at once to fantasy and reality. Hayashi's subjects were often involved in some form of care work (e.g., taking care of aging parents) and stressed the drama's healing character (Hayashi, *"Fuyusona" ni hamatta watashi-tachi*, 29-33).

unseemly, unfitting for a housewife, mother, *obasan*. Strategies of dealing with the past life are manifold. A woman in her 30s decided to sleep separately from her husband so that she could indulge in her passion for South Korean drama and music to her content at night, even at the risk of endangering her marriage. Another woman in her 50s revealed that her husband and children thought that she had gone mad (*kurutta*) over *Fuyusona* in particular and *Kandora* in general. Hasegawa Seiko expresses her sense of guilt over her neglect of her husband and children while she pursues her passion for South Korean popular culture.[20] The conflict between the reality principle and the Korean Wave upends many women's lives, generating not only quotidian tensions but also psychic conflicts. What rescues the loneliness or the guilt is the existence of like-minded people and fan clubs that connect them into a larger community: they "come out" individually and collectively.[21] Fixation on the same star hardly generates jealousy; the stars are love objects in part because they are in reality unattainable. Rather, the commonality of sharing the same fantasy object generates a form of solidarity that is at once ideal and material: ideal because fantasy likes company (there's not much joy in a lonely quixotic quest), and material because fellow fans provide information, sounding boards, and social bonds. The resulting women's networks often function as support groups not only in terms of their shared interests but also for advice and counsel in everyday life.[22]

The social convergence of the Korean Wave fandom manifests itself physically as *geographical convergence*. Shin Ōkubo, an area near the bustling Shinjuku in Tokyo, is the mecca of the Korean Wave fandom in Japan. From a concatenation of Korean restaurants and grocery stores— as well as some concentration of recent South Korean immigrants and sojourners—it refashioned itself from a slightly disreputable district into a fashionable one in the course of the 2000's. Not only are there bookstores, music shops, and specialty-goods stores for all things South Korean popular culture but there are cafes and karaoke establishments. In particular, otherwise ordinary South Korean young men perform as *ikemen* waiters and singers to serve the largely Japanese clientele.

The network is also virtual. *Technological convergence* allows fans enter the terra incognita of cyberspace motivated by their newfangled interest.

---

[20] Hasegawa Seiko, *Hanryū joshi hajimemashita* (Tokyo: Ei Shuppansha, 2012), 140-141. See also Tanaka, *Kanryū*, 70-75, 78-79.

[21] The rhetoric of "coming out" is frequently employed, along with that of *"hamaru."* See, for example, Tanaka, *Kanryū*, 34-36, 44.

[22] See Yi, *Kanryū no shakaigaku*, 21-22.

They become proficient with the laptop and the internet in order to collect information about their favorite stars and to connect with other fans.[23] An elderly and avid fan said that she had never touched a keyboard until her immersion in the world of South Korean television drama. Not only did she acquire a laptop computer but also learned to navigate a satellite television system and acquired two mobile phones (one for the exclusive purpose of her fan-related activities). That is, technological convergence accompanies the Korean Wave fandom. Indeed, almost all *Kandora* fans become avid users of the internet and mobile phones (to access websites).

Many *Kandora* fans embarked on language learning and location tours (packaged tours to filming sites of *Fuyusona* in South Korea).[24] *Linguistic and cultural convergence* become the ultimate badge of devotion and enthusiasm. The ne plus ultra of individual and collective enthusiasm is that some even consider moving to South Korea. Some engage in intensive Korean language instruction, becoming basically fluent over time (honed by repeated trips to South Korea). A housewife with two children who had been studying Korean intensively said: "After my children leave home, I want to live in South Korea and be immersed in *Kandora* and K-pop." With regular airing of South Korean drama, South Korea had become less alien in urban Japan. Indeed, even the place of the Korean language in Japan changed. Rather than employing the Japanese rendering of the Chinese script (instead of the Korean reading), the new norm was to use *katakana*. In one sense, Korean was now on par with Americans: foreign but familiar. Moreover, as Japanese fans picked up Korean, they often employed Korean readings of the Chinese characters.[25] Hence, those immersed in the Korean Wave often talk of *Hanryū* (the Japanese adaption of the Korean *Hallyu*) rather than *Kanryū*.

Furthermore, there is *genre convergence. Fuyusona* and Bae were at the epicenter of the Korean Wave but the swelling tide soon carried ever larger numbers of stars, styles, and genres from South Korean popular culture. From the mid 2000s *Kandora* fans began to follow K-pop in particular. Bae was merely the first icon, the pioneering K-pop boy band Tōhō Shinki (Tongbang Singi in Korean; TVQX, DBSK, and other names elsewhere) also exemplified the same *ikemen* ideal.[26] One fan recounts that after her immersion in *Fuyusona*, her encounter with Tōhō Shinki shook her up,

[23] Hasegawa, *Hanryū joshi hajimemashita*, 38-39; Yi, *Kanryū no shakaigaku*, 29-33.
[24] See, for example, Hayashi, *"Fuyusona" ni hamatta watashi-tachi.*
[25] See, for example, Hasegawa, *Hanryū joshi hajimemashita*, 48-49.
[26] Furuya Masayuki, *K GENERATION* (Tokyo: DHC, 2005), 60-61. See also Hasegawa, *Hanryū joshi hajimemashita*, 10-13; and Yamakawa Chii, *Tōhō Shinki no namida* (Tokyo: Īsuto Puresu, 2010).

leading to a "dangerous" level of fanaticism.[27] In the short-run, devoted *Kandora* fans fueled the initial enthusiasm for Tōhō Shinki and other South Korean popular-music acts knowing that they were South Korean. Devoted *Kandora* fans, who are overwhelmingly middle-aged women, are at times avid K-pop fans, who talk of having "affairs" (*uwaki*) with younger male singers (meaning that they become devoted fans of boy bands while their true relationship remains with a *Kandora* star, such as Bae). Their long-run impact, however, was to carve a niche for South Korean popular music and make it a legitimate genre. That is, *Kandora* was the foundation upon which K-pop could thrive as a distinct, South Korean brand. *Kandora* fans not only provided a core of K-pop fans but more importantly made South Korean popular culture a legitimate presence in Japan. In short, genre convergence occurred.

Finally, there is *generational convergence*. One discernible recent trend is the rise of mother-daughter tourism to South Korea, underscored by a plethora of special travel guides geared for them. These guidebooks suggest several common activities for mothers and daughters, such as touring iconic sites, shopping, beauty stops (cosmetics and spas), and art.[28] Others suggest seeking fashionable cafes and restaurants.[29] Mothers and daughters then can go on to pursue their individual interests, usually South Korean drama in the case of mothers and K-pop for daughters. Although beginning as a group of middle-aged and older women, the Korean Wave fandom has increasingly incorporated younger women and girls, especially with the rise of K-pop.

Needless to say, there are divisions among fans of South Korean popular culture: for example, middle-aged and older women's interest in *Kandora* as opposed to the generally younger demographic of K-pop fans. Yet these differences pale in significance to the gendered character of South Korean popular culture's appeal in Japan. There is a set of common aesthetic principles that animate fans of South Korean popular culture, including physical attractiveness—tall, slim, *ikemen*, resonant voice—as well as behavioral ideals—kind and loving, gentle and gallant, sensitive and thoughtful.[30] They are also embedded in a world

---

[27] Hasegawa, *Hanryū joshi hajimemashita*, 11.

[28] See Bekkan Sukkara, ed., *Oyako de Kannamu!*, vol. 5 (Tokyo: Asuku, 2012).

[29] Hasegawa, *Hanryū joshi hajimemashita*, 70-71, 80-82.

[30] BL manga provide another form of displacement (same-sex love) but valorize the same set of male ideals, the genealogy of which can be traced to *Berubara* and even earlier. Yoshinaga Fumi's post-BL manga play with two polarized types: the aggressive, rough rapist sort against the gentle, kind, sensitive male type in, for example, *Seiyō kottō kashiten*, 4 vols. (Tokyo: Shinshokan, 2000-2002). The same thematic contrast can be seen in her masterpiece, *Ōoku*, 11 vols. to date (Tokyo: Hakusensha, 2005-).

of affluence: a rich, elegant, and sophisticated environment of high life exemplified by Kangnam. What do Japanese female fans of South Korean popular culture want? Whatever the differences based on education or employment, age or generation, there is a dominant thread that speaks to at least one common set of desirable characteristics in men. Although individual variations are significant, and it would be a simplification to cast the contrast between the actual and the desirable as either antipodal (as opposing) or complementary (as lacking), there is no better way to summarize them briefly as qualities that are lacking among actually existing Japanese men, as husbands and fathers, brothers and boyfriends. This tendency manifests itself in actively seeking boyfriends or husbands who are South Korean. Judging by the plethora of internet discussions and published books and articles, it is a non-trivial, albeit minor, phenomenon.[31] The cultural distance, and the suspension of disbelief that I mentioned, is breaking down for some Japanese women. One may very well speak of the convergence of fantasy and reality as well as sexual convergence.

The Gender Divergence

One sphere in which the Korean Wave has generated a major divergence is in terms of gender. By gender divergence, I refer not so much to the persistent inequality—educational achievement, job advancement, income and wealth, and social prestige and political power—between women and men but rather the humdrum reality of the two genders leading separate lives: occupying distinct spaces and pursuing separate interests. Although an excessive focus on gender may occlude internal heterogeneity and bypass other dynamics, the gender divide articulates a deep distinction in Japanese society.

There are of course male fans of South Korean popular culture but *Kandora* and K-pop have remained the province of women. A predictable corollary is the predominantly male constitution of the anti-Korean Wave (*Ken-Kanryū*) movement. The discourse of *Ken-Kanryū* spans a range of criticisms: the lack of originality of South Korean drama or music and the artificial character of South Korean stars (such as the prevalent use of plastic surgery) to the political criticism of the South Korean state and big business and the generalized dislike of things

---

[31] See Chisa, *Koishita hito wa Kankokujin* (Tokyo: Sutandādo Magajin, 2010); Shindō Yukie, *Shin-Ōkubo no toshishita ōji to kekkon shimashita* (Tokyo: Shōgakkan, 2011); and Kankoku Danshi Kenkyūkai, ed., *Kankoku danshi to koi shitāi* (Tokyo: Takarajimasha, 2012).

Korean and Korean people.[32] The most visible political action so far has been a series of demonstrations in front of Fuji TV Station, which has been closely associated with *Kandora*.[33] A common refrain is that most Japanese are not interested in watching *Kandora* and that the Korean Wave is manufactured by South Korean political and business interests as well as Japanese promoters bent on profit.[34] The discourse manifests a mixture of chauvinism ("Japanese culture is superior") and xenophobia ("I don't want foreign shows on Japanese TV"). Hollywood movies have been shown on primetime TV, though it should be noted that they are almost always dubbed in Japanese. What underlies a visceral dislike is a baffling reality that "their" women—mothers, sisters, and friends—have been smitten by South Koreans, threatening at once their patriarchal and patriotic longings. Usually lumped together with other *netto uyoku* (the internet-based right wing) voices, anti-Korean Wave men tend to seek family-like solidarity with other forces that are xenophobic to counter the threat to the purity of the family and the nation.[35]

Contemporary rightwing nationalism in Japan is noteworthy for its appeal to young men but the salient fact is its almost completely male constitution. The post-bubble economy (in fact, almost all the conscious life of many young Japanese men) has been a relentless mixture of longing for the good old days of rapid economic growth and of resignation that the future may be stable or possibly stagnant. Almost no one believes in the post-World War II social order—sometimes called the 1955 system after the year in which the Liberal Democratic Party became consolidated and coinciding with the beginning of rapid economic growth after the Korean War—in which most men could look forward to steady jobs, if not life-time employment with steadily rising standards of living. It was also the time when the nuclear family became the indisputable norm, consolidating the gender divide between working husband-fathers and housewife mothers. By the beginning of the twenty-first century, few could entrust their faith in the postwar 1955 system. Many young men, especially those unable to attend college, find uncertain and unstable economic future, as the mass media constantly pontificate on the rise of *furītā* (the contraction

[32] Yamano Sharin's *Manga Ken Kanryū* (Tokyo: Shin'yūsha, 2005) focuses in fact on progressive Japanese intellectuals and their interpretation of Japanese history and war crimes. Introducing a Zainichi protagonist, by volume 4 the manga deals with Zainichi political demands, such as for local suffrage rights (Tokyo: Shin'yūsha, 2009).

[33] See Furuya Tsunehira, *Fuji terebi demo ni itte-mita!* (Tokyo: Seirinsha, 2012).

[34] Bessatsu Takarajima Henshūbu, ed., *Ken "Kan" dai-nimaku: tsukurareta Hanryū būmu* (Tokyo: Takarajimasha, 2012).

[35] See Yasuda Kōichi, *Netto to aikoku* (Tokyo: Kōdansha, 2012), 320-325.

of the English "freelance" and the German *"arbeiter"* [worker]) and *nīto* (NEET, as in "not in education, employment, or training"), those without any obvious place or prospect in Japanese economy or society. In turn, some of their mothers (and wives) seek lives beyond taking care of their quotidian needs to explore, if only in the realm of fantasy, other possible lives beyond the confines of domesticity. The Korean Wave, in this sense, is an interloper for some young men just as much as it is an escape for some women. The unusually passionate hatred for South Korean popular culture expresses, if only in part, the collapse of the postwar order of male superiority and domestic stability.

It would be misleading to dwell on rabid rightwing nationalists, for as vocal as they are they remain a small minority. What are other men doing? The most visible counterpart to the Korean Wave is the fanatical enthusiasm for AKB48, a female idol group of more than 200 girls. As a *reductio ad absurdum* of *American Idol* or *X Factor* style elections, girls who aspire to be in AKB48 and ascend its hierarchy through election campaigns. Each CD purchased allows a fan—almost all men, not all of them young—to cast one vote, and the annual election result eclipses all the other news in Japan. Indeed, one commentator has suggested that the most popular AKB48 member, Maeda Atsuko, "has transcended Christ."[36] It is a popularity contest in which it is not so much beauty or talent that prevails but rather someone who achieves the ideal of the girl next door: cute but not beautiful, sings and dances well but not too well. Non-Japanese observers usually remain baffled and mystified by AKB48 for their musical performance is amateurish, lacking the polish and professionalism of Girls' Generation (Shōjo Jidai).[37] However, it is precisely the lack of polish—the apotheosis of the demotic impulse—that pervades the AKB48 phenomenon.[38]

AKB stands for Akihabara, formerly an area known for electronics shops, but is now much better known as the mecca of otaku culture. Otaku is a term that surfaced in the late 1970s, referring at the time to fanatical followers of science-fiction manga and anime.[39] Soon it came to signify

---

[36] Hamano Satoshi, *Maeda Atsuko wa Kirisuto o koeta* (Tokyo: Chikuma Shobō, 2012). John Lennon notwithstanding, what is remarkable is the intensely involuted—and almost untranslatable—nature of the AKB48 phenomenon.

[37] Fortunately, readers can judge for themselves. Compare, for example, the two music videos, both big hits in Japan: https://youtu.be/lkHlnWFnAoc; and https://youtu.be/fhseD2tRLUY.

[38] For a debate on the source of AKB48's popularity, see Kobayashi Yoshinori et al., *AKB48 hakunetsu ronsō* (Tokyo: Gentōsha, 2012).

[39] For a general introduction, see Okada Toshio, *Otakugaku nyūmon* (Tokyo: Shinchōsha, 2000). For an interesting chronicle of the 1980s by one of its architects, see Ōtsuka Eiji, *"Otaku" no seishin-shi* (Tokyo: Kōdansha, 2004).

any single-minded subcultural pursuit. Younger Japanese social theorists often connected otaku culture to the breakdown of the master narrative and the arrival of the postmodern.[40] Yet what has come to characterize a particular otaku culture at Akihabara is not so much anime and manga—for they are ubiquitous in Japan—but rather two interrelated phenomena: erotic manga, especially on the theme of *Rorikon* (an abbreviation of the Lolita complex, signifying sexual interest in adolescent or prepubescent girls), and *meido kissa* (maid cafes) in which girls dressed as French maids serve their *go-shujin-sama* ("lords" or "masters" as customers are called). In both instances—and AKB48 as well—young and old Japanese men seek limited relational and erotic gratification in dealing with, whether in the imaginative realm or as role playing, very young girls who are ideally at once cute and buxom, modern but submissive. The commonly expressed ideal is *dōgan kyonyū* (infantile face, big breasts), sort of a sexual Chimera that exemplifies the ambivalent desire of the men in this particular slice of otaku culture. The contained nature of interaction is critical. Any Japanese city is replete with *mizu shōbai* (literally "water business") or *fūzoku* (sex work), from hostess bars and *kyabakura* ("cabaret clubs") to *deriheru* ("delivery health"), meaning women who make house calls to offer erotic massage and sometimes more) and *sōpurando* ("soap land," a bath house that is often a brothel).[41] What maid cafes or AKB48 offer is a much more attenuated form of interaction: no extended conversations, no tactile exchanges, no intercourses of bodily fluids. That is, there is a substantial section of young (and old) Japanese men who do not wish to or are incapable of interacting with independent women—those who are educated, pursue professional careers, and express desires and opinions—who in fact constitute the norm among young Japanese women. Sure enough, the proportion of women who do not want to become housewives or even to be married at all exemplify at once a desire for independence and an unwillingness to compromise marrying just any man for the sake of social respectability and intergenerational reproduction.[42] The social phenomenon is well captured in the 2012 Fuji TV drama *Kekkon shinai* (literally "I Won't Get Married," subtitled in English "Wonderful Single Life").

As many Japanese women are wont to express their disappointment with the general lot of Japanese men, Japanese men too, vocally or silently,

---

[40] Azuma Kōki, *Dōbutsu-ka suru otaku* (Tokyo: Kōdansha, 2001). For an earlier, more empirical articulation, see Miyadai Shinji, Ōtsuka Akiko, and Ishikara Hideki, *Sabukarucha shinwa kaitai* (Tokyo: PARCO Shuppan, 1993).

[41] For overviews, see Kadokura Takashi, *"Yoru no onna" wa ikura kaseguka* (Tokyo: Kadokawa Shoten 2006); and Kadokura Takashi, *"Yoru no onna" no keizai hakusho* (Tokyo: Kadokawa Shoten, 2009).

[42] See, for example, Asahi Shinbun Shuppan, ed., *Kekkon, shinai?* (Tokyo: Asahi Shinbun Shuppan, 2012).

express preference for another, more archaic version of femininity (though it is important to note that the ideal appearance is thoroughly modern). The Korean Wave, in this context, becomes contested, and the fundamental divide occurs along gender lines. However different, Korean-Wave fans and Akihabara otaku both reside snugly in their respective worlds of fantasy. The two ideals are alas incompatible and sustain the gender divergence.

Works Cited

Asahi Shinbun Shuppan, ed. *Kekkon, shinai?* Tokyo: Asahi Shinbun Shuppan, 2012.

Asahi Shinbunsha, ed., *Ikeda Riyoko no sekai*. Tokyo: Asahi Shinbunsha, 2012.

Azuma Kōki. *Dōbutsu-ka suru otaku*. Tokyo: Kōdansha, 2001.

Bekkan Sukkara, ed. *Oyako de Kannamu!*, vol. 5. Tokyo: Asuku, 2012.

Bessatsu Takarajima Henshūbu, ed. *Ken "Kan" dai-nimaku: Tsukurareta Hanryū būmu*. Tokyo: Takarajimasha, 2012.

Chisa. *Koishita hito wa Kankokujin*. Tokyo: Sutandādo Magajin, 2010.

Chua, Beng Huat, and Koichi Iwabuchi, eds. *East Asian Pop Culture*. Hong Kong: Hong Kong University Press, 2008.

Ei Shuppansha, ed. *Seoul hon-Kanryū K-Pop 2013*. Tokyo: Ei Shuppansha, 2012.

Furuya Masayuki. *K GENERATION*. Tokyo: DHC, 2005.

Furuya Tsunehira. *Fuji terebi demo ni itte-mita!* Tokyo: Seirinsha, 2012.

Hamano Satoshi. *Maeda Atsuko wa Kirisuto o koeta*. Tokyo: Chikuma Shobō, 2012.

Hasegawa Kei. "Kanryū būmu to jendā." In *Kanryū sabukarucha to josei*, edited by Mizuta Muneko, Hasegawa Kei, and Kitada Yukie, 47-57. Tokyo: Shibundō, 2006.

Hasegawa Seiko. *Hanryū joshi hajimemashita*. Tokyo: Ei Shuppansha, 2012.

Hayashi Kaori.*"Fuyusona" ni hamatta watashi-tachi*. Tokyo: Bungei Shunjū, 2005.

Hirata Yukie. *Han'guk ŭl sobi hanŭn Ilbon*. Seoul: Ch'aek Sesang, 2005.

Hori Gorō. *BL Shin Nihonshi*. Tokyo: Gentōsha, 2006.

Ikeda Riyoko. *Berusaiyu no bara*, 5 vols. Tokyo: Shūeisha, [1972-1973] 2009.

Ishita Saeko, Kimura Kan, and Yamanaka Chie, eds. *Posuto Kanryū no media shakaigaku*. Kyoto: Minerva Shobō, 2007.

Iwabuchi Kōichi. *Toransunashonaru—Japan*. Tokyo: Iwanami Shoten, 2001.

Jung, Sun. *Korean Masculinities and Transcultural Consumption*. Hong Kong: Hong Kong University Press, 2011.

Kadokura Takashi. *"Yoru no onna" no keizai hakusho*. Tokyo: Kadokawa Shoten, 2009

"Yoru no onna" wa ikura kaseguka. Tokyo: Kadokawa Shoten 2006.

Kankoku Danshi Kenkyūkai, ed. *Kankoku danshi to koi shitāi*. Tokyo: Takarajimasha, 2012.

Kinema Junpōsha, ed. *Seoul de 100% tanoshimu K-Pop kanzen gaido*. Tokyo: Kinema Junpōsha, 2012.

Kiryū Misao. *Sekai bōizu rabu taizen*. Tokyo: Bungei Shunjū, 2012.

Kobayashi Yoshinori, Nakamori Akio, Uno Tsunehiko, and Hamano Satoshi. *AKB48 hakunetsu ronsō*. Tokyo: Gentōsha, 2012.

Kwon Yongseok. *"Kanryū" to "Nichiryū."* Tokyo: NHK Bukkusu, 2010.

Lie, John. "The Transformation of Sexual Work in Twentieth-Century Korea." *Gender & Society* 9, no. 3 (1995): 310-327.

Lie, John. *Zainichi (Koreans in Japan): Diasporic Nationalism and Postcolonial Identity.* Berkeley: University of California Press, 2008.

Mikazuki Kanna. *Kankoku onna hitoritabi.* Tokyo: Chūkei Shuppan, 2012.

Miyadai Shinji, Ōtsuka Akiko, and Ishikara Hideki. *Sabukarucha shinwa kaitai.* Tokyo: PARCO Shuppan, 1993.

Mizuta Muneko. "Gendai no otogibanashi 'Fuyu no sonata' no monogatari no kōzō." In *Kanryū sabukaruchua to josei,* edited by Mizuta Muneko, Hasegawa Kei, and Kitada Yukie, 93-110. Tokyo: Shibundō, 2006.

Mōri Yoshitaka, ed. *Nisshiki Kanryū.* Tokyo: Serika Shobō, 2004.

Okada Toshio. *Otakugaku nyūmon.* Tokyo: Shinchōsha, 2000.

Ōtsuka Eiji. *"Otaku" no seishin-shi.* Tokyo: Kōdansha, 2004.

Pak Chang-sun. *Hallyu, Han'guk kwa Ilbon ŭi dŭrama chŏnjaeng.* Seoul: K'ŏmyunik'eisyŏnbuksŭ, 2008.

Paku Sun'e [Pak Sun-ae] and Tsuchiya Reiko, eds., *Nihon taishū bunka to Nikkan kankei.* Tokyo: Sangensha, 2001.

Robertson, Jennifer. *Takarazuka.* Berkeley: University of California Press, 1998.

Russell, Mark James. *Pop Goes Korea.* Berkeley: Stone Bridge Press, 2008.

Shindō Yukie. *Shin Ōkubo no toshishita ōji to kekkon shimashita.* Tokyo: Shōgakkan, 2011.

Tanaka Chizuko. *Kanryū desu ga sore ga nani ka?* Tokyo: Gamu Shuppan, 2009.

Tanaka Hikaru. *"Obasan" wa naze kirawareru-ka.* Tokyo: Shūeisha, 2011.

Tatar, Maria. *The Hard Facts of Grimms' Fairy Tales.* Princeton: Princeton University Press, 1997.

Tei Taikin. *Kankoku no imēji*, exp. ed. Tokyo: Chūō Kōron Shinsha, 2010.

Yamakawa Chii. *Tōhō Shinki no namida*. Tokyo: Īsuto Puresu, 2010.

Yamano Sharin. *Manga Ken Kanryū*. Tokyo: Shin'yūsha, 2005.

Manga Ken Kanryū, vol. 4. Tokyo: Shin'yūsha, 2012.

Yasuda Kōichi. *Netto to aikoku*. Tokyo: Kōdansha, 2012.

Yi Hyanjin [Yi Hyang-jin/Lee Hyangjin]. *Kanryū no shakaigaku*. Translated by Shimizu Yukiko. Tokyo: Iwanami Shoten, 2008.

Part IV:
Convergence of the Virtual and Real

On Two-Dimensional Cute Girls: Virtual Idols

Yoshida Masataka

Editor's Introduction: The Convergence of the Fictional and Real[*]

Starting with the publication in 2000 of Saitō Tamaki's *Sentō bishōjo no seishin bunseki* (translated into English as *Beautiful Fighting Girl*), which sparked debate among Azuma Hiroki and his circle, Japan saw an outpouring of new academic interest in "otaku."[1] While primarily an analysis of "otaku sexuality," Saitō's book contains a chapter titled "A Genealogy of the Beautiful Fighting Girl," which breaks down the *bishōjo*, or cute girl character, into 13 subcategories including witch, sporty, Pygmalion, cross-dressing and so on. While fans had been doing similar character genealogies and typologies for decades, Saitō's attempt to understand the *bishōjo* and its significance opened the door for publications such as Sasakibara Gō's *"Bishōjo" no gendai-shi: Moe to kyarakutā* (Contemporary History of "Cute Girls:" On Characters and Affection for Them) and Yoshida Masataka's *Nijigen bishōjo-ron: Otaku no megami sōzōshi* (On Two-Dimensional Cute Girls: The Creative History of Otaku Goddesses). While both Sasakibara and Yoshida eschew Saitō's psychoanalytic approach, the former focuses more on cultural criticism and the latter on art history.

Born in Tokyo in 1969, Yoshida is an associate professor at Tohoku University of Art and Design and chairman of the Japanese Association for Contents History Studies. Originally specializing in early modern Japanese history, particularly the urban culture of Tokyo and its art, Yoshida's entry into the field of postwar popular culture was somewhat unexpected. Tending to historicize content and engage in textual analysis, Yoshida identifies and explores exciting connections as few others can. In this excerpt from *Nijigen bishōjo-ron*, available here for the first time in English, Yoshida turns his critical gaze to "virtual idols" (*vācharu aidoru*). His main focus is *bishōjo* characters seen in anime and games, but he

[*] This chapter is a translation by Keiko Nishimura of "Vācharu aidoru," in *Nijigen bishōjo-ron: Otaku no megami sōzōshi* (Tokyo: Futami Shobō, 2004), 175-218. Reprinted with permission of the author and publisher. The introduction is by Patrick W. Galbraith.
[1] Azuma Hiroki, ed. *Mōjō genron F-kai: Posutomodan, otaku, sekushuariti* (Tokyo: Seidōsha, 2003).

draws connections to "real" (*riaru*) idols, who in some way or another are related to the virtual. This fascinating connection opens into questions about the convergence of fiction and reality, which Yoshida has continued to explore in his career.

For example, on September 9, 2014, Yoshida spoke at the Eighth Meeting of the Illusion Workshop (Dai-8-kai Sakkaku Wākushoppu) at Meiji University in Tokyo. Unlike colleagues presenting on optical illusions and the like, Yoshida took up the relationship between "virtual idols" and the "media mix," the latter being a key phrase in Japanese media studies related to convergence (for more, see the Introduction of this volume). Among many memorable points, Yoshida argued that idol anime intentionally confuses fiction and reality, or encourages their convergence, in order to stimulate fan labor to work through connections and layered meaning. To Yoshida's mind, this "illusory scheme" (*sakkaku-teki kufū*) is at the heart of recent media content such as *Love Live!* (from 2010), which features virtual idols who are frequently seen in the anime hanging out in Akihabara, the "otaku" district of Tokyo. When these virtual idols appear in music videos, they are animated characters, but at live performances it is their voice actresses that appear—dressed as the characters, singing and dancing with (as?) them, in synch with music videos projected onstage. The virtual idols are, Yoshida argues, reproduced by the voice actresses' bodies (*namami de saigen suru*), which act as media. This convergence of the fictional and real is apparently stimulating. In 2015, *Love Live! The School Idol Movie* was the number one film in Japan during its opening weekend, grossing ¥400 million (US$3.42 million).

In this chapter on virtual idols, Yoshida lays the groundwork for his approach to virtual idols and the media mix, raising important issues about the relationship between "real" idols and virtual ones, body and image. Not content to stick to the usual narrative of *Creamy Mami, the Magic Angel* (1983-1984) being the first anime to stage a convergence of real and fictional idols, whose careers overlap, Yoshida takes the reader back to *Super Dimensional Fortress Macross* (1982-1983) and "otaku" culture (playing with "virtual reality" [*kasō genjitsu*] was in some ways characteristic of fans in the 1980s)[2] and, further still, to *Star of the Giants* (1968-1971), a TV animation remembered for a gritty style that appealed to older audiences. More importantly, scholars are now looking to *Star of the Giants* as an early example of "vertical integration," where something real—namely the

---

[2] Ōtsuka Eiji, *"Otaku" no seishin-shi: 1980-nendai-ron* (Tokyo: Kōdansha Gendai Shinsho, 2004), 17-20.

Yomiuri Giants baseball team—is integrated into a fictional narrative to create promotional discourse.[3] Here we observe not only a convergence of audiences—younger and older men watching the same TV animation—but also of fiction and reality in the narrative of the Giants and their virtual star, Hoshi Hyūma. As Yoshida points out, *Star of the Giants* is also where the first virtual idols, the Aurora Sisters, appeared, which speaks to the emerging culture of idols in Japan in the early 1970s. From the beginning, idols, as products of media and consumer capitalism, were always fiction, but the connection to anime makes this all the more explicit and opens paths to critical inquiry. For example, Yoshida resonates with an approach to the fictional character as "regulatory mechanism" to produce divergent series and force "their convergence at the level of economics and desire."[4] In the virtual idol, we see both convergence and divergence with "reality," and—by highlighting this—Yoshida draws attention to how fiction and reality are brought into productive relation.

We are not including this translated chapter in the volume because Yoshida is right about everything, which he clearly is not. His declaration that virtual idols are "dead and extinct" is belied by not only the success of *Love Live!*, but also series such as *The Idol M@ster* (from 2005), *Pretty Rhythm* (from 2010), *Aikatsu!* (from 2012), *Wake Up, Girls!* (from 2014) and more. The value of Yoshida's work is its ability to highlight unexpected connections and hint at their significance—for example, the narrative similarities of sports and idol anime and the shared context of their emergence. Similarly, Yoshida's underscoring of an audience desire for more "real" fantasy, which resonates with the demand for "dark" comic book films and TV series in North America, might suggest that there is little room left for "fantasy aware of itself as fantasy." Stated another way, channeling Saitō, can the object of desire be fiction in and of itself? What might that mean for evolving relations with "reality?" The following excerpt marks the beginnings of Yoshida's exploration of what he called in 2014 the "diverse illusory techniques" (*taiyō-na sakkaku-teki shuhō*) of media mixes featuring virtual idols and is sure to stimulate discussion and debate for years to come.[5]

---

[3] Jonathan Clements, *Anime: A History* (New York: Palgrave, 2013), 139.
[4] Marc Steinberg, *Anime's Media Mix: Franchising Toys and Characters in Japan* (Minneapolis, MN: University of Minnesota Press, 2012), 190.
[5] See Chapter 8 for more on the unfolding of the virtual idol.

Chasing After Virtual Idols

A former idol, who dropped out of a second-tier group to become an actress, reconciles herself to a minor role in a TV drama, which includes a scene where she is nude and sexually assaulted. This is not how she imagined her life as an actress. At a time when she is psychologically spent, the woman is stalked by a fanatic follower from her idol days and gets lost in a bizarre world where someone posting information not only about her, but as her, seems more authentic than the person that she has become. This is part of the story of *Perfect Blue*, a novel by Takeuchi Yoshikazu, which in 1998 was adapted into an animated film by a powerhouse team including Kon Satoshi as director and Eguchi Hisashi as character designer. Given the unfairly warped portrayal of fans (*otaku*), which is persistent in the film, *Perfect Blue* can be painful to watch, but that is not the point to focus on.[6]

Rather, the major point is that the abasement of the idol-ness of idols as images is depicted so candidly in a mainstream work distributed with average people as its target audience, which is a turning point in the subcultural world of postwar Japan. Until recently, idols were seen as sacred and, while something to long for, recognized as an existence that was mentally, and of course physically, untouchable. This was even more so for idols created in virtual worlds (anime, comics, games). Whether or not it is the case in the real world, why is it that even the idols of virtual worlds have been made into warm-bodied, raw existences that can be played around with? This chapter explores the vicissitudes of the fortune of idols in unreal worlds, primarily focusing on animation. How have the attributes of the "idol" become components of the virtual cute girl?

The Invisible Bond Between Fighting Spirit and Idols

In 2003, WOWOW broadcast *Star of the Giants Special: Hanagata Mitsuru, the Raging Tiger* (*Kyojin no hoshi tokubetsuhen mōko Hanagata Mitsuru*). At a time when the Hanshin Tigers baseball team was celebrating victory, new animation was added and the work organized to make Hanagata Mitsuru the central character. Also different from the original broadcast

---

[6] Translator's Note (hereafter TN): In part, Yoshida seems to suggest that *Perfect Blue* is a "painful work" (*itai sakuhin*) because the portrayal of demented and twisted fans is consistent with so-called "otaku bashing" in Japanese media more generally in the 1990s. See Sharon Kinsella, "Japanese Subculture in the 1990s: *Otaku* and the Amateur *Manga* Movement," *Journal of Japanese Studies* 24, no. 2 (1998): 289-316. One of the most common anxieties about fans in Japan since this time is that they have lost touch with reality and might hurt people. Yoshida, like many others, is not convinced. See Saitō Tamaki, *Beautiful Fighting Girl* (Minneapolis, MN: University of Minnesota Press, 2011).

is the ending theme song, "Cool Love" (*Kūru-na koi*),[7] which is sung by the Aurora Sisters (*Ōrora sannin musume*). Listening to the ending theme song in 2003 brought back a rush of memories. Who would have thought that at the start of the new millennium I would be reunited with these idols from the past?

In the special, the Aurora Sisters, who appear as idol singers in the original *Star of the Giants* TV animation (1968-1971), end up bowling with the Hanagata, Hoshi Hyūma and Samon Hosaku, three male baseball players. When Samon's throw goes out of control and seems like it is going to hit Tachibana Rumi, a member of the Aurora Sisters, Hoshi protects her, which leads to them becoming closer. After that, the two meet up at a go-go club, which becomes fodder for the broadsheets. Rumi is a top idol and Hoshi a pitcher for the Giants, a top baseball team. Soon after, the Giants go to train in Miyazaki Prefecture, which seems like the perfect escape from the rumor mill and chance for Hoshi to clear his head. However, Rumi shows up in Miyazaki Prefecture to cheer for Hoshi, who, upon seeing her, loses his concentration when throwing a baseball, which hits a child. Hoshi goes to see the child in the hospital, where he meets Hidaka Mina, a nurse and another potential love interest.

In the manga version of events, Rumi tries to smooth things over with money, which upsets Hoshi. Rumi calls him names and leaves, which is the end of her minor part in the story. The TV animation portrays the characters quite differently. In a scene where the Aurora Sisters are performing, Rumi has hurt her leg before the show, but still puts on her high heels and sings powerfully, covered in cold sweat. In a far cry from the manga, Rumi shows her professionalism and spirit. Hoshi notices her pain and rushes to the stage, but Rumi turns to him and says, "Don't! This is my mound." This stops Hoshi, a pitcher for the Giants, because he understands that Rumi's struggle is the same one he faces during games. This important moment in the TV animation comes when Rumi shows Hoshi, who has been losing his passion, a professional's way of life. Where she was a minor and spoiled character in the manga, Rumi plays an important role in the TV animation—she is an idol who inspires an athlete with the strength of her character. It is not uncommon for characters from popular manga series to change in the anime adaptation, but a character with a gap this massive between media representations is rare indeed.

---

[7] The song sung by the Aurora Sisters, "Cool Love" (Kūru-na koi), which features lyrics by Matsushima Yuka and music by Murai Kunihiko, is a cover of The Golden Cups, one of the top acts in what the Japanese industry called Group Sounds. The song that plays in the go-go club where Tachibana Rumi of the Aurora Sisters meet Hoshi Hyūma is "To You, My Love" (Ai suru kimi ni), also by The Golden Cups.

With the addition of music and movement, which are important factors in animation that are not part of comics, it seems clear that people felt it a waste to have the Aurora Sisters disappear after only playing a minor role in *Star of the Giants*, which explains their return in the special. However, the addition of Rumi's story in the original TV animation about an idol who shows her professionalism and guts seems to reflect the animation staff's view of idols as people who struggle, like them, in the world of entertainment. The labor, both mental and physical, devoted to keeping an idol an idol is massive.

There is something in common between the effort on display in sports, which take competition as a foundational principle, and an idol's effort to win the fierce competition with other idols to claim the top spot in the special field of entertainment. At a glance, the connection between the fighting sprit of sports drama and idols seems thin, but if one focuses on "effort" (*dōryoku*)—"compete, crawl up to a higher position and defend it to the end"—the existence of the idol is the same as the protagonists of works such as *Star of the Giants*. Kajiwara Ikki, the writer of *Star of the Giants* and a distinguished name in sports manga, could not have anticipated that the virtual idol, born in the fictional space of anime, would first appear in an adaptation of his work, but in fact it is a natural progression. Effort is at the foundation of the existence of idols, and it continued to be key to the unfolding drama of core works featuring idols for many years after *Star of the Giants*. Later works also showed the darker side of effort in the entertainment world. In this way, the Aurora Sisters became the first virtual idols, born from the genre of sports anime. This factor became the driving force behind the establishment of the first domestically produced idol anime, which was about guts and glory (*konjō mono*).

The Impact of the First Domestically Produced Idol Anime

> *Even the grass in the field that someone steps on*
> *Will someday look up at the sky*
> *Even at times when you cannot see anything for the tears*
> *We are alive*
> *Wandering*
> *Wounded*
> *Searching for tomorrow's sun*

These are the lyrics to the theme song of *Wandering Sun* (*Sasurai no taiyō*, 1971), which tells the story of a young woman's journey to become an idol. Moments after her birth, Mine Nozomi is replaced with another baby, Kōda Miki, by Nohara Michiko, a nurse in the maternity ward who has a complex about her state of poverty. As a result, Miki becomes the daughter of a wealthy family, while Nozomi lives in abject poverty. When Miki and Nozomi turn 17, these two young women, who have lived completely different lives, both set out with the goal of becoming idol singers. *Wandering Sun* is Japan's first domestically produced idol anime. In the opening animation sequence, with the above theme song in the background, we see Nozomi, the sun behind her, wearing white bellbottoms and clutching her beloved guitar as she sings. The 1970s were a different time, but even so it is hard to think of this opening animation as "idol anime."

In terms of story, *Wandering Sun* shares much with stereotypical girls' comics of the day, as opposed to what we might call idol anime. In fact, *Wandering Sun* is based on an original manga by the same name serialized in *Weekly Girls Comics* (*Shūkan shōjo komikku*).[8] Given its origin in comics, a medium to read rather than hear, the original emphasizes story, which is about true love and overcoming a cruel fate. In contrast, the anime might be described as focusing on "straight-up gutsy idols" (*dokonjō aidoru mono*). For example, the characters engage in special training to build lung capacity by working as female shell divers. A strong emphasis is placed on improving skills as a singer, which is their main profession.

As the first idol anime, which constructed an image of idols in an already virtual world, *Wandering Sun* is a significant work. Like the manga, the anime displays the beauty and illusion of idols alongside their darkness and reality, but it is the latter that moves the story forward. For dramatic purposes and to capture viewer interest, even a success story must have the protagonist face adversity. For that reason, in manga and anime that take up idols, there is a stereotypical plot: A protagonist, who starts her activities aiming for success after a life of poverty and misfortune, withstands the challenges of the entertainment world and rises up as a star. The storyline sets an unspoken regulation at the foundation of idol anime whereby the virtual idol is a "tragic idol."

Overlap with the Real World

In the late 1970s, the anime industry, searching for new markets and forms of expression, started paying attention to idols active in the real

---

[8] The original manga version was written by Fujikawa Keisuke and drawn by Suzuki Mayumi. A complete set of four volumes in trade paperback has ben published by Wakagi Shobō and costs between ¥20,000 and ¥30,000.

world. As the name suggests, *Pink Lady Story: Angels of Glory* (*Pinku redī monogatari: Eikō no tenshi-tachi*, 1978) is a TV animation focusing on the most popular idols of the time, Pink Lady. The anime itself was unremarkable, although I did watch it because of the inclusion of Pink Lady, who also hosted the puppet show *Fly! Son Gokū* (*Tobe! Son Gokū*), which starred The Drifters.[9] I vividly remember the theme song, "The Two Came from the Stars" (*Hoshi kara kita futari*), which is a masterpiece, and scenes of the characters learning to dance and sing, which displayed their guts in the face of adversity. (At one point, they are made to sing while tied up.) I also remember thinking that it was rather odd that we should watch an animated version (and it was not even a good one) of Pink Lady, who were at the height of their popularity, when we could just change the channel and see the real thing on a TV variety show. Indeed, the ratings were not great.

"If Pink Lady doesn't work, then try the Candies." Maybe that was the thinking of the producers behind the anime *Sue Cat* (*Sū kyatto*, 1980), the story of three sisters—Sue, Ran and Miki—who aim to become Candies, a real idol group active in Japan in the mid-1970s.[10] Perhaps thinking that the audience would not accept animated versions of human idols, *Sue Cat* has the role of the three idol girls played by humanoid cats, which makes this entry into the history of idol anime unforgettable in its own way. The story is a dark melodrama along the lines of *Wandering Sun*, minus the part about baby switching. Sue Cat, who works at a downtown diner, enters the world of showbiz, where she experiences hardships, including being used by corrupt producers, put into a cabaret, entering into a rivalry with the daughter of rich financiers, becoming a wandering musician and more. In the end, Sue Cat sings at the "Cat Kōhaku Song Contest" and lives happily ever after. In addition to motifs seen in early girls' comics and a side story about the protagonist's search for her father, *Sue Cat* stepped into the dark side of the entertainment industry and explored how mass media builds up the idol as fantasy. As you watch this problematic work, it is hard to think of it as an idol anime, because of the darkness oozing out of it,

[9] *Fly! Son Gokū* (*Tobe! Son Gokū*) is a puppet show based on the Chinese story *Journey to the West* (*Saiyūki*) with characters modeled off of the comedy group The Drifters. Ikariya Chōsuke played Sanzō, Shimura Ken played Son Gokū, Takagi Bū played Cho Hakkai and Nakamoto Kōji played Sagojō, which was perfect casting. What about the last member of The Drifters, Katō Cha? He became a well-known character too, namely a bald mask named "Katochan."

[10] TN: The Candies were formed in 1973 and disbanded in 1978, while Pink Lady was active from 1978 to 1981. The fact that an anime about the Candies came out after one about Pink Lady, and after the group had disbanded, is strange to say the least.

which is characteristic of the 1970s. Even the humanoid cat characters are creepy rather than cute.[11]

TV animation featuring extremely popular real idols failed miserably because it added another layer of fiction by animating "idols," who were already virtual entities separate from reality. What is the "real" being introduced by using "real" idols in anime? Using popular idols and relying on animation technology moves both away from their sales points. After *Sue Cat*, a new method appeared in the anime industry, which was to use not the likenesses of popular idols, but rather the voices of newly debuted idols for characters and theme songs. The focus was thus on the *character*, with voice as a key component of characterization, rather than the image of the "real" idol.[12] The otaku population, awakened by *Mobile Suit Gundam* (1979-1980), were ready for two-dimensional virtual idols, as opposed to idols from the "real" world.[13]

Robot Anime and Virtual Idols

After the trials of the 1970s that presented animated depictions of real idols, the virtual idols that otaku had been waiting for finally appeared on screen in 1982. The anime featuring these virtual idols have gone down in the history of Japanese postwar subculture as masterpieces that represent the 1980s.

The revolution begins with Lynn Minmay, heroine of *Super Dimensional Fortress Macross* (*Chō jikū yōsai makurosu*, 1982-1983). In the story, the Zentradi Army attack the Macross, a gigantic spaceship, on the day of its launching ceremony. The ship's defense system malfunctions, warping it and everyone and everything on and around it to the orbit of Pluto. Civilians caught in the crossfire build a town inside the Macross, which is several hundred meters in length. A nobody when the attack happened, the aspiring singer Lynn Minmay wins the "Miss Macross Contest," held to entertain the stressed civilians onboard, which results in her debut as an idol singer and movie star. Minmay's role as an idol is an important plot point. The Zentradi, who are attacking the humans to reclaim the

---

[11] The skills of illustrators working in TV animation greatly improved from 1979 to 1981. Various efforts by TV animation producers to expand markets and expression include *Dora Taro, The Balloon Vagabond* (*Fūsen no dora tarō*, 1981), *It's Tough Being a Man* (*Otoko wa tsurai yo*), featuring cat characters and with scripts by Yamada Yōji himself, and *Manga Mito Kōmon*, an animated version of the popular samurai series.

[12] TN: For more on this, see Chapter 7 in this volume.

[13] TN: For more on this, see Patrick W. Galbraith, "'Otaku' Research and Anxiety about Failed Men," in *Debating Otaku in Contemporary Japan: Historical Perspectives and New Horizons*, ed. Patrick W. Galbraith, Thiam Huat Kam and Bjoern-Ole Kamm (London: Bloomsbury, 2015), 21-34.

Macross, are an alien species breed for war, which means that they do not understand other aspects of culture such as singing and love. Indeed, hearing music or seeing men and women kissing both confuses and upsets them. In the final episode (Episode 27, "Love Flows"),[14] Minmay is positioned at the front of the Macross and her voice amplified so that the Macross can charge into the confused enemy armada and destroy their flagship.[15]

The most notable characteristic of Lynn Minmay as a virtual idol is her sophisticated character design. Compared with *Sue Cat*, released just two years prior, the improvement is startling. Minmay's face, designed by Mikimoto Haruhiko,[16] is in no way inferior to that of real idols. Furthermore, Iijima Mari, a rising young singer who not only sang Minmay's songs but also voiced her character grabbed attention. The idea of having a young singer sing the main theme of anime and/or voice a character caught on and became a key component of the marketing strategies that were later called "media mix."

Computers and Information Society

It is necessary to mention the OVA *Megazone 23* (1985) in the context of robot anime and idols.[17] In the story, Tokimatsuri Eve is an extremely popular 15-year-old idol in the city where *Megazone 23* takes place, which appears to be Tokyo in the 1980s. Through a series of events, the protagonist Yahagi Shōgo, a regular guy who likes motorcycles, happens upon the secret of his world. The earth went extinct a few centuries ago, and human survivors are traveling in a huge spaceship to find a habitable planet. A central computer called Bahamut controls this spaceship and creates the illusion of a peaceful earth from the 1980s to keep its human passengers happy. The army, however, is executing an operation to take control back from the computer to prepare for war with an approaching ship, which they

---

[14] Actually, there are several episodes after the final battle, which focus on the crew of the Macross helping to rebuild the earth.

[15] The scene of fighter planes firing dozens of missiles—the infamous "Itano Circus" by Itano Ichirō— scored by Minmay's singing is a classic fusion of *bishōjo* and "military." This symbolic expression characterizes the 1980s and influenced many works thereafter. In addition, Minmay's expressive eyes as she smiles were extremely difficult to achieve, speaking to the skills of the talent behind the series. The scene in question was improved greatly for the animated film *Do You Remember Love?* released in 1984.

[16] TN: Mikimoto, who was himself an idol fan, based Minmay on Matsuda Seiko, a popular idol of the time.

[17] TN: *Megazone 23* was directed by Ishiguro Noboru, who also directed *Super Dimensional Fortress Macross*. Given the shared production team, the emphasis on robots and idols makes a good deal of sense. Yoshida touches on this later.

assume is hostile. They pursue Shōgo, who has stolen a motorcycle called the Garland that contains information important to the operation, even as Shōgo debates whether he should help and protect Bahamut.

Shōgo's impulse to help Bahamut is easier to understand when we take into consideration that the computer interfaces with him as Tokimatsuri Eve, a completely virtual idol created by Bahamut by manipulating information and computer graphics. Shōgo initially contacts Tokimatsuri Eve through her TV show "Eve's Only You," which has a corner where the audience can call in and video chat with the idol. He tries to expose the army's plans by showing the Garland on live TV, but the broadcast is interrupted, ostensibly by the army. In this way, Shōgo comes to know Tokimatsuri Eve and the truth, only to see her killed in a dramatic scene where the army takes over Bahamut and erases the idol Tokimatsuri Eve, who screams, "Help me, I'm getting killed!" The army then creates a new Tokimatsuri Eve to use to manipulate the populace into volunteering for the army and to raise troop morale.[18]

Many of the staff of *Super Dimensional Fortress Macross* also worked on *Megazone 23*, and the two works share much stylistically. Significantly, *Megazone 23* further extended the Lynn Minmay character into Tokimatsuri Eve as a virtual idol. Tokimatsuri Eve was voiced by Miyasato Kumi, an upcoming idol, who also sang the main theme song, thus making use of the media mix strategy developed by *Macross*. The scene in the anime where the Bahamut computer draws Eve's image leaves a strong impression that this is a "virtual idol." It is surprising that a work so vividly depicting the fiction and unreality of idols existed in the 1980s. This trend continued with Katsura Masakazu's *Video Girl Ai* (*Den'ei shōjo*, 1989-1992), which created an image of "cute classmate-type virtual girls" and incorporated the evolution of expressional techniques such as computer graphics. What followed was actual "virtual idols," separate from any manga or anime text and operating in the real world, such as Date Kyōko (DK-96) and Terai Yuki.

Tokimatsuri Eve is a computer-generated idol with no subjectivity. She is an image created by the computer Bahamut and circulated among the people. The tragedy that she has to completely change her attitude and

---

[18] In the mid 1980s, many anime and manga with the theme of living in a world that is not real appeared. Examples include not only *Megazone 23*, but also Oshii Mamoru's *Beautiful Dreamer* (1984), the second feature-length film in the *Urusei Yatsura* anime series, *AI City* (1983-1984) by Itahashi Shūhō, a popular manga done in the style of American comics, and Aran Rei's *Forever and Wherever* (*Itsumademo dokomademo*, 1992, but originally serialized in the 1980s). One may wonder about the reasons behind the prevalence of this adolescent theme expressing anxiety towards the world one lives in. In the history of postwar Japan, we might say that subculture reached its "adolescence" in the 1980s.

actions because of a change in the controlling subject—from Bahamut to the army, from peace to militarism—brings to mind the reality of idols, who must go along with the will of production and advertising agencies, especially the trauma of being transferred from one "producer" to another. This commentary on the reality of idols, and expression of their political use, elevates *Megazone 23* to the status of masterpiece. To quote from the main theme of the sequel, *Megazone 23, Part II: Please Give Me Your Secret*, which is titled "Tragic Idol":

> *Everyone is deceived*
> *I'm just an illusion*
> *I'm tired of singing about women in love*
> *When I don't even know love*
> *Alone as an idol trapped in the TV screen*
> *Find me*
> *Pierce me with burning love*
> *You were born for me*

The Metamorphosis of Virtual Idols

So called "magical girl anime" (*majokko anime*), represented by works such as *Sally the Witch* (*Mahōtsukai Sarī*, 1966-1968), are typically made for girls and have at least one episode devoted to idols. Such was the case with *Magical Princess Minky Momo* (*Mahō no purinsesu Minkī Momo*), which aired from 1982 to 1983. In 1983, *Creamy Mami, the Magic Angel* (*Mahō no tenshi Kurīmī Mami*) started its run on TV, but this time the entire show was devoted to idols. *Mami* continued the trend of "a magical girl anime where a child protagonist transforms into an adult," but with key differences. Where *Momo* was a fantasy story set in a mysterious country, *Mami* was set in the fictional town of Kurimigaoka, which resembles Yokohama; it was more realistic, for example depicting school life. The characters were life-sized and human. Compared to Ashida Toyoo, who did the designs for *Momo*, Takada Akemi's character designs for *Mami* were more realistic in terms of proportion, hairstyle, fashion and so on.

In the story of *Mami*, the child protagonist Morisawa Yū discovers a magical ship called "Feather Star" and receives the ability to transform, but only for a limited period of time. Using this ability, Yū becomes an adult woman and performs street-corner karaoke is scouted by a production agency, where she becomes the super idol Creamy Mami. Much of the story explores what it is like for Yū to be Creamy Mami, including belonging to an agency and working as an idol. In some sense, this is the direct successor of *Wandering Sun*. The final episode of *Mami* features Creamy Mami's very last concert during Yū's limited time with the transformation ability, and it is one of the most cathartic final episodes in the history of idol anime.

The same media mix strategy seen in *Super Dimensional Fortress Macross* and *Megazone 23* returns in *Creamy Mami, the Magic Angel*, where a newly debuted idol provides the voice of the protagonist and sings songs attributed to the character throughout the series. Ōta Takako, then just starting her career as an idol, provides the voice of both Morisawa Yū and Creamy Mami, but this time the release of Ōta's new singles (as a real idol) was scheduled to synchronize with Creamy Mami's new releases in the story (as a fictional idol). The relation between fictional and real idols in the form of the virtual idol was perfected for this series, which took the media mix further than ever before. The strategy seen in Mami returns in later idol anime such as *Idol Legend Eriko* (*Aidoru densetsu Eriko*, 1989-1990) and *Idol Angel Yōkoso Yōko* (*Aidoru tenshi yōkoso Yōko*, 1990-1991), which I will touch on later.

Following *Creamy Mami, the Magic Angel*, Studio Pierrot put out *Persia, the Magic Fairy* (*Mahō no yōsei Perusha*, 1984-1985), which is not about idols, but then returned to form with *Magical Emi, the Magic Star* (*Mahō no sutā majikaru Emi*, 1985-1985), which features a magical girl idol. While helping out at her grandfather's theater company, the protagonist Kazuki Mai obtains a magical mirror called "Magi-carat," which specializes in magic tricks. It turns out that a fairy lives inside the magical mirror, and Mai receives magical powers from the fairy, which she uses to transform into the super magician Magical Emi and patch up some mistakes that occurred during a show where "Magi-carat" was helping out. Mai is spotted by a talent scout and makes her debut as an idol who does magic tricks, the star of a new generation. *Emi* is the same story as *Mami* except for the part about magic tricks, and it also shares the media mix strategy, with freshly debuted idol Obata Yōko doing the voice of Kazuki Mai and Magical Emi.

Emi does not build to a dramatic climax, but rather focuses on the everyday troubles that the characters face and nostalgic, somewhat mysterious stories, which make *Emi* a wonderful "healing type" (*iyashi-kei*) anime. However, it features a remarkable plot point in Mai's realization, as she responds to the requests of those around her, that the virtual idol Emi is fiction. In the final episode of *Emi*, despite the plot containing no device such as *Mami*'s limited period of magical transformation, Mai decides to abandon the magic and return to her life as a normal girl. The

Mami TV animation contains no comparable scene in which Yū struggles with playing Creamy Mami as an idol and fiction, nor does she reject the magic that makes her transformation into an idol possible. It is only in the OVA, *Long Goodbye* (1985), at the very end of Yū's monologue, that she does reject the magic.[19] That was 1985, the same year that the final episode of the *Emi* TV animation aired. In these two conclusions, we see protagonists who reject life as an idol when that existence depends solely on magical power. With the element of transformation, these two works depict idols as ephemeral figures. In these works, magic hints at the special something that idols must have beyond actual ability. In other words, rejection of magic is also a rejection of the idol. By having girls reject their idol personas created by magic, the figure of the magical girl idol disappeared from TV animation for a time. In its place emerged somewhat bizarrely realistic stories that reject elements such as magic and affirm the effort of ordinary girls to become idols.

Neo-Virtual Idols

After *Magical Emi, the Magic Star,* virtual idols all but disappeared from TV animation in Japan. When they returned, it was as pure idol anime without robots or magic. These series with their neo-virtual idols employed the same media mix strategy, but with a twist (more on this later). *Idol Legend Eriko* is a dramatic, heroic idol anime that seems like a return to the roots of *Wandering Sun.* Tamura Eriko, daughter of the head of Tamura Productions, a large entertainment company, loses her parents in a traffic accident. Pushed to the edge of despair, Eriko decides to start her career as an idol. She grows through hardships, for example her uncle's attempted takeover of the company, but also through friendship and rivalry with the singer Asagiri Rei. In the way that she is visited by trouble upon trouble, every time dubbed with dramatic narration by Takizawa Kumiko, which makes it sound like a traditional Japanese melodrama, *Idol Legend Eriko* is something of a mix between *Little Princess Sarah* (*Shōkōjo Sēra*) and *Sue Cat.*[20] One might see it as the becoming-meta of idols, or almost a grand parody of the drama of idol anime. The dark

---

[19] In the climatic scene of *Long Goodbye*, Pino, a messenger from the magical ship Feather Star, tells Yū that if she does not tell anyone that she can use magic, then it is hers to use forever. Yū rejects Pino's offer, responding that there is no reason to hide if the power of magic is truly wonderful and everyone is happy with it.

[20] This was an entry in the series World Masterpiece Theater, founded after the success of *Heidi, Girl of the Alps* (1974). Sarah, daughter of a wealthy family who entered boarding school in Britain, becomes a servant after her father's death and family's financial ruin. The story depicts the bullying of Sarah by her former teachers and classmates, which resonated with the situation in Japan, where bullying was coming to be recognized as a social problem.

worldview has its own appeal as a caricature of the light and darkness that we all imagine in the entertainment industry. Perhaps because *Eriko* was so hard-edged, the idol anime that followed back off,[21] including *Idol Angel Yokoso Yōko*, which caught people's attention with its bright and happy drama and stark contrast to *Eriko*. Tanaka Yōko, who comes to Tokyo on a steam train from the countryside to become an idol, meets and befriends Yamamori Saki, who wants to be an actress. The story is about the two young women following their dreams, in turn cheering for and competing with one another. The protagonist Yōko does not carry the dark side that heroines in idol anime had up to this point. She is notable as the first cute-dopy (*tennen-kei*) character, which is distinct from past idols in anime.

Both *Eriko* and *Yōko* took up the media mix, but, unlike other idol anime, the protagonists had the same names as newly debuted idols. That is, the real idol not only shares a singing voice and song list with the fictional idol character, but also a name. However, unlike *Mami* and *Emi*, their speaking voices are provided by professional actresses.[22] Though we do not see much of her on TV these days, Tamura Eriko was once called the next Miyazawa Rie and became the topic of much discussion with the release of a calendar featuring erotic photos of her. She was certainly an idol of some sort when *Idol Legend Eriko* aired on TV. Tanaka Yōko, the namesake of *Yōko*, was also an idol, but soon ran into trouble with her production agency, made a dramatic announcement of her retirement, and left the entertainment world with a fiction-like picture of perfection.

It might be surprising, but if we compare the real idols that provided their names for these two anime and the fictional idol characters themselves, the latter are the more popular. The existence of virtual idols that exceeded the real person in terms of popularity is clear from the record of fanzines (*dōjinshi*). While *Eriko* fans produced a number of fanzines, including the famous *POYOYON* by Amagi Kei and his circle Eriru Dō, *Yōko* fans showed even more excitement. Even though the real Tanaka Yōko had not released a solo photo album, the sign of an idol's fan base, Tanaka Yōko the anime character did release a "photo album" (actually an illustration book) titled *Tanaka Yōko Photo Book High!*, which was a fanzine by Morino Usagi's circle System Gizzy. The different fates of real idols (Tamura Eriko and Tanaka Yōko) and their

---

[21] Similar to the way that *Invincible Steel Man Daitarn 3* (*Muteki kōjin daitān 3*, 1978-1979) backed off after the hard and hot drama of *Invincible Super Man Zambot 3* (*Muteki chōjin zanbotto 3*, 1977-1978).

[22] Eriko is voiced by Yashima Akiko, and Yōko by Kanai Mika.

anime idol characters (Tamura Eriko and Tanaka Yōko) is symbolic of the 1990s, when real idols were in decline and anime idols were on the rise. To put it another way, idols could only be successful as fiction. Perhaps the rawness or fleshy reality of idols had become an obstacle, but it is nonetheless ironic that the media mix strategy to prolong an idol's life by translating her into the world of animation accelerated the disappearance of actual idols, as well as the becoming-meta of idols in the real world.

The Evolutionary Vector of Meta-Idols

Once a month, deep in confinement, Tamahime Princess' spasms occur...
From the central nervous system, moving to the uterus, hundreds of
thousands of horse power of destructive force...Mystery, mystery—a
mysterious phenomenon!

As seen in the video of her live performance at Laforet in Harajuku in 1984, Togawa Jun's sensibility is caustic and even somewhat neurotic. In contrast to Nomiya Maki, a member of Pizzicato Five, who kept a low profile because of her awkwardness and lack of fashion sense but flourished as an idol in the 1990s, Togawa Jun hit the ground running and had incredible momentum from the time of her debut. Togawa thrived in her environment and made it by herself. She had a unique position as a woman in the indies rock scene, but nevertheless appeared in stereotypical 1970s idol costumes and sang lyrics such as "love, love, I love you," thereby appropriating the idol, which existed only as a symbol. This appropriation came with a twist. In the video for "Tamahimesama," Togawa performs in different costumes for each song, changing from a shrine maiden to an insect to an elementary school student (complete with a yellow hat and traditional backpack). It is all too clear that, for Togawa, the *bishōjo* that her male fans desire is an object of ridicule. Operating from the world of indies, Togawa's performance of idol-ness hit the nail on the head. Her performance was, paradoxically, only effective insofar as idols could, at least possibly, remain as idols, which is to say in the 1980s.

A year after Togawa Jun's powerful performance, in December 1985, out of the blue, Koizumi Kyōko released a new single titled "Idol All the Way" (*Nantettatte aidoru*). The song contains lyrics such as "I can't stop being an idol" (*aidoru wa yamerarenai*), which reveals the awareness of Koizumi, herself an idol, of the objectification of idols. This marks a moment when the comprehensive structure of idols was deconstructed, turning "idol" into an attribute or pure sign. As a complete idol, from the top of her head to the tips of her toes, deconstructed, Koizumi Kyōko had to abandon being an idol. Her title changed to "artist," she became the "queen of TV commercials," and finally she sank into the sea of subculture. When an idol knows that she is an idol, the critique launched by Togawa Jun loses its power and she must become something else.

The year 1985 also saw the birth of Onyanko Kurabu (Kitty Cat Club), a massive group of idols produced out of the raw materials of normal girls, neighborhood high-school girls dressed up to appear as idols, which shook the significance of "idols" as a sign to its core. The last blow to idols came in 1986 with the tragic suicide of Okada Yukiko, "the last orthodox idol." These events ushered in an era when idols could no longer survive, whether at the psychic or physical level. What followed was parody and celebration of fabrication. For example, Moritaka Chisato, who debuted in 1987, sang the song "Stress" (1989) wearing a costume that made her look like a plastic doll. She then performed her infamous "anti-ability declaration" (*hijitsuryoku-ha sengen*) and was picked up and played with as an actual doll by Taku Hachirō, thereby drawing attention to the constructed attributes of "idol" and, in the process, erasing the un-ironic existence of the "idol."[23]

In the entertainment world, idols have become self-aware and meta. The existence of "everyone's idol" (*minna no aidoru*) has disappeared, which leaves us with idols breaking down into specific attributes to target narrow subsets of idol fans.[24] It was at this time that we observed the birth of Artemis Promotion[25] and the beginning of so called "underground

---

[23] TN: Taku Hachirō famously also performed a parody of the otaku, which was taken seriously by the media, much as Moritaka had parodied the idol. For more on Taku, see Ōtsuka Eiji, "Otaku Culture as 'Conversion Literature'," in *Debating Otaku in Contemporary Japan: Historical Perspectives and New Horizons*, ed. Patrick W. Galbraith, Thiam Huat Kam and Bjoern-Ole Kamm (London: Bloomsbury, 2015), xiii-xxix. For more on Moritaka, see Patrick W. Galbraith, "Idols: The Image of Desire in Japanese Consumer Capitalism," in *Idols and Celebrity in Japanese Media Culture*, ed. Patrick W. Galbraith and Jason G. Karlin (London: Palgrave, 2012), 185-208.

[24] However, I am keeping an eye on Matsu'ura Aya, who recognizes herself to be an "idol" and performs with the aim of being "everyone's idol."

[25] The company became legendary for producing Mizuno Aoi, the last idol who performed as an idol. Entertainment personalities associated with Artemis Promotion all pursued an "idol-like" image, for example wearing frilled skirts, and gained enthusiastic followers. However, while writing this book, I was informed that "Artemis Promotion will permanently suspend activity on June 27, 2004." Artemis Promotion consistently pursued the traditional idol, which has declined in the mainstream. Their efforts even involved underground and online idols. The end of Artemis Promotion demonstrates this chapter's conclusion about the "complete disappearance of idols."

idols" (*chika aidoru*).[26] At a time when idols were denied by the general public, producers realized that those who still prefer them had a rather unique taste. By responding to the demands of otaku, idols have subdivided themselves into ever more specific performers—catering to small audiences at live houses, disappearing into the darkness of spaces tucked away beneath office buildings and family restaurant.

Idol Attributes Becoming Chaotic

Idol attributes, now recognized as an expression of *bishōjo*, or cute girl characters, appeared in anime, especially comedy and parody, during the 1990s. In *Cat Ninja Legend Teyandē* (*Kyattō ninden teyandē*, 1990-1991), heroines Omitsu and Bururun, the only female members of the secret team Nyanki, form an idol unit called Mipple and sing in the series. The heroine of *NG Knight Ramune & 40* (*NG kishi ramune & 40*, 1990-1991) was voiced by Yokoyama Chisa, who sang the first ending theme song. After that, the new ending theme was sang by not only Yokoyama, but also two other voice actresses. Together, these three actresses provided the voices for the "three maiden sisters"—Milk, Cocoa and Leska—who together make up "Cafe au Lait."

Given these trends, Ashi Production, the makers of *Idol Legend Eriko* and *Idol Angel Yōkoso Yōko*, could not stay silent. In contrast to their previous two works, which used new idols, their third idol anime, *Idol Defense Force Hummingbird* (*Aidoru bōeitai hamingubādo*, an OVA series released between 1993 and 1996), featured the idol unit Hummingbird, comprised of the five *bishōjo* characters in the series. Utilizing the media mix strategy, the five voice actresses for the idol characters also formed a unit called Hummingbird in the real world and performed live. In the virtual world of the anime, set in the near future, the self-defense forces have been privatized and merged with the entertainment industry, resulting in new concepts such as the idol fighter pilot. The five Toriishi sisters form the unit Hummingbird to join the military-entertainment industry and fulfill their parents' dream. They face various obstacles from the military and entertainment worlds, including competition with rivals such as the Fever

---

[26] Around the mid-to-late 1990s, idol groups such as Minami Aoyama Shōjo Kagekidan and Seifuku Kōjō l'inkai were forced to scale back their activities, moving from large public halls to smaller live houses. It was at this time that the term "underground idol" came into use. Though records of these underground performances are limited, there are no shortage of legends and rumors. For example, a group called "Cutie Lemon" appeared on stage in school uniforms and loose socks, the costume of "compensated dating" *(enjo kōsai)*, or stripped down to gym shorts. Underground idols tend to work individually rather than in groups, and are close to online idols. TN: For more on underground idols, see Chapter 9 in this volume.

Girls, but they continue to fight to win the coveted Japan Pilot Award. Not only is the story of *Hummingbird* the direct descendant of *Sue Cat*, but the connections between the military and entertainment, fighter planes and idols, brings to mind *Super Dimensional Fortress Macross.*[27] *Hummingbird* ends with a punchline that Petol, the enemy character, is just a crazed idol fan. Compared to *Idol Legend Eriko* and *Idol Angel Yōkoso Yōko*, there is a clear division of the main theme of *Hummingbird* into "idols" and "pilots." Idols are not ultimately necessary for the story, but rather are an attribute expected to function as a keyword. Ashi Production's idol anime series, which had started to regain the absoluteness of idols with *Eriko* and *Yōko*, threw themselves at the feet of the symbolism of idols in the real world.

However, the idol unit Hummingbird, comprised of five voice actresses in the real world, gained more meaning with the subsequent start of the voice actor boom (*seiyū būmu*) in the 1990s. The voice actor boom, which reverberates in voice actor magazines, is easy to understand if we conceptualize it as the result of otaku desiring "voice actor type idols" (*seiyū-kei aidoru*). Voice actor type idols operate at the level of "voice" (*koe*), which is to say that they occupy a position with a high degree of unreality. Rather than idols with real female bodies (*namami no josei*), otaku, on first meeting these idols, associate them with the world of anime, which feels familiar. That is, the voice actor type idol has her attributes determined by anime. While the idolization of voice actors is commonly seen among male otaku, there is clearly a similar dynamic at work with female fans of male voice actors—for example, those of the idol group NG5 from *Ronin Warriors* (*Yoroiden samurai torūpā*, 1988-1989), who rose to fame a few years before the members of Hummingbird.[28] Soon after Hummingbird, however, even the voice actor idol became unstable. The moment is marked by the hit single "Please tell Me, Mr. Sky" ("Oshiete Mr. Sky," 1996), which is sung by Fujisaki Shiori, a heroine from the dating simulation game *Tokimeki Memorial* (1994, released on the Sony PlayStation in 1995). This debut single CD ranked in at number 27 on the Oricon Charts, which suggests that the general population, and

---

[27] TN: Yoshida also mentions *Hummingbird*'s similarities to *Sakura Wars* (*Sakura taisen*), where a troupe of idols known as the Teikoku Kagekidan (Imperial Opera/Shooting Troupe), pilot steam-powered robots to fight threats to the nation, but the series began later, namely as a game released on Sega Saturn in 1996. It would seem, then, that *Hummingbird* influenced *Sakura Wars*, not the other way around.

[28] This group was formed by the voice actors who played the five main Samurai Troopers in *Ronin Warriors*, namely Kusao Takeshi, Takemura Hiroshi, Sasaki Nozomu, Nishimura Tomohiro and Nakamura Daiki. They appeared at live shows in various locations and were popular enough to release their own CD.

not just gamers, were exposed to the name "Fujisaki Shiori," who was a hit singer in Japan. Note that it was not Kingetsu Mami, the actress who voiced Fujisaki Shiori, who made her debut as a singer, but rather Fujisaki Shiori, a fictional character. Following this success, songs sung by anime and game characters (i.e., their voice actors, but often uncredited) have been released one after the other. In the late 1990s, the trend was for virtual idols to avoid any association with voice actors, who were somehow too real.

Entering the new millennium, relations between voice actors, idols and virtual idols became even more complicated. This is exemplified by child idol Segawa Onbu, who is associated with the anime *Ojamajo Doremi* (*Troublesome Witch Doremi*, also *Magical DoReMi*, 1999-2003). This show continued for four years with only minor changes in the title, and each new iteration features an opening theme song by MAHO Dō, a unit comprised of the three voice actors of the main characters Doremi, Hazuki and Aiko. That is, this magical girl show essentially functions as idol anime. The members of MAHO Dō have grown from three to five, including Segawa Onbu, introduced as a popular "child idol" in the series. The voice actor behind Segawa Onbu is Shishido Rumi, who was a major idol when she debuted, but is known as an indie idol, which for her not only means not belonging to a production agency, but also making appearances at the Comic Market as an independent seller. We can observe here the complex knot of relations, with a former top idol becoming a voice actor and playing the role of a super popular child idol. Because Shishido Rumi is active as a member of MAHO Dō in the real world, the relation between virtual and real is made even more chaotic. As we have seen, "idols" in recent anime are the object of parody. In *Ojamajo*, the thinking goes that in a group of *bishōjo*, one should be an idol, with "idol" made even more of a type than in *Hummingbird*. As Segawa Onbu becomes more involved in the story, her character is revealed as an idol; she is characterized as an idol.

The Idol as Sex Object

Sometime around the end of December 1985, a legendary radio show appeared. All of a sudden, on Saturday, past midnight, a voice announced: "*Onīchan* (big brothers) all over Japan, how are you?" So began the radio show "Tonight Smoothly with Cream Lemon" (*Konya wa sotto kurīmu remon*). The voice belonged to Nonomura Ami, the heroine of *Be My Baby* (1984), the first volume of *Cream Lemon*, a legendary series of adult animation produced in Japan.[29] *Be My Baby* is a shocking story. Ami is in love with her stepbrother, Hiroshi, and, even as they realize their forbidden love in sexual union, their mother knocks on the door (and is implied to have walked in on them). No one thought that this kind of story could exist in a medium other than fanzines, but the OVA release of *Cream Lemon* shocked audiences with sex scenes featuring anime-style *bishōjo* characters. When "Tonight Smoothly with Cream Lemon" aired, the second volume of *Cream Lemon* was released under the title *Ami Again* (1985). In the story, Hiroshi is forced by his mother to study abroad in London in an attempt to separate him from Ami, who is left alone. Kawano, a talent agent, sneaks in to steal Ami's lonely heart. Ami gets extremely drunk at a disco, and Kawano rapes her. Without settling anything, Ami nevertheless debuts as an idol.

In the real world, gossip about the sex lives of female entertainers is a common genre of tabloid journalism, which revels in the dark side of the industry. Such articles can be found in sports and evening newspapers as well as gossip, photo and subculture magazines. While there had been works featuring virtual idols that explored the dark side of the entertainment industry in Japan, it was impossible to talk directly about idols and sex, especially in the mainstream, with all of the usual restriction of (sexual) expression. However, in the new genre of adult anime, it was suddenly possible to depict sex scenes. Ami was the first victim, the original "violated or fallen idol" (*okasareru aidoru*). Owing to Ami's popularity, her series was lengthened, which encouraged increasingly dramatic storytelling and the development of mature characters, ironically diminishing its "utility" as an adult anime.[30] Indeed, the Ami series of *Cream Lemon* ends on an extremely serious and sad note, as the pure love story featuring Hiroshi collides with the fallen idol story featuring Kawano.

The release of *Be My Baby* (1984) and *Ami Again* (1985) occurred in a period when the *raison d'etre* of idols was blurring and change was inevitable. As the success of Onyanko Club in 1985 suggests, the existence of an "idol" was not longer that of a far away "sacred being" (*shinsei-na*

[29] In terms of the release date, the very first adult OVA was *Crimson Maquillage/Girl's Rose Punishment (Yuki no beni geshō/Shōjo bara kei,* 1984), a few months before the release of *By My Baby*. However, the character designs were more realistic (approaching the so-called gekiga style) and the popularity of these works did not reach that of the *Cream Lemon* series. Adult anime from Wonder Kids featured anime-style *bishōjo* from the third episode, *"Shop with a Kitten" (Koneko-chan no iru mise,* 1984), which captured the attention of audiences.

[30] The character design of Ami became more and more adult, including an enlargement of her breasts, which became standard for adult animation. However, the style was diverging from what the audience desired, namely their cute little "Ami-chan," drawn in the *bishōjo* style.

sonzai), but rather amateurish, familiar and accessible. A new type of idol (*atarashii aidoru*) was becoming common. In the story, Ami initially appears as a high school girl troubled by forbidden love, which seemed to be setting her up as a new idol, but this was abandoned to transform her into an "idol-like idol" (*aidoru-rashii aidoru*). Putting Ami, a regular high school girl, on a pedestal/stage as an idol, and turning her series into a look at the dark side of the entertainment industry from her eyes, introduced discrepancy between what she became and what the otaku audience wanted—namely, the cute girl next door. In other words, there was a huge gap in terms of the "idol" image of anime producers and audiences. This is a clear harbinger of the collapse of the idol in the late 1980s, even in the world of virtual eros.

Erotic Game Type Idols

In the 1990s, there emerged a medium to take in the negative aspects of virtual idols—erotic games (*erogē*), also known as adult computer games. A masterpiece of erotic games and a record holder for sales, *Classmate 2* (*Dōkyūsei 2*, 1997) features among its cast of female characters one defined as an "idol." Maishima Karen is a super idol who happens to attend the same high school as the protagonist (the playable character). Debuting at the age of eight, Karen commutes to work from her mansion, but is troubled because she does not have time to go to school and no one treats her like a regular girl. The protagonist encounters Karen being forced to do a swimsuit photo shoot against her will. He intervenes and together with Karen escapes to their high school. Karen is delighted to be able to remove the idol mask, return to her normal self and attend high school. The protagonist confesses his love to her on the rooftop and they have sex in the nurse's office. There are two important things to note here: first, the dark side of the entertainment industry, in the form of a forced photo shoot, is an integral part of the plot; and second, sex occurs only after Karen takes off her idol mask in the more "real" setting of high school. The story emphasizes that the protagonist falls in love with his classmate Maishima Karen and not with the idol. "Idol" is certainly the defining characteristic of Maishima Karen, but the game producers decided that the unreality of the idol is not suitable for a sex scene, which cannot occur until the situation is brought closer to reality. It is also necessary for the idol to confess her true thoughts in the dramatic scene. If the normal girl Ami was distanced from her fans by becoming an idol in the *Cream Lemon* series, then it is exactly the opposite in *Classmate 2*, where Karen goes from an idol back to a normal girl. The sex scene needed to occur in pseudo-reality, namely the nurse's office of a familiar high school, which is separated from the darkness of the entertainment industry.

A high point in the history of erotic games—which explored the intersection of the entertainment industry, idols and eros—is *White Album* (1998). In the game, the protagonist/player begins with a kindhearted and devoted girlfriend, Morikawa Yuki, who is an idol. If the player, through his choices, decides to take a route that brings him into relation with other female characters in hopes of having sex, then the player must treat Yuki harshly and coldly. (If the player is nice to her, then events with other characters cannot occur.) In this "cheating type" game, the player is encouraged to check out other girls, but this becomes emotionally difficult when and if the player develops deep emotional attachments to a given character, such as Yuki.[31] The game takes place at the university that the protagonist attends, which means that the story can be completed without introducing the entertainment industry or idols. The presence of Ogata Eiji, president of an entertainment production company, reminds the player of this outside world, but the game itself ultimately starts and ends as a typical novelesque erotic game (though it has few sex scenes). In other words, "the entertainment industry" and "idols" only function to superficially differentiate this game world from others. The film *Perfect Blue* (discussed earlier in the chapter) was released the same year as *White Album* (1998). It seems that virtual idols—who have come to be treated harshly, ignored or thrown away, who are stalked, violated and dumped—are dead and extinct.

Virtual Idols, Forever!

Once again, idols, who seemed to have died and disappeared in all kinds of media, are reborn in the new millennium. Despite their popularity, the revival is not reducible to Morning Musume, who got their start in 1997 by revealing the backstage drama of auditions. Rather, the revival of idols can be traced to the emergence of online idols (*netto aidoru*), who publish content on their own websites. There are basically two types of online idols: those trying to express themselves and those expressing other selves. The first type publishes diaries to share their inner feelings with readers; they stick to natural content in terms of text and photographs. The second type objectifies themselves at the level of gaze and constructs and expresses different selves; cosplayers are the most prominent. The unique unreality

---

[31] The other female characters are a rival idol, manager, *senpai* (senior schoolmate), *kōhai* (junior schoolmate), and a childhood friend. The last three of these are the golden pattern of relational possibility in games such as this one.

and sense of distance provided online, where your cute neighbor can be an idol, is a reflection of a reality where the sender and receiver are one in the same. This was seen throughout the entertainment industry in the mid-1980s, when, for example in Onyanko Kurabu, the difference between amateurs and celebrities was approaching zero. Both types of online idols erase the distance between idols and their audience, and establish themselves without production companies or producers. This is an ideal situation for those interested in avoiding the artificiality of idols.

Disdain for the artificiality of idols signals a shift in the perception and desire of audiences away from fantasy aware of itself as fantasy and toward more "real" fantasy. This shift has consequences that reverberate across the board with producers of idols working in the entertainment, anime and game industries. The trend is to produce the "idol" in a more realistic manner, but when a third party (i.e., producer) intervenes in the process, the audience reacts with anger and scorn. Given these circumstances, special types—such as online idols and voice actors—are receiving more attention.

From their beginnings in TV animation, virtual idols have gone in multiple directions following the segmentation of taste. Finally, they ended up on individual computer screens as erotic game and online idols. Virtual idols used to capture the attention of large audiences, but these audiences broke down into smaller and smaller groupings until they were effectively only individuals. As the taste for virtual reality (*kasō genjitsu*) has segmented, the notion of a virtual idol for everyone has transformed. In other words, "everyone's idol" has become "an idol for everyone." The "idol" has already become an aspect of the subcultural scene. Relentlessly parodied as a meta-discourse permeated the media, the *raison d'etre* of the idol diminished. In the end, even elements of the virtual idol such as the "dark side of the entertainment industry" and "tragedy" also disappeared. Here we see that the beloved and deified "idol" has completely disappeared, even in the virtual world.

Works Cited

Azuma Hiroki, ed. *Mōjō genron F-kai: Posutomodan, otaku, sekushuariti.* Tokyo: Seidōsha, 2003.

Clements, Jonathan. *Anime: A History.* New York: Palgrave, 2013.

Galbraith, Patrick W. "'Otaku' Research and Anxiety about Failed Men." In *Debating Otaku in Contemporary Japan: Historical Perspectives and*

New Horizons, edited by Patrick W. Galbraith, Thiam Huat Kam and Bjoern-Ole Kamm, 21-34. London: Bloomsbury, 2015.

———. "Idols: The Image of Desire in Japanese Consumer Capitalism." In *Idols and Celebrity in Japanese Media Culture*, edited by Patrick W. Galbraith and Jason G. Karlin, 185-208. London: Palgrave, 2012.

Kinsella, Sharon. "Japanese Subculture in the 1990s: *Otaku* and the Amateur *Manga* Movement," *Journal of Japanese Studies* 24, no. 2 (1998): 289-316.

Ōtsuka Eiji. "Otaku Culture as 'Conversion Literature,'" In *Debating Otaku in Contemporary Japan: Historical Perspectives and New Horizons*, edited by Patrick W. Galbraith, Thiam Huat Kam and Bjoern-Ole Kamm, xiii-xxix. London: Bloomsbury, 2015.

———. *"Otaku" no seishin-shi: 1980-nendai-ron*. Tokyo: Kōdansha Gendai Shinsho, 2004.

Saitō Tamaki. *Beautiful Fighting Girl*, translated by J. Keith Vincent and Dawn Lawson. Minneapolis, MN: University of Minnesota Press, 2011.

Sasakibara Gō. *"Bishōjo" no gendaishi: Moe to kyarakutā*. Tokyo: Kōdansha Gendai Shinsho, 2004.

Steinberg, Marc. *Anime's Media Mix: Franchising Toys and Characters in Japan*. Minneapolis, MN: University of Minnesota Press, 2012.

Yoshida Masataka. *Nijigen bishōjo-ron: Otaku no megami sōzōshi*. Tokyo: Futami Shobō, 2004.

Ensoulment and Effacement in Japanese Voice Acting

Shunsuke Nozawa

Introduction

The work of Japanese professional voice actors, or *seiyū*, covers a wide range of texts, events, and media that in various ways contribute to the larger structure of "convergence culture" in Japan or the "media mix."[1] One may encounter this work, often generically and informally referred to as "*koe no shigoto*" (literally, voice work), in such diverse contexts as jingles in radio shows, voiceovers in TV commercials, and announcements on subways and in other public spaces. While the examples just cited are usually uncredited work, *seiyū*'s usually credited work includes anime production (often described as *afureko*, a portmanteau of "after" and "recording," viz. "post"-production recording), videogame production, character-related merchandise such as "character songs," foreign film dubbing, promotional events, fan events, theatrical performance (especially in the style of *rōdokugeki*, a style akin to reader's theater), and radio and internet talk show hosting. These and other instances of voice work address an intersection of voice, technology, and characterization. More direct examples of this intersection include the featuring of *seiyū*'s anime character voices in car navigation systems and, at a deeper level of technical involvement, the development of singing voice synthesizers such as Vocaloids.[2]

While these diverse contexts, conditions, and consequences of voice work in Japan call for more proper description (especially given that scholarly work on voice acting as a distinct topic seems relatively lacking), and the question of how voice and discourses about it in particular are related to issues of affect and communication in the contemporary media ecology in Japan and elsewhere deserves more careful treatment than I

---

[1] For convergence culture see Henry Jenkins, *Convergence Culture: Where Old and New Media Collide* (New York: New York University Press, 2006). For media mix, see Marc Steinberg, *Anime's Media Mix: Franchising Toys and Characters in Japan* (Minneapolis, MN: University of Minnesota Press, 2012).

[2] For Vocaloids, see Ian Condry, "Miku: Japan's Virtual Idol and Media Platform," MIT Center for Civic Media, July 11, 2011 accessed January 23, 2015, http://civic.mit.edu/blog/condry/miku-japans-virtual-idol-and-media-platform. For car navigation systems "characterized" through voice work, see—, for example—, the following sites: http://lei-kirishima.jp/ and http://maplus-navi.jp/index/voice.

could give in this chapter, my discussion here is more limited in scope. I would like to offer a preliminary sketch of the culture of voice acting. I hope to show voices as potent semiotic objects in the context of "character-centric" Japanese convergence culture. Of particular interest to this sketch is the subcultural metaphor for *seiyū* as *"naka no hito"* (person inside) and its ritualized instantiation as *"naka no hito nado inai!"* (no way there's a person inside!). I examine how this metaphor informs and is informed by *seiyū*'s own discourses about voice acting, their "native" theorization. I particularly pay heed to these reflexive discourses as they emerge from radio shows—a fact which will interest us later. It is as though radio constitutes *seiyū*'s natural habitat.[3]

The metaphor of *naka no hito* frames *seiyū* as mediators or *mediums* of the character-driven convergence culture. It conjures up an imagination of the *verge*, where reality and fantasy meet but never merge. As subcultural participants often say, *seiyū* are seen as inhabiting an interstitial dimension between "3D" reality and "2D" fantasy—"2.5D." *Seiyū* are mediums on the verge. They are enchanters of convergence, relaying characters' voices to fans and animating characters' bodies in narratives and events. They are an interface between different forms of media, between fans and characters. And as I argue below, they imbue their voice with this mediating capacity through techniques of "becoming-inside," of effacing and encasing themselves "inside" their characters. To anticipate my discussion below, I argue that this work of *effacement* is closely tied to a logic of *ensoulment*. Thomas Lamarre's discussion of characterization and thus character "design" in "limited animation" as generative of "soulful bodies"—"bodies where spiritual, emotional or psychological qualities appear inscribed on the surface"—is particularly helpful to my argument here, motivating the question of how, indeed, characters get ensouled. The task of this chapter is to initiate ethnographic discussion of voice acting and its contribution

---

[3] For character-centrism see Hiroki Azuma, *Otaku: Japan's Database Animals*, trans. Jonathan E. Abel and Shion Kono (Minneapolis, MN: University of Minnesota Press, 2009); and Patrick W. Galbraith, "Moe and the Potential of Fantasy in Post-Millennial Japan," *Electronic Journal of Contemporary Japanese Studies*, October 31, 2009, http://www.japanesestudies.org.uk/articles/2009/Galbraith.html. Radio has always been of practical importance to *seiyū* as workplace. And in terms of its historical importance as well, the online and televisual coverage of the 8th Annual Seiyū Awards, held on March 1, 2014, opened with a statement that included the following assertion: "The culture of *seiyū* was born about 80 years ago upon the commencement of radio broadcasting" (http://seiyuawards.jp/201402/18130500.php). For a sociopolitical history of how radio and other communicative technologies have organized phonosonic encounter in modern Japan, see Kerim Yasar, "Electrified Voices: Media Technology and Discourse in Modern Japan" (PhD diss., Columbia University, 2009).

to media convergence by linking the "becoming-inside" of *seiyū* to the "becoming-ensouled" of characters.[4]

Before delving into my main discussion, let me introduce some of the conceptual distinctions to be further illuminated in the rest of the chapter.

Theoretical Framework

This chapter is partly experimental in that it proposes that we deliberately resist the analytic framework of "embodiment" and "performance" in our theorization of voice and acting. We seem to have been rather thoroughly inculcated into these and other related anthropocentric notions. In proposing this, I am informed directly by Teri Silvio's theorization of "animation" as a concept that is distinct from, and as worthy of critical attention for its historicity as, "performance." I will return to "animation" shortly, but here let us note how Silvio explains the relative ineffectiveness of idioms of "performance" in her research on remediation in Taiwanese cosplay. The anthropologist invokes an ethnographic encounter:

> [W]hen I started doing fieldwork with the producers and fans of a popular video puppetry series in 2002 [in Taiwan, *Pili*], I kept running into places where the concept of performance just didn't help. For instance, I found that standard questions which had elicited detailed stories and explanations from opera actresses and their fans [with whom she had worked in her previous research on Taiwanese folk opera]—questions like, "How do you get into character?"—made no sense at all to fans who were cosplaying puppet characters.[5]

Silvio's initial question about relations of identity, one informed by the embodied unity (or "lamination") of performer and character, turned out to be, ethnographically speaking, the wrong question to pose to these cosplayers. Their aloofness prompted the anthropologist to rethink

---

[4] Thomas Lamarre, *The Anime Machine: A Media Theory of Animation* (Minneapolis, MN: University of Minnesota Press, 2009), 184-208, 201. For 2.5D, see Galbraith, "Moe and the Potential of Fantasy in Post-Millennial Japan;" and Patrick W. Galbraith, "Maid in Japan: An Ethnographic Account of Alternative Intimacy," *Intersections: Gender, History and Culture in the Asian Context* 25 (February 2011), http://intersections.anu.edu.au/issue25/galbraith.htm. Discussion of "effacement" presented in this chapter is partially informed by my earlier treatment in Shunsuke Nozawa, "The Gross Face and Virtual Fame: Semiotic Mediation in Japanese Virtual Communication," *First Monday* 17, no. 3 (March 5, 2012), doi: 10.5210/fm.v17i3.3535; and Shunsuke Nozawa, "Characterization," *Semiotic Review* 3 (November 5, 2013), http://www.semioticreview.com/index.php/open-issues/issue-open-2013/21-characterization.

[5] Teri Silvio, "Animation: The New Performance?" *Journal of Linguistic Anthropology* 20, no. 2 (2010): 423.

critically the pervasiveness of performance and embodiment in scholarly and popular language, which had led her to formulate the question this way in the first place. With this rethinking, she was able to redesign her questions to better understand the practice from within the analytic framework constructed by the practitioners themselves. Silvio argues that these cosplayers' own understanding is better approached in terms of "animation"—"a range of technologies and skills that are used to create the 'illusion of life'"—the process of "'breathing life' into a thing" that, as its necessary condition, creates a complex *gap* or "layering" between actors (here, cosplayers) and characters, the animator and the animated.[6]

The case of Vocaloids, like Hatsune Miku, may be productively seen as analogous to Silvio's cosplayers in this vein. It would be rather ludicrous, or analytically rather uninspiring, to speak of Fujita Saki, the *naka no hito* (*seiyū*) who contributed voice samples to the program's phonic library, as an actor who "performs" Miku. In this instance, we must rather ask how Fujita's voice helps "animate" Miku precisely because of—not despite—its disembodiment. Rather than relations of embodiment, what matters are relations of disembodiment, control, operation, and play distributed across different actors, including Fujita as well as a massive number of users and fans who together generate the culture of convergence around Miku.[7]

We may perhaps go one step further in this analogy to suggest that Vocaloids in fact encapsulate something of the essence of voice acting, not least because the empirical reality of *seiyū* work points rather plainly to Vocaloid-like practical and technical processes. While Vocaloids may perhaps represent an extreme in the mode of disembodiment, it is quite literally the case that *seiyū* live disembodiment every day as a matter of professional labor. Their artistic virtuosity derives from the *skills* with which they disengage their voice from their body, and their work is thoroughly mediated by *technological* apparatuses, most notably the microphone. This should at least invite us to complicate our commonsensical idea that sees the acousmatized split between character and actor, between voice and body, as an injury and a source

---

[6] *Ibid.*, 425-426. I borrow the contrast between "lamination" and "layering" from Alaina Lemon's ethnography of a Moscow theatre academy, GITIS: "I prefer the image of 'layering' over 'lamination' to describe this aesthetic value, whereby theatrical practitioners at GITIS aim not to reconcile difference from the other, to 'become the character,' but first to *disarticulate* the other's 'then-and-there' from the actor's 'here-and-now'" (Alaina Lemon, "Sympathy for the Weary State?: Cold War Chronotopes and Moscow Others," *Comparative Studies in Society and History* 51, no. 4 (2009): 845). For "layering," see also Lamarre, *The Anime Machine*; and Erving Goffman, *Frame Analysis: An Essay on the Organization of Experience* (New York: Harper & Row, 1974).

[7] The "ludicrousness" or laughableness of the performance interpretation in this instance often figures as a *joke* in subcultural milieus. See Nozawa, "Characterization."

of anxiety caused by technology against the background of which organic and psychological repair becomes an object of desire. Rather than unwittingly following what Mary Bucholtz describes as our presupposed "ideological project of vocal reattachment, anchoring the voice to socially definable embodied subjects," I believe a closer look at the practitioners' reflexive discourse of voice acting will reveal a different ideological project, one in which the dislocation of voice is the practical condition of its possibility.[8]

While we note that "performance" and "animation" do not neatly map onto empirical boundaries but rather participate in complex interactions in practice (as Silvio herself suggests), in this present discussion I would like to purposefully exaggerate the difference for the sake of conceptual experimentation. What new insights would we be able to gain from voice acting if our analysis consciously puts into question terms like embodiment and performance and the live-theatrical or oratorical humanism these notions presuppose? What if we refashion our usual habit of talking about actors as "performing" characters, a habit very much informed by the identitarian language of "people performing identities?"[9]

Following the foregoing discussion, I would like to make another experimental move to suggest that we consider voice acting, like Vocaloids as well as puppetry and ventriloquism, as a sociotechnical hybrid embedded in imaginaries and techniques of what Victoria Nelson calls "ensoulment"—"practices of en-souling matters." Again following Silvio, I use the idea of ensoulment to refer to processes of "animation" that distribute and project life-forces, *anima*, onto various types of actants. The "matters" of ensoulment that concern us in this chapter, however, are characters, the empty body of a character that encloses a "person-inside." How do characters acquire anima? How do they become "soulful"? How does a shell long for a ghost?[10]

It makes eminent sense to explore ensoulment in this instance not least because *idioms of spiritualism* are widely distributed in Japanese popular culture more generally.[11] I have just made a reference to *Ghost in*

---

[8] Mary Bucholtz, "Race and the Re-Embodied Voice in Hollywood Film," *Language & Communication* 31, no. 3 (2011): 256.

[9] One anonymous reviewer cautioned that this line of thinking may unwittingly invite an unproductive, dichotomous view, and I appreciate this feedback.

[10] Victoria Nelson, *The Secret Life of Puppets* (Cambridge, MA: Harvard University Press, 2003), 30; and Silvio, "Animation," 426.

[11] See, for example, Laura Miller, "Extreme Makeover for a Heian-Era Wizard," *Mechademia* 3, no. 1 (2008); Hirofumi Katsuno, "The Robot's Heart: Tinkering with Humanity and Intimacy in Robot-Building," *Japanese Studies* 31, no. 1 (2011): 93-109; and Michael Dylan Foster, *Pandemonium and Parade: Japanese Monsters and the Culture of Yōkai* (Berkeley: University of California Press, 2011).

the Shell, but ideas such as "spirit," "possession" and "summoning" figure prominently as narrative resource in many manga, videogames, and anime works along with the fabulously dense intertextual references to magic and myth. Perhaps most obvious in "magical girls" and "horror" genres, they are however observed in genres and media forms across the board: from *Neon Genesis Evangelion* (1995-1996) to *Hikaru no Go* (2001-2003), from *Digital Devil Story* (1987, 1995) to *Natsume's Book of Friends* (2005-), from *Spirited Away* (2001) to *Shugo Chara!* (2006-2009). The spiritual idioms also offer artists a way of theorizing characterization. In a TV interview Araki Hirohiko, author of manga works such as *Jojo's Bizarre Adventure* and *Baoh*, once remarked that it is when a character's mouth is drawn that the character comes to life.[12] On the other hand, artists and fans also speak more abstractly of "putting a spirit in a character." (More generally, Japanese speakers use the phrase "putting a spirit [in some container]" in a variety of contexts.) It is in such abstract spiritual terms that, for example, fans of MikuMikuDance (MMD), a freeware 3D-model animation program, praise a well-made MMD character as being "with a spirit already equipped" (*tamashii jissōzumi*)—that is, as if an animating spirit is already bundled together with the software right out of the box.[13]

In what follows, two general points will animate my discussion. First, our commonsensical idea that actors give voices to characters merits reconsideration. Not that it is incorrect. Obviously, it is humans who do the speaking. Rather, I suggest an alternative idea, which, while maybe absurd, will help us better understand the relation between voice and spirit. The idea may be summed up by Bruno Latour's commentary on ventriloquism: "we, the human subjects, are the *dummies* toward which other entities are projecting their real voices *as if* they were coming *from us*" (emphasis in the original).[14] Second, my discussion will revolve around the logic of effacement and the duality it indexes—a façade that seems to hide

---

[12] Araki Hirohiko, interview by Funakoshi Eiichirō, *Shūkan Shōnen Kagikakko* (Fuji TV CS), April 15, 2003. It is safe to assume that what empirically counts as ensoulment is itself highly variable across cultures, genres, artists, and even contexts. In her ethnography of Belgian puppetry Joan Gross reports: "A puppeteer told me that Liège puppets have hearts like humans because they are made of logs which were living trees. The core (*coeur*) of the tree remains the heart of the puppet." See Joan Gross, *Speaking in Other Voices: An Ethnography of Walloon Puppet Theaters* (Philadelphia: John Benjamins, 2001), 120.

[13] The phrase first originated in viewer comments on an MMD video posted on Niconico (http://www.nicovideo.jp/watch/sm7525588); see also http://dic.nicovideo.jp/a/%E9%AD%82%E5%AE%9F%E8%A3%85%E6%B8%88%E3%81%BF.

[14] Bruno Latour, "Forward: Who is Making the Dummy Speak?" in *Action and Agency in Dialogue: Passion, Incarnation and Ventriloquism*, ed. François Cooren (Amsterdam: John Benjamins, 2010), xiii-xvi.

something, a mask that divides its interior and exterior. But my point will be that voice acting involves a strange mask that does not produce a secret nor a desire for spectacular revelation; the *seiyū*'s face is not a secret, and yet it is effectively effaced by characters, *personae*. Rather than spectacles, voice acting makes possible an art of going unnoticed, a counter-spectacular art. It protects the dignity of the one who says, like Herman Melville's Bartleby and one of the *seiyū* discussed below, "I would prefer not to be seen."

Effacement-work: *Naka no Hito* and *Maiku Mae*

The metaphor of *naka no hito*, highly stylized and emblematic of the subculture, sees *seiyū*—like costumed performers—occupying a space "inside" the character. Or to put it the other way around, the idiom configures the character as an outer structure with a hollow interior, like the "body" of a violin or the air columns of an aerophonic instrument. While such a spatial metaphor is not foreign to English ("getting *into* character"), this Japanese subcultural idiom exhibits a different configuration of meaning. Most interestingly, the topology of *naka no hito* is itself metaphorically linked to actions and entities having apparently nothing to do with voice or acting. For example, people sometimes use the metaphor to talk about an operator of a machine, an administrator of a website, or a staff member that works for a company. The official Twitter account holder of the public relations division of NHK (Japan's public broadcasting company) is characterized as the account's *"naka no hito."*[15]

Irreducible to terms of embodied representation, the metaphor encompasses acts of mechanic operation and institutional delegation as well. In his analysis of character merchandising Marc Steinberg aptly suggests that "character" is a "connective technology" of socioeconomic circulation in the context of "media mix" convergence. Following his suggestion, then, we might say that *seiyū* are skillful operators of this technology who animate its connectivity, like the "pilot" in the post-*Mazinger Z* mecha/robot genre who operates a robotic body from within.[16]

The metaphor of *naka no hito* apprehends *seiyū* and characters in a relation of enclosure. It is noteworthy that *seiyū* often describe the

---

[15] Note, further, this account holder is not an anthropomorphic but roboticized figure—with a *serial number*. See NHK PR 1-gō, *Naka no hito nado inai @ NHK kōhō no Tweet wa naze yurui?* (Tokyo: Shinchōsha, 2012). One online glossary suggests more concretely that the phrase *naka no hito* refers to indexical role-inhabitance: "someone taking up a particular role" (http://d.hatena.ne.jp/keyword/%C3%E6%A4%CE%BF%CD).

[16] Marc Steinberg, "Anytime, Anywhere: Tetsuwan Atomu Stickers and the Emergence of Character Merchandizing" *Theory, Culture & Society* 26, no. 2-3 (2009): 5.

place of their work as *maiku mae* ("in front of the microphone"), ie., the sound studio. They habitually engage the technological mediation of the microphone (and related technologies of amplification and editing) as well, it should be noted, as the script, a text-artifact. Quite in contrast to the stereotypic image of oratorical openness associated, certainly in the US with authoritative public speakers and performers ("speaking without a script"), the stereotypic image of a *seiyū* at work depicts the actor holding the script in one hand and flipping the pages with another, speaking into or "in front of" the microphone with their gaze going back and forth between the script and the screen to achieve synchronization.[17]

The enclosed space of *maiku mae*, a space of characterization, is iconic and indexical of *naka no hito*: an actor doubly enclosed. In her autobiography, voice actor Nozawa Masako (whose characters include Hoshino Tetsurō in *Galaxy Express 999* and Son Gokū in *Dragon Ball*) notes that she felt sound studios were "dark," "tiny," and "suffocating" when she first started focusing on "voice work" in her acting career (probably circa 1960). "I had this association with darkness because the studio needed to keep it dim so images could be projected," she says. "In contrast, I had a brighter image for drama studios [for TV and film shootings] because they had lots of lights."[18] Incidentally, this contrast recalls counter-spectacularity in "maid cafés," a space of characterization, as perceptively analyzed by Patrick W. Galbraith: "unlike the myriad reflective surfaces found in hostess clubs, there are no mirrors in a maid café, both literally and figuratively, and visitors do not see themselves."[19]

While *seiyū*'s bodies are necessarily effaced in the narrative text in which their characters appear, the force of effacement-work lingers on even when they are in public. At promotional events for anime

---

[17] See, for example, some of the images in the following pages (note these are all taken from official blogs for *seiyū* vocational schools): http://school.athuman.com/132430/archives/21229.html, http://yoanisapporo.blog49.fc2.com/blog-entry-1576.html, http://www.amgakuin.co.jp/contents/animation/blog/?p=913. In a neoliberal wonderland, speaking without a script ("your own voice") produces value of various sorts while such valorization is haunted by its own ideology of technology and speech. The use of a teleprompter in American politics, for example, motivates an anxiety over the dream of self-regulating, responsible speech in public. And in private too, as seen in this *The Onion* report on a telling (non-)incident: http://www.theonion.com/video/obamas-home-teleprompter-malfunctions-during-famil,14383/.

[18] Nozawa Masako, *Boku wa seiyū* (Tokyo: Opt Communications, 1995), 54.

[19] Galbraith, "Maid in Japan." Another directly pertinent analogy may be made to the sociotechnical environment that led pianist Glenn Gould to rely exclusively on studio recording for his work (and to the thick layers of clothing that enveloped his body).

productions where *seiyū* are often asked to "do the voice" of their character for the audience, diverse forms of effacement-work are routinely observed: showing their back to the audience, shielding their face with an image of the character, asking the audience to close their eyes, etc. Such moments of effacement are also a function of the general *mise-en-scène* of these events. These events often include "on-stage" reenactments of the studio recording (*afureko*). Variations permitted, the reenactment typically involves the cast lined up on stage, each standing in front of his or her microphone and holding a script (often in such a way that the text obstructs the audience's view of their face), *à la* readers theater; behind them is a giant screen on which a clip from the anime is projected. The projected image gets primary visual attention of the audience. The *seiyū* usually receive only dim lighting during the enactment, removing them from the audience's clear visual access while giving them sufficient light for their reading.

On a recent radio show Sugita Tomokazu and Hayami Saori briefly touch on this sensibility to effacement. Sugita plays Sakurai Ruka, the main "target" character in *Tokimeki Memorial Girls' Side 3rd Story*, a dating simulation game produced by Konami. He says that he "deeply appreciates the philosophy" held by Uchida Akari, the game's producer. Sugita suggests that for Uchida the gap between "characters" and "*seiyū*" is so crucial that he often sets up promotional events in such a way that *seiyū* do not directly "perform" their game characters. In turn Hayami, who plays Takamine Manaka in the *LovePlus* series, another popular dating sim produced by Uchida, corroborates Sugita's statement by providing a concrete example: "At *LovePlus* events, I have never appeared on stage as myself," she says. "I provide the voice from behind a screen."[20]

Another example to demonstrate the same point: character songs, or *kyarason*. One concrete manifestation of the Japanese media mix character merchandising, *kyarason* are marketed as songs sung in the voice *and the name* of a particular anime/videogame character; they are stipulated to be a sign indexing *not* the *seiyū* who plays the character but the character. For example, the packaging (e.g., CD cover design) of *kyarason* created for the vastly popular anime *K-on!* displays only the character names. More generally, *seiyū* names are often *enclosed* in parenthesis: [Character Name] (CV. [*Seiyū* Name]); "CV" refers to "character voice." As voice actor Satō Satomi, who has worked on *kyarason* for many anime titles including *K-on!*, put it in an interview, crucial to the creative process of *kyarason* is

---

[20] "Hayami Saori no Free Style" 143, JOQR Chō! A&G+ (Tokyo: Bunka Hōsō, December 24, 2013).

the recognition that "characters and narratives already exist" *kyarakutā toka sakuhin ga ariki*) and the "work of eliminating the [singer-actor's own] self" (*jibun o kesu sagyō*).[21]

More commonly, when expected or forced to "perform" their character in public, voice actors tend to rely on the existing lines of the character, instead of "speaking" freely in the character voice. These lines are verbal masks, an object of dense ritualization, usually clearly demarcated by reflexive cues (what John Gumperz called "contextualization cues"), such as "Here we go" or a subtle postural pause that induces a momentary silence from the audience.[22] The use of such fixed texts in an event cues participants to a fantasy frame. That is, participants are invited in such an instance to apprehend actors as being separable from and inside of their characters, "operating" them from behind the mask. The virtuosity with which *seiyū* accomplish such a complex movement "into" and "out" of the characters is often the object of fans' praise. This is well demonstrated by one fan-created compilation video uploaded on Niconico, a Japanese video-hosting site. The pseudonymous video producer, a *seiyū* enthusiast, collects various *seiyū* appearances on radio shows that capture the fleeting, sometimes rapid-fire, alternation back and forth between *seiyū*'s "own" voices and their characters' voices. The video aptly describes these two moments as "OFF" and "ON," respectively, as if taking a mask "off" and putting it "on," or switching a technical device "off" and "on." *Seiyū* are "placed in the position of the switchboard."[23]

Two observations may be made from the foregoing examples. First, effacement-work helps produce a gap between actors and characters (and maintains it across different contexts), and this split is seen by practitioners and fans as central and conducive to the pleasure of encountering characters in the media ecology created by and sustaining media convergence.

Second, these examples make it clear that the "true" identity of *naka no hito* is ordinarily not a secret at all in the usual sense of classified,

[21] "Anispa" 516, JOQR Chō! A&G+ (Tokyo: Bunka Hōsō, February 22, 2014). According to *LisAni!*, a multimedia portal for anime music, the first instance of what is now recognized as *kyarason*—sung in the name of a character—may be traced back to the character Otonashi Kyōko in *Maison Ikkoku* (1986), voiced by Shimamoto Sumi. See "History of Character Song," *LisAni!* 10, no. 1 (October 2012): 102-125.

[22] John Gumperz, *Discourse Strategies* (Cambridge, UK: Cambridge University Press, 1982), 131.

[23] See http://www.nicovideo.jp/watch/sm12072787. This video is only one of numerous fan-generated works that creatively reassemble *seiyū*'s voices and recombine them with other phonosonic entities; see Nozawa, "Characterization," fn11. The dense ritualization of character language recalls similar processes in cosplay; see Galbraith, "Moe and the Potential of Fantasy in Post-Millennial Japan"; and Silvio, "Animation," 433. The "switchboard" reference is taken from Steven Connor, "The Machine in the Ghost: Spiritualism, Technology and the 'Direct Voice'," in *Ghosts: Deconstruction, Psychoanalysis, History*, ed. Peter Buse (London: Macmillan, 1999), 215.

confidential information—unlike the *naka no hito* of Mickey Mouse at Disneyland, or in the psychoanalytic sense of repression or interdiction. The dialectic of depth and surface, truth and revelation, repression and symptom—none of this is at issue here. Rather, the truth of identity is made elaborately *irrelevant* through effacement-work for the sake of appreciating *seiyū*'s aesthetic effort to give characters *sui generis* realness. The often-expressed claim that anime fans feel disillusioned by the face of voice actors playing their favorite characters is analytically of little value in understanding effacement as a patterned practice, it misleadingly glosses over different kinds of "fans," and it is quite often factually false. When fans utter the ritualized collocation *naka no hito nado inai!* ("No way there's a person inside!"), this is framed as playful because it is obvious to everyone that there *is* a "person inside." To put it in another way, *seiyū*'s work involves an art of going unnoticed through which they achieve a particular kind of *nobodyness* without becoming a secret in our usual sense, that is, without being desired as an object of spectacular revelation and representational salvage. This is an act of hiding whose accomplishment renders the usual denunciation, "You must have something (bad) to hide," rather ineffective or irrelevant to both the execution and interpretation of the act.[24]

A subtler perspective on the nature of pleasure in voice acting for actors as well as fans is presented in the following episode.

Exuding

Voice actors Shintani Ryōko and Kitamura Eri were called upon as guest hosts for the June 12, 2009 episode of the online radio show *Radio Kusarikake*, replacing the show's regular hosts who had a scheduling conflict on that day. Shintani and Kitamura are both very skilled *seiyū*, starring in a countless number of anime, videogames, and drama CDs.

---

[24] *Seiyū*'s effacement-work may be productively compared to a perhaps relatively lesser-known Victorian phenomenon of the so-called "hidden mother" photographs. See Linda Fregni Nagler, *The Hidden Mother* (London: Mack, 2013). The publisher's notes on Nagler's compilation describe these photographs as "examples of a now redundant practice: to cloak or hide a parent within the background of a child's portrait, a common procedure from the advent of photography up until the 1920s, when exposure times were relatively slow, and a hidden parent was required to hold the child still...The images hold a certain degree of comedy—albeit unintentional—because the viewer is asked to suspend their disbelief, to 'not see' the hidden figure. Some contemporary onlookers would have simply not seen the portrait's hidden mother, indicative of the cultural nature of the act of seeing. For other viewers, the hidden figure was an essential part of the picture: high infant mortality rates meant that posthumous portraits were the norm, and thus the hidden mother would signify to the viewer that this child was alive" (http://www.mackbooks.co.uk/books/1006-The-Hidden-Mother.html). See also, "civil inattention" in Erving Goffman, *Behavior in Public Places: Notes on the Social Organization of Gatherings* (New York: Free Press of Glencoe, 1963), 83-88; and "de-selfing" *(Entselbstung)* in Georg Simmel, "The Secret Society," in *The Sociology of Georg Simmel*, ed. and trans. Kurt H. Wolff (New York: The Free Press, 1950), 373.

But most immediately relevant to our discussion, they are—like Sugita Tomokazu mentioned earlier—known to fans as themselves being deep "otaku," enthusiastic fans of anime, manga, games, and related texts that constitute the general character-centric subculture. They are as much on the production side of otaku culture as they are themselves deep connoisseurs of things subcultural. The episode basically consists of a 40-minute "free talk" (as it would be described in Japanese entertainment culture) between the two actors freely drawing on their subcultural knowledge from both professional and fan perspectives, resulting in a text very much reminiscent of the emblematically otaku discourse genre of *moe-banashi* or "*moe* talk."[25]

Kitamura introduces herself to the audience by explaining how she became interested in voice acting:

> I've been a fan of anime and manga since childhood—I was unable to detach myself from 2D (*datsu-nijigen*). The reason why I wanted to become a *seiyū* is...because, well...I get to see this business from a special perspective, I mean, because I've long known since childhood that there *is* a person inside a 2D character![26]

The intriguing expression *datsu-nijigen*, "de-2D-ification," emphasizes Kitamura's deep immersion in otaku culture since when she was a child. She narrates this immersion through her emphatic twisting of the phrase discussed above: "I've long known that there *is* a person inside a 2D character!" (*naka no hito nado iru!, tte iu koto*). The ease with which this phrase surfaces and is improvised upon in this largely unscripted talk suggests the extent to which it has become part of habitual talk about otaku culture.

For Kitamura, the awareness of *seiyū* as *naka no hito* is not a fantasy-breaker at all. To the contrary, the gap continues to be an invitation to fantasy-making. Shintani chimes in, and in turn shares her own story of becoming-otaku/becoming-*seiyū*. She recalls she liked listening to *Motto! Tokimeki Memorial*, a radio drama version of Konami's classic dating simulation game *Tokimeki Memorial*, although she had at that point not played the game itself. In fact, she was a fan of the radio host, voice actor Tange Sakura. Upon hearing that Shintani entered the subcultural

---

[25] Patrick W. Galbraith, "Fujoshi: Fantasy Play and Transgressive Intimacy among 'Rotten Girls' in Contemporary Japan," *Signs* 37, no. 1 (2011): 222.

[26] "Ryōko to Eri no Rajio Kusarikake," *Radio Kusarikake* 53, Radio Tomo (Tokyo: Power Pop Studio, June 12, 2009).

---

world through *radio* dramas, Kitamura immediately suggests that she was already capable of feeling *moe* (characterological empathy) toward auditory signs without the aid of other immediate sensorial inputs. Kitamura infers that this sensibility to acousmatic relations prefigured Shintani's career as a *seiyū*.

Later on in the conversation, the two actors discuss what is "most fascinating" about voice acting. This elaboration is triggered by Shintani's following comment: "Nowadays, [people expect] *seiyū* to expose their face [*kaodashi*] in their media appearances."[27] The idea of *kaodashi*, "face-exposing," refers in this context to a type of work that requires *seiyū* to expose their face in public, including promotional events, press conferences, television appearances, and stage performances. Even though it is increasingly common nowadays for *seiyū* to engage in such work (perhaps most clearly exemplified by such recent productions as *Love Live!* and *THE IDOLM@STER*)—the kind of work she herself has done a number of times (she is also a singer in her own name and regularly performs at live concerts)—Shintani implies that the pleasure of voice acting derives centrally from acts of effacement. Observe how Kitamura follows up on this implied message.

> *Kitamura*: A situation where the actual personality [of *seiyū* themselves] doesn't get revealed 100%—[they express themselves] only through the sound of their voices, but it's as if the personality gets exuded (*shimideteiru*)—this is what's most fascinating.
> *Shintani*: Totally! [laughing enthusiastically][28]

Voice acting relies on an aesthetics of "not revealing one's self 100%" and operates on an acousmatic distillation of communication to "the sound of voices only." Most importantly, the rather fabulous metaphor of "exuding" or *simideru* suggests that the actor-character gap is configured like a non-transparent textile material, like those disposable ear-loop face masks that Japanese people habitually wear. This "mask" frames "*seiyū*'s expression" as the oozing-out of moisture, as it were, through numerous but imperceptibly tiny interstices of the gauze that conceals the face.

Immediately adjacent to the above exchange, Shintani concludes this segment of the conversation with a pointed observation.

---

[27] *Ibid.*
[28] *Ibid.*

Shintani: Totally! [laughing enthusiastically] That's like the privilege of being an anime otaku and a *seiyū* otaku simultaneously, don't you think?
Kitamura: Yes.
Shintani: Anime fans might [complain] "What? This [voice] is totally wrong for this character..." and *seiyū* fans might demand more *kaodashi* [from their favorite *seiyū*], but fans in-between [*aida no fan*] love that kind of thing.[29]

If *seiyū* make the space of 2.5D imaginable and inhabitable, it appears that their art transposes the interstitial quality to fandom as well, creating "fans in-between," who enjoy a "privilege" that escapes the more fundamentalist kinds of fans. Indeed, with her laughter Shintani enacts such a pleasure of interstices in this very interaction as an *aida no fan* herself.

Character-Actor Split

Before moving on, let me pause here and consider the character-actor split in a more analytic way. How can we situate voice acting in a comparative perspective with respect to diverse genres of expression and social action in terms of how the split is calibrated?[30]

There are forms and genres of discourse and social action where the split is a problem to solve, a worrisome distance that is better minimized, or where the very minimizing of it is an object of desire or a normative standard. The tradition of American "method acting" is quite explicit in this respect. According to the Lee Strasberg Theatre & Film Institute website, in this tradition actors "use their imagination, senses, and emotions to conceive of characters with unique and original behavior, creating performances grounded in the human truth of the moment."[31] The character is to be embodied by the actor inside the actor's socio-biographical and psychophysical self. This process is encapsulated perhaps most vividly in one of the core ideas of the tradition, "affective memory." A notion of characterization presupposed here involves an actor- or human-centered view.

In contrast, quite different orientation to the split is observed in such diverse forms and genres of action and discourse as puppetry, ventriloquism, paper theatre, doll play, cosplay, sadomasochistic play, game character/

---

[29] *Ibid.*

[30] This section heavily draws on Paul Manning and Ilana Gershon, "Animating Interaction," *HAU: Journal of Ethnographic Theory* 3, no. 3 (2013): 107-137, which is a further elaboration of Silvio's work on animation.

[31] "Method Acting Technique," The Lee Strasberg Theatre & Film Institute, accessed June 1, 2015, http://www.methodactingstrasberg.com/methodacting.

player relation, impersonation and mimicry, Brecht's epic theatre, etc. (We note *the ludic*—or perhaps more generally *the fantastic/absurd*—as a recurring theme here.) Far from being a distance to be minimized, the split is an integral part of what it means to participate in these actions.[32]

My point is not to impose a hard typology upon these diverse actions and practices; rather, I am interested in comparing *default* conceptualizations that they differentially index. In this vein, I think puppetry offers a particularly productive comparative insight for thinking about voice acting.[33] Following Frank Proschan's discussion of puppetry and voice, we can see that this second treatment of the split makes *voice* a salient site of semiotic-aesthetic intervention.[34] Proschan explores "voice modifiers" in puppetry traditions across the world (like the swazzle in England). These technical devices are designed to "impede" or "distort" what would otherwise be perceived as "natural" speech in live theatre (and in our hegemonic language ideology). That is, the devices help secure the non-congruence of puppets' and puppeteers' worlds: puppetry would be nothing if relations of identity govern these worlds. Here we note puppetry's affinity with more recent technologies of voice modification, like Vocaloids and similar applications. Puppetry and

---

[32] For ventriloquism, see David Goldblatt, *Art and Ventriloquism* (New York: Routledge, 2006); and François Cooren, *Action and Agency in Dialogue: Passion, Incarnation and Ventriloquism* (Amsterdam: John Benjamins, 2010). See Don Kulick, "No," *Language & Communication* 23 (2003): 139-151, for a pointed exposition of the difference between "performativity" and "performance" (with concrete examples including sadomasochistic scenes). For gaming, see Paul Manning, "Altaholics Anonymous: On the Pathological Proliferation of Parasites in Massively Multiple Online Worlds," *Semiotic Review* 1 (March 17, 2013), http://www.semioticreview.com/index.php/thematic-issues/issue-parasites/10-altaholics-anonymous-on-the-pathological-proliferation-of-parasites-in-massively-multiple-online-worlds. For cosplay, see Silvio, "Animation." Numerous studies may be cited for dolls, but see A. Caswell Ellis and G. Stanley Hall, "A Study of Dolls," *Pedagogical Seminary* 4 (1896): 129-175; see also the two-part documentary "My Schoolgirl Fantasy" *(Sailor-fuku Ojisan), VICE Japan*, June 10, 2013, accessed June 1, 2014, https://youtu.be/PsPo8jZpncQ. Mimicry is another widely researched topic, but see Michael Taussig's classic *Mimesis and Alterity: A Particular History of the Senses* (New York: Routledge, 1993).

[33] The literature on puppetry is extremely rich and diverse: see, for example, Roland Barthes, "On Bunraku," *The Drama Review: TDR* 15, no. 2 (1971): 76-80; Petr Bogatyrev, "The Interconnection of Two Similar Semiotic Systems: The Puppet Theater and the Theater of Living Actors," *Semiotica* 47, no. 1-4 [1973] 1983): 47-68; Kenneth Gross, *Puppet: An Essay on Uncanny Life* (Chicago, IL: University of Chicago Press, 2011); Victoria Nelson, *The Secret Life of Puppets* (Cambridge, MA: Harvard University Press, 2003); and Christopher A. Bolton, "From Wooden Cyborgs to Celluloid Souls: Mechanical Bodies in Anime and Japanese Puppet Theater," *positions* 10, no. 3 (2002): 729-771, just to name but a few works directly informing my argument. For ethnographies, see Joan Gross, *Speaking in Other Voices: An Ethnography of Walloon Puppet Theaters* (Philadelphia: John Benjamins, 2001); and Jane Marie Law, *Puppets of Nostalgia: The Life, Death, and Rebirth of the Japanese Awaji Ningyō Tradition* (Princeton: Princeton University Press, 1997). For a discussion of how puppetry has animated such diverse modes of theorization, see Scott Cutler Shershow, *Puppets and "Popular" Culture* (Ithaca: Cornell University Press, 1995).

[34] Frank Proschan, "Puppet Voices and Interlocutors: Language in Folk Puppetry," *Journal of American Folklore* 94, no. 374 (1981): 527-555.

Vocaloids are a gap-creating/-maintaining *techne*. To say that technical mediation of language, especially in the realm of phonic articulation, is "unnatural" because it involves modifying devices and external forces (nonhuman actants) is as fraught with ideological interests as evaluating a sexual act as "bad, abnormal, unnatural, [and] damned" when it involves "manufactured objects," as Gayle Rubin suggested long ago.[35]

Proschan writes that "the larger dramatic problem of providing appropriate characterizations for each actor is complicated, for not only must each figure have a distinct and fitting voice and speaking style, but these must all be produced by only one or two people."[36] This "many-to-one" character/ actor ratio is common in voice acting as well. Anime and videogames frequently deploy dual roles, sometimes by technical and economic necessity, sometimes as narratively motivated (e.g., Katō Emiri playing Kinoshita Hideyoshi and Kinoshita Yūko, twins, in *Baka and Test*). Actors who already play specific characters in a production often share usually uncredited roles such as walla (or *gaya* in Japanese, that is, crowd murmurings).

How about the "one-to-many" character/actor ratio? Clear examples of this involve multiple *seiyū* distributed in a temporal series, as in the case of high-profile characters like Doraemon or Arsène Lupin III, where different *seiyū* "inherit" the character as an "incumbent" ensouler, as if in a dynastic succession, or the case of temporary cast change due to illness or other reasons. These are cases where the (nonhuman) character exceeds the life of (human) actors, requiring these actors for its characterological (and "spiritual") sustenance over time. I have not been able to give adequate thought to the terms of such recruitment, inheritance and incumbency, but as a theoretical first approximation it is safe to assume that they are never constant but always contingent upon ongoing interpretation. For, while we tend to assume such recruitment operates on the logic of similitude—i.e., that the candidate actor would have to phonically "resemble" the incumbent (and certainly this is often the case, as shown by instances where fans denounce cast choice precisely on this basis)—it is possible to imagine a different logic as well. It is instructive in this instance to see that, in the talk between Kitamura and Shintani analyzed above, Shintani—an *aida no fan*—discusses the joy of hearing the same character being voiced by different actors between the "CD

---

[35] Gayle Rubin, "Thinking Sex: Notes for a Radical Theory of the Politics of Sexuality," in *Pleasure and Danger: Exploring Female Sexuality*, ed. Carole S. Vance (Boston: Routledge & Kegan Paul, 1984), 267-319. For *techne* and gaps, see Tom Boellstorff, *Coming of Age in Second Life: An Anthropologist Explores the Virtually Human* (Princeton: Princeton University Press, 2008).

[36] Proschan, "Puppet Voices and Interlocutors," 528.

drama version" and the "TV anime version." For her, these "variations" hardly destroy the integrity of the character and its "world"; rather, they enchant the world even more effectively.[37]

As Silvio suggests, such non-correspondence in the character/actor ratio (many-to-one or one-to-many) is the practical, *default* condition of "animation." Just as in Japanese *bunraku*, where multiple operators are assembled into the "striation" of media in the animation of one puppet, one anime character assembles multiple actants *in praesentia*: voice actor, character designer, in-betweens animator, etc. At the same time, each of these actants also participates separately in disparate characters, creating for itself a distinct set of characters *in absentia* or what might be called characterography (à la "discography," "filmography," etc.).[38]

It is understandable, then, that characterological diversity is a frequent object of talk about voice acting. Questions such as "How do you create different character voices?" and "How many voices do you have?" are commonly asked to skilled *seiyū* like Yamadera Kōichi. Nicknamed by fans as "the man with the voice of seven colors" ("seven colors" is a metaphor for "diversity"), Yamadera's characterography is not just exceedingly long and illustrious but exhibits an almost impossible ontological diversity across sociocultural boundaries as well as species boundaries that conventional live theatrical acting just cannot afford without anthropomorphism. His animal and zoomorphic characters such as Cheese in the *Anpanman* series and Watchdog Robot in *Ghost in the Shell SAC* are particularly notable. While Yamadera's talent is clearly exceptional, many *seiyū* regularly exhibit such diversity in their characterography as well (to a certain extent). Characterological diversity is certainly an accomplishment but it is also an almost normal state of affairs in *seiyū* work.[39]

What interests us here, however, is not the fact of diversity itself, but the way in which *seiyū* theorize it when, for example, they are asked

---

[37] I thank Jason G. Karlin and Dennis Washburn for pointing me to this issue. For variation and world, see Ōtsuka Eiji, "World and Variation: The Reproduction and Consumption of Narrative," trans. Marc Steinberg, *Mechademia* 5, no. 1 (2010): 99–116.

[38] Silvio, "Animation," 428; see also Manning and Gershon, "Animating Interaction," 122.

[39] I thank an anonymous reviewer for referring me to works such as *Yukinojō henge* (Mikami Otokichi's 1934 novel and its many live-action iterations in film and theatre) and Tezuka Osamu's *Nanairo inko* (1981-1982) that make full use of characterological diversity as a narrative element. Further, the reviewer's comment points more generally to the symbolism of *henge* (transformation) inscribed in the Kabuki tradition. Note, however, these instances of characterological diversity are narratively motivated. As the reviewer also notes, at the core of *seiyū*'s characterological diversity is the way in which they quite often—not just as a narrative necessity but almost by default—transcend the boundary of sociocultural, human "identities."

what makes this diversity possible. As we will see below, having the voice of "seven colors" may not be enough, apparently, to make this characterological difference.

Scanning and Tuning

In a 2011 radio interview with radio and television writer Imanami Yūsuke, voice actor Sawashiro Miyuki describes voice acting as "backstage work" (*urakata no shigoto*); as we have seen, such a description is consistent with the general ethos of effacement-work. Even after more than ten years of her career in the show business, she says she still does not feel accustomed to the idea of exposing herself to the media. "I entered this business not expecting to be famous," she says.[40] Imanami, feeling skeptical of this claim, suggests that she should realize she is indeed a celebrity, but she does not seem to buy it. She rather prefers not to be seen:

> I'm in this business because I can eliminate all these moments where I have to be myself. I'd rather want to live someone else's life. I shouldn't be seen—it startles me when I notice I'm being watched.[41]

Like Yamadera, and many other *seiyū*, she has indeed lived many lives that are not only not her own—a preteen boy (Tegamibachi), a *fujoshi* (Fujoshi Kanojo), an undocumented immigrant of unspecified nationality (Sayoyara Zetsubō-sensei), etc.—but also those lives which she, as a "3D" human being, could not possibly live otherwise: the life of a doll (*Rozen Maiden*), an extraterrestrial cat-girl (Di Gi Charat), a headless monster who lacks the speech organ (Durarara!!), a bear-like but otherwise unspecified animal, often misunderstood as a dog, that carries gemstone (labradorite) that has magical power (the *Jewelpet* series).

One way of living a life that is not one's own and is not for one to live is to lose oneself and rely on others. Sawashiro states:

> I'm better at talking about my partner character, because it's him that [I am/my character is] looking carefully at. So I don't know how to react when I'm asked about my character...I could talk endlessly about the boy that [I am/ my character is] in love with, but if it's [about me/about my character], I'd be like "Well, I don't know."

[40] "Seiyūdō" 46, JOQR Chō! A&G+ (Tokyo: Bunka Hōsō, January 16, 2011).
[41] *Ibid.*

The process of characterization produces *ignorance* as positive evidence of its successful operation. Her first-person narrative here draws on perspectival underdetermination between the character and the actor (here certainly assisted by the Japanese language itself—e.g., its frequent featuring of nominal ellipsis in discourse).[42]

Later on in the interview, she links this effacement-work to her own theory of acting in a response to Imanami's question, "So, how many voice colors do you have?"

> Well, people often talk about *kowairo* (voice colors), but...how should I put it—it's better to have seven different *kokoro* (heart, spirit) [than seven voice colors]...So, I really don't think about voice qualities, to tell you the truth.

This is an odd response. The question presupposes—as, I think, we usually do—that characterological diversity is based on *phonic-material* difference, but her answer twists this presupposition, implying that it is based rather on *spiritual* difference. She thinks it is better to have a multiplicity of *kokoro*. Why?

> So, for example, when there is...a drawing of my character already, I'd look at the drawing, and it's like I start hearing a voice coming out of this character (*kikoete-kuru*). Does that make sense? It's like I'm scanning for the voice, and then I'd tune myself with it. I often work like that. So, sometimes, it is a real problem when I happen to pick up the voice of a different character in the process of tuning [with my character]. I'd say to myself, "Oh no, I can't do that voice!"

According to this scenario, one needs to "scan" the character for the voice, and "tune" one's own body with it so as to amplify, modify, and redistribute it accordingly. The compound verb used here, *kikoete-kuru* (lit., "coming-to-be-heard") is particularly telling in its deictic topology: the voice does not originate from the actor's body *here*, but it is coming from *elsewhere*. The actor's body is a telegraphic access point for signal transmission. She receives the voice sent from the character across the "dimensional" divide at a particular frequency, as through a radio receiver. The series of ideas linked together here—"scanning," "tuning," and "hearing a voice from elsewhere"—are rather stunningly reminiscent

---

[42] For more on "no consciousness" of the puppet, see Heinrich von Kleist, "On the Marionette Theatre," trans. Thomas G. Neumiller, *The Drama Review* 16, no. 3 [1810] 1972): 22-26.

of the Spiritualist tradition of the 19th century, which is "one clear manifestation of the Victorian cult of the dead" that emerged in response to, among other things, technologies of disembodied communication such as photography and, more relevant to our discussion, wireless telegraphy, such as radio.[43]

Sawashiro's framework assumes that the character *already* has some sort of voice. This presumed ontology of character voice is instructive in revealing an interesting contrast within the Spiritualist discourse. Her ontology of character voice seems to go against the ideal of angelic, bodiless, and thus "voiceless" communication, inherited from Thomistic angelology and presupposed and modified, directly or indirectly, in various modernist theories of communication, Saussure included.[44] Rather, her vision recalls a genre of Spiritualist séances called "direct voice," which (though it is called "direct") emphasizes the *mediating* role of mediums closely related to communicative technology. In direct voice séances, the claim is made that the spirit directly issues the voice (which does not belong to the medium) and the medium occupies the role of facilitator, transferring or (as in what is known as "trumpet mediums") "amplifying" the spirit voice. Sawashiro's invoking of scanning and tuning is explicitly framed in relation to material apparatuses (i.e., radio), just as direct voice séances deployed material objects such as the trumpet and the phonograph horn. If for direct voice séances "the more 'direct' the voice, the more indirect the agency of the medium becomes," then we might apply a similar equation to Sawashiro's explicit orientation to self-ignorance as just discussed above.[45]

Such quasi-spiritualist logic of what we might call *character direct voice* motivates a notion of *exchange* as well in Sawashiro's explanation, an economy of spirit and voice. In receiving the character voice, she gives the character a spirit to animate its empty body. Having many spirits, a diversity of *kokoro*, is a professional asset because the actor can then enter multiple exchange relations with characters. Whether the "true" location of the voice can be identified in the actor's body turns out to be a less relevant question (even when the question makes sense or is answerable). The question

---

[43] John Durham Peters, *Speaking into the Air: A History of the Idea of Communication* (Chicago, IL: University of Chicago Press, 1999), 97. For Spiritualism, I draw here on Peters' work as well as Steven Connor, "The Machine in the Ghost: Spiritualism, Technology and the 'Direct Voice'," in *Ghosts: Deconstruction, Psychoanalysis, History*, ed. Peter Buse (London: Macmillan, 1999), 203-225. See also Tomoko Masuzawa, "Troubles with Materiality: The Ghost of Fetishism in the Nineteenth Century," *Comparative Studies in Society and History* 42, no. 2 (April 2000), 242-267.

[44] See Peters, *Speaking into the Air*, 63-108.

[45] Conner, "The Machine in the Ghost," 217.

of real practical and theoretical import to *seiyū* and to fans is: "How can I access the voice, proper to the character?"—just like when you adjust your devise setting to tune in a radio station or a wireless connection at a café.[46]

Appropriately enough, this segment of Sawashiro's interview concludes as follows:

> *Imanami:* So, you are in a way pulling your character voice out, taking it out.
> *Sawashiro:* Pulling it out this way, yes.
> *Imanami:* That's *itako*!
> *Sawashiro:* [laughter]

Itako refers to blind female shamans in northern Japan who communicate with, and in the voice of, the dead for the sake of and upon the request of the living.[47] To be sure, it remains to be seen whether this theorization is not simply due to Sawashiro's idiosyncrasy. But our final example below, of a *seiyū* on the verge of mediation, does seem to suggest a similar economy of voice and spirit.

Overensoulment

Hayashibara Megumi is perhaps one of the most notable *seiyū* in the business today. However, despite her wide popularity not only as *seiyū* but also as singer (in her own name), she is carefully effaced in her engagement with the mainstream media. This is crucial to keep in mind: she is a celebrity whose job centrally involves an art of becoming a nobody.[48]

---

[46] One anonymous reviewer raised a question regarding the tension between singularity and typicality, i.e., whether the "character" whose voice Sawashiro tunes herself with is a singular one or—to quote the reviewer's apt phrase—an "archive of 'appropriate' voices accumulated and standardized through a generation of voice actors before her." I could not find statements in this interview and other sources that help me properly respond to this question, but I find it extremely intriguing especially in terms of the folk taxonomy of voice qualities according to which such "appropriateness-to-context" may be evaluated and enacted, something I have not looked into carefully in my research. I thank the reviewer for drawing my attention to this issue.

[47] As in shamanic practices across the world, the ritual textuality of *itako* mediumship is supposed by default to involve technical mediation of objects such as bows and puppets. See Carmen Blacker, *The Catalpa Bow: A Study of Shamanistic Practices in Japan* (London: G. Allen & Unwin, 1975), 147-150. See also Law, *Puppets of Nostalgia*. Also, as many scholars have pointed out, *itako* do not display stereotypic shamanistic bodily signs of trance nor, more interestingly, do they consistently exhibit difference in voice quality when animating the dead. See Marilyn Ivy, *Discourses of the Vanishing: Modernity, Phantasm, Japan* (Chicago, IL: University of Chicago Press, 1995), 141-191 for a particularly insightful discussion.

[48] Hayashibara's prime tool for connecting with fans and the public generally is radio. Her long-running radio talk shows have been particularly important to her in maintaining communication with her fans.

On many occasions Hayashibara has described herself, playfully as much as seriously, as an "*itako seiyū*," remediating her art to spirit mediumship. In one brief interview in an entertainment news magazine, she says she uses this phrase because otherwise she would not know how to explain her experience of characterization. "While keeping my own intentionality intact, it is as if I lend my vocal organ and body to the character so as to allow the character to speak."[49] The original Japanese phrase for this last clause—*kyarakutā ni shabette-morau*—involves a ditransitive verb of receiving (*morau*). The expression stipulates the "speaking" (*shaberu*) as an object given to (to the benefit of) a beneficiary: the character "gives" the speaking "to" the actor. It has the connotation of "begging the character to speak." The economy of voice and spirit implied in Sawashiro's theory is here given a bit more concrete picture: the character-actor split is configured as a relation of *debt*. The following episode will demonstrate this.

Hayashibara is the *naka no hito* of Kyōyama Anna, one of the main shaman characters in Takei Hiroyuki's manga *Shaman King*—in other words, an *itako seiyū* playing an *itako* character. (Her characterography is not foreign to characters with direct engagement with spiritual practices and idioms: e.g., Lina Inverse in *Slayers*, a sorcerer; Ayanami Rei in *Neon Genesis Evangelion*, a clone endowed with a human spirit; Paprika in *Paprika*, a technologically enhanced dream-world double.) The manga obtained huge popularity through its serialization in the weekly *Shonen Jump* from 1998 through 2004; a TV anime series ran almost concurrently (2001-2002). In the manga, a little poem called "Osorezan Revoir" is featured, a song for and about Anna. In 2010, an amateur musician who goes by the name Kapitaro composed a musical piece to this pre-existing poetic text, as a personal homage to the character Anna. Then a middle school student, Kapitaro had Hatsune Miku, a Vocaloid, sing the song, and on October 3, 2010 he uploaded this Miku version to Niconico. This derivative fan work was well received by Niconico viewers; Takei, the artist, also praised Kapitaro for the creation.[50]

About a year later in 2011, it was decided much to the delight of the fans that Takei would resume the manga series with new episodes. In celebration, a singing video of Kapitaro's rendition of "Osorezan Revoir"

---

[49] Hayashibara Megumi, "Seimeiryoku: Hito ga nanto ittemo 'Sukinamono wa suki'," November 29, 2010, accessed June 10, 2014, http://www.zakzak.co.jp/people/news/20101129/peo1011291511000-n1.htm.

[50] "[Hatsune Miku] Osorezan Revoir [Original]," Niconico, March 13, 2010, accessed June 10, 2014, http://www.nicovideo.jp/watch/sm10009443. See also this Twitter aggregation page created on October 24, 2011, http://togetter.com/li/204430, which I partly draw on in this section.

was uploaded on Niconico on October 21—in a manner now familiar in the global fan practice of sharing the singing of Vocaloid songs.[51] Besides being totally mesmerized by the sheer quality of the singing, the fans and other Niconico viewers were noticeably disoriented by this video, because the singing voice sounded exactly like Anna, that is, exactly as she would be voiced by Hayashibara, although there was no mention of Hayashibara on the video. The singer only identified herself as Kyōyama Anna (the user profile attached to the video only showed Anna's character image as the user's avatar). The play of ambiguity ensued: is it Hayashibara or someone else? But then, it sounds exactly like Anna's voice—does that mean that it is Hayashibara after all? But do we need to know who the voice really belongs to in order to be moved by it? Indeed, did we not already apprehend it as Anna's in our first encounter and were we not *in fact* moved by it? Why are we asking this question at all, then? Why should we be so fussy about the true location of the voice, when the voice is already so vividly available for our access and our pleasure? (Recall Sawashiro's perspectival underdetermination discussed above: "me/my character.")

About a few weeks after the upload, Hayashibara revealed in an official statement, rather matter-of-factly, that she was indeed the singer. She said that her production agency had asked her to sing Kapitaro's song, telling her that the fans of the manga would really appreciate that. She immediately agreed to sing it. A recording session was arranged, Kapitaro was contacted for permission to use his music, and the staff would take care of the uploading. Hayashibara just rushed to the recording studio.[52]

Interestingly, while this unmasking of the "true" identity may have satisfied some curious minds, it did not take away the mysterious allure of the singing at all. While some of the comments to the video had heatedly debated on the identity before the revelation was made, in the statement on her website Hayashibara gestured playfully, but also most endearingly, to the *unimportance* of the truth: "For those who thought this wasn't me, no need to feel ashamed by your misunderstanding. For those who thought this was me, no need to accuse those who misunderstood. For in both of you I see love."[53]

In fact, it appears that most people had already sensed it coming. The comments on the video included statements like "no surprise" and "it

---

[51] "Hatsune Miku-Osorezan Revoir [Official Cover by Anna Kyōyama/CV: Megumi Hayashibara," Niconico, October 21, 2011, accessed June 1, 2014, http://www.nicovideo.jp/watch/sm15947771.

[52] Hayashibara Megumi, "Megu san yori: Kyōyama Anna, 'Osorezan Revoir' o utattemita no Hayashibara-teki shinsō!" *Starchild*, November 8, 2011, accessed June 10, 2014, http://www.starchild.co.jp/artist/hayashi/news/2011/1108.html.

[53] *Ibid.*

makes sense that it's Hayashibara." To use Kitamura's image discussed earlier, many viewers perhaps already felt Hayashibara's persona "oozing out" through Anna's singing, behind which the actor concealed her name and her body without it becoming a secret. She was able to demonstrate the robust realness of the character by concealing herself, and the realness retained its force even when the veil was lifted precisely because the effacement was not at all a trick. There's no hoax, and there's no iconoclasm. If anything, her effacement-work induced "love." Viewers still come back to Kyōyama Anna's/Hayashibara Megumi's singing video to pay homage, an act often construed in the image of pilgrimage.[54]

In her statement Hayashibara relates a further backstory.

> As I stared singing, I was already overflowing with tears.
> Myriad things came to my mind: about Yoh and Matamune [main characters of the story], about myself [working on this anime] back then [c. 2001-2002]. Towards the end of the session, my singing almost sounded like crying.
> I got out of the booth and listened to the recording. "Wow, this is great! So moving!" I praised myself. And then all of sudden, in my head, Anna was there, staring at me.
> "Your tears are cheap. Don't show your tears to others so easily. Don't communicate [tsutaeruna]. In this song, you must tuck your sorrow away. And at the height of sorrow, do not cry." She scolded me.
> "Nooo...was it really cheap...? Sorry, Anna. It's been a while..." All this was happening in my head.
> I went back to the booth.
> The snow, the candle, the fiend...Yoh, Yoh, Yoh...
> Anna's gaze infiltrates me. I'm looking mindlessly at what she sees. As I sing at the height of sorrow, I feel a thin layer of hope. Ah, this trippy feeling, it's been a while. Oversoul indeed.[55]

This last phrase, "oversoul," refers to a fictional shamanistic technique featured in the manga *Shaman King*, where it essentially means a high

---

[54] The viewers' repeated acts of "pilgrimage" cumulatively affirm the consecrated nature of the voice, amplifying its transmissive power. While I have not closely examined how audience uptake contributes to character ensoulment so far in my research (and I thank an anonymous reviewer for pointing me to this direction), one may start investigating this dimension by bringing into sharper analytic focus fan communities formed around voice. For example, the social network site Koebu (http://koebu.com/) offers its users a virtual space to share their voice productions in a range of forms, from impersonation (*monomane*) of existing characters and original character contents to singing performances and internet radio shows (see also fn23).

[55] *Ibid.*

degree of spiritual possession. While Ralph Waldo Emerson used the same phrase to envision a universal spiritual unity, "that common heart," here, in contrast, the prefix *over-* signals intensity and excess, leaving room for imagining a multiplicity of the heart.[56]

Hayashibara has not animated Anna *for a long while*. There is a period of inaction since the initial moment of exchange when she first ensouled Anna for the anime series in 2001. As she now confronts Anna, ten years later, in the dark enclosure of the recording studio, it is Anna who remembers the terms of exchange. Anna demands proper ensoulment, not with those "cheap tears"—a sign she interprets as indexing the actor's affective state, not *hers*—but by means of effacing what the actor feels: "don't communicate."

This is perhaps as far removed as it could be from the Method's anthropocentric model of "affective memory," where it is ideal that actors communicate their genuine feeling, the "human truth" of the moment. Hayashibara's reflexive discourse, made explicit in this instance of overensoulment, suggests that the character is not simply "conceived" of by the actor's imagination. Rather, the imagination, in order to be aesthetically effective, must first commit itself to the belief that the character exists, waiting to be/having been ensouled, as an exchange partner, a speech actant capable of speech acts like demanding, reminding, and scolding. A rather absurd belief, to be sure, but it is a belief in the absurd more than anything else, and what matters is that it produces real effects. To recall Latour's commentary on ventriloquism, cited earlier: "we, the human subjects, are the *dummies* toward which other entities are projecting their real voices *as if* they were coming *from us*" (emphasis in the original).[57] Anna is the "other entity" that projects her "real voice" toward Hayashibara. Their exchange transpires at a heightened moment of excessive resonance. It is as if the actor allows the character to resonate through her at her own natural frequency, creating an exceptionally high degree of transmissibility.

Conclusion

Hayashibara's story presupposes an already circulating ideology, a larger framework of aesthetics locally made relevant to discourses about voice acting, while at the same time reorienting subcultural participants to such a framework. This ideology may be summed up in terms of its

---

[56] Ralph Waldo Emerson, "The Over-Soul," *Essays: First Series* (New York: James Munroe & Co., 1847), cited from http://www.emersoncentral.com/oversoul.htm.

[57] Latour, "Forward: Who is Making the Dummy Speak?" xv.

argument for an economy of voice and spirit. Hayashibara's story differs from Sawashiro's explanation, however, in that the latter more strongly presupposes the ontology of character voices, analogous to the Spiritualist "direct voice," while Hayashibara's case makes her experience appear relatively closer perhaps to possession and channeling. (*Hyōi*, a term that emerged as a translation of the English word "possession," as in possession by animals or quasi-animals like foxes, is often used to describe *seiyū* like Hayashibara with a tendency to draw on such possession-like techniques. Sawashiro is usually not associated with this style.) The difference notwithstanding, in this preliminary analysis I would like to emphasize how the two cases point to a general logic. One relies on the belief that, first, the hollow body of a character exists; and second, that this body can be animated from inside through an economy of voice and spirit. *Seiyū*'s art is irreducible to the humanist-organic-theatrical metaphor of embodiment but requires a dialogic imagination of voices and spirits, the gap created between characters and actors through effacement-work.

Earlier in the chapter I used the metaphor of musical instruments for explaining *naka no hito*, albeit only in passing, suggesting that we see the character-actor split as analogous to the relation between instruments and their players. To the extent that this vision of characterization is convincing ethnographically speaking, we may take advantage, for the sake of our description, of the fact that in English we use the verb "play" to describe aesthetic, mechanical, and ludic acts. To say that *seiyū* "play" their characters, in the same way we say one plays a piano, a DVD, or a videogame, helps us capture the culture of voice acting in a way that is in fact consistent with how its participants themselves understand and act on it. It might strike many of us as rather counterintuitive to see an act that looks like theatrical "performance" as being analogous to an act that looks like pressing buttons and adjusting knobs on a mechanical device. But holding on to this view of play is a good ethnographic antidote, I think, against the naturalization of the human and the body as well as the doctrine of immediacy that we often presume upon when it comes to the question of voice.

Let me add one last note about radio. We have witnessed various ways in which *seiyū* actively engage the technology of radio and its remediation in the form of, for example, internet radio. Several important dimensions of *seiyū*'s *radio act* have been identified: radio as an infrastructure of subcultural discourse (most of my examples in this chapter rely on this infrastructure of information), radio as *seiyū*'s workplace, and radio (and the recording booth) as an emblem of effacement-work (the image and reality of enclosure). On the other hand, oozing out in these sites of radio act is an economy of spirit and voice through which *seiyū*'s voice work is remediated to spirit mediumship. The abundance of spiritual idioms in the culture of voice acting should prompt us to contextualize it in the larger historical process of modernity where the emergence of technologies of disembodiment has invited reinvigoration of spiritual imaginaries.

A larger, rather ambitious goal in my ongoing research on voice acting is to show how an ethnography of Japanese voice acting might contribute to what John Durham Peters would call a "more robust vision of spirit" to the broader problematique of "communication."[58] In this chapter, however, my specific aim has been to initiate an ethnographic description of the logic of Japanese voice acting and the way it animates the structure of contemporary convergence culture. I hope that some of the conceptual and empirical issues outlined here will invite further discussion and critical reexamination for such a vision of spirit and communication.

Works Cited

Azuma, Hiroki. *Otaku: Japan's Database Animals*. Translated by Jonathan E. Abel and Shion Kono. Minneapolis, MN: University of Minnesota Press, 2009.

Barthes, Roland. "On Bunraku." *The Drama Review: TDR* 15, no. 2 (1971): 76-80.

Blacker, Carmen. *The Catalpa Bow: A Study of Shamanistic Practices in Japan*. London: G. Allen & Unwin, 1975.

Boellstorff, Tom. *Coming of Age in Second Life: An Anthropologist Explores the Virtually Human*. Princeton: Princeton University Press, 2008.

Bogatyrev, Petr. "The Interconnection of Two Similar Semiotic Systems: The Puppet Theater and the Theater of Living Actors." *Semiotica* 47, no. 1-4 [1973] 1983: 47-68.

Bolton, Christopher A. "From Wooden Cyborgs to Celluloid Souls: Mechanical Bodies in Anime and Japanese Puppet Theater." *positions* 10, no. 3 (2002): 729-771.

---

[58] Peters, *Speaking into the Air*, 109-136.

Bucholtz, Mary. "Race and the Re-Embodied Voice in Hollywood Film." *Language & Communication* 31, no. 3 (2011): 255-265.

Condry, Ian. "Miku: Japan's Virtual Idol and Media Platform." MIT Center for Civic Media, July 11, 2011. Accessed January 23, 2015. https://civic.mit.edu/blog/condry/miku-japans-virtual-idol-and-media-platform.

Connor, Steven. "The Machine in the Ghost: Spiritualism, Technology and the 'Direct Voice'." In *Ghosts: Deconstruction, Psychoanalysis, History*, edited by Peter Buse, 203-225. London: Macmillan, 1999.

Cooren, François. *Action and Agency in Dialogue: Passion, Incarnation and Ventriloquism*. Amsterdam: John Benjamins, 2010.

Ellis, A. Caswell, and G. Stanley Hall. "A Study of Dolls." *Pedagogical Seminary* 4 (1896): 129-175.

Emerson, Ralph Waldo. *Essays: First Series*. New York: James Munroe & Co., 1847.

Foster, Michael Dylan. *Pandemonium and Parade: Japanese Monsters and the Culture of Yōkai*. Berkeley: University of California Press, 2009.

Galbraith, Patrick W. "Moe and the Potential of Fantasy in Post-Millennial Japan." *Electronic Journal of Contemporary Japanese Studies* (October 31, 2009). http://www.japanesestudies.org.uk/articles/2009/Galbraith.html.

————. "Fujoshi: Fantasy Play and Transgressive Intimacy among 'Rotten Girls' in Contemporary Japan." *Signs* 37, no. 1 (2011): 211-232.

————. "Maid in Japan: An Ethnographic Account of Alternative Intimacy." *Intersections: Gender, History and Culture in the Asian Context* 25 (February 2011). http://intersections.anu.edu.au/issue25/galbraith.htm.

Goffman, Erving. *Behavior in Public Places: Notes on the Social Organization of Gatherings*. New York: Free Press of Glencoe, 1963.

————. 1974. *Frame Analysis: An Essay on the Organization of Experience*. New York: Harper & Row.

Goldblatt, David. *Art and Ventriloquism*. New York: Routledge, 2006.

Gross, Joan. *Speaking in Other Voices: An Ethnography of Walloon Puppet Theaters*. Philadelphia: John Benjamins, 2001.

Gross, Kenneth. *Puppet: An Essay on Uncanny Life*. Chicago, IL: University of Chicago Press, 2011.

Gumperz, John. *Discourse Strategies*. Cambridge, UK: Cambridge University Press, 1982.

"History of Character Song." 2012. *LisAni!* 10, no. 1 (October): 102-125.

Ivy, Marilyn. *Discourses of the Vanishing: Modernity, Phantasm, Japan*. Chicago, IL: University of Chicago Press, 1995.

Jenkins, Henry. *Convergence Culture: Where Old and New Media Collide*. New York: New York University Press, 2006.

Katsuno, Hirofumi. "The Robot's Heart: Tinkering with Humanity and Intimacy in Robot-Building." *Japanese Studies* 31, no. 1 (2011): 93-109.

Kleist, Heinrich von. "On the Marionette Theatre." Translated by Thomas G. Neumiller. *The Drama Review* 16, no. 3 [1810] 1972: 22-26.

Kulick, Don. 2003. "No." *Language & Communication* 23 (2003): 139-151.

Lamarre, Thomas. *The Anime Machine: A Media Theory of Animation*. Minneapolis, MN: University of Minnesota Press, 2009.

Latour, Bruno. 2010. "Forward: Who is Making the Dummy Speak?" In *Action and Agency in Dialogue: Passion, Incarnation and Ventriloquism*, edited by François Cooren, xiii-xvi. Amsterdam: John Benjamins, 2010.

Law, Jane Marie. *Puppets of Nostalgia: The Life, Death, and Rebirth of the Japanese Awaji Ningyō Tradition*. Princeton: Princeton University Press, 1997.

Lemon, Alaina. 2009. "Sympathy for the Weary State?: Cold War Chronotopes and Moscow Others." *Comparative Studies in Society and History* 51, no. 4 (2009): 832-864.

Manning, Paul. "Altaholics Anonymous: On the Pathological Proliferation of Parasites in Massively Multiple Online Worlds." *Semiotic Review* 1 (March 17, 2013). http://www.semioticreview.com/index.php/thematic-issues/issue-parasites/10-altaholics-anonymous-on-the-pathological-proliferation-of-parasites-in-massively-multiple-online-worlds.

Manning, Paul, and Ilana Gershon. "Animating Interaction." *HAU: Journal of Ethnographic Theory* 3, no. 3 (2013): 107-137. doi: 10.14318/hau3.3.006

Masuzawa, Tomoko. 2000. "Troubles with Materiality: The Ghost of Fetishism in the Nineteenth Century." *Comparative Studies in Society and History* 42, no. 2 (2002): 242-267.

Meyerhold, Vsevolod Emilevich. "The Fairground Booth." In *Meyerhold on Theatre*, edited by Edward Braun, 119-143. New York: Hill and Wang, [1912] 1969.

Miller, Laura. "Extreme Makeover for a Heian-Era Wizard." *Mechademia* 3, no. 1 (2008): 30-45.

Nagler, Linda Fregni. *The Hidden Mother*. London: Mack, 2013.

Nelson, Victoria. *The Secret Life of Puppets*. Cambridge, MA: Harvard University Press, 2003.

NHK PR 1-gō. *Naka no hito nado inai @ NHK kōhō no Tweet wa naze yurui?* Tokyo: Shinchōsha, 2012.

Nozawa Masako. *Boku wa seiyū*. Tokyo: Opt Communications, 1995.

Nozawa, Shunsuke. 2012. "The Gross Face and Virtual Fame: Semiotic Mediation in Japanese Virtual Communication." *First Monday* 17, no. 3 (March 5, 2012). doi: 10.5210/fm.v17i3.3535

———. 2013. "Characterization." *Semiotic Review* 3 (November 5, 2013). http://www.semioticreview.com/index.php/open-issues/issue-open-2013/21-characterization.

Ōtsuka, Eiji. "World and Variation: The Reproduction and Consumption of Narrative." Translated by Marc Steinberg. *Mechademia* 5, no. 1 (2010): 99-116.

Peters, John Durham. *Speaking into the Air: A History of the Idea of Communication*. Chicago, IL: University of Chicago Press, 1999.

Proschan, Frank. "Puppet Voices and Interlocutors: Language in Folk Puppetry." *Journal of American Folklore* 94, no. 374 (1981): 527-555.

Rubin, Gayle. "Thinking Sex: Notes for a Radical Theory of the Politics of Sexuality." In *Pleasure and Danger: Exploring Female Sexuality*, edited by Carole S. Vance, 267-319. Boston: Routledge & Kegan Paul, 1984.

Shershow, Scott Cutler. *Puppets and "Popular" Culture*. Ithaca: Cornell University Press, 1995.

Silvio, Teri. 2010. "Animation: The New Performance?" *Journal of Linguistic Anthropology* 20, no. 2 (2010): 422-438.

Simmel, Georg. "The Secret Society." In *The Sociology of Georg Simmel*, edited and translated by Kurt H. Wolff, 345-78. New York: The Free Press, 1950.

Steinberg, Marc. "Anytime, Anywhere: Tetsuwan Atomu Stickers and the Emergence of Character Merchandizing." *Theory, Culture & Society* 26, no. 2-3 (2009): 113-138.

———. 2012. *Anime's Media Mix: Franchising Toys and Characters in Japan*. Minneapolis, MN: University of Minnesota Press, 2012.

Taussig, Michael. *Mimesis and Alterity: A Particular History of the Senses*. New York: Routledge, 1993.

Yasar, Kerim. "Electrified Voices: Media Technology and Discourse in Modern Japan." PhD diss., Columbia University, 2009.

Producing Hatsune Miku: Concerts, Commercialization, and the Politics of Peer Production

Alex Leavitt, Tara Knight, and Alex Yoshiba

Introduction

Five thousand fans in a packed, sold-out concert hall. From total darkness, projected green sparks fly out of the stage as a young girl with long, teal pigtails seems to materialize before their eyes. Glowsticks beat in time to the rhythm as swelling screams and cheers drown out her accompanying band members. Hatsune Miku has entered the building.

The concerts of Hatsune Miku have captured the imagination of the world. They have inspired numerous press from Japanese television broadcasts to German newspapers to celebrate Miku, celebrating the nostalgia of science fiction techno-futures like William Gibson's *Idoru* or Sharon Apple of Kawamori Shōji and Watanabe Shinichirō's *Macross Plus*. But Hatsune Miku is more complex than a parading musical avatar: she is the sum of many creative contributions from people all over the world. Primarily connected through the internet, Miku is the result of creative peer production.

As with any collaborative project, creative control remains a core problem. Miku's live concerts can be used to illustrate a number of critical tensions within the peer production process: individual participation versus collective effort, local Japanese community versus global networked audiences, and fan-generated content versus corporate-controlled branding. Therefore, this chapter focuses on the concerts of Hatsune Miku produced by Crypton Future Media, Inc. (hereafter, Crypton) as one lens through which we can view the politics of contemporary media convergence. In particular, these live concerts represent an entry point to understanding how the hybrid dynamics of top-down (producer-to-audience) and bottom-up (audience-to-producer) creative peer production play out between large companies and creative individuals, from artists that lead crowds to produce their artwork ("artistic alpha creators") to ordinary media consumers and everyone in between.[1]

While a number of authors have examined Miku as an image,[2] a persona,[3] a phenomenon,[4] and a collection of media,[5] none have deeply examined the full extent of Miku's creative ecosystem, the global network of artists and media that usually remain hidden behind Miku's stardom. To explain this creative ecosystem, we describe the details of the Hatsune Miku franchise as a unique example of creative peer production, showing how a distributed network of artists and audiences is able to fashion Miku into a media artifact. To explain how these collaborations work, especially in relation to corporate control of Miku's franchise, we look at one of the more-visible facets of the franchise—Miku's professional concerts. These concerts are produced by Crypton—the company that produces Miku's software and (more importantly) controls Hatsune Miku's franchise— and they illustrate various politics of participation between producers and consumers of Hatsune Miku, especially along commercial and cultural divisions. These conflicts illustrate how a hybrid grassroots-corporate, peer-production franchise operates, contributing to the literature and theory about collaborative media, convergence culture, and the contents industry in Japan and abroad.

Throughout the chapter, we situate ourselves as both researchers and participants within the franchise, drawing from documentary interviews, participant observation, and media and audience analyses. We situate our case study of grassroots participation in the Hatsune Miku franchise primarily through over 70 interviews with creators, fans, and scholars conducted by Knight since 2010, along with her animated documentary, the *Mikumentary* series,[6] and her recent participation with Crypton backstage on the American leg of the 2014 Miku Expo Tour. Additionally, Knight

---

[1] Ioana Literat, "The Work of Art in the Age of Mediated Participation: Crowdsourced Art and Collective Creativity," *International Journal of Communication* 6 (December 17, 2012), http://ijoc.org/index.php/ijoc/article/view/1531/835.

[2] Thomas Conner, "Rei Toei Lives!: Hatsune Miku and the Design of the Virtual Pop Star" (MA thesis, University of Illinois at Chicago, 2013).

[3] Jelena Guga, "Virtual Idol Hatsune Miku: New Auratic Experience of the Performer as a Collaborative Platform," *Lecture Notes of the Institute for Computer Sciences, Social Informatics, and Telecommunications Engineering* 145 (2015): 36-44.

[4] Ian Condry, "Miku: Japan's Virtual Idol and Media Platform," MIT Center for Civic Media, July 11, 2011, accessed June 10, 2014, https://civic.mit.edu/blog/condry/miku-japans-virtual-idol-and-media-platform.

[5] Masahiro Hamasaki *et al.*, "Network Analysis of an Emergent Massively Collaborative Creation Community," in *International AAAI Conference on Web and Social Media*, North America, July 7, 2009, 222-225, http://www.aaai.org/ocs/index.php/ICWSM/09/paper/view/226.

[6] For more on the *Mikumentary* series, including episodes of the documentary, see Mikumentary.com.

and Leavitt have interviewed and participated in industry events with members of Crypton Future Media, and since 2010, all three researchers have also conducted additional interviews and participant observation at Japanese- and English-language concerts, fan events, conventions, expos, and participated in and talked to members of online forums, internet communities, and social media platforms. Finally, Yoshiba and Knight have been involved in content creation, including production of fan concerts and songs, as part of their participant observation activities.

Peer Production, Japanese Convergence, and Hatsune Miku

Hatsune Miku is one of the most successful cases of convergence, at least in the Japanese media industry, in the twenty-first century. Over the course of more than seven years, hundreds of thousands of people participated in creating some part of her franchise alongside millions more viewers and fans. But unlike traditional ideas of convergence, Hatsune Miku exists—and continues to be successful—because of peer production.

Hatsune Miku embodies a new form of media production that combines grassroots artistic participation alongside corporate sponsorship and partnerships. Each side exists in a hybrid creative economy,[7] supporting the franchise as it grows in popularity and global reach. In examining Hatsune Miku's live concert events, we show how and why both fan creators and Crypton negotiate a balance between traditionally opposed forms of creative production. These sides, however, are inextricably linked: fan creations could not get the international recognition without Crypton's corporate power. Crypton also would not have a popular software without the free contributions of Miku's fan producer community. And some fans do push back against the "mainstream" image that Crypton must follow to promote a clean, simple image of Miku to the general public. Broadly, we explain how Crypton caters to participant needs and how fans both praise and oppose Crypton's involvement in Hatsune Miku's technical and social infrastructure.

To contextualize these practices within the Hatsune Miku community, we describe how Miku represents a new form of convergence. In Japan, she is part of an extended and networked version of the *media mix*, where the creative control over the media is distributed across a potentially infinite number of collaborators at a global scale.

---

[7] Lawrence Lessig, *Remix: Making Art and Commerce Thrive in the Hybrid Economy* (City of Westminster, UK: Penguin Press, 2008).

What Is Convergence?

Convergence, according to media scholar Henry Jenkin, is a cultural shift that occurs when consumers' relationships are constructed across disparate media platforms.[8] This shift in the entertainment industry can also result in an increase in participation of media consumers, impacting the production processes of that media as those consumers become more involved in creating parts of creative works. As Jenkins explains, "The power of the media producer and the power of the media consumer interact in unpredictable ways."[9]

Culture and media, of course, are not beholden to creative media companies and industries. In recent years, however, companies' control over media artifacts, especially through copyright, has led to various issues around creative participation with corporate media. Convergence has led to new, productive avenues for the industry, though not all of the industry's experiments have been successful. "Sometimes, corporate and grassroots convergence reinforce each other, creating closer, more rewarding relations between media producers and consumers. Sometimes, these two forces are at war."[10] Convergence is a moment in this recent political atmosphere where audience members can become co-producers and participants in the production process of creative works.

Peer production is one process underlying convergence. For economist Yochai Benkler, peer production is the practice of a collective of people working together, each on small parts, to create something much larger.[11] Benkler and other scholars have focused on peer production examples mainly related to information and systems, such as open-source software and participatory knowledge projects like Wikipedia. Compared to these examples, Hatsune Miku represents a unique type of peer production: the peer production of creative, artistic works.[12]

Another concept, *produsage*, extends the idea of peer production to both producers and consumers of information. Produsage describes the ecosystem around peer production and how people interact with peer-produced goods. A blend of the words *producer* and *usage*, it highlights the evolving relationship between media producers (creators) and media consumers (audiences): for instance, the cycle between millions of people

---

[8] Henry Jenkins, *Convergence Culture: Where Old and New Media Collide* (New York: New York University Press, 2006), 3.

[9] *Ibid.*, 2.

[10] *Ibid.*, 16.

[11] Yochai Benkler, *The Wealth of Networks* (New Haven, CT: Yale University Press, 2006).

[12] Alex Leavitt, "The Open-Source Cult(ure) of Hatsune Miku" (paper presented at South by Southwest, Austin, TX, March 12, 2012).

reading and thousands of people contributing articles on Wikipedia. Building off of the idea of creative peer production—ie., media artifacts or franchises, like film, music, or video games, built by thousands of participants—creative produsage focuses on the evolving relationships between the audiences and creators of these peer-productions. The audience has an audience; in other words, audiences become co-producers of products that are then further consumed by other people.

Produsage is important, because it highlights the distributed nature of certain types of peer production. For example, imagine the traditional way someone creates a book or painting: a primary author or artist, or a team, collaborates on the artifact and leads the direction of the story or design. Distributed creative peer production allows many participants— really, anyone—to contribute to the creation and distribution of the media. Given this structure of media creation, issues emerge around creative control of the media property and,[13] more generally, what makes up the franchise (e.g., how boundaries are drawn around what is in and out).

In particular, Japan has witnessed a form of convergence specific to the economic, cultural, and historical contexts of the nation's postwar media industry known as the *media mix*. Japan's media mix draws historically from commercial collaborations with media franchises to produce a narrative beyond the realm of the media itself, similar to what Jenkins calls "transmedia entertainment,"[14] though the media mix traditionally involves branded advertising as well. For example, Japanese media scholar Marc Steinberg details the evolution of the Japanese media mix specifically around Japanese animation, showing how early collaborations between chocolate manufacturers and child-oriented animated television programs produced peripheral commercial goods (*omake*).[15] These goods serve as a means of financing content production, for instance for the storyworld of Osamu Tezuka's *Astro Boy* (*Tetsuwan Atomu*), by developing new kinds of promotional relationships between companies, while also helping extend Astro Boy's world far beyond the program's weekly scheduled show times into kids' everyday lives.

Not all convergence within Japan relates to the media mix; notably, Japan houses one of the most vibrant creative peer production economies in the world through *dōjin*, or self-published, works. *Dōjinshi*, probably the

---

[13] Literat, "The Work of Art in the Age of Mediated Participation."

[14] Jenkins, *Convergence Culture*.

[15] Marc Steinberg, *Anime's Media Mix: Franchising Toys and Characters in Japan* (Minneapolis, MN: University of Minnesota Press, 2012).

most popular type, refers to publications such as comics, magazines, or novels, and usually these creative endeavors are found in fan communities: fan content, mostly derivative works of corporate intellectual media properties, that are by-fans, for-fans.[16] In addition to comics and art, other *dōjin*—like video games and music—are popular at fan conventions, the most notable of which is the bi-annual Comic Market (or Comiket). In recent years, the fervor of Japanese *dōjin* communities has also extended online, propagating on Japanese art websites (like Pixiv, akin to the English-language DeviantArt) and video sharing websites (like Niconico, which is similar to YouTube). These types of creative fan networks and grounded set of derivative practices form perhaps the greatest strength behind contemporary media franchises in Japan, and therefore Hatsune Miku directly emerged from these *dōjin* subcultures with a similar network of creators, audiences, and ethos.[17]

Figure 1. Crypton's official image of Hatsune Miku.

Who, and What, Is Hatsune Miku?

Hatsune Miku, though an international pop star, is at her core a peer-produced creative franchise that originated in Japan and spread internationally, primarily through online social media sites. For context, we explain her origin, how her franchise works, and the social and technical infrastructures that allowed her to reach her current popularity.

[16] Nele Noppe, "Dōjinshi Research as a Site of Opportunity for Manga Studies," in *Comics Worlds and the World of Comics: Towards Scholarship on a Global Scale*, ed. Jaqueline Berndt (Kyoto: International Manga Research Center, Kyoto Seika University, 2010), 123-142; and Hichibe Nobushige, "'Dōjinkai' no ronri: kōisha no rigai, kanshin to shihon no henkan," *Kontentsu bunka-shi kenkyū* 3 (2010): 19-32.

[17] Mizuko Ito, Okabe Daisuke, and Izumi Tsuji, *Fandom Unbound: Otaku Culture in a Connected World* (New Haven, CT: Yale University Press, 2012).

Hatsune Miku (which means "first sound of the future") first appeared in 2007 as a piece of box art on a voice synthesizer, in a series of software called Vocaloid.[18] Vocaloid software allows anyone using the program to drag and drop phonemes on specific musical notes, which are then strung together into words and melodies to form the particular software's singing voice. Produced by Crypton as part of the Character Vocal Series of synthesizer products (featuring a number of other characters), Hatsune Miku was first developed by recording the voice of popular anime voice actress Saki Fujita (figure 1).[19] An anime-style image was printed on the software's packaging to provide a visual representation for the synthesized voice, and this image (rather than the software itself) is now most associated with Hatsune Miku: she has become a character.[20] Crypton produces and sells other versions of Vocaloid software with other character images, but Miku is by far the most recognizable and popular.

Miku's image—her box-art icon (created by well-regarded Japanese illustrator, Kei)—is the forefront of her persona.[21] Though her software allowed musicians to adopt her into their music, Miku's image has flourished exponentially. And the popularity of this image could not have happened without the foundations of Japanese *dōjinshi* subculture, allowing Miku to spread far and wide, remixed and reimagined in a multitude of ways. Miku also emerged as a peculiar moment that bolstered her success: the cultural boom in otaku fandom, the peak of Tokyo's pop mecha Akihabara, the rise of inexpensive and intensive home computing hardware, and the launch of video sharing websites like Niconico and YouTube.

Miku was initially distributed through niche social networks on the Japanese video sharing site Niconico as well as Japanese social networking sites (like the now-defunct Vocaloid Nyappon) as musicians began sharing their songs.[22] Using Vocaloid software, musicians, composers, and lyricists (collectively known as Producers,[23] vocaloP's, or simply P's)

---

[18] Ian Condry, "Post-3/11 Japan and the Radical Recontextualization of Value: Music, Social Media, and End-Around Strategies for Cultural Action," *International Journal of Japanese Sociology* 20, no. 1 (November 2011): 4-17.

[19] Crypton used Fujita's voice again to record an English-language version of the software that was released in 2013.

[20] Eiji Ōtsuka, "World and Variation: The Reproduction and Consumption of Narrative," trans. Marc Steinberg, *Mechademia* 5, no. 1 (2010): 99-116.

[21] Conner, "Rei Toei Lives".

[22] Hamasaki et al., "Network Analysis of an Emergent Massively Collaborative Creation Community." Experimental covers began appearing publicly only a few days after the release of the software.

[23] Producers names are often chosen by the Vocaloid community—more evidence of the social ties that connect this network of creators and audiences.

collaborated on songs and videos, publishing them for free online. Early songs appeared with title cue cards, short animated sequences, lyrics, or static images of Miku.

Eventually, technologies were built around Miku—most notably MikuMikuDance, a fan-created, free software by Yu Higuchi (Higuchi_U) that allows people to use 3D models of Miku and pose them for video capture—that inspired video creators to reach out and collaborate with song artists. As Miku's songs gained audiences, Miku's image became more well known. While Crypton gave Miku a few "official" character traits, like height and musical tenor,[24] fan artists began adapting her image in a variety of ways (usually imagining Miku with different fashion designs or personality traits). Sometimes these images would be uploaded on new versions of song videos, but mostly fan artists, cosplayers, dancers, and singers iterated on her design, creating derivative (or original) works, attributing inspiration to and from each other, and interpreting Miku in their own creative ways. In an interview with one of the authors, an American mother of a teenaged fan explained involvement in Miku's franchise: "Disney is something you go and look at. Miku is something you go and become." Her daughter not only became part of Miku through cosplaying as Miku at conventions, but she became part of Miku's network of creators and larger community. For many creator-fans, it is this "becoming" that is a central appeal of Miku: she is a means of self-expression, access to a network of peers, and ability to become a participant in a novel type of media collective.

As people remixed Miku more often, she became more popular, and more people talked about her by word of mouth, online via social media platforms (like social networks such as Mixi, Facebook, and Twitter or subcultural forums like 2channel, Reddit, and 4chan), and offline at fan events or with friends. People then continued to contribute to her entity through video sharing sites (Niconico and YouTube), art sharing web communities (Pixiv and DeviantArt), and other locations on the internet. Crypton also strategically catered to these fan networks by creating online platforms to support them, such as Piapro.jp (a fan art website[25]) and KarenT, a label to help Vocaloid musicians sell music and collect royalties on their works, both further generating value for the franchise. Again, without the rise and adoption of this ecosystem of social media platforms, Miku could never have spread in this way.

---

[24] See http://www.crypton.co.jp/miku_eng.
[25] The term PiaPro is a Japanese derivation of the term "peer production."

As mentioned above, Vocaloid Producers upload their songs on Niconico and YouTube for free, gathering dozens or millions of views, depending on the particular song and video. For some artists, the music videos they uploaded to Niconico became the foundation for record deals, while thousands of others garnered smaller audiences, but audiences with whom they could interact with at fan events and local venues (for instance, Mogra, a small club in Tokyo's Akihabara neighborhood, or the VOCAROOM,[26] an impromptu meet-up at a bar in Tokyo where Vocaloid producers and fans can talk, according to one interviewee, "on the same level"). As these songs became more popular, the songs gained widespread appeal in Japan. Notably, karaoke businesses began stocking more and more Vocaloid-sung songs, and many of these songs remain as top-sung songs on karaoke rankings, especially amongst teenagers.[27]

The spread of early concert videos significantly influenced Miku's international success on a general level, supported by transnational Japanese pop culture fan communities. While new songs and music videos have been few, given their complexity compared to simpler artistic contributions like illustrations, thousands of international fans participate in fan art communities, cosplay, and especially watching sharing, and localizing music videos across platforms. As Crypton has recognized more audiences outside of Japan, Miku's appearances around the globe have increased. In 2011, Crypton brought Miku to Los Angeles for her first international concert, and recently, Miku has also appeared in other concerts in numerous countries. Crypton has also marketed her in various ways, appearing in the US in Toyota commercials, touring as an opening act for Lady Gaga, and appearing as a guest on the *Late Show with David Letterman*.

Grassroots vs. Corporate: Crypton's Involvement in the Miku Franchise

Given the bottom-up peer production ecosystem that emerged around Hatsune Miku, Crypton still owns her intellectual property. According to Hiroyuki Itoh, the company's CEO, the small company never anticipated Japan's (or the world's) fanaticism with Miku; at the time of launch, the company was "just releasing software." But over time, Crypton has had to make strategic decisions that would affect the future of the Hatsune Miku franchise and brand. Gina Neff and David Stark argue that in contemporary organizations, "responsiveness" is designed into how companies operate, like the "permanently beta" products they create

---

[26] VOCAROOM is featured in Knight's *Mikumentary*, Episode 4 at Mikumentary.com.
[27] See, for example, http://joysound.com/ex/st/songlist/annual_age_2014/index.htm.

that are constantly evolving for the consumer.[28] Crypton essentially was forced to adopt these strategies while recognizing the potential that Miku could have as a distributed creative franchise.

As Hatsune Miku's popularity grew, rather than shutting down the derivative creative works featuring Miku, Crypton embraced creators' passion and assumed a hierarchical, administrative role over the evolution of Miku (a tension we explore in further detail later in this chapter). The challenge was maintaining the proper ecosystem for continued peer production while still maintaining copyright control. One approach they took was to implement a unique copyright license over Miku's image. This license is known as the Piapro Character License, and it allows a variety of free and open uses of Miku's imagery.[29] Basically, the agreement allows anyone to use Miku's image in mostly any non-commercial, derivative way. If anyone wants to use Miku in a commercial manner, they must contact Crypton for a licensing agreement.

As a for-profit company, finances remain a concern, and Crypton keeps a careful watch over how it can ensure profit in relation to the sustenance of the creative community and its volunteered, free contributions to the franchise. Over time, Crypton has released numerous, updated versions of the Hatsune Miku (and other Vocaloid) software. Crypton also wants to support artists, and the company had taken innovative steps to help their contributing artists. Notably, the company worked with JASRAC (the Japanese Society for Rights of Authors, Composers, and Publishers) to create a flexible license where producers could release their music for free but still receive royalties—for instance, through karaoke. Crypton will license Miku's image to large companies too as a core part of their business model, putting Miku in convenience stores (Family Mart), in video games (SEGA), and in hundreds of ancillary commercial goods (from expensive Louis Vuitton branding to generic food and toys in convenience stores). For some fans, partnerships with companies like SEGA, Coca Cola, Toyota, Domino's, and Google are positive symbols of how widespread and successful Hatsune Miku's franchise—driven by everyone's collective creativity—has become. And Crypton's expressed goals emphasize the importance of collective creativity in this commercial ecosystem. As Hiroyuki Itoh described, related to how Crypton decides who to collaborate with, the company prefers focusing on the opportunities where creators can contribute:

---

[28] Gina Neff and David Stark, "Permanently Beta: Responsive Organization in the Internet Era," in *Society Online: The Internet in Context*, ed. Philip N. Howard and Steve Jones (Thousand Oaks, CA: Sage, 2004), 173-188.

[29] Though the Vocaloid software remains strictly proprietary.

If someone wants to make a T-shirt and sell it, the answer is no, because there is no reason to do it, for us. There are people who want to use Hatsune Miku as a tool to express their creativity. *They* can be our partners. For example, Sega made a game which has music and cosplay, and the music and costumes were created by our users. So this game is an opportunity for the creators to express their work...Crypton, as a company, makes a deal if it's possible to be an opportunity for expression...We will create it in order to make an opportunity for the art to be expressed, from a creative point of view.

On the other hand, these large corporate partnerships leave other fans—especially a number of those participants who formed the foundation of the Japanese community in its early years—feeling that she is too commercialized and is controlled artistically more by huge companies (Crypton, and other collaborators like SEGA) than by the artists, producers, and fans (a theme we explore at the conclusion of this chapter).

Alongside voluntary peer production (as structured by Crypton), there exists another form of participant involvement—social relationships. Many fans, especially those who do not create music or videos and mainly view the output of others, find appeal in how Crypton architects Miku's franchise by controlling the order of the ecosystem through financial means and sustaining fan relationships. Media researcher Nancy Baym describes the work around producing and maintaining these social relationships as "relational labor," connections between creators and audiences codified as work and commercialized.[30] These fans see an increase in visibility of Miku brought about by the success of the peer production model as beneficial and exciting, even at the potential expense of over-commercialization, because the work they put into community relationships continues to be supported by Crypton (even though the corporate decisions and agreements are not necessarily transparent to these fans).

Commercialization, for these fans, generally acts as a type of infrastructure for greater attention and expanded participation. While participants in the franchise frequently contribute free labor, and it is possible that some have made agreements with Crypton to get compensated for these contributions, the transparency behind these

---

[30] Nancy Baym, "Connect with Your Audience! The Relational Labor of Connection," *The Communication Review* 18, no. 1 (2015): 14-22.

negotiations are unclear, particularly for fans. Crypton of course gains profit in the aggregate, given the *sum* of all peer contributions and audiences' relations. The aggregate is then multiplied further: as more people participate, the "value" of Miku continues to increase, and the company is able to profit off of selling the concept of the peer production model. While some onlookers might view audiences' enthusiasm for this growth as a sort of false consciousness about exploitative participatory labor, the central role of relational labor in this type of ecosystem is appreciated by a large amount of participants that were interviews.

What is important for this case study's connection to convergence is that the Hatsune Miku franchise is a unique extension of the traditional Japanese "media mix," drawing from an ecosystem of branded content. Except now, in the case of Miku, the original media is created and distributed not in a hierarchical process by the original company but by a creative collective of individuals on the internet. Hatsune Miku's concerts are one example where these corporate collaborations produce acclaimed events and opportunities for fans to engage with the franchise directly and in more traditional, familiar media formats (ie., concerts).

Hatsune Miku in Concert: Going Pro with Peer Production
Crypton Future Media, Inc.'s live Hatsune Miku concerts represent a small slice of Miku's franchise. Yet we focus on them in this chapter as a way to investigate the tensions at play between the bottom-up and top-down dynamics within a creative peer production ecosystem. We also focus on the concerts because, out of all of the facets of Miku's franchise, they have captured the attention and imagination of the world, from hardcore fans to casual, but fascinated, internet onlookers. While only a few thousand fans are able to attend the concerts every year, due to money and especially geography, millions of people have viewed videos of the concerts online.

A Hatsune Miku concert is unique because, instead of writing or commissioning songs, Crypton enlists the contributions of the community for the creative core of the production. Each song performed on stage was at one point uploaded for free to Niconico; popular songs each year are included in the few concerts' lineups. The concert draws from so many places in Crypton's media mix strategy: collaborating with community Producers to include their songs, the fashioning of computer-generated models to be projected on stage,[31] merchandise sales, and even

---

[31] SEGA contributes some models from their video games and assists in creating others with a team called Marza Animation Planet Inc.

recognition of fan engagement (coordinated dancing and cheering by the audience). All of this revolves around that core element of the franchise: its main media content—unlike other media mix franchises in Japan—draws from open participation of distributed creators.

Below, we walk through facets of Crypton's concerts, to examine how these productions combine a unified version of Miku, the contributions of creators, and the fervor and subcultural practices of the franchise's audiences into an approachable, singular performance. Still, as we explain further in this chapter, the concerts highlight various tensions and politics between the professional commercialization of these concerts by Crypton and the grassroots, peer production practices of the Vocaloid community. This case of distributed creative peer production in the context of corporate control reproduces anxieties from traditional production practices within the creative industries.

We examine 14 of Crypton's Hatsune Miku concerts.[32] While Crypton collaborates in various ways to produce some smaller concerts, the 14 we focus on in this chapter are the major productions by the company. Miku's debut concert appearance occurred at the *Animelo Summer LIVE 2009* event in August, while her first solo concert was a week later at the *Miku FES'09* concert in Tokyo. Since then, Crypton has held over a dozen and a half concerts (some collaborations with other companies and using other Vocaloids) both in Japan and abroad, such as in Singapore, Hong Kong, Taiwan, Indonesia, Los Angeles, and New York City (as well as live streams of those concerts to other venues globally). Each concert features music sung by Miku and other Crypton-created Vocaloid characters,[33] for which the number of songs range per event. Crypton works in collaboration with the Producers of each song to create a set list, and then—through various agreements with SEGA and others—has 3D models created or adapted for each song performance.

Song Selection and the Politics of Participation

For the most part, the songs chosen for the concerts draw directly from the Vocaloid community's contributions, with permission by the creators. In particular, the song choices tend to reflect the popularity of the various VocaloidP's songs on Niconico (also including their relative sales

---

[32] For the purposes of this chapter, we will be focusing only on Crypton's concerts for which Miku was the headlining act and were evening-length concerts. The 14 concerts included for this chapter were based on the time of the chapter's writing, and additional concerts have since been produced. The authors would also like to thank *jrharbort* of Mikufan.com for reviewing all the factual information throughout and for this section in particular.

[33] See http://www.crypton.co.jp/mp/pages/prod/vocaloid/.

rankings). However, Crypton as the curator and producer of the concerts decides what the song list will be for each and every concert.

Because Crypton uses the concerts to attract all sorts of audience members, from the most hardcore Miku fans to those new to the franchise, the company becomes tasked with forming a universal Miku: something that anyone can understand as a common "identity" for the singer. The creative community of course may for the most part reinterpret Miku in any way they see fit. Owning the proprietary software and also controlling the copyright license that allows producers and fans to remake Miku, Crypton can also tweak Miku's brand and franchise in any way they see fit.

While community members express both beneficial or detrimental effects on the community, Crypton's strategy is to create a balance between grassroots peer production and maintaining a growing international franchise. In order to maintain control of this corporate branding, in the concerts, Crypton has never presented an extreme version of Hatsune Miku. While drastic redesigns of Miku are also uncommon across the peer production ecosystem (mostly she encounters slight fashion changes or reworked personality types), Crypton is tasked with creating a social face for the singer that is easily identifiable and relatable. Further, Crypton needs to pay homage to songs that are popular within the community while slowly introducing new pieces, giving longtime fans novel moments to celebrate without alienating new audience members. The additional challenge for Crypton is accounting for the network of creators and audience members that maintain the Miku franchise.

Looking across the 14 concerts, we can see how Crypton has made decisions in the evolving landscape of its peer-produced franchise. For instance, Crypton uses criteria such as a song's musicality, themes, popularity, release date, and even costumes to consider its concern (and marketing) potential. Amongst the most-played tunes from all of the concerts, the audience encounters songs like "Melt" (by ryo), "PoPiPo" (by LamazeP), "Yellow" (by kz), "When the First Love Ends" (by ryo), and "Romeo & Cinderella" (by doriko): all songs that are upbeat and sound like contemporary pop music. These songs are included due to their popularity. They rose to prominence within Japanese online communities, and as they gained additional visibility from appearing in the earliest concerts, in addition to being songs with high production value to begin with, their videos exponentially garnered increased view counts and—with them—additional fans.

While some songs are included in the concerts for their notable status within the franchise's core Japanese fan networks, some songs have entered a cultural canon. For example, the internationally popular "World is Mine" (by ryo) has been included in about half of the concerts, though it does appear in every single international concert. "World is Mine" became popular especially via YouTube because of its appearance in a video uploaded from a recording of one of the original Crypton concerts. It was shared often amongst American media outlets as an iconic example of Japanese technophilia,[34] and the inundation of views from American and other international audiences skyrocketed this song into Miku's oeuvre. Further, the song is featured prominently in Crypton's video game collaboration with SEGA (the *Project Diva* series), and it has also been adapted for numerous marketing cross-promotions (for example, in the American Toyota commercials).

Other lesser-known songs have been adapted too, though usually for marketing purposes. For example, in Indonesia's 2014 Miku Expo concert, Miku sings a song in Indonesian, "Venus di Ujung Jari" (by Mohax-2000), allowing for local talent to gain exposure and inspire local fans to buy and try out the Vocaloid software. Also quite recently, the relatively unknown song "Glass Wall" (by Guitar Hero Piano Zero) was adopted into Miku's headline appearance for Lady Gaga's 2014 ArtRave concert tour. An English-language song with few views on YouTube, but with lyrics that expressed Miku's digital nature well and with a dubstep soundtrack that appealed to a changing musical taste with younger American audiences, "Glass Wall" was adapted for Crypton's Los Angeles and New York Miku Expo concerts. Afterward, the song has gained a fair bit of popularity within the English-language fan community (with about 185,000 views on YouTube at the time of this writing; though the song only has about 5,000 views on Niconico). Even more, "Sharing the World" (by BIGHEAD), an English-language song, was adopted by Crypton as the theme song of the 2014 Miku Expo concerts, even though BIGHEAD was relatively unknown as a musical producer within the community (and there were other songs in English already created by some artists).

To note, there are also numerous songs that Crypton has not considered to be representative enough of Miku's ideal public persona for inclusion in the concerts. First, there are tens of thousands of pieces that are never included in the concerts. These songs appear on video sharing sites, and they gain small fan followings, but they do not necessarily break into any major limelight. Crypton has occasionally introduced songs from this less popular end of the Vocaloid spectrum

---

[34] Koichi Iwabuchi, "'Soft' Nationalism and Narcissism: Japanese Popular Culture Goes Global," *Asian Studies Review* 26, no. 4 (2002): 447-469.

into their concerts, though they tend to have many more views than thousands of others. For instance, the song "Dōbutsu Uranai" (Animal Divination, by Sukoppun-san) was performed in Magical Mirai 2013, and while it has received hundreds of thousands of views on Niconico, it hasn't received as many of the more-popular concert regulars. In total, out of the hundreds of thousands songs that have been created featuring Hatsune Miku and published online, only 129 songs have appeared in any Crypton-produced concert. And out of these 129 songs, a group of 24 songs are sung once and never appear again.

The Invisibility of Peer Production

While Crypton's Vocaloid concerts are perhaps one of the most popular ways that people first encounter Hatsune Miku (especially for those outside of Japanese pop culture communities), it remains difficult for the concert to demonstrate the intricacies of the peer production process, ethos, and especially community. Many people, especially internationally, encounter her through YouTube videos of the concerts: a dancing young girl in front of thousands of adoring fans. However, these encounters with the concerts by the general public make peer production invisible. Further, as Miku becomes further commercialized as a character and brand, she becomes iconic without a strong reflection of her creative community. Below, we explore the tensions between the professionalization of Miku and the core foundation of the franchise's content in peer production.

For Crypton's Vocaloid concerts, most attendees have at least seen a video or piece of fan art of Miku before attending; however, they may not yet be active participants in the creator community. The concerts can therefore be entry points for new fans into the peer production community, engaging them further with fan art, cosplay, or even creating videos and music themselves (figure 2). Still, while the concerts are one pinnacle within the creative franchise—a professional concert that people can attend, rather than only engaging with Miku by watching videos at home—they do not promote peer production to its fullest, even though this aspect of the franchise is most important.

Figure 2. Fan cosplay of Calne Ca. Reproduced with permission from Yuriros.

The first point of tension revolves around the agency of the creative peer community. While the concerts reflect the community's preferences, it is not necessarily possible for anyone from the peer production community to "produce" a part of these concerts. Instead of promoting peer production as the core tenet behind Hatsune Miku's existence, the concerts boost the franchise's brand and clout, bringing more attention to only a subset of producers and songs. Crypton has attempted to highlight the community in some prior concerts—for instance, Vocaloid producers and other artists joined the band onstage during the 2012 Thanksgiving Day concerts in Tokyo—though it is uncommon.

The second point of tension manifests from this filtering of the peer production community's spectrum of works. Crypton's choice of songs for the concerts follows a set of decisions around presenting Miku with a clean public face. As we reiterated above, the concerts tend to avoid presenting Miku in any extreme version (as can happen from any particular peer-produced work). For the concerts, Crypton wants to fashion an approachable and relatable Miku.

The social face that Crypton gives Miku avoids particular themes and overtones, such as those that are too grotesque, sexual, or violent.

Various artists have toyed with Miku's personality and image over time, creating an evolving portrait for who Miku was, is, and can be. One of the more radical examples is 3D artist Deino's grotesque rendition of Miku, dubbed Calne Ca, where Miku's body is transmogrified into a deformed half-insect, half-metal-skeleton. Crypton has been able to use most of the popular songs, videos, designs, and personalities in their official brand image because the extreme ones from the community never dominate. And Calne Ca will likely never make it into a concert, because the image requires a deeper interest in Miku's fandom and an appreciation of radical derivatives, thus alienating any newcomers in the audience.

In other words, there are no extremes presented in the concerts because Crypton wants and requires a universal—yet flexible—Miku. As we argued earlier, crafting Miku as a brand necessitates Crypton finding a common identity for Miku as an "individual" performer, but they also want to maintain her aura as an "editable" character, preserving the connection back to peer production.

Therefore, the third point of tension relates to how Crypton presents a singular version of Miku. Unlike the unlimited variations that emerge from the creative community, the Miku on stage is restricted. Crypton frequently adopts color schemes and fashion design styles from popular videos, but they all adhere to Miku as if she were changing costumes (rather than becoming a different entity). As a professional production, the concert portrays Miku acts as the "official" version against the community's varied iterations. When commenting on the naturalism of Miku's animation style, Hiroyuki Itoh explains, "it was created by a computer, and it's difficult to make [the computer animation seem] natural. We want to make her as cute as possible, and also relatable as much as possible so that people feel familiar with her." Familiarity is important: when asked why the company does not create extreme versions of Miku in the concerts, Itoh continues that the concerts are Crypton's opportunity to create an environment where fans can feel like they are able to be in Miku's presence: "The concert is the only one occasion that fans can meet Miku, there are no other places to meet...They don't want anything deformed,[35] they want something as real as possible. [They want] the same height [as Miku], as accurate as possible, they want to see a reproduced Miku, they want something like that." An American fan echoes this desire for a familiar idol, "you can celebrate the participatory aspect of it, but at the same time you can celebrate the fact that you're

---

[35] Referencing a style of Japanese caricature, see http://en.wikipedia.org/wiki/Super_deformed.

going to a concert and you can cheer for Miku much the same way you can cheer for an actual idol." This intentional act of legitimation does two things: while it allows the audience to experience Miku as a familiar performer, it simultaneously limits the ethos of peer production to be present (where Miku can be anything).

In a way, the concerts reiterate a canon of creative works that has emerged from the Vocaloid community, produced in concert with the algorithms of video sharing platforms. As certain songs and videos become popular, they gain more visibility, thus lending points to recommendation algorithms, leading to more people seeing those videos and their view counts increasingly exponentially. When the viewer community shows dramatic appreciation for particular songs, these songs (and related videos, designs, etc.) become embedded in Miku's cultural canon. Given these songs' high-ranking status, Crypton adopts them in the concerts, further cementing their popularity. Thus, the concerts act as a nod to the creators of these songs. But this nod operates at the expense of other songs (and therefore other creators), reproducing a style of traditional hierarchy for these cultural goods: some songs remain as the chosen ones recognized by Crypton, over the other, lesser-valued ones. All in all, the concerts as a traditional form, format, and genre of performance don't synthesize well with the unlimited possibilities that come from the peer production community.

Crypton has even shifted away from earlier experimentation with songs popular with zealous fans. Notable among this small collection of songs are those by niche Vocaloid producer DeadballP, who created many songs for Miku in her early years, though he tends to write lyrics of a blunt, sexual nature (even though the melodies and rhythms of his songs are cute and catchy). For instance, one of his popular songs, "*Watashi wa ningen ja nai kara*" (I'm not a Human, So...) has Miku singing about having sexual intercourse with the listener and how she won't get pregnant. Surprising to some, a few of DeadballP's uploaded videos were removed from Niconico after moderators felt the lyrics were too risqué (he later re-uploaded toned-down versions). Importantly, though, a handful of DeadballP's songs were prominently featured in one of the earliest Crypton concerts. However, only one of his songs appeared in a later concert in 2011, and none have won a spot on any set list since.

Crypton aims to foster an image that demonstrates Miku's potential to be a shared, collaborative artifact for the community. A clean version of Miku often resulting in songs about youth, fun, and romance instead of perverse or socially-complex themes such as violence, sexuality, and morbidity. In crafting a public persona for Miku, Crypton will acknowledge but not openly promote peer productions that toe the line of respectability.[36] To reiterate, this decision helps protect Miku's brand: it fashions Miku into something that all new consumers can easily approach upon their first introduction to the franchise. That said, they cannot actively ignore fan productions—whether the songs are stranger than expected or, more often than not, just not as popular as others—since all of them represent important steps in the historical progression of Miku's brand. Yet this tension re-emphasizes that Crypton, in the concerts, must value a commercial perspective over that of the peer production ethos.

The Social Versus the Commercial

Though we have argued that peer production remains fairly invisible and limited in these concerts, what do the concerts represent for the Vocaloid community, and what role do the concerts play in Cryptons' media mix? Below, we explore the connection between performance and social event that drive the fervor behind these concerts, and how the convergence of social connections into media franchises contributes to a new form of the Japanese media mix.

Crypton's concerts have become a ritual for Vocaloid audiences and Hatsune Miku fans. They are allowed to—in a rare moment—experience being *with* Miku, individually and collectively, in the same time and place. In an interview with one of the authors, Hiroyuki Itoh stated that fans are interested in the concerts because they can be in a moment where they can finally connect with Miku. The appeal, of course, is for fans to experience—as with any concert—the performer "in the flesh," though there remains a disconnect in Miku's case between her live audiences and herself as a "non-real" performer. Media researcher Philip Auslander identifies this friction of liveness back to televised performance, and he argues that the values that we assume are the unique elements of live media events (such as connecting with the performer and building community) are just as present in mediated performances.[37] And many Miku fans do experience her presence at these concerts. As one American male fan describes, "She's not a real person, but she's a real performer...If

---

[36] This is of respectability is also a line in Crypton Future Media Inc.'s Piapro Character License: "When you copy or modify the Characters, please do not distort, mutilate, modify or take other derogatory action in relation to the Characters that would be prejudicial to Crypton's honor or reputation (please see Section 4e. of the full license). Some examples of prohibited uses include use in an overly violent context or in a sexual context." For text of the "Creative Commons Public License to the illustrations of Crypton Future Media's Characters," see http://piapro.net/en_for_creators.html.

[37] Philip Auslander, *Liveness: Performance in a Mediatized Culture* (London: Routledge, 1999).

you ever see her on stage, she interacts with the audience, she introduces the band, she gets a little emotional. That's the only thing that's important. You're there to be entertained. It's a bit like watching [a movie], you suspend belief. You go in there and see her on stage, and for that hour and a half she's real. And that's the way it should be." And as a Japanese male fan describes, "Yes, we all know that she is not an individual that exists, but seeing her disappear from the stage like that makes us recognize that she has a virtual existence. She has a strong presence on the stage but we feel that she is also virtual." By staging her in the format of a proscenium-framed rock concert, Crypton also helps further spotlight audience members' sense of presence. Even though Miku is animated in proportion to the human band members, Crypton helps tweak her performance—such as through extremely fast costumes changes or transitions that make her body explode into bits or sparkles—to emphasize the unique digital nature of her existence and again to highlight that her origins lie in technology and especially online collaborations.

In the concerts, fans are also able—in another rare moment—to connect with other members of the Vocaloid community in person and offline, and to build the networks of community often promised by live performance.[38] Though they are less successful at promoting peer production, the concerts do highlight the shared energy and excitement of being involved in the franchise—social aspects that are difficult to experience in unison with others solely online. Usually each concert provides a standing space for avid fans and a recessed seating area for other concert goers. Fans will memorize dances and coordinate glowstick dance movements (*otagei*) for each song, depending on the song's musical content, costume design, and sometimes even song producer (figure 3). Community socializing is common in *dōjinshi* culture: a frequent fan custom in Japan is the *ofukai*, or post-event meetups, where friends (or sometimes strangers) gather together to drink, sing karaoke, and enjoy each others' company.[39] As one Vocaloid instrument engineer explained in an interview with one of the authors, Miku represents a connection between members in a subculture because she "is the social glue that binds

---

[38] Lucie Vágnerová, "Liveness and Labor and Hologram Singers" (paper presented at Bone Flute to Auto-Tune: A Conference on Music & Technology in History, Theory, and Practice, University of California, Berkeley, April 24-26, 2014).

[39] When Japanese fans go abroad (e.g., to the concert in Los Angeles), they also bring over fan goods, which they will sometimes distribute to other fans: for example, we saw customized fan shirts circulating amongst Japanese audience members, a fan-created comic (drawing from interactions with American fans), and some fans brought sets of homemade glowsticks to hand out to Americans who had not thought to bring any. At the 2014 Los Angeles concert, a small group of Japanese fans actually brought over a small projector and screen, setting up their own miniature concert in a local bar.

people together." A Chinese-American Vocaloid fan explained: "Maybe this whole time when we thought live performance were about the bands themselves, maybe we should rethink the fact that live performances were about being with other fans, about being connected to other people. In that case, maybe it is the fact that Miku is a database that is bringing people together." Simon Reynolds similarly described 1990s rave culture and participation in these live performances in a similar way: "intimacy is dispersed into a generalized bonhomie: you bond with the gang you came with, but also people you've never met."[40] For many fans, simply being present at the concert is their form of participation, compared to other peer production creators (who become directed involved in contributing).

Figure 3. Screenshot from Hatsune Miku Live Party 2013 in Kansai during a performance of "Love Colored Ward." (*Hatsune Miku Raibu Pātī 2012 in Kansai*, Blu-ray (2013; Tokyo, Japan: Kadokawa Shoten). http://5pb.jp/mikupa/index_kansai.html.

Crypton's concerts additionally allow fans their one moment per year to focus their fan energy and experience Miku with many similarly-energetic others, collective moments that the community audiences embrace. As Lucie Vágnerová demonstrates, Hatsune Miku's "holographic" concerts challenge a central assumption of contemporary live performance: the unique aura of the live body performing on stage.[41] The disruption of

---

[40] Simon Reynolds, *Energy Flash: A Journey through Rave Music and Dance Culture* (Berkeley: Soft Skull Press, 2012), xxxi.

[41] Vágnerová, "Liveness and Labor and Hologram Singers." Many fans and media colloquially use the term "hologram" when describing Miku's concerts. In the strictest sense, Miku is technically not a hologram; she appears on stage as a video projected onto a plane of glass.

"realness" embodied by the concerts is one that is shared by the majority of attendees, Japanese and foreign, at their first concert. The familiar staging of a rock concert production only deepens this discord: a live band appears on stage, performing and improvising live with Miku's predetermined songs amidst a proscenium stage and a setup of multiple projectors beam Miku's character image onto the screen. For seasoned fans, the surprise of her projected form has become normalized; they share a common excitement for her physical presence, in addition to debating the song choices, costumes, and technology on display. Though Miku is unresponsive to audience interactions in real time, the semblance of liveness incites a shared, community response: a suspension of disbelief and reverence of Miku's constantly transforming, animated figure, because a central draw for these concerts is the overriding sense of community *with one another*. Many fans interviewed have articulated even a sense of collective accomplishment: each audience member has played some role in bringing Miku to the stage. Every artwork made, every video watched, every "share" and every "like" online, each piece has contributed to the production, even if Crypton was responsible for compiling it.

From a commercial standpoint, Crypton must architect Hatsune Miku to fit a particular brand image that the company can use to its benefit. Any effort the company puts toward this goal, of course, helps the peer production community, since Crypton maintains the software, its social media platforms, and the engineering of Miku's professional image. Underlying these concerts, Crypton uses savvy marketing: they *depend* upon and therefore *must* involve fan participation in their entire international branding effort. Crypton's productions can be viewed as a successful balancing of user-generated content, popularity triggered by audiences, and commercial branding. This combination is unique to Hatsune Miku, as a creative conduit and platform for self-expression, and especially unique to the media mix within Japan, which is slowly acclimating to the networked creative productions that propagate online in networked communities.

In an interview with one of the authors, Hiroyuki Itoh—when asked about Crypton's main priority in developing new products or services—explained that they must take care of the fans. This "taking care" involves responding to new directions and opportunities created by the community and making sure that peer-production is primary to the company's focus. This focus is evident in the guidelines Crypton uses when selecting new companies to partner with and Itoh's focus on using Miku as a "tool to express...creativity" (as explained earlier in this chapter). Such an unusual reply reflects Crypton's unique history as a small, "beta" company: when they first released the Vocaloid software, they had no idea that Miku would inspire an international phenomenon. When they saw what people were creating with Miku, rather than shutting down this bottom-up fan production, they built a whole company around fostering participation and creativity. Supporting hundreds of thousands of people's creative use of the character remains the crux of Crypton's business model, and much of Miku's success is based on fans recreating, remixing and recirculating her character in this bottom-up way. At the same time, however, Crypton wants to maintain top-down commercial copyright control over Miku as a character. If Miku were truly "owned by everyone," then anyone could create, say, a Miku fashion line or produce their own concert. Crypton still has a vested interest in allowing her identity to remain open and participatory rather than as one corporate, fixed identity. In a successful, hybrid-commercial model of creative peer production like Hatsune Miku's franchise, bottom-up participation relies on an ethos of participatory culture, emphasized by a belief in the value of contributing to a collective work made available to a free public commons. But because Crypton is forced to navigate the contemporary landscape of the creative industries and copyright, the company must maintain the role of a top-down guiding force over how and where the brand of Miku develops over time.

Peer Production at a Global Scale

This chapter has addressed Crypton's Vocaloid concerts featuring Hatsune Miku as one of the pivotal examples of convergence in contemporary peer-produced media franchises and the Japanese contents industry. Crypton has faced new types of decisions as it tries to internationalize the peer production community beyond its core in Japan.

The majority of Miku's primary creator community and consumer audience resides within Japan. Due to her inherently Japanese persona, there are a number of cultural elements to Miku that may not translate well abroad: namely, Miku's image is drawn in an anime-style that is situated within an otaku subcultural design aesthetic. The software, of course, existed for years only in Japanese. From a production standpoint, Miku also exists within an aura of "cute"-ness, extending again from Japan's otaku subculture, in which young female performers are venerated as idols.[42] Miku also depends on a culture of fan works and

---

[42] See Patrick W. Galbraith and Jason G. Karlin, *Idols and Celebrity in Japanese Media Culture* (London: Palgrave, 2012).

the close relationships between fan artists connected by local events and online communities. These aspects combine to form a uniquely Japanese environment within which Miku predominantly operates.

For many fans outside of Japan, Miku's perceived "Japaneseness" is a central part of her appeal. For example, in late 2013 one of Crypton's primary strategies for expanding the international spread of Miku was to release an English-language version of the software (both the interface and Miku's spoken phonemes) to consumers. During fieldwork while attending a panel at Anime Expo (the largest anime convention in the US) that hosted representatives from Crypton Future Media in 2011, one of the authors noted that, when asked by the panel if they were interested in an English-language Miku, the audience—a few thousand fans of Japanese pop culture—did not express much interest: only about a dozen or so individuals raised their hands. For this crowd, which makes up a significant portion of Hatsune Miku followers, the idea of a non-Japanese Miku was less appealing. This attraction to Miku's distinct Japanese identify conflicts strongly with ideas of "fan homology," where fans of this pop media can "select out Japanese representations" and embrace foreign fan identities,[43] and other intermeshed theories of transcultural fan practice.[44]

With the recent Miku Expo tours in Indonesia and the US, we have seen that Crypton's concerts have been accepted with passion in numerous countries. Yet sustaining Miku long-term depends on whether or not Crypton can foster an international foundation of creators, in addition to audiences. An increase in the saturation of commercial goods geared toward the general public in Japan—for example, Miku's licensed image appears regularly on buses, billboards, food products, and even AA batteries in Japan—has led many dedicated Japanese peer community participants to view this shift from underground music production to mainstream commercial acceptance as a mixed blessing at best. As reflected in the songs selected for Crypton's concerts, while certain artists may gain international exposure, they tend to be the artists who already work in popular genres and for pop audiences. Some Japanese producers who found success in the early years of the Miku have since stopped featuring Miku in their music; either turning completely to mainstream music production, or using other niche, non-Crypton (or open-source) Vocaloids; or ceasing music

---

[43] Matt Hills, "Transcultural *Otaku:* Japanese Representations of Fandom and Representations of Japan in Anime/Manga Fan Cultures," in *Proceedings of MiT2* (Massachusetts Institute of Technology, Cambridge, MA, May 10-12, 2002), http://cmsw.mit.edu/mit2/Abstracts/MattHillspaper.pdf.

[44] Bertha Chin and Lori Hitchcock Morimoto, "Toward a Theory of Transcultural Fandom," *Participations: Journal of Audience & Reception Studies* 10, no. 1 (May 2013): 92-108.

production altogether. Other fans have even taken it upon themselves to curate fan concerts, where they choose the singers, set lists, and content without the oversight of Crypton's control (figure 4).

Figure 4. A fan concert against a fly net set up in a restaurant in Downtown Los Angeles in 2014. Reproduced with permission from stephieku.

These tensions between peer production and commercialization are not unique to Crypton: almost all underground artistic movements historically experience tension-filled re-workings when entering the mainstream (for instance, the history of punk as both a musical and social movement).[45] A Vocaloid producer describes his own experience moving from making Vocaloid music as his hobby to making his music for

---

[45] Dick Hebdige, *Subculture: The Meaning of Style* (London, England: Routledge, 1979).

commercial purposes this way: "I actually got [commercially] sponsored many times. I feel regrets about doing it. Whenever you are sponsored by someone that means there is no compromise, and you have to make the best-selling songs for them. But most of the time I want to make my own music." Similar contemporary peer production projects, like Wikipedia, have come under scrutiny in recent years as scholars have noted declines in participation that could jeopardize their ultimate sustainability.[46] Just as with these examples, Hatsune Miku as a sustainable peer-produced artifact depends on continued participation by musicians and artists, who will continue her legacy by creating more media. Yet, even for Vocaloid producers in Japan who have been inside these communities for years, these question are open. As one producer said, "Imagine if such a minority culture [like Vocaloid] takes over the mainstream culture. I think it's very incredible...I would be very happy if normal people start liking this culture, but now I still don't have the confidence to say that." It remains to be seen if and how music production will continue to be bottom-up collaborations in the Miku ecosystem, such as some open-source projects that either died out completely or were bought by commercial enterprises.

Miku's image acts as a conduit for individuals to form bonds through collaboration and inspiration. Creators project their qualities and values onto Miku's iterative narrative. Audiences also relate to her on an individual level, using her as a platform for personal expression and identification.[47] Miku will continue to exist as a platform for commercial production: Crypton has adapted her image to suit the needs of hundreds of thousands of fans and capitalized on the productive efforts of those participants. But what underlie the concerts are the tensions, conflicts, and politics of creative peer production and a transnational community network of millions of fan participants that will continue to impact how Miku matures in the near future.

Works Cited

Auslander, Philip. *Liveness: Performance in a Mediatized Culture*. London: Routledge, 1999.

Baym, Nancy. "Connect with Your Audience! The Relational Labor of Connection." *The Communication Review* 18, no. 1 (2015): 14-22.

---

[46] Aaron Halfaker *et al.*, "The Rise and Decline of an Open Collaboration System: How Wikipedia's Reaction to Popularity Is Causing Its Decline," *American Behavioral Scientist* (December 28, 2012), doi: 10.1177/0002764212469365.
[47] Condry, "Miku."

Benkler, Yochai. *The Wealth of Networks*. New Haven, CT: Yale University Press, 2006.

Bruns, Axel. *Blogs, Wikipedia, Second Life, and Beyond: From Production to Produsage*. Bern, Switzerland: Peter Lang Publishing, 2008.

Chin, Bertha, and Lori Hitchcock Morimoto. "Toward a Theory of Transcultural Fandom." *Participations: Journal of Audience & Reception Studies* 10, no. 1 (May 2013): 92-108.

Condry, Ian. "Miku: Japan's Virtual Idol and Media Platform." MIT Center for Civic Media, July 11, 2011. Accessed June 10, 2014. https://civic.mit.edu/blog/condry/miku-japans-virtual-idol-and-media-platform.

———. "Post-3/11 Japan and the Radical Recontextualization of Value: Music, Social Media, and End-Around Strategies for Cultural Action." *International Journal of Japanese Sociology* 20, no. 1 (November 2011): 4-17.

Conner, Thomas. "Rei Toei Lives!: Hatsune Miku and the Design of the Virtual Pop Star." MA thesis, University of Illinois at Chicago, 2013.

Galbraith, Patrick W., and Jason G. Karlin. *Idols and Celebrity in Japanese Media Culture*. London: Palgrave, 2012.

Guga, Jelena. "Virtual Idol Hatsune Miku: New Auratic Experience of the Performer as a Collaborative Platform." *Lecture Notes of the Institute for Computer Sciences, Social Informatics, and Telecommunications Engineering* 145 (2015): 36-44.

Halfaker, Aaron, R. Stuart Geiger, Jonathan T. Morgan, and John Riedl. "The Rise and Decline of an Open Collaboration System: How Wikipedia's Reaction to Popularity Is Causing Its Decline." *American Behavioral Scientist* (December 28, 2012). doi: 10.1177/0002764212469365.

Hamasaki, Masahiro, Hideaki Takeda, Tom Hope, and Takuichi Nishimura. "Network Analysis of an Emergent Massively Collaborative Creation Community." In *International AAAI Conference on Web and Social Media*, North America, July 7, 2009, 222-225. http://www.aaai.org/ocs/index.php/ICWSM/09/paper/view/226.

Hebdige, Dick. *Subculture: The Meaning of Style*. London, England: Routledge, 1979.

Hichibe Nobushige. "'Dōjinkai' no ronri: kōisha no rigai, kanshin to shihon no henkan." *Kontentsu bunka-shi kenkyū* 3 (2010): 19-32.

Hills, Matt. "Transcultural *Otaku*: Japanese Representations of Fandom and Representations of Japan in Anime/manga Fan Cultures." In *Proceedings of MiT2*, Massachusetts Institute of Technology, Cambridge, MA, May 10-12, 2002. http://cmsw.mit.edu/mit2/Abstracts/MattHillspaper.pdf.

Ito, Mizuko, Daisuke Okabe, and Izumi Tsuji. *Fandom Unbound: Otaku Culture in a Connected World*. New Haven, CT: Yale University Press, 2012.

Iwabuchi, Koichi. "'Soft' Nationalism and Narcissism: Japanese Popular Culture Goes Global." *Asian Studies Review* 26, no. 4 (2002): 447-469.

Jenkins, Henry. *Convergence Culture: Where Old and New Media Collide*. New York: New York University Press, 2006.

Lessig, Lawrence. *Remix: Making Art and Commerce Thrive in the Hybrid Economy*. City of Westminster, UK: Penguin Press, 2008.

Literat, Ioana. "The Work of Art in the Age of Mediated Participation: Crowdsourced Art and Collective Creativity." *International Journal of Communication* 6 (December 17, 2012). http://ijoc.org/index.php/ijoc/article/view/1531/835.

Leavitt, Alex. "The Open-Source Cult(ure) of Hatsune Miku." Paper presented at South by Southwest, Austin, TX, March 12, 2012.

Neff, Gina, and David Stark. "Permanently Beta: Responsive Organization in the Internet Era." In *Society Online: The Internet in Context*, edited by Philip N. Howard and Steve Jones, 173-188. Thousand Oaks, CA: Sage, 2004.

Noppe, Nele. "Dōjinshi Research as a Site of Opportunity for Manga Studies." In *Comics Worlds and the World of Comics: Towards Scholarship on a Global Scale*, edited by Jaqueline Berndt, 123-142. Kyoto: International Manga Research Center, Kyoto Seika University, 2010.

Ōtsuka, Eiji. "World and Variation: The Reproduction and Consumption of Narrative." Translated by Marc Steinberg. *Mechademia* 5, no. 1 (2010): 99-116.

Rao, Mallika. "Meet Hatsune Miku, The Sensational Japanese Pop Star Who Doesn't Really Exist," *Huffington Post*, October 8, 2014. Accessed November 10, 2014. http://www.huffingtonpost.com/2014/10/08/hatsune-miku-letterman_n_5956420.html.

Reynolds, Simon. *Energy Flash: A Journey through Rave Music and Dance Culture*. Berkeley: Soft Skull Press, 2012.

Schneider, Rebecca. *Performing Remains: Art and War in Times of Theatrical Reenactment*. London: Routledge, 2011.

Steinberg, Marc. *Anime's Media Mix: Franchising Toys and Characters in Japan*. Minneapolis, MN: University of Minnesota Press, 2012.

Vágnerová, Lucie. "Liveness and Labor and Hologram Singers." Paper presented at Bone Flute to Auto-Tune: A Conference on Music & Technology in History, Theory, and Practice, University of California, Berkeley, April 24-26, 2014.

Part V:
Affective Convergence

The Labor of Love: On the Convergence of Fan and Corporate Interests in Contemporary Idol Culture in Japan

Patrick W. Galbraith

Introduction

In the past decade, Japan has experienced an idol boom. The number of idols performing today is "the greatest in the history of Japanese entertainment" (*Nihon no geinō shijō saidai*).[1] In 2013, Japan was the second largest music market in the world, with a total retail value of US$3 billion, and 46 of the top 50 bestselling singles came from Japanese artists; the top 10 bestselling singles all came from idols, with one group, AKB48, responsible for numbers one through four.[2] At a time of global media convergence, how can we account for the persistence of idols, whose popularity seems to be stubbornly local? On reflection, proximity to, and relations with, fans seem to be key. In the case of celebrities, we have seen that regular exposure tends to make people know and care more about them, which in turn makes Japanese media with Japanese celebrities more appealing in Japan.[3] Celebrities, especially idols, mobilize fan audiences, which tend to overlap with national boundaries, but not necessarily so. Celebrities from outside Japan are more successful at developing fan audiences and finding a place in the market if they regularly appear in Japan.[4] If, as some suggest,[5] we are now in the "idol warring states period" (*aidoru sengoku jidai*)—a provocative turn of phrase that brings to mind a

---

[1] Tanaka Satoshi, "Posuto AKB wa dō suru? Aidoru sengoku jidai no yukue," *Yomiuri shinbun*, October 9, 2012, accessed October 12, 2015, http://archive.is/DIOFrl.

[2] Oricon Style, "Nenkan CD shinguru rankingu: 2013," accessed October 12, 2015, http://www.oricon. co.jp/rank/js/y/2013/. For a comparable discussion of the electronic gaming industry in Japan, which is also dominated by local producers, see Chapter 3 in this volume.

[3] Gabriella Lukács, *Scripted Affects, Branded Selves: Television, Subjectivity and Capitalism in 1990s Japan* (Durham, NC: Duke University Press, 2010), 23-24.

[4] Guy de Launey, "Not-so-Big in Japan: Western Pop Music in the Japanese Market," *Popular Music* 14, no. 2 (1995): 208; and Ho Swee Lin, "Emotions, Desires, and Fantasies: What Idolizing Means for Yon-sama Fans in Japan," in *Idols and Celebrity in Japanese Media Culture*, ed. Patrick W. Galbraith and Jason G. Karlin (London: Palgrave, 2012), 177-179.

[5] Okajima Shinshi and Okada Yasuhiro, *Gurūpu aidoru shinka ron: 'Aidoru sengoku jidai' ga yatte kita!* (Tokyo: Mainichi Komyunikēshonzu, 2011).

history of multiple groups struggling for control of Japan, which is largely a domestic affair—then one has to be an idol to have a fighting chance, and idols are characterized by proximity to and relations with fans.

While production logic and marketing strategies do much to explain the phenomenon of idols, an idol's existence depends on cultivating and maintaining relationships with fans. This is absolutely clear when we consider "underground" (*chika*), "street" (*rojō*) and "net" (*netto*) idols, who do not have the luxury of production and advertising agencies pushing them and instead labor in relation to fans.[6] Thousands of underground idols and idol groups exist, but only a handful can draw 500 people to a live performance.[7] Most depend on about 20 core fans, whom they appeal to directly to buy multiple copies of CDs to support them as well as to spread the word and recruit new fans. Underground idols spend so much time interacting with these core fans that it is not surprising that some describe their fans as "closer to me than any of my friends."[8] Idols and their fans stay in touch through social media, as many of us do with friends, but for them this is also work—related to making a living. Although the intimacy of relations with fans is most obvious when observing underground, street, and net idols, this is the defining characteristic of idols in Japan. Indeed, AKB48 became the bestselling group in Japan precisely because it focused on proximity to and relations with fans—"idols that you can meet" (*ai ni ikeru aidoru*)—and harnessed the productive social activity of idols and fans relating to one another.[9]

This chapter examines how the interests of fans and corporations converge in contemporary idol culture in Japan, where both fans and corporations support idols in different but complementary ways. In the social activities of fans and idols relating to one another, we see another convergence: fans become performers. In their convergent form, some idol-fans become idols, while others support idols in ever more active ways. In her ethnographic account of fandom, Christine R. Yano notes that idols performing onstage are faced with fans performing elaborate cheers and dances for them: "The two performances face one another...and converge in

---

[6] Gabriella Lukács, "The Labor of Cute: Net Idols, Cute Culture, and the Digital Economy in Contemporary Japan," *positions: asia critique* 23, no. 3 (2015): 487-488, 492-496.
[7] Bekku Jun'ichi, "In the Quest for Fame, Underground Idol Groups Slog It Out with Just a Few Fans," *Asahi shinbun*, March 31, 2015, accessed October 12, 2015, https://ajw.asahi.com/article/cool_japan/style/AJ201503310011.
[8] Bekku, "In the Quest for Fame."
[9] Patrick W. Galbraith, "AKB Business: Idols and Affective Economics in Contemporary Japan," in *Introducing Japanese Popular Culture*, ed. Alisa Freedman and Toby Slade (London: Routledge, forthcoming).

a spectacle of intimacy."[10] As the performances of fans and idols converge, so do the interests of fans and corporations; as Yano argues, "Shared intimacy becomes a marketing tool."[11] That is, the social activities of fans and idols relating to one another and fans supporting idols becomes a source of value for corporations, which in turn support idols and fans and their social activities and relations. Fans do not perceive corporations to be exploitative because they engage in social activities for their idols and themselves, which is to say for their own interests, but this is also in the interest of corporations. To indicate the convergence of material and emotional interests, I call what fans and idols do in relation to one another the labor of love; they labor doing what they love and labor for love. Corporations act as apparatuses to capture some of the value generated by fans, who labor for love in relation to idols; idols, fans, and their relations are supported by corporations, which they in turn support. As a case study of the labor of love, this chapter examines UNIDOL, a competition for university students who form groups and perform as idols. University idols are idol-fans who practice and perform idol dances as a form of fan activity and after-school club activity, but this is also serious business that involves long practice sessions and performances for paying customers. These performances not only advertise existing idols, whose music and moves idol-fans reproduce, but also feed into the expanded idol industry by preparing new performers and fans. To demonstrate this, the chapter follows SPH mellmuse from Sophia University in Tokyo, who were voted the top group at UNIDOL in summer 2014.[12] Following from the gender of performers at UNIDOL generally and the members of SPH mellmuse specifically, the chapter discusses primarily female idols and fans, or the convergence of female idols and fans into female idol-fans. Instead of the production logic of idols, this chapter focuses on the idols themselves and their own productive activities.[13] It concludes with a discussion of the labor of love in terms of affect and autonomous Marxism.

---

[10] Christine R. Yano, "Letters from the Heart: Negotiating Fan-Star Relationships in Japanese Popular Music," in *Fanning the Flames: Fans and Consumer Culture in Contemporary Japan*, ed. William W. Kelly (New York: State University of New York Press, 2004), 54.

[11] *Ibid.*, 49.

[12] Observations of SPH mellmuse (originally SPH48) and interviews were conducted in Tokyo from summer 2013 to summer 2014. Interviews were conducted in Japanese; all translations are my own. For issues of privacy, names, photographs, and identifying details are withheld.

[13] Focusing on the industry and marketing tends to make idols appear as "images," which is clear in phrases such as "image alliances" and "image commodities." See Saya S. Shiraishi, "Doraemon Goes Abroad," in *Japan Pop! Inside the World of Japanese Popular Culture*, ed. Timothy J. Craig (New York: M.E. Sharpe, 2000), 289; and Lukács, *Scripted Affects*, 24, 47. In this approach, the image can be a cartoon character (Doraemon, a robot cat from the future) or a human being (Kimura Takuya, an idol from the boy band SMAP). In my own work, I have encountered a limit to approaching idols as images, which seems to risk ignoring the people living, loving, and laboring in relation to the image.

The Idolization of Youth

In her recent article based on interactions with net idols in Japan, Gabriella Lukács underscores the enormous amount of effort that goes into being attractive to fans, which she calls "the labor of cute."[14] Idols labor to be cute, or *kawaii* in Japanese, a word that combines ideographs meaning "possible" (*ka*) and "love" (*ai*). To be cute is to be lovable, able to be loved, and idols labor to be so. Since cute became a media and consumer culture phenomenon in Japan in the 1970s, idols, who not coincidentally first appeared in that same decade,[15] have become role models for many girls and women.[16] In his ethnography of idol culture in Japan, Hiroshi Aoyagi suggests that the role of an idol is to successfully navigate social maturation and develop a persona that is "publically adorable."[17] Idols are introduced in magazines and on television as ideals for the youth of their time. They are also carriers of information about lifestyle and fashion for people more generally.[18] Especially as models, singers, dancers, personalities and actresses, idols also embody the ideal of a creative, communicative subject who works well with others and gains their love and support, an ideal that began to rise in many post-industrial nations in the 1970s and took hold in Japan in the wake of economic recession and flexible employment in the 1990s.[19]

Now more than ever, idols are role models for the publically adorable subject, and women interact with them from a young age. Ever since *Creamy Mami, the Magic Angel* (1983-1984) told the story of a 10-year-old girl who magically transforms into a 16-year-old girl and becomes a "mega idol" (*daininki aidoru*), animation and idol culture have been deeply intertwined.[20] *Creamy Mami* was a pioneering work in the development of the media mix,[21] which is related to the spread of media worlds.[22] Works

---

[14] Lukács, "The Labor of Cute," 487, 496.

[15] Patrick W. Galbraith and Jason G. Karlin, "Introduction: The Mirror of Idols and Celebrity," in *Idols and Celebrity in Japanese Media Culture*, ed. Patrick W. Galbraith and Jason G. Karlin (London: Palgrave, 2012), 4-5.

[16] Sharon Kinsella, "Cuties in Japan," in *Women, Media, and Consumption in Japan*, ed. Lise Skov and Brian Moeran (Honolulu: University of Hawai'i Press, 1995), 225-237.

[17] Hiroshi Aoyagi, *Islands of Eight Million Smiles: Idol Performance and Symbolic Production in Contemporary Japan* (Cambridge, MA: Harvard University Asia Center, 2005), 63.

[18] Lukács, *Scripted Affects*, 29-31, 43, 51-52.

[19] Anne Allison, "The Cool Brand, Affective Activism and Japanese Youth," *Theory, Culture and Society* 26, no. 2-3 (2009): 90-91; and Lukács, *Scripted Affects*.

[20] For more on this, see Chapter 6 in this volume.

[21] "Mahō no aidoru Kurimī Mami tanjō," *Animax*, March 13, 2003, accessed October 12, 2015, https://web.archive.org/web/20030313205635/http://www.animax.co.jp/program/m_creamymami.html.

[22] Marc Steinberg, *Anime's Media Mix: Franchising Toys and Characters in Japan* (Minneapolis, MN: University of Minnesota Press, 2012).

such as *Creamy Mami* helped spread images of idols and make them part of a ubiquitous media environment; girls grow up relating with and through idols, in media worlds anchored by idols.[23] In the media mix world, fantasy overlaps with reality, for example when 15-year-old Ōta Takako, who sang as the idol character Creamy Mami for the hit TV anime, became an actual idol simultaneously with her fictional counterpart. In recent years, in line with the ongoing boom, idols appear in multimedia franchises for young female audiences such as *Pretty Rhythm* (from 2011) and *Aikatsu!* (from 2012), for older male audiences such as *THE iDOLM@STER* (from 2005) and *Wake Up, Girls!* (from 2014), and cross-gender and cross-generation phenomena such as Vocaloids (popular from 2007) and *Love Live!* (from 2010).[24] A mainstream anime series targeting young girls and broadcast in prime time by TV Tokyo, Bandai's *Aikatsu!*, an abbreviation of *aidoru katsudō* (idol activities), takes place in Starlight Academy, a prestigious middle and high school where girls train to become idols and take part in various auditions. Originally a collectible card game and now spanning manga, anime, merchandise, and more, *Aikatsu!* became a megahit media franchise—earning Bandai an estimated ¥14.1 billion in the first quarter of 2014[25]—by trading on girls' fantasy of becoming idols, as well as the broader social fantasy of girl idols.[26] At many middle and high schools in Japan, one hears talk of classroom rankings of the attractiveness of peers and talk of class idols, which speaks to the idolization of youth. One cannot help but notice how many idols perform wearing costumes that resemble school uniforms, even when they have long since graduated from compulsory education, which reinforces associations of youth, school, and idols. The massively successful media franchise *Love Live!*—which spun out an animated film

[23] Although there is not sufficient space to develop it here, I will point out that media mix strategies made strong connections between idols and manga, anime, and games in the 1990s in the forms of virtual idols such as Fujisaki Shiori, voice actor/actress idols such as Hayashibara Megumi and idols performing as manga/anime characters such as F4. See Ōtsuka Eiji, *"Otaku" no seishin-shi: 1980-nendai-ron* (Tokyo: Kōdansha Gendai Shinsho, 2004), 18; Thomas Lamarre, "Regional TV: Affective Media Geographies," *Asiascape: Digital Asia* 2 (2015): 95; and Chapter 7 of this volume.

[24] If there is any doubt that young people are attracted to these virtual worlds and idols, consider the following. In 2014, 11 of the top 20 songs requested by teens through the popular Joysound karaoke system were Vocaloid tracks; the remaining nine were anime tracks. Audrey Akcasu, "Vocaloid Takes Over Teen Karaoke Scene, More than Half of 2014's Top 20 Songs Synthetic," *Rocket News*, December 23, 2014, accessed October 12, 2015, http://en.rocketnews24.com/2014/12/23/vocaloid-takes-over-teen-karaoke-scene-11-of-2014s-top-20-songs-synthetic/. For more on Vocaloids, see Chapter 8 of this volume.

[25] "'Aikatsu!' daininki de shijō ikkyo kakudai: Bandai/Namco gurūpu de konki 141 oku en mikomu," *AnimeAnime*, February 8, 2014, accessed October 12, 2015, http://animeanime.jp/article/2014/02/08/17392.html.

[26] Media franchises featuring idols seem to be targeting young girls as their main audience, but are also notoriously popular with not-so-young men. These two audiences converge as idol-fans.

that was number one at the Japanese box office for three weeks in June 2015—captures this perfectly in its fantasy of regular schoolgirls from across Japan becoming "school idols" (*sukūru aidoru*).[27] Young women in Japan perform as idols at special events, if not in everyday interactions with peers, and this continues into university years, when there is less pressure to perform academically and more pressure to perform socially, which includes after-school club activities and school festivals.

Unsurprisingly, many young women are scouted by production agencies to become idols in the time between middle school and university, but what is surprising is the level to which young women aspire to be idols. A 2008 survey asked young women between the ages of 15 and 22 what are the "jobs you want to do, wanted to do, or would like to try" and found that the top three choices were actress or model; singer or musician; and entertainer, talent, or comedian.[28] All these dream jobs involve celebrity and things that idols do. Analyzing these survey results, Miura Atsushi argues that such work responds to young women's desire to work in relation to others who value them, or a desire to be recognized (*shōnin saretai*). These young women are the ones founding or joining underground idol groups, the number of which ballooned from an estimated 50 groups in Tokyo in 2008 to over 350 in 2015.[29] A few might make it big, most will transition into more realistic occupations after graduating from school, and some will continue in their idol activities while working part-time jobs and living with their parents or partners.

Embarking on a career as an idol has become something casual, which is even supported by institutions of higher learning. In the wake of AKB48's stunning commercial success and the subsequent idol boom, universities across Japan from 2011 began to register new after-school clubs, whose activities included watching idol music videos, learning the dances and performing them for others. These clubs wanted to come together and perform for larger audiences, and, in 2012, UNIDOL was born.[30] Short for "university idol," UNIDOL is an event that brings together student groups that perform "copy dances of idol groups" (*aidoru*

---

[27] "Love Live Film Earns 260 Million Yen in 2nd Weekend, Beats Out *Mad Max* for Tickets Sold (Updated)," *Anime News Network*, June 22, 2015, accessed October 12, 2015, https://www.animenewsnetwork.com/news/2015-06-22/love-live-film-earns-260-million-yen-in-2nd-weekend-beats-out-mad-max-for-tickets-sold/.89558.

[28] Miura Atsushi and Yanauchi Tamao, *Onna wa naze kyabajō ni naritai no ka? "Shōnin saretai jibun" no jidai* (Tokyo: Kōbunsha, 2008), 107. The survey was conducted by cell phone and received 1,154 responses. Respondents could choose as many occupations as they wanted, and these were the top three with 43.95%, 40.6%, and 38.1% respectively.

[29] Bekku, "In the Quest for Fame."

[30] See the official website at http://unidol.jp/.

gurūpu no kopī dansu) and puts them in competition with one another for the honor of being named number one in Japan. Okada Kōhei, chairman of the UNIDOL Executive Committee, explains that, "In the 1990s, during the band boom, a lot of copy bands appeared in Japan. In the same way, copy idols (*kopī aidoru*) have increased during the idol boom. Some of them don't stop at the hobby and go on to be active as underground idols."[31] Okada stresses that members of the idol copy dance groups that perform at UNIDOL are university students and idol-fans (*menbā wa aidoru fan*); indeed, these groups sometimes evolve out of fan clubs.[32] Idol-fans engage in copy dance performances because it is "fun" (*tanoshii*) to do so; their idol activities are part of after-school club activities, which are engaged in as students and idol-fans. Nevertheless, UNIDOL has grown to become a major media event covered by an estimated 150 outlets, including TV Tokyo and BS Fuji; *Mainichi shinbun, Sankei shinbun,* and *Weekly playboy*; Jiji.com, Mantan TV, and MSN Video; Yahoo! News, Niconico News, and Excite News; and many others.[33] The event has expanded to twice yearly, and there are also plans for HIGHDOL, which will feature high school idols. Interest in university and high school-aged women as potential idols is certainly not without precedent in Japan—there were sequential media booms in the 1980s[34]—but now normal young women are producing and performing themselves as idols. This is a phenomenon of fandom, not agencies and advertisers, and it is spreading across the nation. In 2015, UNIDOL attracted 47 teams from 40 universities.[35] We are not far from the media world of *Love Live!*, where normal young women become school idols and compete against other school idols from across Japan.

Sophia University and SPH mellmuse

Located in central Tokyo, Sophia University is an elite private school founded by Jesuits in 1928. Well known for its department of foreign

---

[31] Quoted in Ōnishi Motohiro, "Joshidaisei, aidoru ni naritai: Nihon ichi kettei-sen ni 40 daigaku," *Asahi shinbun*, March 16, 2015, accessed October 12, 2015, http://www.asahi.com/articles/ASH3B5F22H3BUCVLo1R.html. The connection to copy bands is suggestive. Mōri Yoshitaka points out that the band boom occurred in the 1990s, a time when Japan was undergoing an economic crisis and individuality and creativity came to be valued as part of a post-Fordist regime of flexible accumulation. See Mōri Yoshitaka, "J-Pop: From the Ideology of Creativity to DiY Music Culture," *Inter-Asia Cultural Studies* 10, no. 4 (2009): 479-481. This line of inquiry anticipates my discussion of affect and autonomous Marxism later in this chapter.

[32] Ōnishi, "Joshidaisei."

[33] Tada Copy, "UNIDOL Summer 2014," July 25, 2014, accessed October 12, 2015, http://www.tadacopy.com/download/2014unidol.pdf.

[34] Okada Toshio, *Otaku wa sudeni shindeiru* (Tokyo: Shinchōsha, 2008), 93.

[35] Ōnishi, "Joshidaisei."

languages, Sophia University is attractive to "returnees" (*kikoku shijo*), or Japanese who lived overseas in their youth, "descendents of Japanese" (*nikkeijin*), so-called "half Japanese" (*hāfu*), and "foreigners" (*gaikokujin*). In a global age, the relatively mixed and multilingual population of Sophia University might seem ideal, although in this context there is always the danger of failure to establish one's self as publically adorable in/as/to Japanese. Some students are disparagingly referred to by peers as "weird Japanese" (*hen japa*). However, those who successfully establish themselves in this environment become a pool of attractive talent. Consider that Agnes Chan, a singer from Hong Kong who became a hit in Japan in the 1970s, enrolled in the international program at Sophia University in 1974, a legacy that was followed by singers and personalities such as Beni, Crystal Kay, Dave Spector, Aoyama Teruma, and many more. In addition, talent scouts often attend campus beauty and popularity contests, for example the Mister and Miss Sophia Contest, which is known among students as a launching pad for a career in media and entertainment.[36] Sophia University's main traffic artery on campus—a straight line from Shinjuku Street past the library—is something of a runway, with immaculately groomed students on parade throughout the day.

Once scouted and signed by production agencies, a young person is referred to as an "egg" (*tamago*), but this somewhat misleadingly places the emphasis on industry producers who supposedly hatch said egg and masks *social* incubation and production. The proverbial egg is laid and hatched by parents, and the hatchling grows to maturity in interaction with teachers and classmates, peers and media. From fashion to makeup, communication skills to charisma, the idol-in-training develops a cute persona, and learns and labors to be lovable in relation to others in everyday social interactions. These small moments add up to one's power in relation to (not necessarily over) others, which can be seen in school popularity contests and festivals. Those who successfully produce and perform themselves are school idols, who are "discovered" by scouts and connected to industry "producers." It is somewhat telling that one of Sophia University's slogans is "Men and women for others, with others" or, more literally from the Japanese, "For the sake of others, we live with others" (*tasha no tame ni, tasha to tomo ikiru*). Cynically, it almost appears that the value of living for and with others is tapped by the idol industry, which does no more than select and promote idols that emerge out of

---

[36] Because the majority of students at Sophia University are female, the Miss Contest has produced more famous winners. For a list of winners who landed jobs in media and entertainment, see https://ja.wikipedia.org/wiki/ミスキャンパス - .E4.B8.8A.E6.99.BA.E5.A4.A7.E5.AD.A6.

social relations—that are produced in the *social factory*—and manage and capitalize on social relations.

In 2010, students at Sophia University formed a new after-school club called SPH48. Unique among the many dance and performance clubs already on campus, SPH48 is a fan club formed during the idol boom and linked in name to its inspiration: AKB48. SPH48 stands for "Sophia 48," just as AKB48 stands for "Akihabara 48," the name of the neighborhood in Tokyo where that infamous idol group was formed.[37] Like AKB48 before them, SPH48 did not originally have 48 members, but rather about a dozen young women who came together to perform at a school festival. When a larger than expected crowd came to see them, Sophia University's idol-fan club decided to continue its activities. SPH48 introduces itself as a "group that copies idol performances" (*aidoru pafōmansu o kopī suru gurūpu*), which means concretely that they mimic the dance routines of famous idol groups beginning with AKB48 and extending to Morning Musume, Girls' Generation, and more. The "dance division" (*dansu-bu*) meets regularly to watch videos and practice moves. At these meetings are also members of the "management division" (*unei-bu*), who are in charge of planning, operations, and marketing. Journalist Ōnishi Motohiro explains the role of the management division: "They release videos of performances on video sharing sites and, if there is a request, will arrange for the group to appear at industry events."[38] As Ōnishi sees it, SPH48 captures "the hearts of fans with communication just like professional idol groups" (*puro no aidoru gurūpu no yō na komyunikēshon de, fan no kokoro o tsukamu*).[39] This copy idol group, an idol-fan club, has its own fan club. Members stay in touch with fans through social media, maintain a website, and hold events where they pose for photographs.[40] Their website proudly restates an abbreviated English slogan of Sophia University as an idol slogan: "For others, with others." In Japanese, they are even more direct: "For you, with you" (*anata no tame ni, anata to tomo ni*).

SPH48 is acutely aware of the need to meet the demands of idol fans. They scan media channels for feedback on their performances, a practice that began in May 2011, when, in conjunction with their appearance at the All Sophians' Festival, a photograph of SPH48 was made public and received harsh criticism online. For some idol fans, especially a subset of AKB48's extremely passionate and vocal supporters, SPH48 appeared

---

[37] Galbraith, "AKB Business."

[38] Ōnishi, "Joshidaisei."

[39] *Ibid.*

[40] See the group's website at http://sph48.is-mine.net/.

to be "too uncute idols" (*kawainasasugi aidoru*).[41] If an idol labors to be cute and lovable, then the rejection of SPH48 as "uncute" by these haters was taken by the group to be a failure. In response to the perceived crisis, SPH48 made renewed efforts to improve the quality of their idol performances, which is to say to be as cute and lovable as the idols that they mimic. They also changed their name to SPH mellmuse to create some distance from AKB48 and avoid negative comparisons.[42] Finally, the group resolved to eliminate seniority and vertical relationships of hierarchy (*jōge kankei*) and to decide who performs based on merit. This restructuring, essentially neoliberal in character, was intended to motivate and embolden younger members, who would now have the chance to rise to the top in free competition, which would ultimately lead to higher quality performances overall.

Today, SPH mellmuse's idol activities range from "classroom performances" (*kyōshitsu kōen*) to "industry events" (*kigyō ibento*). In the latter, which take place in commercial venues outside of the school, SPH mellmuse performs alongside and is essentially indistinguishable from underground idols, who are idols that have yet to break into mainstream commercial and media outlets. In June 21, 2013, six members of SPH mellmuse performed two songs at an industry event in Harajuku, where I asked about their idol activities. One responded:

> Before I started going to Sophia University, I got accepted to some other schools. When I was researching about Sophia, I thought that the school festival was quite interesting. I always wanted to dance, especially copying idol dances, so I decided to go to Sophia University because of SPH48.

Another member added:

> When I went to freshman week at Sophia University, I received information about SPH, and I was like, wow! So I went to Twitter and found out that there would be an information session and decided to go. I thought this club seemed like fun. I had wanted to do copy dancing from before I encountered SPH.

---

[41] Others said that SPH48 was "bringing shame on their alma mater" *(bokō no haji sarashi)*.

[42] The name was officially changed at a meeting on June 30, 2013. The leader of SPH48 at the time pointed to "flaming" *(enjō)* on 2channel, a massive online bulletin board known for attracting deep fans who engage in anonymous discussion, as a reason to create some distance from AKB48. The new name, "SPH mellmuse," combines "mell," which means honey or sweetness, with "muse," which means "goddess of music." The logo was also changed from a clear AKB48 copy.

Finally, a third member:

> During the welcoming event for incoming students, I received a
> school magazine that introduced all the clubs at Sophia University.
> I was looking for one related to stage performances. When I was
> in high school, I used to be in the acting club, and I thought that I
> should continue to do something related with stage performances.
> There are other dancing circles, but SPH seemed to be the best fit
> for me in terms of cost and the amount of days and hours of practice
> required per week. At first, I was worried that I would not be able to
> copy idol dances, and wanted to join the management division, but
> when I went to the welcoming party, I sang a song and received a
> message directly from seniors in the club telling me to use my skills
> and join the dance division instead.

Two of the members interviewed already had an interest in idols and
joined SPH mellmuse to be involved in copy dancing, and the third
had experience with stage performance. All three, to differing extents,
were self-produced idols performing alongside underground idols as
part of school activities. In this way, we see a blurring of amateur and
professional, play and work, classroom performance and industry event.

However, even as SPH mellmuse overlaps with underground idols—
and even mainstream idols (more on this below)—members insist that
they are not "real" idols. Not only do they consistently and unambiguously
state that they "copy idol performances" (*aidoru pafōmansu o kopī shimasu*),
but they also cleverly parody and undermine the role of the production
agency, which we are told turns the raw material of the normal schoolgirl
into an idol. Members of SPH mellmuse's management division refer to
their imaginary production agency as DeI, where "de" is a prefix from
Latin indicating negation and "i" is the first letter of the English word
"idol." Despite the insistence that they are not real idols, both the dance
and management divisions agree that SPH mellmuse should take to heart
that what they do is "for the customers"—a slogan that they state directly
in English. The use of "customers" here, despite performing for fun and
not for money, reflects a sense of indebtedness to those who support
them. Even if the members of SPH mellmuse are idol fans and not "real"
idols, they have real fans who pay real money to see them, which means
that they must do their best to perform as real idols. Members invest
time, energy, and money to practice for the sake of self-improvement and
ensuring fan satisfaction.

Among their many performances, arguably the most important for SPH mellmuse is UNIDOL. At the inaugural UNIDOL in 2012, SPH mellmuse took third place out of seven groups; there were 400 people in the audience. In 2013, SPH mellmuse took second place out of 14 groups; there were 850 people in the audience. Finally, in the summer of 2014, SPH mellmuse, which was once derided as too uncute to be idols, worked tirelessly to improve and was voted the number one university idol group in Japan (figure 1). As many as 30 groups participated and drew an audience of 1,850 people (figure 2), who each paid 3,000 yen for a ticket to attend (figure 3). To achieve their win, members of SPH mellmuse's dance division practiced relentlessly leading up to the event, missing scheduled classes at Sophia University and, according to one member, flirting with illness due to mental and physical exertion.[43]

---

[43] Interview by author, Tokyo, Japan, June 25, 2014.

Figure 1. Flier for UNIDOL 2014.

Figure 2. A view of the growth of UNIDOL.

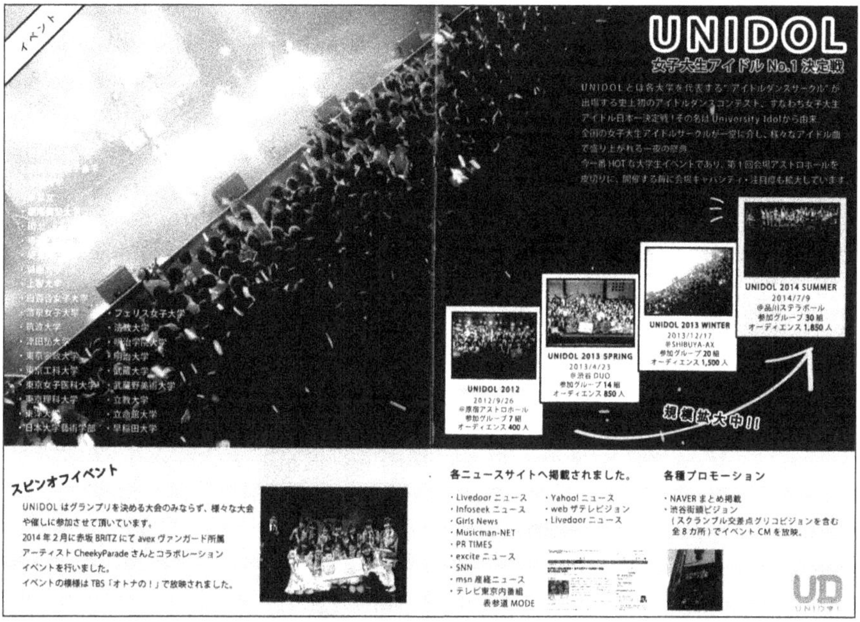

Figure 3. Ticket to UNIDOL 2014.

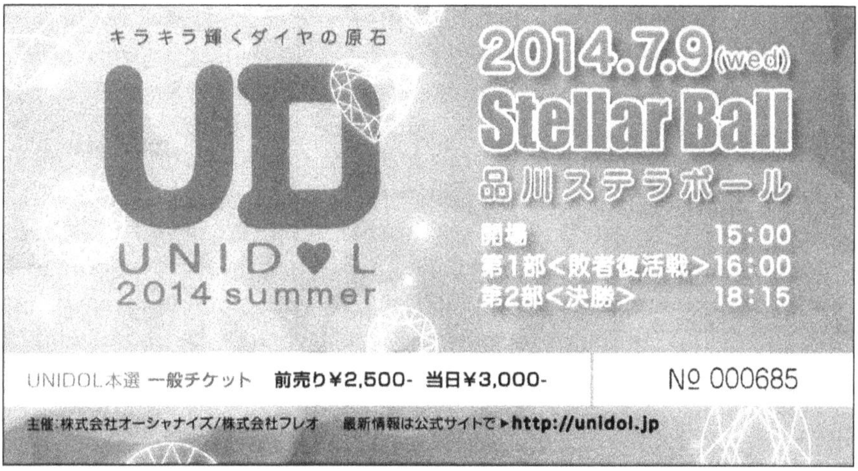

UNIDOL 2014 was a fascinating example of the role of fans in contemporary idol culture in Japan.[44] Not only were the members of

[44] For an overview of the event, see Okkun, "Like a Diamond in the Rough: Female University Students Shine Bright at UNIDOL Summer 2014," *Tokyo Girls' Update*, July 2, 2014, accessed October 12, 2015, http://tokyogirlsupdate.com/unidol-summer-2014-2-20140723231.html.

SPH mellmuse and other groups all idol-fans, but so were all members of the audience, who came not only to see university idols, but also the idols that they copied in projected music videos (or "promotion videos," as they are often called in Japan) and even in person as special guests.[45] When SPH mellmuse performed their idol copy dances, music videos featuring the idols they mimicked were projected on a screen behind them. Members of the audience, both male and female, mimicked the dance moves that SPH mellmuse was itself mimicking. To put it another way, in front of the screen where a video of "real" idols was projected, SPH mellmuse performed a copy dance facing a live audience that was facing them and also performing a copy dance; movements were mirrored and energy circulated in front of the screen. The absence of the "real" idol made it even more surprising when members of the audience shouted the names of the idols on screen rather than the copies on stage. These calls to real/absent idols mixed together with calls to copy/present idols from friends, family, and fans, who saw the university idols as the real thing. One member of SPH mellmuse explained her performance as follows: "I am always nervous at live shows, but I want to give power to everyone (*mina-san ni pawā o ataetai*) like the idols I love."[46] Not only does one give power to the audience, but also is empowered as an idol receiving power from the audience. At UNIDOL 2014, we can observe the exchange of power between idols and fans that is crucial to contemporary idol culture. We see "a spectacle of intimacy"[47] in the convergence of the idol-fan performance. We also see how the power of shared movements is channeled by corporations, who capture some of its value.

Idol-Fans, Labor, and Love

What are we to make of the powerful shared movements of UNIDOL, or the powerful reproduction of idol music and moves by idol-fans? Singing and dancing along with idols, activities engaged in by copy idol performers and fan performers on and off stage, might be understood in terms of what Christine R. Yano calls "*migawari*, which means, literally, 'body exchange' and refers to a person, act, or state of substitution—in short, surrogacy."[48] By Yano's estimation, it is through fan surrogacy that

---

[45] For example, the performers at UNIDOL in the summer of 2014 shared the stage with special guests °C-ute, a professional idol group produced by Hello! Project. At a pre-event, CheekyParade, a professional idol group signed with the Avex Vanguard label, held a "collaboration event" with the university students who would be performing at UNIDOL.
[46] Quoted in Ōnishi, "Joshidaisei."
[47] Yano, "Letters from the Heart," 54.
[48] *Ibid.*, 46.

an idol's music and movements spread and gain power. We can perhaps better understand this by taking a brief detour through media theory. If, as Henry Jenkins has argued, media that does not spread is essentially "dead,"[49] then it must spread to have life. Jenkins points out that it is often fans who do this spreading through copying and sharing activities. To put it another way, spreading occurs through the social activities of fans, which give media its life.[50] Ian Condry has referred to such activities as "the social in media," which is its life, its powerful life force, or what he calls its "soul."[51] As with media, so too with idols—fans copy and share the music and movements of their idols, which contributes to the power of idols.

If we discuss fan and social activities as the soul of contemporary idol culture, then we should also consider how this soul is put to work.[52] Let us examine what goes into fan surrogacy. Yano's example is karaoke, where fans sing the songs of their favorite idols. They are copying and sharing the song in embodied and social ways. On the one hand, the fan forms her lips around the words and vocalizes the sounds of her idol's voice, which is a personal and intimate sharing between idol and fan. On the other hand, the fan shares her performance with a group of friends, which contributes to the spread of the idol's song in her social circle and network. In her fieldwork, Yano found that karaoke is not only a fan activity, but also an important aspect of marketing colloquially referred to by industry insiders as getting the song to "enter the ears" (*mimi ni hairu*) of as many people as possible.[53] Where once this might have been done primarily by getting the song played on the radio or used in a TV show or advertisement, we see this strategy augmented, if not replaced, by idol-fan performances that spread the song in embodied and social ways. The image of a song entering the ear, replicating in the host body (repeating as an "ear worm"), and spreading through contagion might bring to mind the biological metaphor of virality, but as Jenkins notes, the biological

---

[49] Henry Jenkins, "If It Doesn't Spread, It's Dead (Part One): Media Viruses and Memes," Confessions of an Aca-Fan: The Official Weblog of Henry Jenkins, February 11, 2009, accessed October 12, 2015, http://henryjenkins.org/2009/02/if_it_doesnt_spread_its_dead_p.html.

[50] Ian Condry, *The Soul of Anime: Collaborative Creativity and Japan's Media Success Story* (Durham, NC: Duke University Press, 2013), 73-76.

[51] *Ibid.* 2, 29.

[52] Franco Berardi, *The Soul at Work: From Alienation to Autonomy* (Los Angeles: Semiotext[e], 2009).

[53] "Fan club members are thus encouraged by the record company that organizes and controls the club to sing the latest song at karaoke as part of a promotional strategy, spreading its sound to *mimi ni hairu* (enter the ears) of the public and make it a hit" (Yano, "Letters from the Heart," 46). See also Christine R. Yano, *Tears of Longing: Nostalgia and the Nation in Japanese Popular Song* (Cambridge, MA: Harvard University Asia Center, 2002), 45-76.

metaphor makes the host seem passive, if not also somehow sick.[54] Instead, there is perhaps a more suitable metaphor: colonization.[55] Rather than passive hosts, here we see fans as active workers, laboring bodies, whose hearts and minds are cultivated in relation to idols and made productive for capital. If, as Yano suggests, "[s]hared intimacy becomes a marketing tool,"[56] then this certainly applies to UNIDOL, where copy idols and fans share the music and movements of idols and contribute to their spread, life, and power.

In order to understand idol-fan labor, let us follow through Yano's example of karaoke, which has long been seen as a serious endeavor in Japan: "participation expresses a willingness to socialize with fellow group members on an equal basis and is an expression on the part of performers that their own needs are met through their inclusion in the group."[57] In many studies of Japanese culture, shared leisure activity of this kind has been tied to strengthening corporate bonds or the after-hours work of bonding.[58] However, if the surrogacy of idol-fan performances at UNIDOL points to a group, then it is a fan group, which both does and does not overlap with school and work groups. The work of bonding is with and through idols as idol-fans. Practice for idol-fan performances does occur in semi-formal settings such as after-school clubs—that is what SPH mellmuse is all about—but individuals also practice flexibly on their own, over time, in relation to idols and fans.

One underground idol, a first-year university student who was 18 years old, told me that she spends almost all of her "free time" on weekdays after school going to karaoke to practice songs for her regular weekend performances.[59] At the time, this young woman, a self-identified idol-fan, had one original song, but the rest of her repertoire was covers of idol and anime songs. While working as part-time staff at many establishments and events in Akihabara, this underground idol was called on to sing, which she saw as an opportunity to practice. She was not always or necessarily paid to sing, but was nevertheless always "on" as a performer and idol-in-training. Just like her performatively cute (*burikko*) style of

---

[54] Jenkins, "If It Doesn't Spread."

[55] Steinberg, *Anime's Media Mix*, 169.

[56] Yano, "Letters from the Heart," 49.

[57] Bill Kelly, "Japan's Empty Orchestras: Echoes of Japanese Culture in the Performance of Karaoke," in *The Worlds of Japanese Popular Culture: Gender, Shifting Boundaries and Global Cultures*, ed. Dolores Martinez (Cambridge, MA: Cambridge University Press, 1998), 84.

[58] For example, Anne Allison, *Nightwork: Sexuality, Pleasure, and Corporate Masculinity in a Tokyo Hostess Club* (Chicago, IL: University of Chicago Press, 1994), 54-56.

[59] Interview by author, Tokyo, Japan, February 28, 2015 and March 19, 2015.

dress and speech, singing was a skill that she developed on her own over time in relation to others. It was a skill that she brought to the workplace, one that made her a valuable asset for employers. Although ostensibly singing at work was just for practice, this underground idol also saw it as an opportunity to get exposure and potentially win fans. She did not want to be embarrassed by performing (free songs) poorly and alienating potential fans, and hence she practiced at karaoke before she practiced at work and engaging in what she called "karaoke alone" (*hitori karaoke*).[60] In a strangely poetic way, this young woman paid for these karaoke sessions with the money that she earned from her part-time jobs. In the above statement of a junior member of SPH mellmuse who was inducted into the dance division after she wowed seniors by singing karaoke—who had, as it were, developed a skill that gave her an advantage and allowed her to leap frog over the competition and secure a spot in the group and on stage—one can recognize personal investment in practice. While that young woman ended up in an after-school club at an elite private university, if circumstances were different she might be using her skills to make a living. Indeed, SPH mellmuse's activities of copying idols and performing as idols for idol fans is part of some people's job descriptions. At Maidreamin, a chain of cafés in Akihabara, part-time workers, who are university-aged women earning a wage of about ¥900 an hour, are called on to perform copy idol dances to entertain customers. On the café's recruitment page, prospective workers are told, in English, that the "Dreamin world is your stage," "We do an awards ceremony twice a year," and finally just "CD debut!"[61] In the above examples of underground idols, university idols, and part-time workers, we can see the labor that goes into idol-fan performances, and how the surrogacy of fan activities intersects with different economies of value. That underground idols, university students and part-time workers all told me that they "love" (*daisuki*) idols, fans and singing and dancing as idols only underscores the complex entanglements of their labor. (Recall the SPH mellmuse member who wanted to perform like the idols she loves.)[62]

The masses of girls and women as idol-fans who could be idols or are already performing as idols in some capacity are what Furuhashi Kenji

---

[60] While this underground idol's routine may seem a little strange, in fact "karaoke alone" is not entirely uncommon; there are even establishments that specialize in it. See, for example, https://1kara.jp/.
[61] See the company's website at http://maidreamin.com/en/recruit/maid.
[62] Ōnishi, "Joshidaisei."

refers to as the "reserve army of idols" (*aidoru yobigun*).[63] With respect to Furuhashi, and a nod to Marx, we might refer to the reserve army of idols as a reserve army of labor, with the reminder that these are not laborers in reserve, but rather always already laboring bodies who are not fully employed or compensated. The reserve army of idols, the reservoir of idol-fan activity, is the social energy that powers contemporary idol culture. In the case of university idols, who are produced in the factory of social activity, corporations capitalize on the idolization of youth and value of idol-fan performances. These performances are a form of labor, which, as we have seen in university and underground idols, is freely given. Idol-fans are free labor in at least two ways: they are free to labor and labor for free. The university idol, underground idol, and part-time idol worker in Akihabara are all engaged in forms of free labor as idol fans and idols relating to fans. To phrase it somewhat differently, they labor doing what they love and labor for love. To indicate the convergence of material and emotional interests, I call this the labor of love. Capitalism depends on such labor, which, as Tiziana Terranova explains, it "nurtures, exploits, and exhausts."[64]

Affect and Autonomous Marxism

If we follow the lead of autonomous Marxists, who seek to understand the value of life itself, then we might follow Terranova to the issue of "affect."[65] In philosophy, affect refers to a modification or variation produced in a body in interaction with another body, which increases or diminishes the body's power of activity. In his critique of the labor theory of value, autonomist Marxist Antonio Negri connects affect to "the power to act" and "value from below," which precedes and exceeds the relations of capital.[66] In later work with Michael Hardt, however, Negri identifies

---

[63] Furuhashi Kenji, "C-kyū aidoru ni jinsei o ageta seishokusha! Aidoru ga hito kara mono ni natta toki, mania ga umareta!" in *Bessatsu takarajima 104 gō: Otaku no hon*, ed. Ishii Shinji (Tokyo: JICC shuppankyoku, 1989), 26. John Lie implies something similar in a discussion of South Korea's "large reserve army of potential K-pop stars." In his provocative explantion of the phenomenon, Lie argues that K-pop is designed to be memorable, inspire mimicry and spread like a meme. Inescapable and catchy pop songs, karaoke machines and social pressure to perform have prepared a "nation of singers," generated a "surplus" and made "K-pop star" into "the most desirable occupation for a young South Korean girl." Hence just as UNIDOL participants copy idol dances, it is "not uncommon for young people (and even some old ones) to reproduce K-pop dance steps in public." See John Lie, *K-Pop: Popular Music, Cultural Amnesia, and Economic Innovation in South Korea* (Oakland, CA: University of California Press, 2015), 104-107, 130-131, 145.

[64] Tiziana Terranova, "Free Labor: Producing Culture for the Digital Economy," *Social Text* 18, no. 2 (2000): 51.

[65] *Ibid.*

[66] Antonio Negri, "Value and Affect," *boundary* 2 26, no. 2 (1999): 78-79.

"affective labor," which "produces or manipulates affects."[67] Certainly this is an apt description of what idols do: generating "a feeling of ease, well-being, satisfaction, excitement, passion—even a sense of connectedness or community."[68] It is not a coincidence that idols emerged in the 1970s, which is precisely when theorists observed a shift toward forms of labor dealing with the "immaterial"—for example, images, ideas, and information.[69] Idols are uniquely positioned as not only images, which nevertheless can and do affect, but also as the embodied presences more often associated with affective labor.[70] Further, idols mobilize fans, who are in many ways ideal immaterial laborers—active, productive, social, communicative, and networked.[71] If, as Maurizio Lazzarato argues, the corporation profits to the extent that it has "the capacity to activate and manage productive cooperation,"[72] then it does so through the deployment of idols. To put this somewhat differently, idols are the key to activating and managing productive cooperation among fans, as can be observed in the shared movements, spreading, and surrogacy of idol-fan performances at an event such as UNIDOL.

UNIDOL not only demonstrates the "power to act" among idol fans, but also how this "value from below" can be channeled and captured by corporations. Despite the slogan—"UNIDOL: Sparkling Diamonds in the Rough" (*UNIDOL: Kira kira kagayaku daiya no genseki*)—the members of SPH mellmuse do not intend to be cut and polished into precious stones by industry producers. As idol-fans, their labor of love nonetheless serves to invigorate the idol industry by attracting and holding attention, reinforcing fan attachments and affecting audiences. UNIDOL is an event sustained by idol-fan performances, which demonstrates the value of fan activities and audiences, or more broadly what Henry Jenkins has identified as "brand communities," which are comprised of the most loyal and intense supporters that sustain and spread the brand.[73]

---

[67] Michael Hardt and Antonio Negri, *Multitude: War and Democracy in the Age of Empire* (New York: Penguin Press, 2004), 108. Gabriella Lukács adds that "affective labor integrates processes of capital accumulation with practices of self-determination by further blurring the line between paid and unpaid work." See Gabriella Lukács, "Dreamwork: Cell Phone Novelists, Labor, and Politics in Contemporary Japan," *Cultural Anthropology* 28, no. 1 (2013): 48.

[68] Michael Hardt, "Affective Labor," *boundary 2* 26, no. 2 (1999): 96.

[69] Maurizio Lazzarato, "Immaterial Labor," in *Radical Thought in Italy: A Potential Politics*, ed. Paolo Virno and Michael Hardt (Minneapolis, MN: University of Minnesota Press, 1996), 133-134.

[70] Hardt, "Affective Labor," 96.

[71] Lazzarato, "Immaterial Labor," 142.

[72] *Ibid.*, 134.

[73] Henry Jenkins, *Convergence Culture: Where Old and New Media Collide* (New York: New York University Press, 2006), 72-79.

In his interactions with corporations in the United States, Jenkins encountered a discourse on "affective economics," which suggests that desires, connections and commitments can be qualified, measured and commoditized.[74] "Affective economics," Jenkins explains, "sees active audiences as potentially valuable if they can be courted and won over by advertisers."[75] As P. David Marshall argues, celebrities can be compared to brands and are "instrumental in the organization of an affective economy."[76] An idol, however, is more than a brand. Even if brands can be described as "lovemarks,"[77] idol-fans love not brands but idols, human and familiar, which perhaps intensifies the affective economy. The deployment of idols in media and advertising to court fan audiences is a noted phenomenon in Japan.[78]

To point this out is not to say that consumers and fans are duped or exploited, which assumes passivity and weakness. On the contrary, as we have seen in the example of UNIDOL, fans are active and empowered in their support for idols.[79] If, as Marshall suggests, the celebrity, media personality or idol embodies an audience and articulates "social power," then their deployment can be seen as not only *"attempts* to contain the

---

[74] *Ibid.,* 61-62.

[75] *Ibid.,* 64.

[76] P. David Marshall, *Celebrity and Power: Fame in Contemporary Culture* (Minneapolis, MN: University of Minnesota Press, 2014), 247.

[77] Jenkins, *Convergence Culture,* 68.

[78] For example, see Lukács, *Scripted Affects.* In fan communities, talking about idols includes talking about their appearances in commercials, which are sought out online, watched multiple times, and analyzed as idol media. See Jason G. Karlin, "Through a Looking Glass Darkly: Television Advertising, Idols, and the Making of Fan Audiences," in *Idols and Celebrity in Japanese Media Culture,* ed. Patrick W. Galbraith and Jason G. Karlin (London: Palgrave, 2012), 85-86. Idol fans not only watch more commercials, but they also watch more intensely, which some have understood in terms of surplus value from audience labor in relation to the screen. See Sut Jhally and Bill Livant, "Watching as Working: The Valorization of Audience Consciousness," *Communication* 36, no. 3 (1986): 133, 136. For more on the audience commodity, see Dallas W. Smythe, *Dependency Road: Communications, Capitalism, Consciousness and Canada* (Norwood, NJ: Ablex, 1981), 22-51; and Marshall, *Celebrity and Power,* 63, 194.

[79] Consider how corporations deploy idols to activate fans and enfranchise them with the promise of participation—for example, voting for their idols. Henry Jenkins refers to the phenomenon of *American Idol* as the "fantasy of empowerment" and "promise of participation," which "helps build fan investments" (Jenkins, *Convergence Culture,* 64.) I argue elsewhere that a business model that capitalizes on fan investments is behind the commercial success of the idol group AKB48 in Japan, but must stress that this is not new (Galbraith, "AKB Business"). Moreover, Daniel J. Boorstin writes that, "each of us likes a movie star or television celebrity more when we think we have had a hand in making him a celebrity." See Daniel J. Boorstin, *The Image: A Guide to Pseudo-Events in America* (New York: Vintage, [1961] 2012), 221. Everyone understands that this is a media/marketing spectacle, but nonetheless takes pleasure in participating and seeing the results of participation have an impact. So it was, Boorstin points out, that in 1957 an estimated 20 million votes were placed for an attractive model to represent Rheingold beer—the largest "election" in the United States next to the presidency.

mass[es]," but also to channel social power and capture some of its value.[80] To put it another way, if fans can be described as a "collective force"[81] or a "collective force of desire,"[82] then this collective force of desire is for the idol and is productive. Marshall concludes that "the economic power of the pop star is configured around affect" and the pop star is a "personality who can capture youth's affective intensity."[83] Let us somewhat rephrase this to underscore that the power of the pop star or idol is social before it is economic, and corporations deploy idols in *attempts* to capture some of the value of the affective intensity of relations among idols and fans and of idol-fan performances. In idol-fan performances, "The barriers between audience and actors are broken and there is a celebration of active participation."[84] Indeed, active participation is celebrated by fans and corporations alike in a convergence of social and economic interests and values. In relation to the idol, fan activities—labors of love such as copy dances, karaoke, passing out fliers, and moving and vocalizing during live performances to energize the crowd and be recognized—are part of an affective economy. Such is the power to act, which is also value from below partially captured by corporations that support and extract value from idol-fan performances.

Insight into the convergence of fan and corporate interests in contemporary idol culture in Japan comes from an unlikely place: the sex industry. Writing about "hosts," or men paid to provide sexualized services to female clients, Akiko Takeyama argues that the affective economy in Japan is "nested in the service and entertainment industry."[85] By Takeyama's estimation, the affective economy both exploits and satisfies. In her example, on the one hand, men are able to self-produce, perform, and profit by working at host clubs, while on the other hand women are comforted in relation to hosts and realize themselves as beings worthy of recognition and love. Club owners then extract value from the affective labor of hosts and customers in relation to one another.

---

[80] Marshall, *Celebrity and Power*, 63, 243. "Attempts" is italicized in Marshall's original text to underscore that the capture is never certain or complete.

[81] *Ibid.*, 195.

[82] Thomas Lamarre, *"Otaku* Movement," in *Japan After Japan: Social and Cultural Life from the Recessionary 1990s to the Present*, ed. Tomiko Yoda and Harry Harootunian (Durham, NC: Duke University Press, 2006), 359. Lamarre uses Antonio Negri to build his argument.

[83] Marshall, *Celebrity and Power*, 183.

[84] *Ibid.*, 193. Marshall is citing a discussion of identification with heroes in Hans Robert Jauss, *Aesthetic Experience and Literary Hermeneutics*, trans. Michael Shaw (Minneapolis, MN: University of Minnesota Press, 1982), 184.

[85] Akiko Takeyama, "Intimacy for Sale: Masculinity, Entrepreneurship, and Commodity Self in Japan's Neoliberal Situation," *Japanese Studies* 30, no. 2 (2010): 238.

For Takeyama, "the affect[ive] economy satisfies multiple players and institutions in mutual yet asymmetrical ways,"[86] and this also seems true of contemporary idol culture. Idols bring together fans and corporations, who are satisfied in mutual yet asymmetrical ways. Idols, like hosts, are involved in self-production, performance, and promotion in an affective economy, or, as Brian and Gina Cogan nicely put it, idols "are simultaneously commodified objects and producers of a commodity."[87] One can see how affective labor, which is engaged in by both idols and fans, can be rewarding for those involved.[88] Recall the statement by one underground idol that her core fans are "closer to me than any of my friends,"[89] which suggests relationships that are clearly valuable to her and provide her with affirmation, if not also social and economic opportunities. Fans as friends and lovers support idols, and such relationships (seldom if ever consummated sexually) can be sources of affirmation for them, too. This is where affective labor suggests emergent alliances and the power and value of life, which precedes and exceeds capitalist arrangements.[90] At the same time, given the incredible number of idols performing in Japan today, one can easily grasp how the affective

---

[86] *Ibid.*, 238.

[87] Brian Cogan and Gina Cogan, "Gender and Authenticity in Japanese Popular Music: 1980-2000," *Popular Music and Society* 29, no. 1 (2006): 84-85. The Cogans suggest that idols self-commodify and "inject their personalities into the process" (Cogan and Cogan, "Gender and Authenticity in Japanese Popular Music," 86), which is precisely what Lazzarato would expect of immaterial laborers (Lazzarato, "Immaterial Labor," 134-137). For a comparative look at the economics of self-commodifying, see Takeyama, "Intimacy for Sale," 241.

[88] Yano, "Letters from the Heart," 47; Lukács, "Dreamwork," 48; Ho, "Emotions, Desires, and Fantasies," 171-177; and Lukács, "The Labor of Cute," 498-499.

[89] Bekku, "In the Quest for Fame."

[90] Due to issues of space, I will not pursue a full discussion of affect and politics—already underway in Hardt and Negri, *Multitude*; Allison, "The Cool Brand;" Lukács, "Dreamwork"—but would like to draw attention to Marshall's argument that celebrities embody audiences and social power, work at an affective level, and represent "the potential for societal transformation" (Marshall, *Celebrity and Power*, 196, 244). There are structural limitations and seldom "a clear social movement," but Marshall is prescient in connecting the social power of celebrities with politics. One might take this in the direction of a politics of moving bodies, supporting life, and forming new collectivities, but for now I will just offer a few examples from Japan. After the nuclear disaster in Japan in 2011, idol group Seifuku Kōjō I'inkai (founded in 1992) released the single "No! No! No More Nuclear Power Plants!" (Dā! Dā! Datsu genpatsu no uta), which has simple lyrics and dance steps, is performed at live events, and is meant to be copied by the audience and performed together. While Seifuku Kōjō I'inkai is an underground idol group with little mainstream success, such is not the case with popular singer Saitō Kazuyoshi (debuted in 1993). In 2011, in response to the persistent lies of officials in the Japanese nuclear industry and government, Saitō took his own "I Always Loved You" (Zutto suki datta, 2010), used as a TV commerical jingle, and turned it into the viral hit "It Was Always a Lie" (Zutto uso datta, 2011). These examples suggest that celebrities can move fans to act not only as consumers, but also as citizens. For counterpoints, see Chapter 1 and Chapter 2 in this volume.

economy feeds into "the postindustrial national economy,"[91] which is nicely expressed by Sakai Masayoshi's concept of "idol national wealth" (*aidoru kokufu*).[92]

Figure 4. Sponsors of UNIDOL 2014.

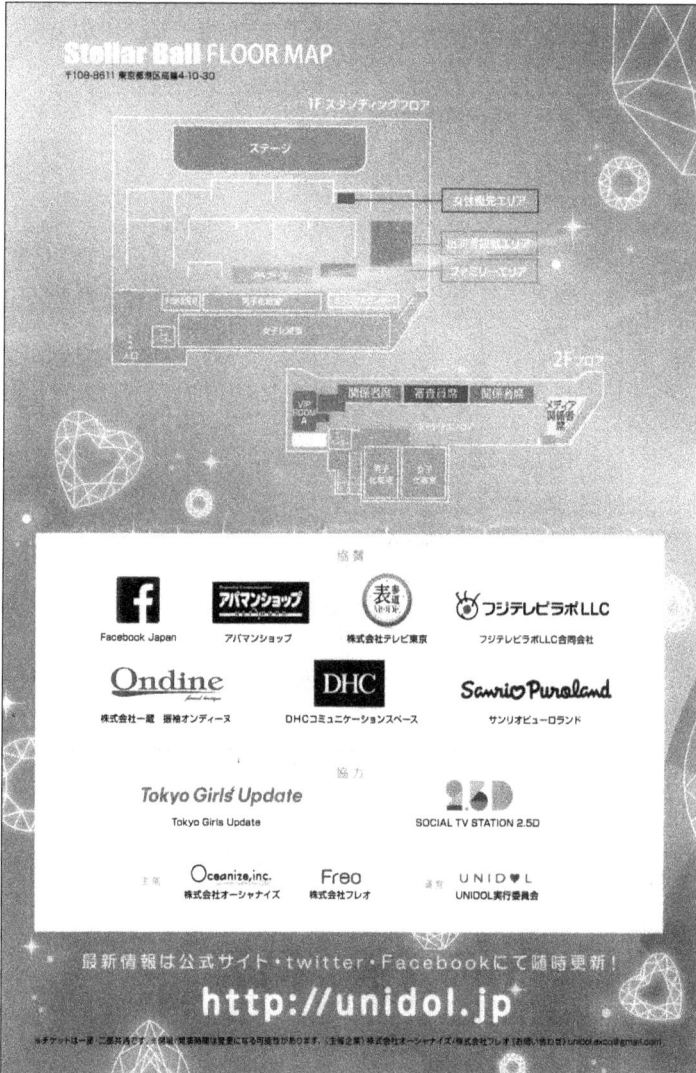

---

[91] Takeyama, "Intimacy for Sale," 238.

[92] Sakai Masayoshi, *Aidoru kokufu ron: Seiko, Akina no jidai kara AKB, Momokuro jidai made toku* (Tokyo: Tōyō Keizai Shinpōsha, 2014). See also Sharon Kinsella, *Schoolgirls, Money and Rebellion in Japan* (London: Routledge, 2014), 26-27.

Figure 5. Cover of the July issue of *Freo* magazine, which features an article on UNIDOL 2014.

UNIDOL shines a light on how not only multiple players but also institutions are satisfied in the affective economy in mutual yet asymmetrical ways. Just as Takeyama's club owners extract value from the affective labor of hosts and customers in relation to one another, at UNIDOL, the idol-fan audience, comprised of performers both on and off stage, is sold to sponsors, who advertise during the event.[93] The sponsors of UNIDOL 2014 included old media outlets such as TV Tokyo, Fuji TV and *Freo* as well as new media outlets such as Tokyo Girls' Update, Social TV Station 2.5D, and Facebook Japan (figures 4 and 5). The inclusion of familiar social media sites such as Facebook serves as a reminder that with the omnipresence of media in our lives and expectation that someone is always watching, not just SPH mellmuse, but all of us are performing "for others, with others."[94] In theory, anyone at any university in Japan can work hard to be cute, win friends, followers and fans and perform at UNIDOL—if not in the dance division, then in the management division, or in some other capacity. Indeed, Okada Kōhei is not only the chairman of the UNIDOL Executive Committee, but also a fourth-year student at Meiji University, which gives the impression that this is an event by and for students and idol fans. The convergence of fan and corporate interests is, however, plain to see. UNIDOL has as "support" a company called Oceanize,[95] which makes a business out of collecting information on university students, which it sells (not unlike how Facebook offers its free service to users, who freely generate information about themselves in free labor in the social media factory, which is valuable to the corporation in aggregate). The slogan of Oceanize may as well be the slogan of UNIDOL: "Move the students, move the world" (*gakusei o ugokasu koto de sekai o ugokashite iku*).[96] If companies such as Oceanize can move the students, then they can move the world, which is to say profit from the movement of students in the world. The shared movements of idol-fan performances at UNIDOL are an example of this. To return to Lazzarato's insight, the corporation profits to the extent that it can "activate and manage productive cooperation,"[97] which it achieves through the deployment of idols.

In this way, idol-fan activities are integrated into broader media economies, which depend on the social factory and the labor of love. Indeed, UNIDOL would not be possible without groups like SPH mellmuse investing time and energy into copying idols to perform as idols in competition with their peers and relations with fans. Although

---

[93] Tada Copy, "UNIDOL Summer 2014."

[94] Social media contributes to self-producing and performing as a way of life. The social media factory is where we "learn to immaterial labor." See Mark Coté and Jennifer Pybus, "Learning to Immaterial Labour 2.0: MySpace and Social Networks," *ephemera: theory and politics in organization* 7, no. 1 (2007). See also Lukács, "The Labor of Cute," 508.

[95] Ōnishi, "Joshidaisei."

[96] See the company's website at http://oceanize.co.jp/.

[97] Lazzarato, "Immaterial Labor," 134.

they insist that they are not real idols, SPH mellmuse performs and functions in much the same way. If members of SPH mellmuse look and sound and perform like "real idols" (*genjitsu no aidoru*),[98] it is because they are real idols, idols in reality, minus production agencies, contracts, and paychecks.[99] This is not, however, a simple story of exploitation. When they were voted the number one university idol group in Japan at UNIDOL in the summer of 2014, not only did SPH mellmuse receive prize money of ¥150,000—handed to them by °Cute, "real" idols who they really idolized[100]—but they also received other less obvious rewards. While not guaranteed compensation for their labor—which they did for love in relations with idols, one another, rivals, fans, the audience—the members of SPH mellmuse expressed not only satisfaction but even joy at being able to perform together, participate in the event, and succeed in their personal and shared goals. SPH mellmuse's performance was for themselves and for others, including but not limited to their teammates, fans, peers, the idols that they copy, and the corporations supporting these idol-fan performances. Value here cannot be understood in strictly or even primarily economic terms, but rather should be approached as a complex entanglement of fan and corporate interests, a convergence of social and economic values, which characterizes contemporary idol culture in Japan.

Conclusion

This chapter has explored how idols and fans, who converge in the form of idol-fans, are engaged in the labor of love in relation to one another. Corporations capture some of the value of social activity, or the power of life that autonomous Marxists such as Antonio Negri link to affect.[101] Idol-fans are thus part of an affective economy, but this is not a simple story of exploitation. As Akiko Takeyama notes, one of the characteristics of the affective economy is that it "satisfies multiple players and institutions

---

[98] Ōnishi, "Joshidaisei."

[99] The situation is not entirely dissimilar to NCAA tournament basketball, a massive business in the United States that does not share its revenues with players. Despite the obvious value of their labor, university athletes are paid nothing, because they are students, not professionals. For a lucid discussion of systemic abuses, see John Oliver on the subject: https://www.youtube.com/watch?v=pX8BXH3SJno. Interestingly, unlike many university athletes, none of the university idols I interviewed saw what was happening to them as exploitation. Copy dancing and performances were described as something done for fun and separate from their occupation, which they insisted was "student."

[100] Okkun, "Sophia University's SPH mellmuse Claims the Crown at UNIDOL Summer 2014," *Tokyo Girls' Update*, July 11, 2014, accessed October 12, 2015, http://tokyogirlsupdate.com/sph-mellmuse-claims-the-crown-at-UNIDOL-2014-20140723925.html.

[101] Negri, "Value and Affect," 78-79.

in mutual yet asymmetrical ways."[102] Idol-fans are not passive dupes, but rather are actively and knowingly laboring in the affective economy; they are active, productive, social, communicative, and networked subjects, which is to say ideal laborers in the current economic situation.[103] Today, corporations profit to the extent that they can "activate and manage productive cooperation,"[104] which they achieve through the deployment of idols. Whether it be members of SPH mellmuse working hard after class to copy idol dances, underground idols practicing at karaoke to cover idol songs, or fans passing out fliers, taking to social media and buying CDs in support of idols, this "power to act" and "value from below" is to some extent captured, but by no means exhausted, by corporations in the affective economy.[105] In contemporary idol culture, convergence softens distinctions between idols and fans, labor and love, independent and corporate. This helps explain the paucity of anti-capitalist movements in Japan, for why would fans refuse what they love—idols—and refuse to do what they love—copy and support idols? Without understanding this convergence of interests, we cannot hope to understand contemporary idol culture, or capitalism, for that matter.

Works Cited

Akcasu, Audrey. "Vocaloid Takes Over Teen Karaoke Scene, More than Half of 2014's Top 20 Songs Synthetic." *Rocket News*. December 23, 2014. Accessed October 12, 2015. http://en.rocketnews24.com/2014/12/23/vocaloid-takes-over-teen-karaoke-scene-11-of-2014s-top-20-songs-synthetic/.

Allison, Anne. *Nightwork: Sexuality, Pleasure, and Corporate Masculinity in a Tokyo Hostess Club*. Chicago, IL: University of Chicago Press, 1994.

———. "The Cool Brand, Affective Activism and Japanese Youth." *Theory, Culture and Society* 26, no. 2-3 (2009): 89-111.

Animax. "Mahō no aidoru Kurimī Mami tanjō." March 13, 2003. Accessed October 12, 2015. https://web.archive.org/web/20030313205635/http://www.animax.co.jp/program/m_creamymami.html.

---

[102] Takeyama, "Intimacy for Sale," 238.
[103] Lazzarato, "Immaterial Labor," 142.
[104] *Ibid.*, 134.
[105] Negri, "Value and Affect," 78-79.

Anime Anime. "'Aikatsu!' daininki de shijō ikkyo kakudai: Bandai/Namco gurūpu de konki 141 oku en mikomu." February 8, 2014. Accessed October 12, 2015. http://animeanime.jp/article/2014/02/08/17392.html.

Anime News Network. "Love Live Film Earns 260 Million Yen in 2nd Weekend, Beats Out Mad Max for Tickets Sold (Updated)." June 22, 2015. Accessed October 12, 2015. https://www.animenewsnetwork. com/news/2015-06-22/love-live-film-earns-260-million-yen-in-2nd-weekend-beats-out-mad-max-for-tickets-sold/.89558.

Aoyagi, Hiroshi. *Islands of Eight Million Smiles: Idol Performance and Symbolic Production in Contemporary Japan.* Cambridge, MA: Harvard University Asia Center, 2005.

Bekku, Jun'ichi. "In the Quest for Fame, Underground Idol Groups Slog It Out with Just a Few Fans." *Asahi shinbun.* March 31, 2015. Accessed October 12, 2015. https://ajw.asahi.com/article/cool_japan/style/ AJ2015033110011.

Berardi, Franco. *The Soul at Work: From Alienation to Autonomy.* Los Angeles: Semiotext(e), 2009.

Boorstin, Daniel J. *The Image: A Guide to Pseudo-Events in America.* New York: Vintage, [1961] 2012.

Cogan, Brian, and Gina Cogan. "Gender and Authenticity in Japanese Popular Music: 1980-2000." *Popular Music and Society* 29, no. 1 (2006): 69-90.

Condry, Ian. *The Soul of Anime: Collaborative Creativity and Japan's Media Success Story.* Durham, NC: Duke University Press, 2013.

Coté, Mark, and Jennifer Pybus. "Learning to Immaterial Labour 2.0: MySpace and Social Networks." *ephemera: theory and politics in organization* 7, no. 1 (2007): 88-106.

De Launey, Guy. "Not-so-Big in Japan: Western Pop Music in the Japanese Market." *Popular Music* 14, no. 2 (1995): 203-225.

Furuhashi, Kenji. "C-kyū aidoru ni jinsei o ageta seishokusha! Aidoru ga hito kara mono ni natta toki, mania ga umareta!" In *Bessatsu takarajima 104-gō: Otaku no hon*, edited by Ishii Shinji, 24-39. Tokyo: JICC Shuppankyoku, 1989.

Galbraith, Patrick W. "AKB Business: Idols and Affective Economics in Contemporary Japan." In *Introducing Japanese Popular Culture*, edited by Alisa Freedman and Toby Slade. London: Routledge, forthcoming.

Galbraith, Patrick W., and Jason G. Karlin. "Introduction: The Mirror of Idols and Celebrity." In *Idols and Celebrity in Japanese Media Culture*, edited by Patrick W. Galbraith and Jason G. Karlin, 1-32. London: Palgrave, 2012.

Hardt, Michael. "Affective Labor." *boundary 2* 26, no. 2 (1999): 89-100.

Hardt, Michael, and Antonio Negri. *Multitude: War and Democracy in the Age of Empire*. New York: Penguin Press, 2004.

Ho, Swee Lin. "Emotions, Desires, and Fantasies: What Idolizing Means for Yon-sama Fans in Japan." In *Idols and Celebrity in Japanese Media Culture*, edited by Patrick W. Galbraith and Jason G. Karlin, 166-181. London: Palgrave, 2012.

Jauss, Hans Robert. *Aesthetic Experience and Literary Hermeneutics*. Translated by Michael Shaw. Minneapolis, MN: University of Minnesota Press, 1982.

Jenkins, Henry. *Convergence Culture: Where Old and New Media Collide*. New York: New York University Press, 2006.

———. "If It Doesn't Spread, It's Dead (Part One): Media Viruses and Memes." Confessions of an Aca-Fan: The Official Weblog of Henry Jenkins, February 11, 2009. Accessed October 12, 2015. http://henryjenkins.org/2009/02/if_it_doesnt_spread_its_dead_p.html.

Jhally, Sut, and Bill Livant. "Watching as Working: The Valorization of Audience Consciousness." *Communication* 36, no. 3 (1986): 124-143.

Karlin, Jason G. "Through a Looking Glass Darkly: Television Advertising, Idols, and the Making of Fan Audiences." In *Idols and Celebrity in Japanese Media Culture*, edited by Patrick W. Galbraith and Jason G. Karlin, 72-93. London: Palgrave, 2012.

Kelly, Bill. "Japan's Empty Orchestras: Echoes of Japanese Culture in the Performance of Karaoke." In *The Worlds of Japanese Popular Culture: Gender, Shifting Boundaries and Global Cultures*, edited by Dolores Martinez, 75-87. Cambridge, MA: Cambridge University Press, 1998.

Kinsella, Sharon. "Cuties in Japan." In *Women, Media, and Consumption in Japan*, edited by Lise Skov and Brian Moeran, 220-254. Honolulu: University of Hawai'i Press, 1995.

————. *Schoolgirls, Money and Rebellion in Japan*. London: Routledge, 2014.

Lamarre, Thomas. "*Otaku* Movement." In *Japan After Japan: Social and Cultural Life from the Recessionary 1990s to the Present*, edited by Tomiko Yoda and Harry Harootunian, 358-394. Durham, NC: Duke University Press, 2006.

————. "Regional TV: Affective Media Geographies." *Asiascape: Digital Asia* 2 (2015): 93-126.

Lazzarato, Maurizio. "Immaterial Labor." In *Radical Thought in Italy: A Potential Politics*, edited by Paolo Virno and Michael Hardt, 133-147. Minneapolis, MN: University of Minnesota Press, 1996.

Lie, John. *K-Pop: Popular Music, Cultural Amnesia, and Economic Innovation in South Korea*. Oakland, CA: University of California Press, 2015.

Lukács, Gabriella. *Scripted Affects, Branded Selves: Television, Subjectivity and Capitalism in 1990s Japan*. Durham, NC: Duke University Press, 2010.

————. "Dreamwork: Cell Phone Novelists, Labor, and Politics in Contemporary Japan." *Cultural Anthropology* 28, no. 1 (2013): 44-64.

————. "The Labor of Cute: Net Idols, Cute Culture, and the Digital Economy in Contemporary Japan." *positions: asia critique* 23, no. 3 (2015): 487-513.

Marshall, P. David. *Celebrity and Power: Fame in Contemporary Culture.* Minneapolis, MN: University of Minnesota Press, 2014.

Miura Atsushi, and Yanauchi Tamao. *Onna wa naze kyabajō ni naritai no ka? "Shōnin saretai jibun" no jidai.* Tokyo: Kōbunsha, 2008.

Mōri, Yoshitaka. "J-Pop: From the Ideology of Creativity to DiY Music Culture." *Inter-Asia Cultural Studies* 10, no. 4 (2009): 474-488.

Negri, Antonio. "Value and Affect." *boundary 2* 26, no. 2 (1999): 77-88.

Okada Toshio. *Otaku wa sudeni shindeiru.* Tokyo: Shinchōsha, 2008.

Okajima Shinshi, and Okada Yasuhiro. *Gurūpu aidoru shinka ron: 'Aidoru sengoku jidai' ga yatte kita!* Tokyo: Mainichi Komyunikēshonzu, 2011.

Okkun. "Like a Diamond in the Rough: Female University Students Shine Bright at UNIDOL Summer 2014." *Tokyo Girls' Update.* July 2, 2014. Accessed October 12, 2015. http://tokyogirlsupdate.com/unidol-summer-2014-2-20140723231.html.

———. "Sophia University's SPH mellmuse Claims the Crown at UNIDOL Summer 2014." *Tokyo Girls' Update.* July 11, 2014. Accessed October 12, 2015. http://tokyogirlsupdate.com/sph-mellmuse-claims-the-crown-at-UNIDOL-2014-20140723925.html.

Ōnishi Motohiro. "Joshi daisei, aidoru ni naritai: Nihon ichi kettei-sen ni 40 daigaku." *Asahi shinbun.* March 16, 2015. Accessed October 12, 2015. http://www.asahi.com/articles/ASH3B5F22H3BUCVL0IR.html.

Oricon Style. "Nenkan CD shinguru rankingu: 2013." Accessed October 12, 2015. http://www.oricon.co.jp/rank/js/y/2013/.

Ōtsuka Eiji. *"Otaku" no seishinshi: 1980-nendai-ron.* Tokyo: Kōdansha Gendai Shinsho, 2004.

Sakai Masayoshi. *Aidoru kokufu ron: Seiko, Akina no jidai kara AKB, Momokuro jidai made toku.* Tokyo: Tōyō Keizai Shinpōsha, 2014.

Shiraishi, Saya S. "Doraemon Goes Abroad." In *Japan Pop! Inside the World of Japanese Popular Culture*, edited by Timothy J. Craig, 287-308. New York: M.E. Sharpe, 2000.

Smythe, Dallas W. *Dependency Road: Communications, Capitalism, Consciousness and Canada.* Norwood, NJ: Ablex, 1981.

Steinberg, Marc. *Anime's Media Mix: Franchising Toys and Characters in Japan.* Minneapolis, MN: University of Minnesota Press, 2012.

Tada Copy. "UNIDOL Summer 2014." July 25, 2014. Accessed October 12, 2015. http://www.tadacopy.com/download/2014unidol.pdf.

Takeyama, Akiko. "Intimacy for Sale: Masculinity, Entrepreneurship, and Commodity Self in Japan's Neoliberal Situation." *Japanese Studies* 30, no. 2 (2010): 231-246.

Tanaka Satoshi. "Posuto AKB wa dō suru? Aidoru sengoku jidai no yukue." *Yomiuri shinbun.* October 9, 2012. Accessed October 12, 2015. https://web.archive.org/web/20130425105945/http://www.yomiuri.co.jp/job/biz/columnculture/20121009-OYT8T00206.htm?.

Terranova, Tiziana. "Free Labor: Producing Culture for the Digital Economy." *Social Text* 18, no. 2 (2000): 33-58.

Yano, Christine R. *Tears of Longing: Nostalgia and the Nation in Japanese Popular Song.* Cambridge, MA: Harvard University Asia Center, 2002.

———. "Letters from the Heart: Negotiating Fan-Star Relationships in Japanese Popular Music." In *Fanning the Flames: Fans and Consumer Culture in Contemporary Japan*, edited by William W. Kelly, 41-58. New York: State University of New York Press, 2004.

Anxious Proximity: Media Convergence, Celebrity, and Internet Negativity

Daniel Johnson

This chapter will focus on the messiness of media convergence. We can approach this issue from an industrial perspective, such as in how a film might suddenly go out of print on video formats and become unavailable as licensing rights to a studio's film library change hands during corporate consolidation. Or how some video games force players into an "always online" mode of play in order to make the most use of a gaming console's integrated features—whether individual users want those features or not. But there are also cultural elements that accompany these industrial changes, and online media presents a rich area for investigating this dimension of the contemporary mediascape. This can include topics such as media piracy and discourses concerning political speech in anonymous communities.[1] But the ways that ordinary users of online media engage in antagonistic behavior with producers and performers from mainstream media signals an especially thorny problem within media convergence.

In Japan, this issue of antagonism in online media is also deeply tied to television. Television occupies a central position in commercial media in Japan and therefore serves as one of the primary nodes for processes and discourses of media convergence. The domestic music industry relies on television in promoting new artists and releases through appearances on variety programs and in coupling songs with weekly dramas. Many feature films are funded by television networks and their affiliated media conglomerates. Online and mobile media can offer alternative networks for the distribution and consumption of content, but in many cases also find themselves being integrated into the televisual apparatus or used in conjuncture with television viewing.[2] But television is also one of the primary objects of discussion for online communities, and in some

---

[1] See Elise Kramer, "The Playful Is Political: The Metapragmatics of Internet Rape-joke Arguments," *Language in Society* 40, no. 2 (April 2011): 137-168, for some of the rhetorics surrounding free speech and offensive speech (often targeting women) in English-language internet culture.

[2] For example, Thomas Lamarre has written on the intersection between mobile phones, Twitter, and television spectatorship. See Thomas Lamarre, "Living between Infrastructures: Commuter Networks, Broadcast TV, and Mobile Phones," *boundary* 2 43, no. 2 (2015): 157-170.

cases these discussions turn antagonistic and veer into campaigns of harassment and abuse against television performers and personalities. This tendency also intersects with how anonymous online social forms are often accompanied by an intensification of actual world categories of identity, such as gender and race.[3]

One of the most prominent areas of fascination within television media for these communities is celebrity. And, as with other facets of the media industry in Japan, television is central to the production and circulation of images of celebrity. Performers such as comedians, idols, and talent use appearances on television variety shows and dramas to promote themselves and reach a wider audience. But more generally, the content of many television programs is seemingly this culture of celebrity itself, with topic of discussion for variety panels often being the latest gossip and developments within the Japanese entertainment world (*geinōkai*).[4] However, the emergence of online celebrity forms on blogs, YouTube, and Niconico might cause us to consider the possibility of a decentering of television within the production and circulation of fame in Japan. This is true even as online media platforms such as Niconico become increasingly akin to television networks in how they develop content as repeating programs, rely on live broadcast formats, and affiliate themselves with powerful media institutions (such as Kadokawa Publishing). But this perceived decentering also contributes to the anxieties surrounding media convergence for those involved with television (see Chapter 4).

In what ways might online forms of celebrity threaten to displace those of television? Television's model of celebrity one that is organized in a roughly vertical manner, with powerful talent agencies (*jimusho*) wielding influence over the images of their performers, the types of programs they can appear on, and the ways that audiences can interact

<hr/>

[3] This chapter will deal primarily with gender-related cases of "messiness" in media convergence. Race will be discussed in the footnotes, focusing on how online communities in Japan respond to Korean media and performers on Japanese television.

[4] Consider a show like *Ariyoshi Hanseikai* (NTV, 2013-), which features celebrity guests who appear on the program in order to explain a personal oddity or quirk and receive a comedic punishment from the show's host, Ariyoshi Hiroiki. This premise ensures that the content of the show is mainly celebrity gossip and introductions of lesser known figures to a larger audience, poking fun at the culture of celebrity while simultaneously promoting it. For more on the ways in which the images of celebrity are circulated through televisual media, see Gabriella Lukács, *Scripted Affects, Branded Selves: Television, Subjectivity, and Capitalism in 1990s Japan* (Durham, NC: Duke University Press, 2010); and Mitsuhiro Yoshimoto, "Image, Information, Commodity," in *In Pursuit of Contemporary East Asian Culture*, ed. Xiaobing Tang and Stephen Snyder (New York: Westview, 1996), 123-138.

with their performers.[5] The models of fame offered by online media often inhabit a very different structure—independently managed performers have emerged outside of mainstream media's networks of power through social media and video sharing websites. This structural and economic alternative is also accompanied by the emergence of new performance genres that have also generated interest among audiences who have turned away from seemingly standard fare offered by mainstream media. The success of these alternative modes of celebrity has in turn caused television producers to try and appropriate these acts for their own programming.[6]

This is where the messiness of media convergence can be reintroduced. Appearances made by internet personalities on commercial television do not always go smoothly. The types of performance they engage with can alienate television audiences expecting something more familiar or accessible. What's more, these appearances on television by net performers can even invite the hostilities of online audiences who feel contempt for mainstream media and the audiences of traditional media. As such, the industrial convergence of television and online media is accompanied by different forms of cultural divergence. This dynamic is one that is constantly reforming as each party tries to take advantage of the opportunities provided by the other while also guarding its own sense of control over content and in the management over images of celebrity.

This dynamic of fame that circulates between television and online media is one that can be characterized in terms of anxiety. But we should also clarify what anxiety means in this context. This includes who might be experiencing it and how these sentiments contribute to other facets of contemporary media culture. On the one hand, anxiety can describe the position of media producers in the television industry. Television's central status in Japanese media is in some cases called into question by the alternative opportunities for performance, production, and distribution allowed for by internet media. This in turn can threaten the

---

[5] For one account of the influence that these agencies can wield, see Noji Tsuneyoshi's biography of Watanabe Shin, *Watanabe Shin monogatari: Shōwa no sutā ōkoku o kisuita otoko* (Tokyo: Magazine House, 2010). The agency that Watanabe founded, Watanabe Productions, began the practice of requiring music variety shows to identify the performers as Watanabe talent in the *telop* (television opaque projector or superimposed titles) captions as part of their agreement for letting their artists perform (Noji, *Watanabe Shin monogatari*, 71-75).

[6] Other factors have contributed to mass media's interest in appropriating internet media, such as declining audiences for television broadcasting and the perceived immediacy and interactivity of online media. Some of the appropriations of net media by television and anxieties about this convergence are covered in a roundtable discussion published in Uno Tsunehiro, ed. "TV no owari to intānetto wandārando?" *PLANETS Special 2011 "Natsu yasumi no owari ni"* (2011): 148-157.

control over content that television producers enjoy within mainstream media industries. But anxiety can also describe the relationship between performers and audiences within new media platforms. This includes the harassment of mainstream figures of celebrity over social media.[7]

But on the other hand, the superior posture held toward mainstream culture by audiences on sites such as 2channel is tempered by the movement of online performers from internet media onto television and the types of reception they receive from mainstream viewers. This trajectory toward television by some net performers gestures toward a renewal of television's dominance in contemporary media, even as it is presumably threatened by alternatives that emerge through online media. Anxiety is therefore something that can be felt on either end of the spectrum(s) of media convergence: from industry professional to ordinary user, or media performer to media consumer.

Given all of the ways in which anxiety might appear in contemporary media, this chapter will draw upon that concept to describe some of the interwoven structures of affect within Japanese television and internet media. One of these is the quality of approaching but not quite reaching or obtaining celebrity. Within media convergence this can also refer to the ability to successfully move between media forms and industries, which often rely on different structures (or sources) of power and authority. But given the ambivalence or hostility expressed by different kinds of media audiences toward one another, there is also a sense in which this excitement about fame is continuously being deflated by negative affects—sentiments of exposure, embarrassment, and so-called ironic detachment. Key to this problem of exposure is the issue of gender, and particularly how different types of performers are received based on their gendered identity or gendered style of performance. This sense of anxiety intersects with the widely circulated fantasy that anyone can become famous, a fantasy that is intensified and complicated by the emergent forms of celebrity made available by internet media.

Characterizing this media environment as one of "anxious proximity," this chapter will approach how these networks of desire and attachment contribute to an ambivalence toward celebrity that is caught on the one hand between fantasies of access to public figures of fame and becoming famous oneself, and on the other the sentiments of suspicion

---

[7] One early, and extreme, example of a television performer being harassed by anonymous users can be found in comedian Smiley Kikuchi's account of his trials with being accused of murder online and his attempts to clear his name. See Smiley Kikuchi, *Totsuzen, boku wa satsujinhan ni sareta* (Tokyo: Takeshobō, 2011).

and antagonism that accompany them.[8] This tension is perhaps most pronounced in acts of exposure that bring into relief the intersections of (micro)celebrity and anonymity in online media. The collision between personal fantasies of becoming famous with the cultivated self-presentation of ironic detachment demonstrates not just the asymmetrical dynamic of identity that is common in online media platforms, but the overlapping value systems that different types of users share.

But what kind of structure of emotion animates these forms of attachment? What do they show us about the convergence of media cultures and platforms as television and internet media compete and collaborate with one another? In exploring these questions, this chapter will introduce two cases studies in which figures of online celebrity make appearances on variety television and, rather than finding a new horizon of success, encounter ambivalence or outright hostility from audiences that follow them online. In both cases, the gendered identity of the performer will be central to their ambivalent (if not negative) reception by online and television audiences. This ambivalence in reception can therefore also be tied to the ways in which the media identities and performance styles of these figures might disrupt the ways that gender is represented, domesticated, and commodified in popular media. Through these examples, this chapter hopes to demonstrate some of the ways in which celebrity circulates through different kinds of media and how these instances of convergence draw out affects of anxiety about contemporary media culture and its rhetorics of fame, identity, and self-presentation.

Contested Celebrity

Shimoda Misaki opened a YouTube channel in 2011 to produce and share videos of herself performing "calls" for drinking parties, singing karaoke, and dancing to popular songs. These genres of recorded performances— "I tried to dance it" (*odotte-mita*) and "I tried to sing it" (*utatte-mita*)—have achieved cult-like popularity among users of video sharing sites like YouTube and Niconico in Japan, where they have provided alternate venues for emerging forms of celebrity that circulate outside of mainstream, televisual media. Shimoda began her career in Japan's entertainment industry as a fashion model but eventually moved toward internet video performance out of her enthusiasm for the *visual-kei* "air band" Golden Bomber. Golden

---

[8] Sianne Ngai characterizes anxiety as having a "spatial dimension" that is also "unfixed." See Sianne Ngai, *Ugly Feelings* (Cambridge, MA: Harvard University Press, 2007), 236. This article will expand upon that observation by considering anxiety alongside narratives of identity/fame and media convergence, qualities which, while not literally spatial, do have an "unfixed" quality in how they can be experienced as trajectories or competing domains of authority.

Bomber themselves achieved a large following online by performing on Niconico before moving on to mainstream success through a commercial tie-up of one of their songs, "Memeshikute."[9] Shimoda's dance-cover of that song won her an award from an online video competition in 2011, which in turn brought her greater visibility and became part of her identity as an online figure of celebrity.

Shimoda's profile as an internet-famous fan of the group spilled over into audience outrage on July 11, 2013, when she made an appearance on the talk variety show *Out X Deluxe* (Fuji TV, 2013-). Here she announced her desire to join Golden Bomber, an all male group, as a new member. The hosts of the show questioned her on this ambition, noting the all-male membership of the group and the unusual manner in which she was going about trying to join.[10] Shimoda responded by noting that two of the current four members of the group were actually former fans who had joined when openings in the line-up had become available, but also escalated her rhetoric, claiming that if she were able to join the group, "If I only have 50 years left to live, I would be fine with two of those years" as long as they were spent as part of the group. She continued to explain her position by saying that she had always had a difficult time establishing emotional connections with other people and artistic forms of expression such as music, also claiming that seeing the band perform live had made her feel like she could belong in a way she had not experienced before. Shimoda's appearance on *Out X Deluxe* concluded with her attempting to address the members of Golden Bomber by facing the camera and declaring, "Ever since I first encountered Golden Bomber I've wanted to join, even to the point where I can't think of anything else." She then asked for a direct answer from the four members of the band as to whether she could join or not.

---

[9] The song was originally released in 2009 but didn't become a hit until it was tied to an energy drink TV advertising campaign in 2011. The lyrics of the song were also changed from "*memeshikute*" (effeminate) to "*nemutakute*" (to become tired) to thematically match the product being sold.

[10] The gender politics of this exchange between Shimoda and the hosts of the show are quite complicated. Part of the hosts' ambivalence toward her bid to join Golden Bomber was due to the exclusively male membership of the group. But at the same time, one of the hosts is the cross-dressing (*josō*) performer Matsuko Deluxe. Different forms of queer performance can be seen every day on television in Japan, although this does not necessarily translate into these identities being recognized in other parts of public life outside of the "character" driven world of the entertainment industry. Similarly, there seems to be an asymmetry in terms of what types of identities or performance styles are readily accepted by television audiences—transgender or transvestite *tarento* who perform or present as women are quite common, but the reverse less so. The resistance to Shimoda's attempt to intrude upon the masculine space of Golden Bomber has some resonance with this dynamic. For more on asymmetrical appropriations of gender identity in contemporary Japan, see Sharon Kinsella, "Minstrelized Girls: Male Performers of Japan's Lolita Complex," *Japan Forum* 18, no. 1 (2006): 65-87.

The online reaction to Shimoda's attempted bid to join the group was immediate. A blog entry she had written about her appearance on the show received over 2,000 comments within the first two days the post had been online, with hundreds more messages sent over Twitter, and coverage in online news magazines and tabloids quickly following.[11] Shimoda had been using her blog to promote her appearance on *Out X Deluxe* leading up to the show's airing, and some of these entries she had posted there appeared to anticipate the backlash she might face. The attempts to clarify and justify her appeal to join Golden Bomber did not, however, stem the tide of outrage from other fans and readers. Some insisted that she should apologize to the group for her petition to join, while others asserted that she must be trying to make fun of them and that she couldn't be a real fan.[12] In some sense these comments were echoing the incredulity of the two hosts, who also suspected that Shimoda might simply be trying to produce a media spectacle for her own benefit. The online responses by ordinary fans of the group were, however, also laced with a sense of personal offense at Shimoda's perceived audacity. Many tried to convince her that she was being rude to both the group and to other fans with her declaration, noting the difference between privately held dreams and things said in public spaces such as blogs or television. More still simply insisted that she was exploiting the popularity of the group to be able to appear on television herself and to promote her own work to a wider audience, essentially piggybacking on the name of Golden Bomber to attract attention through the controversy the appearance was bound to generate (figure 1).[13]

---

[11] See, for example, "'Gōruden Bomubā ni kanyū shitai': Kinbaku ni uttaeru moderu Shimoda Misaki no burogu ga enjō," *Tech Insight*, July 12, 2013, accessed July 29, 2013, http://japan.techinsight.jp/2013/07/kinbakuninaritai-simodamisaki-outdelux20130711.html.

[12] Shimoda responded to readers in subsequent blog posts. She said she would not apologize, also stating that she has enormous respect for Golden Bomber and therefore could never be making light of them. See her blog post "Pinhīru wa hitoashi mo motteinai shi, ashi mo fundeimasen" on July 13, 2013.

[13] These accusations did, in some sense, turn out to be true, as Shimoda was invited to appear on other popular variety shows such as *London Hearts* (TV Asahi, August 20, 2013) due to the media spotlight she suddenly found herself in. Shimoda was also preparing to release her first single, "Ote o haishaku! Mō ichyo!" and heavily promoting her work during this period, so while couched in the aggressive language of anti-ism, the accuracy of these accusations should be recognized to some extent. However, Shimoda's relative absence from television following this debacle also suggests the possibility that she was somewhat of a bystander to net culture's rivalry with television.

Figure 1. Shimoda Misaki appearing on *Out X Deluxe* (Fuji TV) on July 11, 2013. The caption reads "I'd like to have an audition to join the group" (left). A reader posts a reply to Shimoda's blog, spamming "die die die" (*shine*) and "go away" (*kiero*) over and over again (right).

What can the above example show us about contemporary media culture in Japan? This particular case may at first glance appear insignificant in comparison to other clashes between television and internet media in Japan. Shimoda is not a highly visible personality in Japanese mass media, and the dust-up her appearance on *Out X Deluxe* helped to generate did not result in the kind of scandal that many other moments of perceived transgression by celebrities have. However, even with its relatively minor status, what this case can bring into relief is some of the characteristics of online cultures of negativity and their relationship with emerging forms of celebrity in contemporary media culture. This includes distinctions between the modes of fame that emerge in online media and those that have been established in television as well as the increasing integration of online media such as blogs and Twitter accounts into the promotional apparatus of celebrity. The gender identity of the performer being put under the public eye is also significant and provides one of the frames for how "transgression" is interpreted and responded to by online communities.

Embedded within the context of this mediascape is also the network of fantasy that appears around fame, such as the notion that essentially anyone can become famous through events like auditions or by entering special entertainment schools and programs. This fantasy is widely perpetuated in all manner of media in Japan's entertainment industry and is indeed at the core of many of the dominant forms of contemporary celebrity culture, such as idols and comedy performance.[14] Taken alongside the solicitation of access to figures of celebrity through industry promoted online media (e.g., Twitter, Mixi, etc.), this orientation toward fame as something that is always on the cusp of availability to ordinary people is one that can be thought of in terms of proximity to both actual figures of fame—who can sometimes be interacted with through social media—and the proximity of fame itself through emerging forms of performance, spectacle, and media.

But these fantasies of becoming famous or having access to celebrities through social media are also met with ambivalence. This ambivalence can also spill over into outright negativity. In online media this sometimes includes practices such as trolling and flaming, behaviors that are often wound up in affects of suspicion and an orientation toward acts of defacement and exposure. This is perhaps best exemplified in cases of scandal or outrage where the private information of celebrities is revealed by anonymous users through online media, such as sharing photographs or videos of private moments that seemingly contradict a performer's public persona. However, rather than dismissing this behavior as merely a kind of social aberration in online cultures, questions of how the psychic fuel of negativity and suspicion intersects with other facets of contemporary media can lead to a richer understanding of the evolving relationship between mainstream media such as television and online media (and its cultures of anonymity). We can see these dynamics at work in Shimoda's reception from audiences commenting on her blog, where the possibility of her expanding upon her celebrity (and obtaining mainstream visibility) collided with a culture of negativity that anticipates an ulterior motive and tries to resist mainstream media. With those questions in mind, this chapter will approach some of the ways that fame is subject to a continuous re-qualification in spaces of online anonymity (and pseudo-anonymity) and the emerging media and social practices they enable.

---

[14] For more on the fantasy of believing anyone can become an idol, see Ōta Shōichi, *Aidoru shinkaron: Minami Saori kara Hatsune Miku, AKB48 made* (Tokyo: Chikuma Shobō, 2011), 31, 42. In regard to comedy (*owarai*) and the use of tournaments to promote amateur participation, see Yamanaka Ichirō, *'Owarai tarento-ka' shakai* (Tokyo: Shōdensha, 2008), 34, 85. Joel Stocker has also written on how Yoshimoto Kogyo's comedy schools and theaters have been appropriated by fans as ways of trying to meet their favorite performers in addition to trying to enter the entertainment world. See Joel Stocker, "The 'Local' in Japanese Media Culture: Manzai Comedy, Osaka, and Entertainment Enterprise Yoshimoto Kogyo" (PhD diss., University of Wisconsin, 2002). Yamanaka Ichirō also describes comedy tournaments such as the M-1 *manzai* contest as being a space where amateurs and famous professional comedians can share the same stage, which presents another opportunity for fans to try and meet their favorite performers (Yamanaka, *'Owarai tarento-ka' shakai*, 14).

Negativity, Anonymity, and Celebrity

Negativity can encompass a wide variety of practices in internet culture. These can range from harassing and abusing other users through online media such as Twitter or the comment section of YouTube, to more mundane practices such as down-voting videos or social media content in a way that produces a visual trace of opposition to mainstream mass media and entertainment. Given this chapter's focus on the relationship between online anonymity and images of celebrity in mass media, this section will lay out some of the salient qualities of online negativity and its relationship to celebrity and mass media. Negativity in online spaces will therefore not be something that is defined comprehensively, but rather as it pertains to concepts such as celebrity and media convergence.

As part of that task this article will consider fame as an "immaterial form of mediation" that, while being constantly transformed and re-contextualized by new sites of activity (such as social media), has itself properties of a kind of interface or technology that mediates the asymmetrical relationships between different types of users.[15] Fame—as a category of knowledge and way of knowing—can thus be thought of as a kind of "affective cathexis" that manages the social relationships between figures of celebrity and their audiences (or non-audiences) by conjoining commonly circulated sentiments of desire, suspicion, and attachment. This approach can be useful in thinking about anxieties about celebrity in a way that is not bound up in familiar ontologies of producers and consumers, but instead centered on the structures of affect that circulate between and constitute such positions. As Sianne Ngai has noted, negative or "ugly" feelings can appear as "affective ideologemes" that psychically define the stakes of symbolic struggles by producing a meeting ground for various regimes of meaning-production.[16] The value systems that appears through these kinds of struggles over attachment is where this chapter will locate its conceptualization of anxiety and exposure.

Recent work analyzing English-language online cultural forms has frequently observed the complicated (if not antagonistic) relationship between mainstream media and online communities. Whitney Philips has described the relationship between online trolls and mainstream media as one of "cultural digestion" in which trolls appropriate and

---

[15] The language of "immaterial form of mediation" and "affective cathexis" comes from recent work on brands and branding. See Paul Manning, "The Semiotics of Brand," *Annual Review of Anthropology* 39 (October 2010): 33-49; and Constantine V. Nakassis, "Brand, Citationality, Performativity," *American Anthropologist* 114, no. 4 (December 2012): 624-638.

[16] Ngai, *Ugly Feelings*, 3, 7.

parody images and ideas from mainstream media.[17] This is also often tied to an elitist tendency in online communities, with the anonymous users assuming an antagonistic stance toward media—such as television, print, and film—and the audiences who follow said media. As previously mentioned this is also true in the case of television for online users in Japan. This is due to television's role in promoting related entertainment such as music, idols, and comedy, and its function as a nexus for inter-media discursivity and institutional accumulation of brand identity.[18]

Sentiments of offense and suspicion are also common in these communities and the discourses they produce. As Philips observes in her study of English-language online trolling, the aggressive barrage of racist, sexist, and heterosexist language is used to taunt uninitiated visitors into a position of offense or outrage. This then allows for the aggression to continue, as the sincere reaction of the offended party is mocked ruthlessly by the active offenders under the self-presentation of ironic detachment. The combination of unattributed writing and the general atmosphere of irony on sites such as 4chan also leads to a constant sense of suspicion in which everything written is always already trolling and insincere. This mode of abuse and agitation—in which individual users act as a kind of aggregate, non-individualized mass—resonates with how Hamano Satoshi has described participation in threads on 2channel as individual users assuming the "character" of the site and its particular cultural identity.[19]

Media sociologist Kitada Akihiro's analysis on cultures of cynical negativity in Japanese language internet sociality points toward a similar

---

[17] See Whitney Phillips, *This Is Why We Can't Have Nice Things: Mapping the Relationship Between Online Trolling and Mainstream Culture* (Cambridge, MA: MIT Press, 2015).

[18] Fuji TV often finds itself at the center of online "anti-ism" in Japan. The two examples that this chapter will focus on are from programs broadcast on Fuji, but much of the negativity directed toward the station is due to its perceived alliance with South Korean media. These negative responses to media content and performers from South Korea constitute another form of anxiety within media convergence in Japan, one that speaks to the ethnic dimensions of contemporary media culture in addition to the issues of gender, celebrity, and power described elsewhere. Some of this negativity is born from conspiracy theories asserting that *zainichi* Koreans own the network, or that the popularity of South Korean entertainment in Japan has been artificially manufactured (and exaggerated) by elites. There are of course more mundane forms of cooperation between the media industries of Japan and South Korea. Eun-Young Jung has noted how the South Korean music label SM Entertainment has used its partnerships with Avex and Yoshimoto Kogyo to have some of its most popular performers appear on variety shows such as *Hey! Hey! Hey! Music Champ* (Fuji TV, 1994-2012) as well as television advertising spots. See Eun-Young Jung, "Transnational Cultural Traffic in Northeast Asia: The 'Presence' of Japan in Korea's Popular Music Culture" (PhD diss., University of Pittsburgh, 2007), 187.

[19] Hamano Satoshi, *Ākitekucha no setaikei: Jōhō kankyō wa ikani sekkei saretekita-ka* (Tokyo: NTT Shuppan, 2008), 95, 102.

dynamic. Focusing on the bulletin board 2channel, Kitada notes the cynical stance toward mass media among many users of the site, who tend to adopt a position of ironic laughter that renders everything as part of a big in-joke that they can enjoy as they distance themselves from mainstream society.[20] Part of this culture of "anti-ism" can be attributed to feelings of exclusion from the discourse of mass media, which is often perceived as denying a political voice to opposing views and lending a monopoly to powerful institutions.[21] However, in a more abstract sense, we can also think of this kind of cynical laughter as part of a negative, elitist tendency that seeks to antagonize and belittle mainstream society by carving out a distinct space of cultural operation with its own code of (anti-) politics. The emergence of alternative media forms and performance genres on sites like Niconico and YouTube has added to this sense of autonomy in net culture and distance from mainstream society and media.

But this negative energy is not always directed exclusively at media institutions. Individual users, including public figures of celebrity, are also frequent targets for this type of harassment. In Japan this is particularly true for performance genres such as idols, who are often expected to remain romantically single (or at least not publicize their relationships) in order to satisfy fantasies of availability, access, and, frequently, idealized notions of femininity or boyishness. This climate of suspicion has expanded to cover other forms of celebrities, and Ōta Shōichi has noted a kind of "idolification" of other types of female celebrity such as TV announcers and voice actresses (*seiyū*) who in recent years have found their private lives put under the microscope in a way that would normally only be expected of idol performers.[22] The widely perpetuated taboo on relationships among idols has thus found itself being integrated into other genres of performance, accompanied by similar patterns of fan outrage about the discovery of a favorite announcer or voice actress having a romantic life. This becomes another avenue through which audiences attempt to monitor the politics of fame and again gender. Online media such as blogs, Twitter, and 2channel have provided platforms for ordinary audiences to

---

[20] Kitada Akihiro, *Warau Nihon no nashonarizumu* (Tokyo: NHK Books, 2005), 196-200.

[21] Hamano Satoshi and Azuma Hiroki touch on this point in a conversation held during a live broadcast on Genron's channel on Niconico, which was later published in transcription. See Hamano Satoshi and Azuma Hiroki, "'Ākitekucha no setaikei' to sono-go," in *Media o kataru* (Contectures), ed. Azuma Hiroki (Tokyo: Genron, 2012), 165.

[22] See Ōta, *Aidoru shinkaron*, 197-200, 238-240. The circulation of print-club photographs (*purikura*) of voice actresses showing them with friends or boyfriends on sites such as 2channel has lead to new kinds of "idol hunting" in which anonymous users will try to dig up material for provoking sentiments of outrage and humiliation among other users and, of course, for the performers themselves.

contribute to the economies of offense and scandal by discovering and distributing information that can be used to harass performers as well as to offend other audiences.[23] This is part of a more general transformation in how online audiences can use internet media in divergent ways in order to disrupt the expectations of mainstream media institutions that are trying to court them as audiences, presenting an additional instance of the "anxious" antagonism between television and net culture.

Exposure and Attachment

As with trolls in English-language online media, the rhetoric of negativity in Japan is one of detachment that adopts a stance of superiority to the target of its laughter. But is this self-presentation of cynical laughter always so detached? What other forms of investment might this kind of negative energy suggest? In writing on sentiments of optimism and attachment, Lauren Berlant notes that cynical detachment is often "not really detached at all," but rather part of a process of "navigating an ongoing and sustaining relation to the scene and circuit of optimism and disappointment."[24] Here Berlant is referring to the network of attachments that are built around objects or relations of desire, and the work that goes into maintaining those attachments in order to preserve a sense of world or purpose. The ironic, sneering laughter of internet "antis" that persistently hounds mainstream media or celebrity personalities might then be thought of as a kind of rhetoric for maintaining a distinct type of relationship with the cultural environment these users find themselves enmeshed in. In this rhetorical mode, sentiments of suspicion and hostility—even when framed by ironic laughter or cynicism—can be interpreted as a kind of attachment in that they organize the meta-relationship between anonymous audience and mainstream media (namely television) through these intense structures of emotion.

Berlant describes attachment to an object of desire as a "cluster of promises we want someone or something to make to us and make possible

---

[23] As described previously, gender is of great importance to this notion of fame as a site of mediation and its relationship to online self-presentation. Looking at English-language internet culture such as 4chan and Facebook, Whitney Phillips has drawn connections between anonymous trolling with a cultural logic of masculinity, noting the ways that the rhetoric of "rationality" in trolling is often part of a performance of dominance over other users and rehearsal of privilege through imaginations of universalized value regimes. In other words, the insistence by trolls of their own "cool rationality" as they simultaneously project highly encoded emotional qualities of insecurity and anger on their targets (often through the language of sexual violence) is organized around a gendered logic in which the targets of trolls are coded as feminine through their offense to the trolls' harassment. See Phillips, *This Is Why We Can't Have Nice Things*, 124-125.

[24] Lauren Berlant, *Cruel Optimism* (Durham, NC: Duke University Press, 2012), 27.

for us," also noting that this cluster of promises "allow us to encounter what's incoherent or enigmatic in our attachments, not as confirmation of our irrationality but as explanation of our sense of *our endurance in the object*."[25] Approaching cultures of cynical laughter from the perspective of "endurance in the object" might seem counter-intuitive, but the self-presentation of "not caring" by antis can also be taken as a particular kind of investment into a network of attachment.

The fantasy of becoming famous is of course another place where we can locate this network of attachment and the kind of emotional logic it produces. Both mainstream celebrity—such as idols and comedians—and internet-based, alternative forms of fame are animated by this notion that even ordinary people are an audition or chance discovery away from being in the spotlight. As such, the fantasy of potentially becoming famous is something that both brings the audiences for these two types of media together and delineates their differences. The forms that celebrity takes and the networks of prestige they engage with are different, but the logics that organize them are the same. These sentiments are also transformed by the anxiety of media convergence between television and internet culture on the one hand, and gendered identity on the other. Turning to another example can help demonstrate the types of animosity that appear between these media and their audiences.

Hyakka Ryōran is a self-described "internet talent" and well-known performer on Niconico. He developed a character-persona around his talent for sleight of hand performance (*tejina*) and ability to sing in both a high-pitched, anime-character style female voice and a more conventional male voice, achieving popularity through a series of videos and streaming broadcasts he made of himself singing Vocaloid songs while wearing colorful costumes and women's clothing.[26] Based on this popularity online he was invited to appear in character on the talk variety show *Waratte Iitomo!* (Fuji TV, 1982-2014) in October of 2011 as part of a corner used for introducing new talent to a wider audience.[27] For his performance he demonstrated series of card tricks, performed a

---

[25] *Ibid.*, 23 (italics retained from original).

[26] Vocaloid is a voice-synthesizer software that is popular on sites such as Niconico. For more on Vocaloid, see the December 2008 special issue of *Eureka* dedicated to Hatsune Miku and Chapter 8 in this volume. Hyakka Ryōran was recently profiled on *Vice Japan*'s YouTube channel (https://youtu.be/-hZLWc53G6M) in a short documentary about his career as a "net talent." The episode did not, however, cover his appearance on *Waratte Iitomo!*

[27] He was introduced in Japanese as "*otoko no ko Hyakka Ryōran*" on the show. A visual pun in the Japanese writing of the name is unfortunately lost in the transliteration to Romanization. The character used for "*ko*" here is the one for "young girl" or "daughter" (which can also be read as *musume*) rather than the character used in "young boy" (*otoko no ko*).

standing back-flip, and sang a brief excerpt from a Vocaloid song. *Waratte Iitomo!* has long been at the center of mainstream television in Japan, so the sense of visibility to a wider public that it can offer to a generally unknown performer is quite enormous. Comedians and idols have been able to find mainstream success through well-received appearances on the program, meaning that Hyakka Ryōran's invitation to perform serves as an indication of how potentially significant a role Niconico and its cultures of performance are coming to play in Japan's mediascape.

That potential for intruding into the space of mainstream celebrity and finding wider recognition never materialized. Many viewers commenting online noted the relatively cool reception Hyakka received on the show, pointing out the small amount of time he was given to sing (the introduction used up most of the time he had to appear), the puzzled reaction of the live audience, and the lack of real engagement with the style of performance he was taking up among other members of the show's panel.[28] In the context of mainstream television's ambivalent relationship with internet culture, these infringements on Ryōran's performance gesture toward a general discomfort with the media culture he was representing. This includes the style of performance he was engaging with—mixing male and female voices—and his way of presenting himself—a form of cross-dressing. One commenter on 2channel even described the reaction from the live audience and talent panel as a "crushing defeat" (*sanpai*) for internet culture, with many others agreeing that what can achieve popularity on a site like Niconico will not likely find an audience with the mainstream public. As such, while we can certainly consider Hyakka Ryōran's being asked to appear on such an institutional part of Japan's mainstream media culture as a token of alternative media entertainments and internet celebrity being courted by television media as an effort to expand their viewership, his reception among the live audience and other performers would also appear to indicate a very tall barrier between those different venues and audiences.[29]

There are two facets of this case that I would like to highlight. The first is that this example suggests a variation on the anxiety about potentially

---

[28] For example, users posting on the message board of a news story about the appearance note the lack of a reaction among the live audience, while a thread on 2channel about the show has posters claiming that he should have stuck to the net and that there was no way the general public would respond positively. See "Hyakka Ryōran ga Waratte Iitomo! ni shutsuen! Kaijo no kūki ga tsumetakute warota!" October 16, 2011, accessed July 29, 2013, http://desktop2ch.tv/news/1318758578/.

[29] He has also shifted his online persona since the appearance on *Waratte Iitomo!*, now focusing on hosting online radio programs as a disc jockey rather than singing or appearing in cosplay. Niconico has also gone on to become quite mainstream in Japanese media since that broadcast.

anyone being able to achieve fame and success in the entertainment industry in Japan. The fantasy of mainstream success that a small, devoted audience might have for a favorite act or performance style is tempered by an anxiety about rejection or indifference from the general public and the confrontation with opposing networks of prestige and authority that circulate in those media. This is also buttressed by anxieties over exposure: to what degree does the reception of an individual performer or performance function as a representative and extend to the culture that produced and celebrated it? The imagination of "anyone can become famous" is thus confronted with another kind of doubt about just what kind of "anyone" can become famous, and the discomfort of being exposed as investing in a particular fantasy about fame. This again returns us to this issue of gender, and how it relates to exposure for performers and audiences. The second—and perhaps more striking—is the loss of ironic detachment, or, more specifically, a quasi-reversal of the dynamic in which anonymous, online audiences make fun of mainstream culture from a position of detached, elitist contempt. Turning net culture into a spectacle for a mass media audience who reacted with ambivalence compromises the assumption of ironic superiority that allows net users to laugh at that media. In order to preserve their position of detached superiority, they now have to disavow their position and laugh at themselves.[30]

What we have then is a meeting of anxieties about media convergence and different kinds of attachments to fame that they each promote. Among these is a sense of embarrassment over having one's investment or attachment to a fantasy of fame being subjected to exposure, something which is heightened by different media forms trespassing on one another. As with Shimoda's negative reception from other fans of Golden Bomber, Hyakka Ryōran's appearance on *Waratte Iitomo!* suggests an anxiety that is bound up in the investments audiences make into media, genre, and

[30] A related case occurred during the summer of 2011, when protesters picketing Fuji TV's use of Korean-made content and performers on their network assembled at Fuji's Odaiba campus in Tokyo. The protest snowballed out of social media commentary on the network's perceived alliance with Korean media. The commentary on social media included 2channel and Niconico but also, and perhaps more famously, Twitter, where the actor Takaoka Sōsuke kicked off a controversy by posting nationalistic messages about the network's use of Korean media and performers. However, the protest coincided with Fuji's "United States of Odaiba" event, and protesters marching through the network campus seemed to blend in with regular tourists and visitors partaking in the festivities. Commenters watching online noted this, quickly turning their negativity away from Fuji's perceived slights against Japanese media and toward an ironic stance of laughing at the protesters who had showed up. As with the previous footnote that touched on anti-Korean sentiment in Japanese internet culture, this points toward an ethnically charged dimension of media convergence. For more on anti-Korea sentiment in Japanese language internet discourse and the Fuji TV protests, see Yasuda Kōichi, *Netto to aikoku: Zaitokukai no 'yami' o oikakete* (Tokyo: Kodansha, 2012); and Chapter 5 in this volume.

performance among cultures of fame in Japan, a quality that is brought into relief when confronted with a disinterested audience that comes from a different background. While readers of Shimoda's blog fought back against the declaration of her intention to join the group, the perception of the mainstream media's gaze falling upon an alternative media figure like Haykka Ryōran also has connotations for that kind of media culture and its celebration of a particular style of fame or performance being received negatively or exposed as aberrant on a more general level. As mentioned above, this reverses the normal dynamic of online anti-ism cynically mocking mainstream TV through the manner in which underground, online media faced an indifferent reception on mainstream television. We should also keep in mind that—at least in the case of media like 2channel or Niconico—because much of the management of culture is performed anonymously, the exposure of those cultural practices to a general audience also amounts to a kind of unmasking that unsettles the dynamic of asymmetrical representation normally enjoyed by users of internet media.[31] However, rather than thinking of this unmasking only in terms of its relationship to anonymity and visibility, I also want to consider the relationship between unmasking and losing the positionality of ironic distance and being exposed as participating in a network of investments and attachments in fantasies of celebrity.

This sense of exposure represents a final kind of anxiety about media convergence. Underlying this sense of anxiety—and the others that I have discussed—is also a redistribution of power and authority within media culture. To elaborate further, the previously discussed appropriation of internet culture and its alternative aesthetics and performance practices by television represents one instance of convergence anxiety. The way that internet media opens up new ways for anonymous audiences to interact with figures of public celebrity—and often in antagonizing ways organized around gender identity—gestures toward another, and one in which media institutions such as television lose the ability to control how audiences engage with their content and performers. But as we can see, the loss of the privileged way of viewing and laughing that anonymous audiences commenting about mainstream media online have enjoyed becomes disrupted when their self-presentation of ironic detachment is undermined, as they are exposed as audiences invested in particular media forms, cultures, and narratives about fame that betray that self-styled culture of irony and detachment. They become, in a way, like

---

[31] For more on anonymity and unmasking, see Chapter 7 in this volume.

the audiences of traditional media that they express contempt for. In that sense, what is perceived as being lost or threatened by a particular kind of media user (or media identity) also brings into relief some of the affective structures that organize how ordinary users identify themselves in relation to celebrity and institutional power. This in turn can show us something about the different forms of attachment, anxiety, and proximity that circulate between media forms, audiences, and users.

Works Cited

Berlant, Lauren. *Cruel Optimism*. Durham, NC: Duke University Press, 2012.

Hamano Satoshi. *Ākitekucha no setaikei: Jōhō kankyō wa ikani sekkei saretekita-ka*. Tokyo: NTT Shuppan, 2008.

Hamano Satoshi and Azuma Hiroki. "'Ākitekucha no setaikei' to sono-go." In *Media o kataru* (Contectures), edited by Azuma Hiroki, 143-209. Tokyo: Genron, 2012.

Jung, Eun-Young. "Transnational Cultural Traffic in Northeast Asia: The 'Presence' of Japan in Korea's Popular Music Culture." PhD diss., University of Pittsburgh, 2007.

Kikuchi Smiley. *Totsuzen, boku wa satsujinhan ni sareta*. Tokyo: Takeshobō, 2011.

Kinsella, Sharon. "Minstrelized Girls: Male Performers of Japan's Lolita Complex." *Japan Forum* 18, no. 1 (2006): 65-87.

Kitada Akihiro. *Warau Nihon no nashonarizumu*. Tokyo: NHK Books, 2005.

Kramer, Elise. "The Playful Is Political: The Metapragmatics of Internet Rape-joke Arguments." *Language in Society* 40, no. 2 (April 2011): 137-168.

Lamarre, Thomas. "Living Between Infrastructures: Commuter Networks, Broadcast TV, and Mobile Phones." *boundary 2* 43, no. 2 (2015): 157-170.

Lukács, Gabriella. *Scripted Affects, Branded Selves: Television, Subjectivity, and Capitalism in 1990s Japan*. Durham, NC: Duke University Press, 2010.

Manning, Paul. "The Semiotics of Brand." *Annual Review of Anthropology* 39 (October 2010): 33-49.

Nakassis, Constantine V. "Brand, Citationality, Performativity." *American Anthropologist* 114, no. 4 (December 2012): 624-638.

Ngai, Sianne. *Ugly Feelings*. Cambridge, MA: Harvard University Press, 2007.

Noji Tsuneyoshi. *Watanabe Shin monogatari: Shōwa no sutā ōkoku o kisuita otoko*. Tokyo: Magazine House, 2010.

Ōta Shōichi. A*idoru shinkaron: Minami Saori kara Hatsune Miku, AKB48 made*. Tokyo: Chikuma Shobō, 2011.

Phillips, Whitney. *This Is Why We Can't Have Nice Things: Mapping the Relationship Between Online Trolling and Mainstream Culture*. Cambridge, MA: MIT Press, 2015.

Stocker, Joel. "The 'Local' in Japanese Media Culture: Manzai Comedy, Osaka, and Entertainment Enterprise Yoshimoto Kogyo," PhD diss., University of Wisconsin, 2002.

Uno Tsunehiro, ed. "TV no owari to intānetto wandārando?" *PLANETS Special 2011 "Natsu yasumi no owari ni"* (2011): 148-157.

Yamanaka Ichirō. ' *Owarai tarento-ka' shakai*. Tokyo: Shōdensha, 2008.

Yasuda Kōichi. *Netto to aikoku: Zaitokukai no 'yami' o oikakete*. Tokyo: Kodansha, 2012.

Yoshimoto, Mitsuhiro. "Image, Information, Commodity." In *In Pursuit of Contemporary East Asian Culture*, edited by Xiaobing Tang and Stephen Snyder, 123-138. New York: Westview, 1996.

www.ingramcontent.com/pod-product-compliance
Lightning Source LLC
Chambersburg PA
CBHW050109280326
41933CB00010B/1027